# Exploring Effective Municipal Planning and Implementation

Pandelani Harry Munzhedzi
*University of Venda, South Africa*

Erasmus Mathebula
*University of Limpopo, South Africa*

Ntsako Idris Makamu
*University of South Africa, South Africa*

A volume in the Advances in Electronic Government, Digital Divide, and Regional Development (AEGDDRD) Book Series

Published in the United States of America by
IGI Global
Business Science Reference (an imprint of IGI Global)
701 E. Chocolate Avenue
Hershey PA, USA 17033
Tel: 717-533-8845
Fax: 717-533-8661
E-mail: cust@igi-global.com
Web site: http://www.igi-global.com



Library of Congress Cataloging-in-Publication Data

CIP Pending
ISBN: 979-8-3693-3617-5
EISBN: 979-8-3693-3618-2

British Cataloguing in Publication Data
A Cataloguing in Publication record for this book is available from the British Library.

All work contributed to this book is new, previously-unpublished material.
The views expressed in this book are those of the authors, but not necessarily of the publisher.

For electronic access to this publication, please contact: eresources@igi-global.com.

# Advances in Electronic Government, Digital Divide, and Regional Development (AEGDDRD) Book Series

Zaigham Mahmood
University of Derby, UK & North West University, South Africa

ISSN:2326-9103
EISSN:2326-9111

**MISSION**

The successful use of digital technologies (including social media and mobile technologies) to provide public services and foster economic development has become an objective for governments around the world. The development towards electronic government (or e-government) not only affects the efficiency and effectiveness of public services, but also has the potential to transform the nature of government interactions with its citizens. Current research and practice on the adoption of electronic/digital government and the implementation in organizations around the world aims to emphasize the extensiveness of this growing field.

**The Advances in Electronic Government, Digital Divide & Regional Development (AEGDDRD)** book series aims to publish authored, edited and case books encompassing the current and innovative research and practice discussing all aspects of electronic government development, implementation and adoption as well the effective use of the emerging technologies (including social media and mobile technologies) for a more effective electronic governance (or e-governance).

## Coverage

- Current Research and Emerging Trends in E-Government Development
- E-Citizenship, Inclusive Government, Connected Government
- Emerging Technologies within the Public Sector
- Frameworks and Methodologies for E-Government Development

IGI Global is currently accepting manuscripts for publication within this series. To submit a proposal for a volume in this series, please contact our Acquisition Editors at Acquisitions@igi-global.com or visit: http://www.igi-global.com/publish/.

The (ISSN ) is published by IGI Global, 701 E. Chocolate Avenue, Hershey, PA 17033-1240, USA, www.igi-global.com. This series is composed of titles available for purchase individually; each title is edited to be contextually exclusive from any other title within the series. For pricing and ordering information please visit http://www.igi-global.com/book-series/advances-electronic-government-digital-divide/37153. Postmaster: Send all address changes to above address. 

## Titles in this Series

For a list of additional titles in this series, please visit: www.igi-global.com/book-series

*Emerging Developments and Technologies in Digital Government*
Yuanyuan Guo (Tsinghua University, China)
Information Science Reference • copyright 2024 • 423pp • H/C (ISBN: 9798369323632) • US $325.00 (our price)

*Machine Learning and Data Science Techniques for Effective Government Service Delivery*
Olalekan Samuel Ogunleye (School of Computing and Mathematical Science, University of Mpumalanga, South Africa)
Engineering Science Reference • copyright 2024 • 344pp • H/C (ISBN: 9781668497166) • US $265.00 (our price)

*Digital Transformation and Sustainable Development in Cities and Organizations*
Faidon Theofanidis (Australian University, Kuwait) Oualid Abidi (Australian University, Kuwait) Alper Erturk (Australian University, Kuwait) Stephen Edward Colbran (Central Queensland University, Australia) and Erman Coşkun (Izmir Bakircay University, Turkey)
Business Science Reference • copyright 2024 • 304pp • H/C (ISBN: 9798369335673) • US $265.00 (our price)

*Futuristic e-Governance Security With Deep Learning Applications*
Rajeev Kumar (Moradabad Institute of Technology, India) Abu Bakar Abdul Hamid (Infrastructure University Kuala Lumpur, Malaysia) Noor Inayah Binti Ya'akub (Infrastructure University Kuala Lumpur, Malaysia) Madhu Sharma Gaur (G.L. Bajaj Institute of Management and Technology, India) and Sanjeev Kumar (G.L. Bajaj Institute of Management and Technology, India)
Information Science Reference • copyright 2024 • 276pp • H/C (ISBN: 9781668495964) • US $275.00 (our price)

IGI Global
PUBLISHER of TIMELY KNOWLEDGE

701 East Chocolate Avenue, Hershey, PA 17033, USA
Tel: 717-533-8845 x100 • Fax: 717-533-8661
E-Mail: cust@igi-global.com • www.igi-global.com

# Table of Contents

**Preface** ........ xviii

**Chapter 1**
Drawing Lessons From Participatory Budgeting in Brazil for South African Municipal Participatory Budgeting ........ 1
*Ndwakhulu Stephen Tshishonga, University of KwaZulu-Natal, South Africa*

**Chapter 2**
Empowering Residents, Enhancing Services: How Democratic Governance Can Revitalize Service Delivery in Zimbabwean Municipalities ........ 25
*Tendai Kaponda, Central China Normal University, China*

**Chapter 3**
Examining Challenges Impacting the Implementation of an Integrated Development Plan in Selected Townships of Nelson Mandela Metropolitan Municipality ........ 58
*Nandiswa Mpolweni, Durban University of Technology, South Africa*
*Martin Mulunda Kabange, Durban University of Technology, South Africa*

**Chapter 4**
Local Economic Development as a Catalyst for Agricultural Growth and Poverty Relief Strategy: A Rural Eastern Cape Perspective ........ 77
*Tando Rulashe, Nelson Mandela University, South Africa*
*Kutu Ramolobe, Nelson Mandela University, South Africa*

**Chapter 5**
Impact of Corona-Virus on Local Economic Development in Zwelisha Community, Durban, South Africa ........ 109
*Ndwakhulu Stephen Tshishonga, University of KwaZulu-Natal, South Africa*
*Slungile Charity Sigwebela, University of KwaZulu-Natal, South Africa*

**Chapter 6**
Sustainable Provision of Municipal Services Through Community-Led Initiatives: Ratepayers' Associations in South Africa ........................................ 129
*Mpfareleni Mavis Netswera, University of South Africa, South Africa*

**Chapter 7**
Enhancing Rural Governance in Zimbabwe: Exploring the Significance of Inter-Governmental Coordination in Facilitating Collaboration and Communication ........................................ 145
*Tendai Kaponda, Central China Normal University, China*

**Chapter 8**
Leveraging Spatial Data Infrastructure for Enhanced Municipal Planning: A Case Study of Pakistan ........................................ 175
*Munir Ahmad, Survey of Pakistan, Pakistan*
*Asmat Ali, Survey of Pakistan, Pakistan*
*Hammad Hussain, COMSATS University Islamabad, Wah, Pakistan*

**Chapter 9**
District Development Model and Service Delivery in South Africa: Reality or Misnomer? ........................................ 195
*Sanah Tebogo Matloga, University of Venda, South Africa*
*Mahlodi Joyce Sethu, University of Venda, South Africa*

**Chapter 10**
A Critical Appraisal on the Impact Maximization of Integrated Service Delivery Through District Development Model ........................................ 227
*Ndwakhulu Stephen Tshishonga, University of KwaZulu-Natal, South Africa*
*Bernard Karabo Sebake, Nelson Mandela University, South Africa*

**Chapter 11**
Analysis of the Significance of Good Governance in Municipal Planning and Implementation ........................................ 247
*Emmanuel Maemu, University of Venda, South Africa*

**Chapter 12**
Management of Municipal Transport System in South Africa ........................................ 260
*Maijane Mashamaite, University of South Africa, South Africa*

**Chapter 13**
The Impact of Civil Society Organisations (CSOs) on the Effectiveness and Quality of Municipal Service Delivery ........ 283
*Kutu Ramolobe, Nelson Mandela University, South Africa*
*Murendeni Praise Ramaru, Nelson Mandela University, South Africa*

**Chapter 14**
Addressing Corruption and Mismanagement in South African Municipalities: Strategies for Effective Governance........ 294
*Martin Mulunda Kabange, Durban University of Technology, South Africa*
*Hlengiwe Mabizela, Durban University of Technology, South Africa*
*Lesha Joseph Judell, Durban University of Technology, South Africa*
*Zwelithini Michael Zwane, Durban University of Technology, South Africa*

**Compilation of References** ........ 326

**About the Contributors** ........ 384

**Index** ........ 388

# Detailed Table of Contents

**Preface**..................................................................................................... xviii

**Chapter 1**
Drawing Lessons From Participatory Budgeting in Brazil for South African Municipal Participatory Budgeting ............................................................ 1
*Ndwakhulu Stephen Tshishonga, University of KwaZulu-Natal, South Africa*

This chapter interrogates the participatory budgeting model experimented with in Porto Alegre to draw lessons for South African municipalities. Participatory budgeting is a process in which citizens, through their civic associations, volunteer to participate regularly in decision-making about the public budget. The chapter argues that participatory budgeting allows ordinary people to activate and broaden their civic action and further demonstrates the importance of invited spaces, particularly in enabling community practices. The primary lesson for South African municipalities is the experimentation of participatory budgeting that is institutionally based on active participation through regular meetings and deliberation of issues. For example, in the Brazilian city of Porto Alegre, an increase in popular participation and investment in sectors such as housing, education, sanitation, and health was imperative. Case studies have been used as the research method instruments for this chapter.

**Chapter 2**
Empowering Residents, Enhancing Services: How Democratic Governance Can Revitalize Service Delivery in Zimbabwean Municipalities........................ 25
*Tendai Kaponda, Central China Normal University, China*

This research employs a mixed-methods approach, combining quantitative surveys with qualitative case studies, to explore the relationship between democratic governance and service delivery in Zimbabwean municipalities. Findings reveal that while decentralisation empowers local governments, effective governance structures are crucial for improved service delivery outcomes. Challenges in resource allocation and financial viability underscore the need for increased support and transparent mechanisms. Enhancing transparency, accountability, and citizen participation is vital for rebuilding trust and improving governance effectiveness. Strengthening electoral processes is essential for promoting democratic legitimacy. Implementing these recommendations can revitalise local service delivery and empower residents in urban communities. This study contributes to advancing our understanding of the importance of democratic governance in promoting inclusive and sustainable development in municipalities.

**Chapter 3**
Examining Challenges Impacting the Implementation of an Integrated Development Plan in Selected Townships of Nelson Mandela Metropolitan Municipality ........................................................................................... 58
*Nandiswa Mpolweni, Durban University of Technology, South Africa*
*Martin Mulunda Kabange, Durban University of Technology, South Africa*

The South African Integrated Development Plans (IDPs) were established to strategically coordinate development efforts, allocate resources effectively, and improve service delivery across municipalities in the country. Nevertheless, despite adhering to legal obligations, municipalities face persistent challenges that impede the realisation of their strategic goals and the effective execution of their plans. This study explores the barriers obstructing the Nelson Mandela Metropolitan Municipality's (NMMM) efficient implementation of its IDPs, notwithstanding its compliance with legislation. Through qualitative methods, including document review and stakeholder interviews, the study identifies critical challenges such as limited community participation, insufficient budget allocation, human resource constraints, and strained intergovernmental relations. These challenges intersect and impact the municipality's capacity to deliver services effectively and achieve its strategic goals.

**Chapter 4**
Local Economic Development as a Catalyst for Agricultural Growth and Poverty Relief Strategy: A Rural Eastern Cape Perspective ................................ 77
*Tando Rulashe, Nelson Mandela University, South Africa*
*Kutu Ramolobe, Nelson Mandela University, South Africa*

In rural South Africa, the enduring legacies of apartheid, including poverty and limited opportunities, persist. This chapter delves into how agriculture can drive local economic growth and development, despite challenges like resource scarcity and inadequate infrastructure. It explores how leveraging agriculture can alleviate poverty. Drawing on theories like systems theory and community-based development, it examines interventions to uplift rural communities. Using a mixed-method approach with an interpretive paradigm and an exploratory design, the chapter conducts a systematic review of secondary data sources, including scholarly publications and official government documents. Despite persistent challenges, findings indicate governmental efforts to support informal and smallholder farmers in enhancing their livelihoods and contributing to LED. Government support for small farmers is acknowledged, but obstacles remain. The chapter emphasizes stakeholder collaboration to enhance skills, infrastructure, and community empowerment for sustainable development.

**Chapter 5**
Impact of Corona-Virus on Local Economic Development in Zwelisha Community, Durban, South Africa ...................................................................... 109
*Ndwakhulu Stephen Tshishonga, University of KwaZulu-Natal, South Africa*
*Slungile Charity Sigwebela, University of KwaZulu-Natal, South Africa*

Multifaceted impacts of the pandemic on local economies and provided insights into the strategies and policies that can foster recovery and resilience. Furthermore, the chapter used qualitative research methods, such as interviews to capture the experiences and perceptions of local businesses, entrepreneurs, government officials, and community members. The chapter's findings could contribute to understanding the complex dynamics between pandemics, local economies, and economic development. By examining the impact of COVID-19 on local economic development, this chapter found evidence-based decision-making strategies that could contribute to developing strategies that can mitigate the adverse effects of pandemics on local economies, ultimately leading to more sustainable and inclusive economic growth.

**Chapter 6**
Sustainable Provision of Municipal Services Through Community-Led Initiatives: Ratepayers' Associations in South Africa ........................................ 129
*Mpfareleni Mavis Netswera, University of South Africa, South Africa*

This chapter emphases the key role that community-led initiatives play in the absence of sustainable provision of services from the government. Through these initiatives, citizens as individuals or as a formation get involved in the provision of services to improve the quality of their lives. Through secondary data analysis, this chapter examines the prevalence and the role of ratepayers' associations in the sustainable provision of public services in South Africa. The main findings reveal that in the past few years, ratepayers' associations have been holding underperforming municipalities accountable by demanding services due to them. Whereas some took over collapsed municipal services through lawsuits and volunteerism to ensure continues delivery, others managed to address the water pollution dated back to the 1990s when overworked sewage systems were continuously used with little maintenance. The chapter recommends multi-stakeholder partnerships within a municipal area to share knowledge, expertise and support to ensure availability and sustainability of services.

**Chapter 7**
Enhancing Rural Governance in Zimbabwe: Exploring the Significance of Inter-Governmental Coordination in Facilitating Collaboration and Communication ........................................................................................ 145
*Tendai Kaponda, Central China Normal University, China*

Zimbabwe's rural governance involves coordination across different government levels, with distinct roles and responsibilities. The chapter highlights the historical evolution of rural governance in Zimbabwe, which has shifted towards greater decentralisation. The RDDC serves as a platform for coordination across government entities at the district level, but issues such as inadequate participation and conflicting authorities have been noted. Political dynamics, economic constraints, and social traditions influence intergovernmental coordination. Ansell and Gash's collaborative governance model offers insights for stakeholders. Intergovernmental coordination is crucial for facilitating collaboration and communication. There is a need for enhanced information sharing, clarified roles, improved leadership, adequate resources, and better communication mechanisms. Leveraging the lessons from Ansell and Gash's model can significantly contribute to promoting effective intergovernmental collaboration and improving rural governance and development outcomes in Zimbabwe.

**Chapter 8**
Leveraging Spatial Data Infrastructure for Enhanced Municipal Planning: A Case Study of Pakistan.......... 175
*Munir Ahmad, Survey of Pakistan, Pakistan*
*Asmat Ali, Survey of Pakistan, Pakistan*
*Hammad Hussain, COMSATS University Islamabad, Wah, Pakistan*

The significance of spatial data infrastructure (SDI) in municipal planning in Pakistan cannot be overstated, as it can plays a central role in reshaping urban development endeavors. By amalgamating a variety of geospatial datasets and fostering cooperation among government bodies and stakeholders, SDI can facilitate well-informed decision-making, streamlined resource allocation, and heightened citizen involvement. In grappling with obstacles such as procedural delays, insufficient coordination, and limited resources, SDI emerges as a comprehensive framework that tackles the multifaceted challenges of urbanization, transportation, and environmental sustainability. Furthermore, through its emphasis on transparency, accountability, and citizen empowerment, SDI can ensure that planning endeavors are inclusive and attuned to the diverse needs of the populace.

**Chapter 9**
District Development Model and Service Delivery in South Africa: Reality or Misnomer?.......... 195
*Sanah Tebogo Matloga, University of Venda, South Africa*
*Mahlodi Joyce Sethu, University of Venda, South Africa*

The chapter aimed to provide a critical overview of the district development model (DDM) and service delivery challenges in South Africa. South African planning has been characterised by fragmented planning, impacting service delivery. To resolve this, the cabinet adopted the DDM as an innovation to improve integrated planning and service delivery across all spheres of government. The main objective of the model was to solve the silo problem. The study employed the desktop method. Critical theory was adopted to review DDM and service delivery challenges. The findings revealed that DDM is expected to develop, support, and promote entrepreneurs by prioritising service procurement. Government should ensure stakeholders' involvement in the planning and implementation process. Spheres of government should stop working in silos and fight the triple challenges for DDM to become a reality rather than a misnomer. Government must develop mechanisms for accountability across municipalities for the implementation of DDM.

**Chapter 10**
A Critical Appraisal on the Impact Maximization of Integrated Service Delivery Through District Development Model ............................................. 227
*Ndwakhulu Stephen Tshishonga, University of KwaZulu-Natal, South Africa*
*Bernard Karabo Sebake, Nelson Mandela University, South Africa*

This chapter assesses the impact of the district development model (DDM) 's impact in maximizing integrated service delivery in South Africa. This chapter argues that the maximization of service delivery could only occur through proper alignment of resources, closing gaps between the people and the government. The chapter uses DDM objectives to evaluate the potential and challenges in enhancing integrated service delivery and intergovernmental relations at the local government level. DDM objectives are as follows: a) to promote cooperation instead of functioning in silos; b) to attenuate the disassociation between government and people; c) to ensure the delivery of consolidated services. OR Tambo District Municipality, eThekwini Metropolitan Municipality, and Waterberg District Municipality were used as case studies to reflect on the operation of the piloted DDM in South Africa.

**Chapter 11**
Analysis of the Significance of Good Governance in Municipal Planning and Implementation ..................................................................................... 247
*Emmanuel Maemu, University of Venda, South Africa*

This chapter focuses on the significance of good governance in municipal planning and implementation to develop changeable activities that may foster good governance during municipal planning and implementation. This chapter will seek to assess the obstacles that cause developmental projects to fail in South African municipalities. Municipal planning means the control and regulation of land use at a municipal level whereas implementation entails the requirement that all municipalities in the country develop and approve such plans to adequately respond to the needs. Good governance means the capacity of city councils and their partners to formulate and implement sound policies and systems that reflect the interests of local citizens, and to do so in a way that is transparent and inclusive of those with the least power and resources.

**Chapter 12**
Management of Municipal Transport System in South Africa ......................... 260
*Maijane Mashamaite, University of South Africa, South Africa*

Travelling to and from work is the second most popular cause for household travel in South Africa, trailing only educational travels. South Africa's municipal transport system also suffers from fluctuating ridership, with some workers compelled to drive owing to a lack of safe and reliable transport options, while others frequently have little choice but to use public transport, despite the obstacles and unreliability. This chapter explores the current issues confronting the Southern African municipal transport systems and suggests a potential way to address them. The chapter outlined difficulties encountered in municipalities for which a universal solution may be implemented. These difficulties were determined to be primarily the result of government initiatives. The chapter concludes that social outcomes must be better integrated into South African municipal transport system at the strategic, tactical, and operational levels.

**Chapter 13**
The Impact of Civil Society Organisations (CSOs) on the Effectiveness and Quality of Municipal Service Delivery ........................................................... 283
*Kutu Ramolobe, Nelson Mandela University, South Africa*
*Murendeni Praise Ramaru, Nelson Mandela University, South Africa*

Municipalities are the level of government closest to the people, and their primary function is to deliver essential services to local communities. However, effectively achieving this goal requires prioritizing the interests of those communities. A key factor in improving municipal service delivery is strong collaboration with civil society organizations (CSOs). Therefore, this chapter investigates the impact of CSOs on the effectiveness and quality of municipal services. Qualitative research methodologies were used, largely through desktop research to analyse the influence of CSOs on municipal service delivery. CSOs are crucial, in improving the efficiency and quality of services provided by local governments. They engage communities to promote involvement and hold authorities accountable for their actions. Through encouraging engagement and fostering accountability measures CSOs make contributions, to upholding democratic principles and enhancing the welfare of residents.

**Chapter 14**
Addressing Corruption and Mismanagement in South African Municipalities: Strategies for Effective Governance ........ 294
*Martin Mulunda Kabange, Durban University of Technology, South Africa*
*Hlengiwe Mabizela, Durban University of Technology, South Africa*
*Lesha Joseph Judell, Durban University of Technology, South Africa*
*Zwelithini Michael Zwane, Durban University of Technology, South Africa*

Corruption and mismanagement pose significant challenges to effective governance and service delivery within South African municipalities. A systematic literature review was conducted using the preferred reporting items for systematic reviews and meta-analyses (PRISMA) framework to address these issues, and interventions supported by empirical evidence were suggested. The results emphasised the need to address systemic obstacles, encourage community involvement, and strengthen civil society's responsibility. Capacity-building initiatives and institutional reform were also identified as indispensable instruments in the fight against corruption. Municipalities can achieve more transparent, accountable, and effective governance by addressing these issues. Policymakers and stakeholders should prioritise these interventions to restore public confidence in municipal management and promote sustainable development.

**Compilation of References** ........ 326

**About the Contributors** ........ 384

**Index** ........ 388

# Foreword

The extent to which communities attain social, economic and environmental objectives is highly dependent on the functionality and efficacy of its local government systems. Being the sphere closest to communities, municipalities are therefore expected to plan, budget and effectively implement programmes and projects that improve the quality of life of citizens. This is applicable to all municipalities across the globe in that they are expected to structure and manage planning, budgeting and implementation processes in a way that ensures that the developmental objectives are met, and community aspirations are satisfied.

Three decades into democracy, unfortunately, the majority of South Africans are still to enjoy the benefits of being serviced by an ideal municipality. Majority of South Africans struggle with inadequate access to basic services, as well as a decline in the quality of some services. All this is despite the resources made available by national government, especially in the form of conditional grants to address service delivery backlogs as well as to accommodate new growth. Most municipalities are unable to spend the budget allocated to them for infrastructure delivery and maintenance. As a result, access and quality of social and economic services continue to be a challenge. One of the main contributing factors to the below average performance of most municipalities is ineffective planning, budgeting and implementation. While the various legislative and policy prescripts provide a blueprint of the planning and implementation requirements, there are serious challenges in this regard. In some instances, the challenge is perpetuated by lack of skilled officials in key service delivery areas. Corruption and lack of accountability have also ravaged many municipalities in that elected and appointed municipal officials escape scoot free with no consequences whatsoever for transgressing policy prescripts. Institutions mandated to hold these officials to account including but not limited to the municipal councils have often failed in holding these officials to account for their actions and inactions. Many billions of municipal monies have been lost through corrupt practices. To this extent, corruption, lack of accountability, ineffective planning and budgeting contributes negatively to municipal plans not being effectively implemented.

This book edition will therefore contribute immensely to the development of this critical sphere of government closest to the people. By exploring the importance of various elements such as good governance, democratic governance, integrated planning and economic development, the book provides key elements necessary for a complete ecosystem that is critical for an effective local government system.

**Modjadji Malahlela**
*Department of Cooperative Governance, Human Settlements & Traditional Affairs (Limpopo province in South Africa)*

# Preface

In the evolving landscape of global governance, municipalities serve as the critical nexus between government aspirations and community realities. However, municipalities in many third-world countries face persistent challenges that undermine their ability to achieve their set plans and objectives. This compilation, *Exploring Effective Municipal Planning and Implementation*, seeks to delve into these multifaceted issues and offer scholarly insights and practical solutions to enhance the efficacy of municipal governance.

Municipalities are often beset by a confluence of impediments such as inadequate skills and capacity, pervasive corruption, insufficient political will, a lack of consequences for policy violations, and weak accountability frameworks. These issues collectively contribute to the stagnation and dysfunction observed in local governments around the world. Tshishonga (2019) highlights the prevalence of corruption and mismanagement within local government structures, which significantly hampers development efforts and service delivery. Consequently, municipalities frequently fail to meet their constitutional obligations, resulting in persistent negative audit outcomes.

This reference book provides a platform for academics and practitioners worldwide to contribute to the discourse on municipal governance. By examining the factors contributing to the ongoing failures in local government and proposing viable mechanisms for improvement, we aim to foster a deeper understanding and develop strategies to enhance the effectiveness of municipalities.

Each chapter offers a unique perspective and expertise, contributing to a comprehensive exploration of the challenges and opportunities within municipal governance. The diversity of topics and the depth of analysis presented in this book underscore the complexity of municipal planning and implementation and the necessity for a multi-faceted approach to reform.

We extend our gratitude to all contributors for their valuable insights and dedication to this critical field of study. It is our hope that *Exploring Effective Municipal Planning and Implementation* will serve as a vital resource for scholars, policymakers, and practitioners seeking to improve the functioning and performance of municipalities, ultimately leading to better service delivery and enhanced community well-being.

**Chapter 1: Drawing Lessons from Participatory Budgeting in Brazil for South African Municipal Participatory Budgeting,***Ndwakhulu Tshishonga, University of KwaZulu Natal, South Africa*

This chapter examines the participatory budgeting model from Porto Alegre, Brazil, to extract valuable lessons for South African municipalities. Participatory budgeting engages citizens in decision-making about public budgets through civic associations, promoting active civic involvement and community practices. The chapter argues that participatory budgeting can enhance civic action and demonstrates its importance through case studies. The Porto Alegre model shows increased popular participation and investments in essential sectors like housing, education, sanitation, and health, providing a blueprint for South African municipalities to foster active citizen participation and improve service delivery.

**Chapter 2: Empowering Residents, Enhancing Services: How Democratic Governance Can Revitalize Local Delivery in Zimbabwean Urban Local Authorities,***Tendai Kaponda, Central China Normal University, China*

This chapter employs a mixed-methods approach to explore the relationship between democratic governance and service delivery in Zimbabwean municipalities. It finds that while decentralization empowers local governments, effective governance structures are crucial for improved service delivery. The chapter highlights challenges in resource allocation and financial viability, emphasizing the need for transparent mechanisms and increased support. Strengthening transparency, accountability, and citizen participation is vital for rebuilding trust and improving governance. Enhancing electoral processes to promote democratic legitimacy is also essential. The chapter provides recommendations to revitalize local service delivery and empower residents.

**Chapter 3: Examining Challenges Impacting the Implementation of Integrated Development Plan in Selected Townships of Nelson Mandela Metropolitan Municipality,***Nandiswa Mpolweni, Martin Kabange, Durban University of Technology, South Africa*

This chapter explores the barriers impeding the effective implementation of Integrated Development Plans (IDPs) in the Nelson Mandela Metropolitan Municipality. Despite meeting legal obligations, municipalities face challenges such as limited community participation, insufficient budget allocation, human resource constraints, and strained intergovernmental relations. Using qualitative methods, the study identifies these intersecting challenges and their impact on the municipality's capacity to deliver services and achieve strategic goals. The findings highlight the need for improved strategies to overcome these obstacles and enhance the effectiveness of IDPs.

**Chapter 4: Local Economic Development as a Catalyst Agricultural Growth & Poverty Relief Strategy – A Rural Eastern Cape Perspective,***Tando Rulashe, Kutu Ramolobe, Nelson Mandela University, South Africa*

This chapter investigates the potential of agriculture to drive local economic growth and poverty alleviation in rural Eastern Cape, South Africa. It discusses the persistent challenges of poverty and limited opportunities stemming from apartheid and explores how agricultural initiatives can uplift rural communities. Using a mixed-method approach, the chapter reviews secondary data to examine interventions supporting informal and smallholder farmers. Despite ongoing challenges, the findings recognize government efforts to enhance livelihoods and contribute to local economic development. The chapter emphasizes the importance of stakeholder collaboration to improve skills, infrastructure, and community empowerment for sustainable development.

**Chapter 5: Impact of Coronavirus on Local Economic Development in Zwelisha Community, Durban, South Africa,***Ndwakhulu Tshishonga, Slungile Sigwebela, University of KwaZulu Natal, South Africa*

This chapter explores the multifaceted impacts of the COVID-19 pandemic on local economies, with a focus on the Zwelisha community in Durban, KwaZulu Natal Province. Using qualitative research method, including interviews with local businesses, entrepreneurs, government officials, and community members, the chapter captures the experiences and perceptions of the pandemic's effects. The findings provide insights into strategies and policies that can foster recovery and resilience, contributing to evidence-based decision-making. The chapter underscores the importance of developing strategies to mitigate the adverse effects of pandemics on local economies, ultimately promoting sustainable and inclusive economic growth.

**Chapter 6: Sustainable Provision of Municipal Services Through Community-Led Initiatives: Ratepayers' Associations in South Africa,***Mpfareleni Netswera, University of South Africa, South Africa*

This chapter examines the critical role of community-led initiatives, specifically ratepayers' associations, in the sustainable provision of municipal services in South Africa. Through secondary data analysis, it explores how these associations hold underperforming municipalities accountable and sometimes take over collapsed services through lawsuits and volunteerism. The chapter highlights successful examples where ratepayers' associations addressed long-standing issues such as water pollution. It recommends multi-stakeholder partnerships to share knowledge, expertise, and support to ensure the availability and sustainability of services, emphasizing community involvement in improving service delivery.

**Chapter 7: Enhancing Rural Governance in Zimbabwe: Exploring the Significance of Inter-Governmental Coordination in Facilitating Collaboration and Communication,***Tendai Kaponda, Central China Normal University, China*

This chapter explores the coordination between different government levels in Zimbabwe's rural governance, highlighting the historical shift towards decentralization. It discusses the role of the Rural District Development Committees (RDDC) and the challenges of inadequate participation and conflicting authorities. Using Ansell and Gash's collaborative governance model, the chapter emphasizes the need for enhanced information sharing, clarified roles, improved leadership, adequate resources, and better communication mechanisms. It provides insights into promoting effective intergovernmental collaboration and improving rural governance and development outcomes in Zimbabwe.

**Chapter 8: Leveraging Spatial Data Infrastructure for Enhanced Municipal Planning: A Case Study of Pakistan,***Munir Ahmad, Asmat Ali, Hammad Hussain, Survey of Pakistan, COMSATS University Islamabad, Wah, Pakistan*

This chapter underscores the importance of Spatial Data Infrastructure (SDI) in municipal planning in Pakistan. By integrating various geospatial datasets and fostering cooperation among government bodies and stakeholders, SDI can facilitate informed decision-making, streamlined resource allocation, and increased citizen involvement. The chapter addresses challenges such as procedural delays, insufficient coordination, and limited resources, proposing SDI as a comprehensive framework to tackle urbanization, transportation, and environmental sustainability issues. It highlights the potential of SDI to promote transparency, accountability, and inclusive planning processes.

**Chapter 9: District Development Model and Service Delivery in South Africa: Reality or Misnomer?,***Sanah Matloga, Mahlodi Sethu, University of Venda, South Africa*

This chapter provides a critical overview of the District Development Model (DDM) and its impact on service delivery in South Africa. It discusses the fragmented planning that has characterized South African service delivery and the adoption of the DDM to improve integrated planning. Using a desktop method and critical theory, the chapter reviews the challenges and potentials of the DDM. The findings reveal that for the DDM to be effective, there must be stakeholder involvement, and government entities must move away from siloed operations. The chapter calls for mechanisms to ensure accountability and the successful implementation of the DDM.

**Chapter 10: A Critical Appraisal on the Impact Maximization of Integrated Service Delivery through District Development Model,***Ndwakhulu Tshishonga, Bernard Sebake, Nelson Mandela University, South Africa*

This chapter assesses the District Development Model (DDM) and its potential to maximize integrated service delivery in South Africa. It argues that effective service delivery requires proper resource alignment and bridging gaps between the government and citizens. The chapter uses DDM objectives to evaluate its potential and challenges in enhancing service delivery and intergovernmental relations. Case studies from OR Tambo District Municipality, eThekwini Metropolitan Municipality, and Waterberg District Municipality illustrate the model's implementation and impact. The chapter concludes that successful DDM implementation depends on cooperation, reduced governmental disassociation, and consolidated service delivery.

**Chapter 11: Analysis of the Significance of Good Governance in Municipal Planning and Implementation: Municipal Planning and Implementation,***Emmanuel Maemu, University of Venda, South Africa*

This chapter delves into the crucial role that good governance plays in municipal planning and implementation, emphasizing the development of adaptable activities that can foster better governance practices. The chapter assesses the obstacles that hinder the success of developmental projects in South African municipalities. It defines municipal planning as the regulation of land use at the local level and implementation as the necessary development and approval of plans to meet community needs. Good governance is characterized by the capacity of city councils and their partners to formulate and implement sound policies transparently and inclusively, reflecting the interests of local citizens, particularly the marginalized.

**Chapter 12: Management of Municipal Transport System in South Africa,-***Maijane Mashamaite, UNISA, South Africa*

This chapter examines the challenges confronting South Africa's municipal transport systems and proposes potential solutions. It identifies fluctuating ridership and the lack of safe and reliable transport options as key issues. Many workers are compelled to drive due to the unreliable public transport system, while others have no choice but to use it despite the obstacles. The chapter outlines government initiatives and concludes that social outcomes must be better integrated into the transport system at strategic, tactical, and operational levels. It suggests comprehensive strategies to improve the municipal transport system's reliability and safety.

**Chapter 13: The Impact of Civil Society Organizations (CSOs) on the Effectiveness and Quality of Municipal Service Delivery,***Kutu Ramolobe, Murendeni Ramaru, Nelson Mandela University, South Africa*

This chapter investigates the impact of civil society organizations (CSOs) on municipal service delivery in South Africa. It highlights the essential role of CSOs in improving service efficiency and quality by engaging communities, promoting involvement, and holding authorities accountable. Using qualitative research methodologies, the chapter analyzes the influence of CSOs through desktop research. It concludes that CSOs are crucial in upholding democratic principles and enhancing residents' welfare by encouraging engagement and accountability in municipal service delivery.

**Chapter 14: Addressing Corruption and Mismanagement in South African Municipalities: Strategies for Effective Governance,***Martin Kabange, Hlengiwe Mabizela, Lesha Joseph Judell, Zwelithini Michael Zwane, Durban University of Technology, South Africa*

This chapter addresses the challenges of corruption and mismanagement in South African municipalities and suggests strategies for effective governance. Conducting a systematic literature review using the PRISMA framework, the chapter identifies interventions supported by empirical evidence. It emphasizes the need to address systemic obstacles, encourage community involvement, and strengthen civil society's responsibility. The chapter also highlights capacity-building initiatives and institutional reforms as essential tools in combating corruption. By implementing these strategies, municipalities can achieve more transparent, accountable, and effective governance. The chapter calls on policymakers and stakeholders to prioritize these interventions to restore public confidence in municipal management and promote sustainable development.

In compiling *Exploring Effective Municipal Planning and Implementation*, we aimed to address the intricate and multifaceted challenges that municipalities, especially in third-world countries, encounter in their governance and service delivery efforts. Our contributors have meticulously examined various aspects of municipal governance, offering a wealth of insights and practical solutions grounded in rigorous research and diverse case studies.

The chapters in this book underscore the significant hurdles municipalities face, including inadequate skills and capacity, corruption, weak accountability frameworks, and insufficient political will. These factors collectively contribute to the inefficacy of local governments, as poignantly highlighted by Tshishonga (2019), who discusses the rampant mismanagement and corruption within local government structures.

Through the collective expertise of our authors, this book offers a comprehensive exploration of these issues, presenting a range of strategies to enhance municipal governance. From the lessons of participatory budgeting in Brazil to the role of civil society organizations in South Africa, each chapter provides valuable perspectives and evidence-based recommendations aimed at fostering effective municipal planning and implementation.

As editors, we are immensely grateful to all our contributors for their dedication to this critical field of study. Their contributions not only deepen our understanding of municipal governance but also present actionable strategies for overcoming the persistent challenges faced by municipalities. We hope this book serves as a vital resource for scholars, policymakers, and practitioners committed to improving municipal governance and enhancing community well-being.

Ultimately, *Exploring Effective Municipal Planning and Implementation* is more than a scholarly compilation; it is a call to action. It urges stakeholders at all levels to embrace transparency, accountability, and inclusive governance practices. By doing so, we can pave the way for more effective, resilient, and responsive municipalities that are capable of meeting the needs of their communities and fostering sustainable development.

Editors:

**Pandelani Harry Munzhedzi**
*University of Venda, South Africa*

**Ntwanano Erasmus Mathebula**
*University of Limpopo, South Africa*

**Ntsako Idris Makamu**
*University of South Africa, South Africa*

## REFERENCES

Tshishonga, N. (2019). Prospects and challenges of transforming local government into a learning organisation. *African Journal of Public Affairs*, 11(1), 157–175.

# Chapter 1
# Drawing Lessons From Participatory Budgeting in Brazil for South African Municipal Participatory Budgeting

**Ndwakhulu Stephen Tshishonga**
*University of KwaZulu-Natal, South Africa*

## ABSTRACT

*This chapter interrogates the participatory budgeting model experimented with in Porto Alegre to draw lessons for South African municipalities. Participatory budgeting is a process in which citizens, through their civic associations, volunteer to participate regularly in decision-making about the public budget. The chapter argues that participatory budgeting allows ordinary people to activate and broaden their civic action and further demonstrates the importance of invited spaces, particularly in enabling community practices. The primary lesson for South African municipalities is the experimentation of participatory budgeting that is institutionally based on active participation through regular meetings and deliberation of issues. For example, in the Brazilian city of Porto Alegre, an increase in popular participation and investment in sectors such as housing, education, sanitation, and health was imperative. Case studies have been used as the research method instruments for this chapter.*

DOI: 10.4018/979-8-3693-3617-5.ch001

## INTRODUCTION

Since 1994, local government in South Africa has created both challenges and opportunities. The White Paper on Local Government (1998: v) stipulates that local government should impact reconstruction and development. In contrast to apartheid's local government, this mandate renders local government a unique point of entry to government. Hence, some scholars associate local government with the local sphere of government, a decentralized form of government, sub-national government, or democratic local governance (Mokgopo, 2017; Picard & Mogale, 2015). However, the post-apartheid local government is challenged with transforming discriminatory and racially embedded structures into a transparent and responsive sphere of government. Most importantly, the *Constitution of the Republic of South Africa (1996, Section 152[1])* and the *White Paper on Local Government (1998)* assert that local government is purposefully designed to devolve governance to the grassroots. Thus, this affords people a platform to get involved in the political processes affecting their lives (Tobi & Oikhala, 2021). Local government is confronted by various challenges, such as policy formulation, decision-making, and policy implementation aimed at mitigating the adverse effects of an unjust, autocratic, and bureaucratic apartheid local government (Manzini, 2016). Lack of administrative capacity, incompetence, fraud, and corruption; operational deficit rendering many municipalities unable to fulfill their developmental mandate of service delivery and promoting local democracy (Bambo, 2022; Kaywood, 2021; Ntliziywana, 2021). The apartheid government was known for producing subjects instead of active citizens (Matloga, Mahole, and Nekhavhambe, 2024). Additionally, the dismal performance of municipalities hinges on their financial mismanagement, council and administrative instability, and crumbling municipal infrastructure (Basson & Hunter, 2023). As such, local government is challenged to entrench democracy and governance based on the active participation of the local people. Ultimately, the convergence of these challenges undermines the social contract between the local state and the people.

This chapter interrogates the participatory budgetary model experimented with in cities like Porto Alegre and Kerala. Despite its challenges, participatory budgeting has proven to be a success story, particularly in activating active citizenry and deepening local governance through representation, deliberation, and participation (Wampler, McNulty & Touchton, 2021). Considering that South Africa has adopted a developmental approach to local governance, the primacy of this chapter is to draw lessons from participatory budgeting processes for South African municipalities. The methodology adopted for this chapter is qualitative, where a desktop literature review was used as the dominant research instrument. This chapter is divided into the following sections: the first section presents the theoretical conceptions of participatory budgeting. The second section introduces the case study of participatory budgeting in Porto Alegre, Brazil, followed by a section on the framework for participatory budgeting in South Africa. The fourth section puts forward lessons that can be utilized by South African municipalities, followed by the conclusion of the chapter.

## THEORETICAL CONCEPTIONS OF PARTICIPATORY BUDGETING

Globally, nations have experimented with the participatory budgetary (PB) model as part of democracy-deepening and local governance (Gilman & Wampler, 2019). Although participatory budgeting started in Brazil in the city of Porto Alegre, its influence and experimentation have been widespread. In its original or modified form, participatory budgeting emerged as part of a broader participatory instrument institutionalized for empowered participatory governance, countervailing power, participatory publics, and democratic innovations (Sintomer, Herzberg & Rocke, 2008, p. 165). In Brazil, participatory budgeting was equated to delegative democracy (Kapiszewski, Levitsky & Yashar, 2021), and its theoretical foundations border participatory and deliberative models of democracy (Della Porta, 2013; Held, 2010). Participatory democracy is rooted in valuing and promoting citizen participation in decision-making processes (**Musadat, 2023).**

For Political Scientists such as Ly (2023), participatory forms of democracy foster human development, enhance a sense of political efficacy, reduce a sense of estrangement from power centers, nurture a concern for collective problems, and contribute to the formation of an active and knowledgeable citizenry (in Held, 2010, p. 212). **Kraai, Ndevu & Matsiliza (2023)add that t**he PB methods promote public participation and, as such, call for people to have the power to affect collective decisions. **Deliberative democracy is a continuum of participatory democracy and has to do with citizen participation whereby consensus is reached through deliberations, discussions, and persuasive arguments (Della Porta, 2013& Polletta,** 2002). Through d**irect democracy, people are engaged directly in the country's governing procedure in direct democracy, and decisions are made directly by the public. If a new law or regulation is to be enacted, citizens have to vote against or in favour of it, and only then will it be approved or rejected (Germann & Serdult, 2017). It is also known as 'pure democracy' because there is no direct involvement of intermediaries who make decisions on behalf of the citizens (Robert, 2022). Direct democracy represents common sovereignty and citizens' right to make fundamental decisions directly with no intervention of their representatives (Colombo, 2018). No other model of democracy assures a greater degree of transparency and openness among the people and the**

**authorities. Public discussions and debates on major issues are held (Mueller, Vatter & Schmid, 2016).** When such a decision is made, it binds the group unless new reasoning and convincing is tabled for further deliberations. In deliberative democracy, dialogue and arguments resolve problems and conflicts (Curato, Hammond & Min, 2019). Thus, for Sanders (Scudder, 2020), deliberation requires equality in resources and guarantees equal opportunity for citizens to articulate persuasive arguments. Across the world, governments and NGOs are experimenting with a process of participatory budgeting where members of a community help decide how to allocate public expenditure.

The notion of a participatory budget is associated with the collective decision, prioritization of community needs and services, citizen participation, and budget allocation procedures (Baiocchi & Ganuza, 2014). Participatory budgeting allows citizens to deliberate and negotiate over the distribution of public resources through decision-making processes (Dhimitri & Burda, 2019). The distribution of resources is based on democratic institutions where accountability transfers decision-making authority to citizens and empowers promoted and enhanced citizens (Atisa, Zemrani & Weiss, 2021). Viewed from the collaborative theories, participatory budgeting is underpinned by 1) an argument that critiques the rational-dominated development paradigm and its replacement with a humanistic approach that advocates practices where establishing purposes and identifying actions is fundamental (Healey, 1992, p. 154). 2). Proponents of participatory budgeting are anti-rationalist in their views, where change agents are neutral and expected to be uninterested observers (Leduka, 2009). Participatory budgeting locates change agents as active actors, advisors, and shapers of communities. Participatory budgeting is procedural, a space for citizen participation, and requires co-decision-making capacity as the precursors for a 'new form of participatory government' (Sintomer et al. 2008, p. 167). Through participatory budgeting, 'formal institutionalisation of a rights-based approach to development' is entrenched (Beall, 2005, p. 124), 'direct participation options attempts to create the conditions for a more deliberative democracy' (Lafont, 2015), and 'empowered deliberative democracy based on values of participation, deliberation and empowerment' (Hammond, 2021). Importantly, participatory budgeting promotes transparency and reduces the possibility of ineffective government and corruption. Its advantage is that it allows citizens, especially those from the historically disadvantaged, marginalized, socio-economically, and politically excluded, to actively engage in processes that enable them to identify their challenges and explore alternative solutions. The participatory budgeting model is further applauded for improving the quality of democracy by supporting open citizen participation and debates (Marumaholo, Chigwata & Nhede, 2018). Direct involvement of citizens and associations is encouraged in the identification, planning, implementation, evaluation, and monitoring of development projects (Kgobe & Mamokhere, 2021). As an institutional framework, participatory budgeting has proven to have the potential to strengthen people's knowledge about governance issues, improve state functioning, and fight against the squandering of public resources (Leduka, 2009). Participatory budgeting is famous for balancing the prerogatives of municipalities without stifling citizens' voices and their active participation in democratic decision-making processes (Brumatti, 2022).

The cases below are typical examples of participatory democracy, such as the participatory budgeting experimented with in Porto Alegre and Kerala (Baiocchi, 2011; Heller, 2001). The deliberations of these cases entail both the opportunities and some of the challenges in institutionalizing direct and participatory governance through participatory budgeting.

## PARTICIPATORY BUDGETING IN PORTO ALEGRE

Participatory budgeting is thus understood as a process by which citizens, through their civic associations, volunteer to participate regularly in decision-making about the public budget (Džinić, Svidroňová and Markowska-Bzducha, 2016). Thus, democratic decentralisation gave rise to the participatory governance agenda with devolution of power accompanied by regular elections, council hearings, and participatory budgeting (Onyalo, 2021). These cases demonstrated that through community deliberation and citizen input, people can influence the decision-making processes of municipality governance (Baocchi, 2011, p. 306). Despite their low educational levels and being from underprivileged neighbourhoods, with regular meetings and deliberation of issues, people managed to mainstream their issues for consideration in the municipality council. Through participatory budgeting, ordinary people could practice direct democracy, whereby people's assemblies became the forum for citizens to discuss and vote for investment priorities for their respective zones (Hordijk, 2012). According to Baiocchi (2011), these gatherings of ordinary people were able to broaden their civic action and further demonstrate the importance of government-sponsored settings, particularly in enabling community practices.

Case study of Participatory Budgeting in the Brazilian city of Porto Alegre

Historically, the participatory budget in Porto Alegre was introduced by the Partido dos Trabalhadores, known as the Workers' Party, in the early 1990s (Santos, Tanscheit and Ventura, 2020). This trajectory should be envisaged as part of the myriad reforms incorporating citizen input into municipal governance's decision-making processes. For example, the experimentation of participatory budgeting in the Brazilian city of Porto Alegre saw increased popular participation and investment in housing, education, sanitation, and health (Blinova, 2017). Participatory budgeting was pioneered in Porto Alegre nearly twenty years ago. It usually includes four stages: community members identify spending priorities, develop spending proposals, and vote on proposals to fund, which the local government finally implements. In Brazil, participatory budgets emerged from the Porto Alegre municipal government after it faced bankruptcy and chronically inadequate public infrastructure. Their experimentation with democratic governance through participatory budgeting forged a pathway for citizens to assume greater responsibilities in exercising their active citizenship and allocating resources. Since then, according to the Participatory Budget Project, an advocacy NGO worldwide has incorporated some variations of participatory budgeting in their city budgeting.

In Brazil, participatory budgeting has become the vehicle for deepening deliberative democracy and 'empowered deliberative democracy' as espoused by Fung and Wright (2001, p. 7). Participatory budgeting is democratic because it relies on citizen participation and the capabilities of ordinary people, particularly in deliberating on issues and seeking alternative solutions. The second part of the 'empowered deliberative democracy' is deliberative. The participatory budgeting model, by its design, is intrinsically anchored on deliberative and robust debates through citizens' efforts with the outcome of reasons-based decision-making. Essentially, participatory budgets not only facilitate democratic processes and deliberative engagement but empower citizens by integrating actions with collective deliberations. Introspectively, participatory budgeting reflects innovations that encompass provision for participatory planning, citizen monitoring committees, forms of public referenda, and citizen consultation (Gaventa, 2011, p. 257).

This model of planning, implementing, and monitoring the budget has an influential impact as a new framework for democratic local governance that interfaces popular forms of participation with more representative forms of democracy. Porto Alegre is considered one of the most influential and exemplary models for reorienting cloistered bureaucracies, especially at local government levels (Musadat, 2023). By modeling budgets in a participatory manner, Porto Alegre enhanced governance and democracy by 'reverting the priorities' and governing in favour of the poor and marginalized (Beall, 2005, p. 124). Evidence from the experience of participatory budgeting reveals that representation participation and deliberations can transform the lives of the poor and powerless.

## FRAMEWORK FOR PARTICIPATORY BUDGETING IN SOUTH AFRICA

The South African framework for participatory budgeting is guided by constitutional, legislative and policy frameworks such as the Constitution (1996), the White Paper on Local Government of 1998, the Municipal Structures Act of 1998, and the Municipal Systems Act of 2000. These frameworks form part of the legal and institutional framework of governance grounded on transparent, accountable, and democratic society principles. The Public Finance Management Act of 1999 at the national level and the Municipal Finance Management Act (MFMA) of 2003 are mainly related to financial and budgeting processes. These legislative frameworks require all spheres of government to be accountable financially. Sibanda (2017) thus argues that the enacted policy frameworks not only forge the necessary relationships between municipalities and citizens but guarantee the rights of citizens to participate in the budgeting processes. This entails engaging the public through relevant structures and processes whereby ordinary people and civil society structures are afforded a forum to give input through identifying issues and their prioritisation.

As a principal framework, the Constitution of the Republic of South Africa, 1996 (hereafter referred to as the 1996 Constitution) obligates the spheres of government to be distinctive, interdependent, and interrelated as an agreement to work collaboratively to enhance policy formulation and implementation. As such, local government is empowered with its executive and legislative power to make decisions about its core mandate, namely service delivery and local democracy (Amtaika, 2013 & De Vries, 2016). Local governments are the closest to the people, so they must encourage citizen participation in budgeting formulation, implementation, and evaluation (see Sections 151, 152, and 195 of the 1996 Constitution). Thus, citizens' needs and priorities are the foundation upon which decisions are made and deliberated. Second to the 1996 Constitution is the White Paper on Local Government (1998), where office bearers are encouraged to adopt the developmental model of local government, where transparency, accountability, and service and citizen-oriented are fundamental for allowing civic input. In principle, views, needs, and aspirations are strongly influenced by budget formulation, with stakeholders engaged in decision-making.

The participatory budgeting model in South Africa is grounded in the decentralisation policy highlighted above. Political and administrative powers are transferred through decentralization, and resources are shared through fiscal decentralization (Siddle & Koelble, 2018). Thus, the participatory nature of budgeting involves stakeholders such as politicians and officials, including people represented by various national and local organizations. There is an intrinsic link to social mobilization, decentralization, and deepening democracy through citizen participation, especially in seeking alternative development processes in budget development and implementation. (Robbins, 2012, p. 3). Thus, fiscal discrimination prompted the democratic government to enact policies and mechanisms to promote democratic governance and participatory decision-making. Through the legislative processes, inclusive and participatory development processes were institutionalised for local governance and transforming power relations, especially at the local government level. Participatory governance introduces changing power and power relations with the values of transparency, accountability, responsiveness, and inclusion (Kraai, Ndevu & Matsiliza, (2023). The democratization of the South African political environment has created opportunities for increased civic participation in priority setting and decision-making by elected local governments. Nyembezi (2024) notes that due to chronic unemployment, deepening poverty, and widening inequality, social movements have been at the forefront of exposing citizens' discontent against the state's incapacity and non-accountability to carry its developmental democratic mandates. However, fiscal decentralization poses a particular challenge for citizen participation in local governance in its technical complexity and critical significance for the delivery of public services (Arends, 2020). Participation matters for democracy, and the engagement of citizens and civil society is paramount in the quest for a just and inclusive society (Mongae, 2024). Ironically, in most cases, existing structures restrict groups and individuals, thus sowing seeds of discontent and frustration and tend to exclude most citizens who pay local taxes and consume local services provided by local governments.

## DRAWING LESSONS FOR SOUTH AFRICAN MUNICIPALITIES

Lessons could be drawn for South Africa from the case studies of participatory budgeting presented above. Both cases have been experimented with as the pioneers of participatory budgeting from which other nations derived their lessons and modeled participatory budgeting. In this chapter, participatory budgeting lessons are drawn for eThekwini municipality.

Redress through Participatory Budgeting

The participatory budgeting model has been experimented with in Latin America and some countries as an instrument for redress. As documented, participatory budgeting emerged from the people's struggles for inclusion, social justice, and deliberative democracy. With repressive regimes in power, the political elite has utilized the budget to channel public resources for personal gains. The prevalence of autocratic governments underpinned by inequitable structures forced people to form their social movements, civil society organizations, and political organizations to challenge their oppression, exclusion, and socio-economic marginalization. Given this situation, budgets and their participatory nature serve as a weapon to engender social justice based on what Mullay (2007, p. 96) calls 'equal opportunity,' where the distribution or redistribution of resources, income, goods, or services through participatory taxing and budgeting is a fundamental principle. Through people's movements, citizens managed to claim the political space and, with equal opportunity at their disposal, were able to put into practice participatory and deliberative democracy.

The South African government, post-1994, attempted to reform the budget policy where public resources were indiscriminately distributed to the budgetary system that served the needs of the people. Due to the legacy of apartheid, the democratic government, under the leadership of the African National Congress (ANC) Tshishonga (2019) and Welsh (2021), has taken a decisive policy decision to transform the South African financial system to allow access and equal distribution of public resources through the budget. Building a nation based on democratic principles of social justice, equality, and equity entails dealing with the challenge of ensuring redress and promotion of the socio-economic and political affirmation of those previously excluded (Miyandazi, 2023). Participatory budgeting in Porto Alegre is used as a tool to redress the inequalities and inspire innovation (Masiya, Mazenda, Gwabeni, 2021); exclusion and marginalization of the poor and historically disadvantaged, South Africa could learn that redress is a transformative agenda where the people should be primary agents of ensuring that their needs are prioritized and dealt with through their active participation. The current version of the participatory budget practiced in South Africa and eThekwini municipality, in particular, subscribe to what Arnstein (2019, 26) categorizes as 'tokenism,' which comprises consultation, placation, and informing. South Africa and its municipalities are guided by progressive legislation to engender a participatory system to enhance citizen participation (Thompson & Nleya, 2010, p. 232). However, without direct representation by the people and civil society in the local governance council, the agenda to redress the socio-economic and political predicaments facing South Africa became impossible.

Participatory budgeting as an intrinsic value of active civil society

The civil society sector has been the backbone of grounding participatory budgeting in Porto Alegre. They considered that centralized government with a city government was being dominated by what Fung & Write (2001) call a 'clientelistic approach' where public resources were utilized to maintain political power in Porto Alegre. Merging from a government administration dominated by dictatorial politics underpinned by traditional patronage practices, social action, and corruption, the victory of the Workers Party in the mayoral election in 1995 subsequently led to the establishment of democratic rule that saw the adoption of participatory budgeting. Participatory budgeting was populated through a campaign meant to democratise the municipality by extending and deepening forged democracy in Brazil. In particular, the primary intention of participatory budgeting was on financial equity, primarily by ensuring poor citizens have a fair share of the budget or a say in public spending (Franklin and Ebdon, 2020).

Like Porto Alegre, South Africa has a vibrant civil society dating back to the struggle against the apartheid regime (Heller, 2001; Fung & Wright, 2001). The civil society sector, under the auspices of the Mass Democratic Movement (MDM), played a revolutionary role in challenging the only white minority regime, which thrived on discriminating against people based on race, gender, and ethnic grounds (Matebesi, 2023). Racially, local authorities were created under apartheid with more resources directed to white-populated municipalities. Despite the low subsidy given to the local government, funding for black local authorities was small (Bambo, 2022). The more significant portion of subsidies was channeled through white neighbourhoods, providing health, ambulance, and fire brigade services to black communities Van der Waldt, 2020). Subsidies meant for local authorities were allocated along racial and ethnic lines. The participation and social activism culture developed during apartheid continued to the post-democratic era. The institutionalisation of participation through the involvement of civil society is evident in the declaration by the democratic government when embracing the third sector as a crucial partner in the governance framework.

At the national level, through the budget hearing, citizens, individually or within their representative structures, have been encouraged to make submissions on draft policies, including budgetary issues. At the local government level, despite the policies enacted to democratise the local sphere, various participatory governance mechanisms were institutionalised to engage citizens in matters relating to local governance (Amtaika, 2013; Picard & Mogale, 2015). These mechanisms have been established as forums for citizens to express their grievances and, more importantly, enable citizens to participate in and inform governance processes with the budget at the centre (The Presidency, 2019). However, transforming these formal structures into dynamic mechanisms to influence budget allocation and engage meaningfully in community and municipal governance issues remains an insurmountable challenge. In Porto Alegre and Kerala, civil society organizations are a central part of the budgeting process. As such, South African municipalities could learn a valuable lesson by integrating civil society instead of treating them as consultative forums without executive power (Muiu, 2023). For example, in Porto Alegre, participatory budgeting became a success due to the devolution of decision-making power to neighbourhood associations. Significantly, South Africa, including eThekwini municipality, could learn to empower not only invited formal structures such as wards committees and IDP in dialogue but also invest in training and incorporating organs of civil society in the governance framework.

Participatory budgeting as organic social and mass mobilisation

Participatory budgeting was based on organic social and mass mobilisation. Hence, this model of budgeting emerged as a modern urban management and participatory endeavour, with the primary aim of promoting local democratic governance (Ackerman, 2011). Political transformation in Kerala and Porto Alegre was central in mobilising people and structures across gender, class and political lines. PB is vital, especially in funding local governance, and Kraai, Ndevu, and Matsiliza (2023) argue that it formalizes the participation of citizens in decision-making processes. A rights-based approach to development influenced organic social and mass mobilisation, hence its deliberative form of citizen participation. Through the participatory budgeting model, participatory practice and social action are achieved via institutional and structural transformation within the political space created during the social and political engagement (Hickey & Mohan, 2004: 13). Likewise, South Africa experienced organic social and mass mobilisation, especially in the struggle against apartheid's discriminatory regime and laws. However, the democratic era witnessed some vibrant civil society organisations and social movements absorbed into the ruling party. Hence their mobilisation drive was subjugated. The political victory by progressive parties against the autocratic and centralized regimes, for example, in Brazil, presented a fertile ground for mass mobilization in favour of addressing socio-economic and political challenges faced by residents (Baiocchi, 2015).

In the context of South Africa, criticism has been leveled against the Municipal Finance Management Act (2003) for putting more emphasis on insufficient citizen participation in municipal financial management, such as participatory budgeting and robust and regular disclosure requirements, including citizen performance reviews (Sikhosana, 2022). Post-apartheid era, mass mobilisation has emerged to address sectoral challenges such as general housing, health and service delivery issues. The formation of social movements operating locally and nationally, such as Abahlali baseMjondolo (ABM) in 2005 and the Treatment Action Campaign (TAC) in 2005, attest to sector-based mobilization. In these cases, the demand for housing by shack dwellers and accessibility to ARVs by HIV-infected citizens (see Duncan, 2015 & Gibson, 2011). A lesson to be learned from this is that mobilization through invited and invented spaces is crucial for eThekwini municipality to enter into a service agreement with its citizens and their representative structures as decisive partners in service delivery. Thus, paying lip service to participatory and deliberative democracy is costly, resulting in violent service delivery protests that are particularly prevalent in the eThekwini municipality.

Empowerment through the Participatory Budgeting Model

Empowerment of the excluded and marginalised including the grassroots organisations and structures has been central in the participatory budgeting model. Empowerment within the context of Porto Alegre embraced direct participation of individual citizens and democratically elected structures (Baiocchi, 2012). Empowerment was entrenched through local indigenous citizens, and their structures claimed power through winning elections and the adoption of PB not only decentralized decision-making powers to the people, but people could hold elected representatives accountable and transparent. PB was based on actualizing participatory practice, where both support for participatory and deliberative governance is enhanced through engaging and educating citizens and community structures about the rules or policies in which decision-making operates in the contemporary world (Ledwith & Springett, 2022). According to Heller (Pandeya, 2015), strengthening and empowering local government has been justified by making government more efficient and increasing accountability and participation. This implies that civil society organisations must reclaim their space in the governance framework to play a central role in influencing policies. For Coelho, Pozzebon, and Cunha (2022), empowering residents and their organizations is essential as it allows them to play a role in decision-making and has the potential to balance power dynamics.

Local government in South Africa operate within the developmental model, which obligates all municipalities (including eThekwini municipality) to partner with individuals and structures in seeking sustainable solutions to socio-economic challenges (White Paper on Local Government, 1998). Thus, empowerment entails building effective partnerships to strengthen civil society organisations as essential partners in forging a healthy democracy (World Bank Group, 2018). The empowerment of civil society through investing in such structures has social, economic, and political dividends for the municipalities. By collaborating with civil society, municipalities such as eThekwini gain political credibility, address service delivery gaps, and further experiment with new forms of invited and invented spaces for people-centered development and effective local governance (Mlambo & Tshishonga, 2018). Skills and knowledge relating to how municipalities work are fundamental in empowering the councilors, ward committees, and civil society formations (October 2018). Skills and a conducive environment are vital in promoting participation, and for Baholo (2023), participation refers to the involvement of the local people in the actual agenda-setting of development organizations. Such participation, thus, contributes to addressing power inequalities in development and local government alike. At eThekwini municipality, the governance of both councilors and ward committees are orientated and capacitated regarding policies and rules that guide local government (Wallis, 2018). The exclusion and marginalisation of individuals and civil society coupled with the ineptitude of local government fuels the service delivery protests in South Africa. The failure of the municipality to address these challenges has led people and social movements such as Abahlali baseMjondolo to embark on protests and demonstrations in demand for service delivery and fair allocation of financial resources to informal settlements. As channels for financial resources in the form of budgets, participatory budgeting is crucial in both democratization and a community governance process, including tapping into people's energies towards the self-sustainable development of communities (Mansuri & Rao, 2003).

Consolidating local democracy (social contract) through Participatory Budgeting

In Porte Alegre, an influential local state and active citizenry constitute a decentralised and democratic empowerment of local governments. Thus, **Heller (2001: 133)** argues that the success of PB was based on a committed political agenda with associated dynamics and capacities of local actors. Participatory budgeting was known for closing the gap between governments and citizens, resulting in local elites working closely with residents in identifying and deciding on projects and implementing such development initiatives (Souza, 2001: 159). Wampler (2000: 2) advocates participatory budgeting at a local level because it can potentially increase social equity and reduce clientelism, social exclusion, and corruption. PB has been proven to be one of the vehicles used to promote social learning, active citizenship, and ownership, and it can improve local policies and resource allocation (Gordon, Osgood Jr, and Boden, 2017). Despite having succeeded in overcoming authoritarianism and further re-democratise municipal governance, participatory budgeting was institutionalised to build bridges between states and citizens by increasing the participation of its citizens in budget decisions.

For instance, since 1994, many civil society organisations that used to play a vital role in governance by intervening on behalf of citizens and communities where instances of poor government service delivery were a problem either no longer exist or nowadays play an insignificant role (see Lodge, 2001, p. 11-12). One reason is that many of these organizations, which used to challenge the state regarding human rights violations, inadequate service delivery, poor governance, and unjust laws, were demobilized just after 1994, when the new democracy was born. Sadly, the post-apartheid era witnessed the demise of community structures such as the resident associations and street committees, which used to represent the needs and aspirations of the residents (Dosoudil, 2012). These community structures were replaced by institutions such as ward committees, which, despite being recognised, are ineffective in radically representing the needs of the people and are dominated by local political elites. Baud & Nainan (2012, p. 181) argue that ward committees are elected representatives charged with representing the interests of all the citizens in the wards, thereby voicing people's grievances and recommending projects for implementation. However, the authors quickly added that planning and implementing such projects is impossible without financial resources. Moreover, even the international donor community, which used to give substantial financial support to these organizations, suddenly switched focus and redirected their funds to the new government while significantly reducing their support to Non-Governmental Organisations (NGOs) and civil society organizations. It is acknowledged that some NGOs or civil society bodies which largely mobilised communities against apartheid might have thrived in the post-apartheid era; however, Lodge (2001, p. 11) notes that the civic movement of that era generally experienced "fragmentation" as "external resources were being redirected to government and more experienced [NGO] leaders moved out into public office (of private business)." The disempowerment of civil society bodies has contributed to the weakening relationship between citizens and the state.

In essence, the notion of convergence between political and community oversight is underlined and underpinned by active and responsible citizenship empowered not only to demand an effective and proactive state but one capable and competent enough to exercise its responsibilities on the one hand (NDP, 2011). Local democratic governance, on the other hand, demands a social contract between the state and the governed; therefore, a state is responsible and capable of fulfilling its mandate. A social contract is a social pact that underpins the role of civil society in balancing power and relations in the governance equation (Rousseau, 1998). The convergence of oversight through political and civic/community makes practical sense, primarily based on demanding fundamental rights and deepening democracy and people-centered governance. With the decline of democracy, the social contract is often compromised, and citizens are up in arms, demanding efficient and effective performance from tier governments. At the same time, capacitated public institutions can ensure that they deliver on basic needs and provide essential services. The Presidency (2019) noted that this demands the interplay of effective state and active citizenry. In this context, empowered citizens and active structures could prevent governance by Kakistocracy, thus allowing the government to be governed by the worst people in society (Basson & Hunters, 2023, p. 200). In particular, the ward committee system is strategically positioned to link various constituencies and municipal can councils by further consolidating social contracts and community-based governance. Ward councillors can make necessary inputs into decisions about the capital budget through consultations with the communities they represent. This presents a significant opportunity to deepen local democracy and strengthen the social contract between the people and elected representatives. Once community consultation has occurred, ward councillors should work closely with the Council's finance committee to ensure that ward requests are taken seriously.

Due to the challenges of the municipalities, eThekwini municipality witnessed a substantial disconnect between civil society and the local state. Evidence of this disconnect is the frequency of strikes and their violent nature in the municipality. For eThekwini municipality, a lesson to be drawn from this is the renewal of interactive governance, which recognizes the interface of invited spaces and people's invented spaces. The convergence of invited and invented spaces could be instrumental in dealing with multiple deficiencies, such as service delivery and underdevelopment, social capital, skills, and the financial sector (Cebekhulu, 2018, p. 153). Thus, the failure of the local state to keep its promises led voters and citizens, in general, to lose trust in them. Mangcu (2002) states that the promises of delivery have become nothing less than 'the opium of the masses.' Lessons from participatory budgeting for eThekwini is that clear and honest communication by the municipality could go a long way, especially in creating an inclusive governance system based on accountability, transparency, and social justice, especially in distributing resources.

## CONCLUSION

The chapter was premised on the participatory budgeting model adopted by the Porto Alegre municipality. The case study was chosen for its potential to revolutionise and transform the democratic governance systems within the context of budgeting processes through citizen participation. Evidence from various authors on the subject of participatory budgeting applauded Porto Alegre as a participative democratic approach to realize participatory and deliberative democracy. Participatory budgeting showed the pathways through which transparency, formal rules, and accountability procedures (Ledwith & Springett, 2010) are capable of oiling the wheels of actual participatory practice. The achievements achieved through this model have led to the modification of the world model, both in developed and developing nations such as South Africa. Citizens' representation, participation, and decision-making powers enabled them to deliberate on pertinent issues and, through their democratically elected structures such as assemblies and community councils, claim power and influence municipal policies regarding the equitable distribution of financial resources.

Despite their low educational levels and coming from underprivileged neighborhoods, people managed to mainstream their issues for consideration in the municipality council. Through participatory budgeting, ordinary people could practice direct democracy, whereby people's assemblies became the forum for citizens to discuss and vote for investment priorities for their respective zones.

In the countries where participatory budgeting was experimented, success stories have been documented, and lessons have been drawn. Despite its success story, PB has its fair share of criticisms globally. Considering PB was initially driven by civil society in Porto Alegre, in most cases, local government, through municipalities, is at the forefront of creating and channeling public participation. Thus bringing power dynamins and contestation. In this regard, Miraftab & Kudva (2015) argue that meaningful participatory development and practices can only be achieved by scaling up a local-level participatory process if they are scaled out. The powerless-powerful dichotomy was dismissed as misleading since it implies that some forms of engagement are inherently superior (Martin, 2003, p. 192). When participatory mechanisms are state-introduced and sponsored, participatory budgeting and engagement, become a cosmetic, exploitative feature and can become lip service to empowerment (Cornwell, 2011). For instance, the South African budgetary process is elite-led and falls short of engaging constituencies.

South African participatory budgeting is typical of the cosmetic and exploitative nature. Upon drafting the budget, the Mayor and the city administrators would assemble the public and pronounce the budget without meaningful engagement on the actual budget and its priorities. This form of participation subscribed to "tokenism" according to Arnstein's ladder of citizen participation, where people are merely informed and consulted (Arnstein, 2019, p. 5). The existence of participatory mechanisms in South Africa, such as the Ward Committees and Integrated Development Plans do not translate into spaces for genuine engagement, let alone gauging ordinary people's capacity to comprehend the components of the budget itself. In the context of South Africa, the politicisation of these invited spaces contributed to the social exclusion and economic marginalisation especially of the political party non-card caring members of the communities. In Porto Alegre, the budgeting process was a collective affair with accountability and transparency regarding financial allocation; however, in South Africa, budget allocation is the domain of municipal chief financial offers and administrators. Baiocchi (2015) observes that BP was able not only to increase ordinary citizens' voices but also to engage transparency, tap into local sources of information, and further improve the accountability of elected officials. Interestingly, Heller (2012) observed that engaging the public through invited channels offers essential sources of information but is limited in affording people's participatory engagement and power. Unlike the PB as practiced in Brazilian cities (Dagnino, 2008), participatory budgeting in South Africa is short of people's representation and engagement, especially in drafting and prioritizing key budget areas to be funded and the actual budget implementation.

Lessons were drawn from the case studies for South African municipalities. Evidence shows that the strength of participatory budgeting is its commitment to grassroots representation in the governance structures of the municipality and its ability to open a forum for deliberations.

## REFERENCES


Ackerman, J. (2011). Co-governance for accountability: Beyond 'exit' and voice. In Cornwall, A. (Ed.), *The Participation Reader*. Zeb Books.

Amtaika, A. (2013). *Local government in South Africa since 1994: Leadership, democracy, Development and Service Delivery in Post-Apartheid Era*. Carolina Academic Press.

Arends, H. (2020). The dangers of fiscal decentralization and public service delivery: A review of arguments. *Politische Vierteljahresschrift*, 61(3), 599–622. 10.1007/s11615-020-00233-7

Arnstein, S. R. (2011). A ladder of citizen participation. In Cornwall, A. (Ed.), *The Participation Reader*. Zeb Books.

Atisa, G., Zemrani, A., & Weiss, M. (2021). Decentralized governments: Local empowerment and sustainable development challenges in Africa. *Environment, Development and Sustainability*, 23(3), 3349–3367. 10.1007/s10668-020-00722-0

Baholo, N. (2023). *Community participation in an integrated development planning process life cycle: the case of Matlosana Local Municipality* [Doctoral dissertation, North-West University (South Africa].

Baiocchi, G. (2015). The Citizens of Porto Alegre. In Miraftab, F., & Kudva, H. (Eds.), *Cities of the Global South: Reader*. Routledge.

Baiocchi, G., & Ganuza, E. (2014). Participatory Budgeting as if Emancipation Mattered. *Politics & Society*, 42(1), 29–50. 10.1177/0032329213512978

Bambo, S. (2022). *South African Local Government Challenges and Prospects. Polokwane*. Empore Publishers.

Baocchi, G. (2011). Talking politics in participatory governance. In Cornwall, A. (Ed.), *The Participation Reader*. Zeb Books.

Barchiesi, F. (2011). *Precarious Liberation: Workers, the State and Contested Social Citizenship in Post-Apartheid South Africa. Scottsville*. UKZN Press. 10.1515/9781438436128

Basson, A., & Hunter, Q. (2023). *Who will Rule South Africa? The Demise of the ANC and the Rise of a New Democracy*. Flyleaf Publishing & Distribution.

Baud, I., & Nainan, N. (2012). Negotiated Spaces for Representation in Mumbai. In Pouw, N., & Baud, I. (Eds.), *Local Governance and Poverty in Developing Nations*. Routledge.

Beall, J. (2005). *Funding Local Governance: Small Grants for Democracy and Development*. ITDG Publishing. 10.3362/9781780443287

Blinova, E. A. (2017, June). Participatory budgeting and social inclusion in modern Brazil. In *Proceedings of the International Conference IMS-2017* (pp. 230-236). ACM. 10.1145/3143699.3143723

Brumatti, L. M. (2022). *Institutional roots inertia and participatory governance in Brazil* [Doctoral dissertation, Universidade de São Paulo].

Cebekhulu, E. (2018). *Umhlaba Uyahlaba! The World is Thorny. Wandsbeck*. Reach Publishers.

Coelho, T. R., Pozzebon, M., & Cunha, M. A. (2022). Citizens influencing public policy-making: Resourcing as a source of relational power in e-participation platforms. *Information Systems Journal*, 32(2), 344–376. 10.1111/isj.12359

Colombo, C. (2018). Justifications and citizen competence in direct democracy: A multilevel analysis. *British Journal of Political Science*, 48(3), 787–806. 10.1017/S0007123416000090

Cornwell, A. (Ed.). (2011). *The Participation Reader*. Zeb Press.

Curato, N., Hammond, M., & Min, J. B. (2019). *Power in deliberative democracy*. Palgrave Macmillan. 10.1007/978-3-319-95534-6

Dagnino, E. (2008). Challenges to Participation, citizenship, and democracy: Perverse Confluence and displacement of Meanings. In Bebbington, A., Hickey, S., & Miltlin, D. (Eds.), *Can NGOs Make a Difference? The Challenge of Development Alternatives*. Zed Books.

De Visser, J. (2005). *Developmental local government: A case study of South Africa*. Intersentia nv.

De Vries, M. S. (2016). *Understanding public administration*. Bloomsbury Publishing. 10.1007/978-1-137-57546-3

Della Porta, D. (2013). *Can Democracy be Saved? Cambridge CB2*. Polity Press.

Dhimitri, E., & Burda, M. (2019). The participatory budgeting for local governance. Case study municipality of Korca (Albania). *Journal of Applied Economic Sciences*, 2(64), 605–611.

Dosoudil, M. (2012). A case study of street committees in enhancing participatory democracy in the Emfuleni Local Municipality and the need for civil education. *Journal of African & Asian Local Government Studies*, 1(1), 62–85.

Duncan, J. (2015). *Protest Nation: The Right to Protest in South Africa*. Scottville: UKZN Press.

Džinić, J., Svidroňová, M. M., & Markowska-Bzducha, E. (2016). Participatory budgeting: A comparative study of Croatia, Poland and Slovakia. *NISPAcee Journal of Public Administration and Policy*, 9(1), 31–56. 10.1515/nispa-2016-0002

Franklin, A. L., & Ebdon, C. (2020). Participatory budgeting in the Philippines. *Chinese Public Administration Review*, 11(1), 60–74. 10.22140/cpar.v11i1.250

Germann, M., & Serdult, U. (2017). Internet voting and turnout: Evidence from Switzerland. *Electoral Studies*, 47, 1–12. 10.1016/j.electstud.2017.03.001

Gibson, N. (2011). *Fanonian Practices in South Africa: From Steve Biko to Abahlali baseMjondolo*. University of KwaZulu-Natal Press.

Gilman, H., & Wampler, B. (2019). The difference in design: Participatory budgeting in Brazil and the United States. *Journal of Deliberative Democracy*, 15(1). 10.16997/jdd.318

Gordon, V., Osgood, J. L.Jr, & Boden, D. (2017). The role of citizen participation and social media platforms in the participatory budgeting process. *International Journal of Public Administration*, 40(1), 65–76. 10.1080/01900692.2015.1072215

Green, F. M. (2008). *Constitutional Development in the South Atlantic States, 1776-1860: A Study in the Evolution of Democracy*. The Lawbook Exchange, Ltd.

Hammond, M. (2021). Democratic innovations after the post-democratic turn: Between activation and empowerment. *Critical Policy Studies*, 15(2), 174–191. 10.1080/19460171.2020.1733629

Healey, P. (1992). Planning through debate. *The Town Planning Review*, 63(2), 143–163. 10.3828/tpr.63.2.422x602303814821

Held, D. (2010). Models of Democracy (3rd Ed). Cambridge CB2: Polity Press.

Heller, P. (2001). Moving the State: The Politics of Democratic Decentralisation in Kerala, South Africa, and Porto Alegre. *Politics & Society*, 29(1), 131–163. 10.1177/0032329201029001006

Heller, P. (2012). Democracy, Participatory Politics, and Development: Some Comparative Lessons from Brazil, India, and South Africa. *Polity*, 44(4), 643–665. 10.1057/pol.2012.19

Hickey, S & Mohan, G. (2008). Relocating participation without a radical politics of development: insight from political action and practice. In S, Hickey & G, Mohan (eds.) *Participation from 18.*

Hordijk, M. (2012). Citizenship, Local Governance and Democracy. In Pouw, N., & Baud, I. (Eds.), *Local Governance and Poverty in Developing Nations*. Routledge.

Kaplan, A. (1996). *The Development Practitioners' Handbook.* Pluto Press.

Kaywood, L. (2021). Exploring the History and Development of the Local Government System in South Africa. *African Journal of Public Affairs.*, 1(3), 42–61.

Kgobe, F. K. L., & Mamokhere, J. (2021). The value of public participation in land-use planning for redeeming congestion in South African municipalities. *Technium Soc. Sci. J.*, 26, 17–31. 10.47577/tssj.v26i1.5020

Khoza, M. (2003). *Being Yourself, Representing Others: A Guide for Local Government Councillors in South Africa*. Flame Tree Media.

Knight, B., Chigudu, H., & Tandon, R. (2002). *Reviving Democracy: Citizens at the Heart of Governance*. Earthscan Publications Limited.

Kraai, S., Ndevu, Z., & Matsiliza, N. (2023). Participatory Budgeting to Foster Inclusivity, Transparency, and Accountability in Local Government: A case study of the City of Ekurhuleni Metropolitan Municipality of South Africa. *African Journal of Public Affairs*, 14(1), 63–88.

Lafont, C. (2015). Deliberation, participation, and democratic legitimacy: Should deliberative mini-publics shape public policy? *Journal of Political Philosophy*, 23(1), 40–63. 10.1111/jopp.12031

Leduka, M. (2009). *Participatory budgeting in the South African local government context: The case of the Mantsopa local municipality, Free State province* [Doctoral dissertation, Stellenbosch: University of Stellenbosch].

Ledwith, M., & Springett, J. (2022). Participatory practice: Community-based action for transformative change. *Practice*. Policy Press.

Lodge, T. (2001). South African Politics and Collective Action, 1994-2000. In B. Klandermans, M. Roefs, & J. Olivier. (Eds). *The State of the People: Citizens, Civil Society and Governance* (pp, 1-26). Pretoria: Human Sciences Research Council.

Ly, B. (2023). Social media and political involvement in Cambodia. *Cogent Social Sciences*, 9(1), 2194565. 10.1080/23311886.2023.2194565

Mangcu, X. (2002). *The democratic moment: South Africa's prospects under Jacob Zuma*. Sunnyside: Jacana Media.

Mansuri, G., & Rao, V. (2003). *Evaluating community driven development: a review of the evidence*. Development Research Group, World Bank.

Manzini, S. (2016). *The views of government officials on the Integrated Development Plan as a framework for local government that is developmental and responsive to peoples' needs*. Gauteng.

Martin, S. (2003). Engaging with citizens and other stakeholders. In Bovaird, T., & Loffler, E. (Eds.), *Public Management and Governance*. Routledge.

Marumaholo, S., Chigwata, T. C., & Nhede, N. T. (2018). Participatory Budgeting in the City of Kwekwe (Zimbabwe). *African Journal of Public Affairs.*, 10(4), 196–211.

Matebesi, S. (2023). Transactional autism: Effect of the engagement practices of protest leaders on community protest in South Africa. In H, Brooks, R, Chikane & S, Mottiar (Eds.). *Johannesburg: Mapungubwe Institute for Strategic Reflection (MISTRA)*.

Matloga, S. T., Mahole, E., & Nekhavhambe, M. M. (2024). Challenges of public participation in improving basic service delivery in Vhembe District Municipality, Limpopo, South Africa. *Journal of Local Government Research and Innovation*, 5, 11. 10.4102/jolgri.v5i0.160

Miraftab, F., & Kudva, H. (2015). *"Participation" Cities of the Global South: Reader*. London & New York: Routledge.

Miyandazi, V. (2023). Human Rights and Equality Commissions in Kenya and their role in tackling poverty and economic inequality. *Federal Law Review*, 51(4), 422–441. 10.1177/0067205X231212026

Mlambo, P., & Tshishonga, N. (2018). Operation Sukuma Sakhe (OSS) at Ugu District: Towards Democratizing Participatory Spaces for Decentralized Service Delivery. In G, Szell & D, Chetty (eds,). *Making Popular Participation Real* (pp. 227-241). Berlin & New York; Peter Lang.

Moeti, K. (2007). Budget reform and management of public money through budgeting. In Moeti, K. (Ed.), *Public Finance Fundamentals* (pp. 122–133). Juta & Co.

Mokgopo, T. I. (2017). The decentralised nature of the sphere of local government in South Africa. [JPADA]. *Journal of Public Administration and Development Alternatives*, 2(1), 82–102.

Mongae, M. (2024). *30 years: Democracy isn't a once-off achievement*. Mail & Guardian.

Mueller, S., Vatter, A., & Schmid, C. (2016). Self-Interest or Solidarity? *Statistics, Politics, and Policy*, 7(1-2), 3–28. 10.1515/spp-2016-0003

Muiu, M. (2023). *Politics and Government in South Africa*. Routledge, Taylor & Francis Group. 10.4324/9781003377962

Mullaly, B. (2007). The new structural social work (3rd ed.). Don Mills, Ontario: Oxford University Press.

Nel, E. (2004). *Evolving Participatory Governance and Developmental Local Government in Post-Apartheid South Africa. Participatory Governance Planning, Conflict Mediation and Public Decision-Making in Civil Society*. Ashgate Publishing Limited.

Ntliziywana, P. (2019). Professionalization of Local Government Management in South Africa. In C, Chigwata, J, De Visser & L, Kaywood (Eds.). *The Journey to Transform Local Government*. Cape Town: Juta @ Co. Ltd.

Nyembezi, N. (2024). 30 years on, unity in diversity is in trouble. *The Mercury*, 6.

October, L. (2018). *Ward Councillors are key players*. Mail & Guardian.

Onyalo, P. O. (2021). The Decentralised Governance in Kenya: Implications on Citizen Participation in Local Governance. *European Journal of Behavioral Sciences*, 4(4), 22–39. 10.33422/ejbs.v4i4.692

Paderewski, D., Levitsky, S., & Yashar, D. J. (2021). Inequality, democracy, and the inclusionary turn in Latin America. *The inclusionary turn in Latin American democracies*, 1-56.

Pandeya, G. P. (2015). Does citizen participation in local government decision-making contribute to strengthening local planning and accountability systems? An empirical assessment of stakeholders' perceptions in Nepal. *International Public Management Review*, 16(1), 67–98.

Picard, L. A., & Mogale, T. (2015). *The Limits of Democratic Governance in South Africa*. UCT Press.

Robbins, G. (2012). *Public Participation in Municipal Budgeting*. UKZN.

Robert, L. (2022). *"Direct Democracy: Definition, Examples, Pros and Cons." ThoughtCo, Feb. 2, 2022. Accessed from* [thoughtco.com/what-is-direct-democracy-3322038.]. Accessed on. [19 April 2024]

Rousseau, J.J. (1998). *The Social Contract. Hertfordshire SG12 9HJ: Words Editions.*

Santos, F., Tanscheit, T., & Ventura, T. (2020). The Workers' Party and Participatory institutions: The influence of intra-party dynamics in the adoption of Participatory budgeting. *Dados*, 63, e20180152. 10.1590/dados.2020.63.3.202

Scudder, M. F. (2020). The ideal of uptake in democratic deliberation. *Political Studies*, 68(2), 504–522. 10.1177/0032321719858270

Sibanda, M. M. (2017). Control, ethics, and accountability in the financial management performance of Eastern Cape municipalities. *Journal of Public Administration*, 52(2), 313–339.

Siddle, A., & Koelble, T. A. (2012). *The Failure of Decentralisation in South African Local Government: complexity and unanticipated consequences*. UCT Press. 10.58331/UCTPRESS.51

Sikhosana, N. (2022). *Outcomes-based participatory gender planning and budgeting in South African local government context: a case of selected municipalities in the Eastern Cape Province.*

Sintomer, Y., Herzberg, C., & Rocke, A. (2008). Participatory Budgeting in Europe: Potential and Challenges. *International Journal of Urban and Regional Research*, 32(1), 164–178. 10.1111/j.1468-2427.2008.00777.x

Souza, C. (2001). Participatory budgeting in Brazilian Cities: Limits and Possibilities in building democratic institutions. *Environment and Urbanization*, 13(1), 159–184. 10.1177/095624780101300112

Tapscott, C. (2008). The challenges of deepening democracy in post-apartheid South Africa. In *Foundations for local governance: Decentralization in comparative perspective* (pp. 213–231). Physica-Verlag HD. 10.1007/978-3-7908-2006-5_10

Thompson, L., & Nleya, N. (2010). Passivity or protest? Understanding the dimensions of mobilisation on rights to services in Khayelitsha, Cape Town. In Coelho, V. S. P., & Von Lieres, B. (Eds.), *Mobilising for Democracy: Citizen Action and the Political of Public Participation (pp* (pp. 223–242). Zed Books. 10.5040/9781350221413.ch-011

Tobi, A. A., & Oikhala, G. I. (2021). Local government reforms and grassroots development in Nigeria. *The Journal of American Science*, 18(1), 113–133.

Tshishonga, N. (2018). The War Room as a Platform for Public Participation: Views from Stakeholders. In Szell, G., & Chetty, D. (Eds.), *Making Popular Participation Real; African and International Experiences*. Peter Lang.

Tshishonga, N. (2019). The Legacy of Apartheid on Democracy and Citizenship in Post-Apartheid South Africa: An Inclusionary and Exclusionary Binary? AFFRIKA: Journal of Politics. *Economics and Society.*, 9(1), 167–191.

United Nations Development Programme. (2000). *South Africa: transformation for Human Development, 2000*. UNDP.

Van Der Waldt, G. (2020). London Government. In C, Landsberg & S, Graham (Eds.) (5th Eds.) *Government and Politics in South Africa: Coming of Age*. Pretoria: Van Schaik Publishers.

Wallis, M. (2018). Case Studies from eThekwini Municipality. In G, Szell & D, Chetty (eds,). Making Popular Participation Real (pp. 263-275). Berlin & New York; Peter Lang.

Wampler, B. (2000). *A Guide to Participatory Budgeting*. A Paper presented at the third conference of the International Budget Project, Mumbai. www.internationalburget .org/cdrom/papers/systems/ParticcipatoryBudget/Wampler. pdf

Wampler, B., McNulty, S., & Touchton, M. (2021). *Participatory budgeting from a global perspective*. Oxford University Press. 10.1093/oso/9780192897756.001.0001

Welsh, D. (2021). Apartheid and its legacies. In N, De Jager (Ed.). *South African Politics: An Introduction* (pp. 29-55). Cape Town: Oxford University Press.

Young, I. M. (2002). *Inclusion and Democracy*. Oxford University Press. 10.1093/0198297556.001.0001

# Chapter 2
# Empowering Residents, Enhancing Services:
## How Democratic Governance Can Revitalize Service Delivery in Zimbabwean Municipalities

**Tendai Kaponda**
https://orcid.org/0009-0003-3287-4335
*Central China Normal University, China*

## ABSTRACT

*This research employs a mixed-methods approach, combining quantitative surveys with qualitative case studies, to explore the relationship between democratic governance and service delivery in Zimbabwean municipalities. Findings reveal that while decentralisation empowers local governments, effective governance structures are crucial for improved service delivery outcomes. Challenges in resource allocation and financial viability underscore the need for increased support and transparent mechanisms. Enhancing transparency, accountability, and citizen participation is vital for rebuilding trust and improving governance effectiveness. Strengthening electoral processes is essential for promoting democratic legitimacy. Implementing these recommendations can revitalise local service delivery and empower residents in urban communities. This study contributes to advancing our understanding of the importance of democratic governance in promoting inclusive and sustainable development in municipalities.*

DOI: 10.4018/979-8-3693-3617-5.ch002

## INTRODUCTION

Local government plays a crucial role in citizens' daily lives, directly impacting access to essential services like sanitation, water, waste management, and infrastructure. In Zimbabwe, however, concerns persist regarding the effectiveness of municipal service delivery. This research project investigates how promoting democratic governance practices within Zimbabwean municipalities can empower residents and revitalize municipal service delivery. Zimbabwean municipalities face a multitude of challenges in delivering essential services to residents. These include limited resources, inadequate infrastructure, and a lack of transparency and accountability (Mawonde, 2019). Additionally, citizen participation in local decision-making processes is often limited, leading to a sense of disenfranchisement and a disconnect between residents and municipal governments (Crook & Gavboy, 1993).

This research contributes to the ongoing debate about strengthening local governance in Africa. By examining the link between democratic practices and service delivery in Zimbabwe, the paper sheds light on potential solutions for improved service provision. The findings can inform policy decisions at the national and local levels, empower citizens to hold their governments accountable, and ultimately contribute to a more responsive and efficient system of local service delivery.

This research will address the following questions:

1. How do different forms of citizen participation (e.g., budget consultations, and community forums) influence the effectiveness and responsiveness of local service delivery in Zimbabwean municipalities?
2. What is the relationship between the level of electoral competition in local government and the level of accountability they hold towards residents regarding service delivery?
3. How can increased transparency measures (e.g., public service expenditure reports, and accessible grievance procedures) rebuild trust between citizens and municipalities, leading to improved service delivery outcomes?
4. To what extent is Zimbabwe's current decentralization policy effective in empowering municipalities to manage resources and make decisions that directly impact local service delivery?
5. What are the specific democratic governance practices employed by successful Zimbabwean municipalities with demonstrably improved service delivery, and how can these practices be replicated in other areas?

## METHODOLOGY

This research will employ a mixed-methods approach, combining quantitative and qualitative data collection methods. A survey will be conducted among residents in selected municipalities to gauge their level of participation in local government processes, perception of service delivery effectiveness, and trust in municipal governments. Additionally, secondary data on municipal government finances, service delivery indicators (e.g., water access rates, waste collection efficiency), and voter turnout in local elections will be collected and analyzed. Case studies will be conducted on two Zimbabwean municipal governments with demonstrably improved service delivery. These cases will explore the specific democratic governance practices implemented in these municipalities and analyze their contribution to success. Quantitative data will be analyzed using statistical software to identify correlations between citizen participation, transparency, and service delivery outcomes.

## LITERATURE REVIEW

### Decentralisation and Local Governance in Zimbabwe

The Zimbabwean government has undertaken decentralization efforts, devolving some power and resources to municipal governments (Mandela Institute, 2010). However, the effectiveness of these reforms has been questioned, with concerns about limited fiscal autonomy and continued control by central authorities (Moyo, 2011). Decentralization and local governance in Zimbabwe have undergone significant evolution and challenges over the years. Since independence in 1980, the Government of Zimbabwe has prioritized local government reform related to decentralization. The process of decentralization involves the transfer of power from a central authority to lower levels of government, aiming to empower local institutions (Conyers, 2003; Mukoyi, 2021). In Zimbabwe, decentralization has been marked by distinct phases, including the colonial period (1890-1979), the post-colonial era (1980-2008), and the constitutional period (2009 to date). Each phase has shaped the distribution of power and resources within local governance structures. The colonial phase was characterized by a two-tier local governance system divided along racial lines, with limited power for black communities. Post-independence efforts aimed to address these imbalances but faced challenges due to centralized control and limited local autonomy. The constitutional period seeks to extend power to municipal governments through devolution, allowing for more effective governance at the local level (Mukoyi, 2021).

The 2013 Constitution aimed to improve decentralization in Zimbabwe's local government system but faced challenges in implementation by the central government. The study highlighted in one of the sources indicates that full implementation of decentralization has the potential to enhance efficient and effective service delivery, citizen participation, democracy, and accountability within the local government system (Madzimure, 2021). Devolution has been proposed as a strategy to strengthen decentralization in Zimbabwe by transferring powers and resources to local institutions, thereby empowering them to govern more effectively. Devolution is seen as a way to address past weaknesses in decentralization where local governance lacks power and resources for meaningful development (Mukoyi, 2021; Zinyama, 2021). In summary, democratic governance plays a critical role in shaping decentralization and local governance in Zimbabwe by influencing power dynamics between central and municipal governments, promoting citizen participation, enhancing service delivery efficiency, and fostering accountability within the local government system (Madzimure, 2021; Mukoyi, 2021; Zinyama, 2021).

Efforts towards decentralization and devolution in Zimbabwe have been driven by the need to enhance local governance effectiveness, promote citizen participation, and address historical disparities in power and resource distribution. The transition towards devolution represents a significant step in empowering local institutions and fostering more inclusive and efficient governance structures within the country (Conyers, 2003).

## Democratic Governance Theory

The democratic governance theory serves as the foundation for the theoretical framework. Democratic governance theory posits that power should be distributed amongst different levels of government, with local communities having a meaningful role in decision-making processes (Kurebwa, 2015). Democratic governance theory encompasses a diverse range of ideas about how to achieve a legitimate and effective system of rule by the people. John Locke, for instance, emphasized individual rights and limited government power through the concept of consent of the governed (Locke, 1689). Modern liberals like Robert Dahl focused on features like competitive elections and citizen participation, coining the term "polyarchy" (Dahl, 1971). However, theorists like Jürgen Habermas argue that true democracy requires a space for public deliberation, where citizens can engage in rational-critical discourse to reach legitimate decisions (Habermas, 1987). Zimbabwe's political landscape, while marked by democratic elements, raises questions about the extent to which power is truly distributed and exercised at the local level. Democratic governance theory posits that decentralisation, the transfer of power from central authorities to local communities, empowers citizens and fosters democratic participation (Marks, 1993; Schmitter, 2004).

Examining Zimbabwe's decentralisation efforts through this theoretical lens requires a critical analysis of:

· **Power distribution:** Does the decentralisation framework genuinely shift decision-making power to local communities, or does the central government maintain significant control?(Moyo & Ncube, 2014)?

· **Power exercise:** Do municipal governments have the resources and capacity to effectively exercise the devolved powers (Nyikadzino, 2019)?

· **Accountability:** Are local officials held accountable to the communities they serve, and are mechanisms in place to ensure transparency and citizen participation? (CLGF, 2005). Understanding the practical realities of decentralisation in Zimbabwe necessitates a multi-faceted approach acknowledging both theoretical ideals and potential constraints. This includes examining the devolution process in light of:

· **Political context:** How do historical power structures and the existing political landscape influence the effectiveness of decentralisation (Mansuri & Rao, 2013)?

· **Socio-economic factors:** What are the socio-economic conditions of local communities, and how do they affect their ability to participate effectively in decision-making processes? (OECD, 2007)

· **Institutional capacity:** Do local institutions have the necessary capacity and resources to implement devolved functions effectively (Moyo & Ncube, 2014)?

Only by scrutinizing these aspects can we assess whether decentralisation in Zimbabwe truly promotes democratic governance and empowers local communities.

There is no single originator or person who is responsible for the democratic governance notion. It is a collection of knowledge and concepts that have developed over time with the help of many academics, political thinkers, and practitioners. Through their writings on political philosophy, liberalism, participatory democracy, and the foundational ideas and institutions of democratic governance, various political philosophers and thinkers, including John Locke, Jean-Jacques Rousseau, James Madison, John Stuart Mill, Alexis de Tocqueville, and John Dewey, have influenced democratic governance theory. In his writings, including "Politics" and "The Athenian Constitution," the ancient Greek philosopher Aristotle investigated the ideas of democracy and governance. He looked at various kinds of administration and talked about the benefits and drawbacks of democracy. Liberal democracy was founded on John Locke's ideas, particularly his "Two Treatises of Government." He stressed the value of individual liberties, constrained government, and the will of the governed. Both the French philosopher Jean-Jacques Rousseau and the English philosopher John Stuart Mill advocated for the necessity of a social compact with active public engagement in democratic administration as well as the safeguarding of individual liberty. Amartya Sen, an Indian economist, and Nobel Prize winner, broadened the concept of democracy beyond electoral procedures. He stressed the significance of human development, social and economic freedoms, and capacities in democratic administration (Sen, 1999). Sen contends that democracy is an integral component of human freedom and that it is crucial to advancing both the economy and society. Dahl (1971), who is regarded as one of the 20th century's most prominent political scientists, is particularly noteworthy for his work on democratic philosophy. With his idea of polyarchy in particular, he made fundamental contributions to democratic thought. Dahl makes the case in his paper that democracy calls for a variety of civil liberties as well as chances for citizens to participate in decision-making. He looked at the factors and organizations needed to create an inclusive and participatory democracy. According to Nussbaum (2011), democratic government is crucial for fostering the growth of human potential and making sure that everyone has the chance to live happy, full lives. Philosopher Rawls is best known for his writings on political liberalism. In "A Theory of Justice," Rawls makes the case that democratic governance is necessary to ensure that society is structured in a fair and just manner.

## A DEMOCRATIC GOVERNANCE PERSPECTIVE IN DECENTRALISATION

*Figure 1. Applicability of the democratic governance theory to administrative decentralisation*

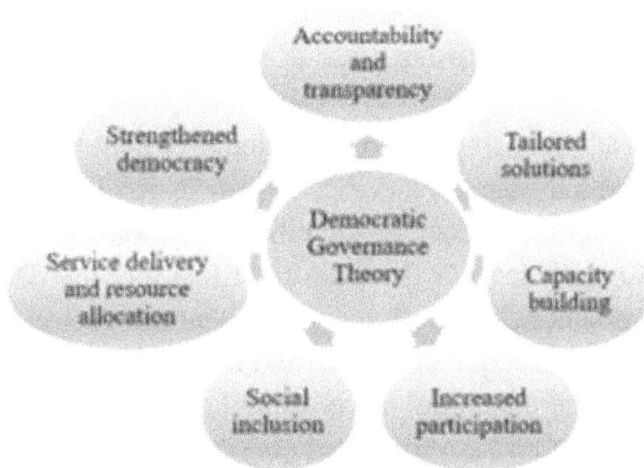


The relevance of democratic governance in the realm of administrative decentralisation is important. It's like a puzzle where each piece represents a different aspect of how we make decisions and distribute resources. The study explores how this idea of democratic governance plays a crucial role in the way we decentralise administration. This section unravels the layers of this concept and sees how it ties into the bigger picture of giving power and control to local communities.

## Increased Participation

The necessity of citizen participation is emphasized by democratic government philosophy. According to Shrestha and Adhikari (2018), democratic governance can boost rural communities' self-sufficiency and participation in decision-making. Decentralization enables greater local engagement, giving rural populations more influence over decision-making that directly affects their lives. Empowering people and communities to actively participate in governance and contribute to the growth of their communities, fosters grassroots democracy. The need to involve citizens in decision-making processes, particularly those who may be impacted by the decisions, is emphasized by theory. As a result, there is now more citizen involvement in rural governance. Amara et al. (2014), claim that democratic governance theory has influenced citizen involvement in rural African governance. The theory, according to the authors, offers a framework for people to demand their rights and hold their government officials responsible. As a result, there is now more citizen involvement in community development initiatives, public meetings, and election monitoring. The Panchayati Raj system, which was implemented in India and is founded on democratic governance principles, has increased citizen involvement in rural governance (Bardhan et al., 2006).

## Accountability and Transparency

The significance of transparency and accountability in decision-making is another crucial component of the democratic governance philosophy. As stated by Houtzager and Koop (2008), democratic governance is about creating mechanisms that enable people to hold elected officials responsible for their decisions and actions. By putting governance closer to the people, decentralization can promote more accountability. Better governance outcomes and more responsiveness may result from this. By highlighting the significance of public engagement, representation, and accountability, democratic governance theory has significantly influenced local accountability in rural governance. Democracy governance theory, according to Bhatnagar (2006), encourages participatory democracy, which enables citizens to have a say in decision-making processes and hold elected officials accountable. According to Ribot (2004), the design and execution of decentralization programs, which aim to move authority and resources from central governments to local communities, have been influenced by democratic governance theory. By allowing residents to participate in decision-making processes and keep tabs on local officials' performance, decentralization can promote local accountability. Fox (2007) explains how instruments for openness and accountability, such as citizen report cards and social audits, have been impacted by the democratic governance paradigm. With the help of these systems, citizens can learn about the performance of their elected representatives and hold them responsible for their deeds and decisions. By ensuring that local interests and needs are taken into account during the design and execution of development projects, this strategy can promote local accountability. By encouraging participatory democracy, decentralization, transparency, and accountability procedures, democratic governance theory has generally had a considerable impact on local accountability in rural governance.

## Tailored Solutions

Local expertise and contextual awareness are valued in democratic government theory. It can support sustainable development and aid in raising the level of governance in rural regions (Sharma and Singh, 2012). Rural communities frequently face particular problems and requirements that call for specialized solutions. Decentralization enables more responsive decision-making procedures that help rural communities effectively address their unique issues and goals. By highlighting the significance of citizen engagement, representation, and accountability, democratic governance theory has inspired the design and implementation of tailored solutions in rural governance. Sarker and Itohara (2018), encourages the creation of solutions that are specifically suited to the requirements and preferences of local communities. This strategy can increase local engagement and ownership in development activities. This strategy may result in the creation of custom solutions that are more receptive to the requirements of regional communities. Brinkerhoff and Goldsmith (2002) explain how the design and execution of participatory development initiatives, which aim to involve local communities in decision-making processes, have been inspired by the democratic governance paradigm. This strategy may result in the creation of more practical and long-lasting custom solutions. The goal of democratic decentralization, which strives to distribute authority and resources from national governments to local communities (Ribot, 2004). Encouraging citizen involvement, network governance, participatory development, and democratic decentralization, democratic governance theory has generally had a substantial impact on the creation of tailored solutions in rural governance.

## Capacity-Building

Building local communities' capacity to take part in decision-making and hold public authorities responsible is crucial, according to the democratic governance idea. This theory contends that initiatives to increase local community capacity can enhance service delivery and foster more efficient and adaptable governance in the setting of rural areas. Wily and Okoth-Ogendo (2007) found that fostering democratic government in rural areas requires capacity-building. Capacity-building is a long-term, ongoing process that involves a wide range of interventions, including training, education, networking, and institutional strengthening (Wily & Okoth-Ogendo, 2007). Capacity-building initiatives can support ensuring that resources are distributed in ways that reflect the needs and goals of those areas by increasing the ability of local communities to take part in decision-making processes and hold municipal governments responsible. The idea of democratic governance isn't just about setting up democratic systems; it's also about making sure that the people in rural areas get the services they need. Brinkerhoff and Goldsmith (2005), pointed out that it's important to provide services that match what the citizens need. They said that democratic governance doesn't only mean creating democratic structures; it's also about giving services that address what the people want. To put it in perspective, the UNDP (2009) also mentioned that for democratic governance to work, it's not just about having the right democratic setup, but also about providing services that meet the needs of the people. It's kind of like making sure both parts of the equation are in sync – having democratic systems and making sure those systems deliver services that help the citizens. This refers to making sure that essential services like infrastructure, healthcare, and education are delivered to local people in a timely and efficient manner in the context of rural governance. According to a South African study, empowering rural communities through capacity-building programs enabled people to take part in the process of making decisions and build the capacity to lobby and advocate for their development (Kriel & Van Wyk, 2017; Akin et al. 2005).

## Social Inclusion

The democratic governance paradigm places a strong emphasis on the value of social inclusion in the formulation of public policy. According to this idea, social inclusion initiatives can assist in ensuring that the needs and objectives of marginalized groups are taken into account when resources are allocated and services are provided in the framework of rural governance. Fostering democratic governance in rural communities requires social inclusion (Schatz & Williams, 2013). By giving marginalized groups, the means to have an impact on local governance, such as indigenous peoples, women, people living with disabilities, and minorities, decentralization can empower them. The democratic governance paradigm emphasizes the value of strengthening excluded groups and giving them access to decision-making processes, according to Rambaldi and Anriquez (2003).

## Resource Allocation and Service Provision

The democratic governance idea places a strong emphasis on the value of citizen responsibility and participation in decision-making. In rural areas, administrative decentralization can enhance resource distribution and service provision. The contribution of democratic governance to community development in rural areas is discussed by Shrestha (2013). FAO (2011) emphasizes the value of democratic governance in rural regions and claims that the principles of democratic governance are crucial for rural development, as they help to ensure that the needs and priorities of rural people are taken into account. According to Fagbemi and Ojo (2017:151), decentralization can improve the distribution of resources and the delivery of services in rural areas. According to the authors' observations, "decentralization of governance has been identified as a strategy for promoting rural development and improving service delivery to rural communities". This assertion suggests that decentralizing governance is a way to help rural areas develop and improve the delivery of services to their communities. Decentralization can lead to more sustainable resource management and better representation of local interests (Agrawal and Ribot, 1999).

## Strengthened Democracy

The strengthening of democracy in rural government has been significantly influenced by democratic governance theory, a concept that carries substantial implications for effective local governance. This theory underscores the inherent value of citizen participation, openness, accountability, and responsiveness in fostering a thriving democratic environment at the grassroots level. According to Agrawal and Ribot (1999), democratic governance theory catalyzes nurturing democratic institutions within local communities. This involves not only encouraging residents to actively engage in decisions that shape their daily lives but also entails constructing streamlined and transparent public administration systems. By affording citizens a voice in local government decision-making processes and establishing mechanisms that ensure accountability, this theory lays the foundation for empowered and participatory local governance. By creating an environment where citizens play an active role in shaping the decisions related to service delivery, this approach paves the way for more efficient and relevant services. This alignment with local needs enables services to be tailored to meet the specific requirements of each community, resulting in more impactful and effective outcomes. The theory resonates as a call to action, urging for the amplification of rural voices, the fortification of local democracy, and the forging of pathways toward more resilient and thriving rural communities.

## EMBRACING THE EVOLUTION OF DECENTRALIZATION: CHALLENGES AND OPPORTUNITIES EXPLORED

In the evolving landscape of governance, a paradigm shift known as decentralization has captured significant attention. This discourse transcends mere administrative rearrangements; it delves into the intricate interplay of challenges and opportunities that accompany this multifaceted evolution. This exploration transcends the confines of theory, akin to scholarly dialogue, as we dissect the complex tapestry of decentralization. Prepare to embark on a journey that unpicks the intricacies of this phenomenon – unearthing the impediments, seizing the prospects, and synthesizing a holistic understanding of the decentralized governance dynamic

## CHALLENGES

### Limited Capacity

Rural areas often lack human and financial resources, limiting their capacity to effectively govern and implement decentralized policies and programs. This includes challenges in training and equipping local government officials and community leaders to carry out their responsibilities. Chikozho and Kanyangarara (2015:1) postulated, "the decentralisation process has been characterised by lack of capacity and skills at the local level" This leads to inefficiencies and ineffective service delivery. Similarly, Bwalya and Mulenga (2015) argue that decentralization efforts in Zambia have been hampered by a lack of capacity at the local level, as well as inadequate financial resources. This has made it difficult to effectively implement decentralized policies and programs, leading to uneven development outcomes across different regions of the country.

### Inadequate Infrastructure

Rural areas may have limited access to basic infrastructure such as roads, electricity, and telecommunications, which hampers the delivery of public services and the implementation of development initiatives. In Zimbabwe, insufficient resources are a major challenge facing delivering decentralized governance. This may also include a lack of basic infrastructure such as roads, water and electricity, health facilities and inadequate educational institutions as noted by Chikozho and Kanyangarara (2015), this can make it difficult to plan and effective implementation of decentralized policies, especially in rural areas. In Zimbabwe, there's a big hurdle when it comes to having enough stuff to make decentralized governance work. We're talking about resources, the things one needs to get things done. But it's not just about money; it's also about basic things like roads, water, electricity, hospitals, and schools. Similarly, Moyo et al. (2019) argue that poor infrastructure is a major obstacle to the effectiveness of decentralization in Zimbabwe. They note that many municipal governments lack the resources needed to operate and maintain basic infrastructure, resulting in uneven development in different parts of the country. The lack of resources and proper infrastructure makes the whole idea of decentralized governance a bit wobbly in Zimbabwe.

## Political Interference

The politicization of rural governance can pose challenges to decentralization. Political interference, such as the selection of local officials based on political affiliations instead of merit, can undermine the principles of good governance and local autonomy (Mamokhere, 2023). Sithole (2013:3) said, "the central government still exercises significant control over municipal governments, including the appointment of senior officials". This undermines the autonomy of municipal governments and limits their ability to independently decide what is in the best interests of their communities. One major challenge is that the original purpose of decentralization can get lost in the shuffle. Instead of empowering local areas to make decisions that benefit their specific needs, decisions might be influenced by political agendas that prioritize other goals. Political interference can undermine the effectiveness of decentralization efforts. Decentralization should be accompanied by measures to ensure that municipal governments have sufficient autonomy to make decisions that benefit their communities Olowu & Wunsch, 2004; Ribot, 2004). Political interference can also lead to favouritism, unequal treatment and hinder transparency. When decisions are influenced by political forces rather than the needs and preferences of the people, it becomes hard to hold anyone responsible when things don't go as planned.

### Inequitable Resource Allocation

The allocation of resources to municipal governments may be inadequate or uneven, leading to disparities in service delivery and development. Insufficient funding and resource distribution can hinder rural governance and perpetuate inequalities between urban and rural areas. As noted by Mawowa and Ndlovu (2014:4), "municipal governments are financially constrained and rely heavily on central government for financial support". This limits their ability to provide services and infrastructure to their communities. However, sometimes these resources aren't divided up fairly. This uneven distribution of resources can create problems when it comes to rural governance through decentralization. The lack of enough funding and resources means that some local areas don't have the means to offer the same level of services as others. Those municipal governments often face financial constraints and rely heavily on the central government for money. This challenge hampers rural governance because it limits the ability of municipal governments to provide essential services and build the necessary infrastructure, leading to inequalities between rural and urban areas.

## Limited Participation and Representation

There may be limited citizen participation and representation in decision-making processes at the local level. This can be due to factors such as low levels of civic education, inadequate platforms for community engagement, and a lack of inclusivity in governance structures. By participation and representation, we mean that people in the community have the chance to express their opinions, needs and concerns, and their voice is considered in decision-making (Foo et al., 2011). The idea is to give more power to communities, including what it includes participatory citizens in the decision-making process. However, this is sometimes not done as well as it should be. This limited participation and representation can be a challenge because it means that the decisions being made do not reflect the true wishes or needs of the community. Low levels of civic education, inadequate platforms for community engagement, and a lack of inclusivity in governance structures can limit citizen participation and representation in decision-making processes at the local level" (Kanyangarara & Chikozho, 2015: 3). In local government, this can lead to decisions that are not equally in everyone's interests. When a choice is made by only a few, the views and interests of the broader community may be ignored. Furthermore, limited participation and representation can also create a lack of trust between communities and local government. When there is limited participation in local government and no representation, it seems that only certain voices are heard while others are left behind. This challenge hinders the true spirit of decentralisation because it does not fully acknowledge the power of different perspectives and the collective wisdom of communities.

# OPPORTUNITIES

## Local Empowerment and Participation

Decentralization provides an opportunity for increased local empowerment and citizen engagement in governance processes. As Sithole (2013) said, decentralisation has created opportunities for citizens to take part in the decision-making process of local government. By involving rural communities in decision-making, planning, and implementation of development projects, decentralization can promote inclusivity, local ownership of initiatives, responsiveness and accountability (Uddin, 2019). This process of empowerment through participation is essential for genuine democratic processes and effective service delivery (Uddin, 2019). Community engagement is vital for promoting sustainable decisions and improving outcomes in local governance. It fosters cohesive communities, ensures access and community empowerment, drives social transformation, and deepens democracies.[1] Through civic participation and empowerment, every citizen has the means to actively engage in public processes, leading to more accountable and transparent governance.[1] Empowering municipal governments is fundamental for strengthening local democracy. It enables citizens to participate in decision-making processes, monitor public service delivery, and create an environment that promotes democracy and improves the quality of life for citizens (Bradley, 2017). Civil society organizations play a crucial role in influencing government decisions, mobilizing the population, educating on rights, and facilitating social reconciliation.[1] Decentralization, community engagement, civic participation, and empowering municipal governments are all interconnected elements that contribute to effective democratic governance and service delivery at the local level.

## Tailored Development Approaches

Decentralization allows for the customization of development approaches to suit the specific needs and priorities of rural areas. Municipal governments and traditional leaders can play a significant role in identifying and addressing the unique challenges faced by their communities, leading to more effective and sustainable development outcomes[1] (Pekkola, Ylinen & Mavengere; 2022). This method enhances collaboration, accelerates schedules, and ensures cost-effectiveness, ultimately benefiting both municipalities and their communities (Martin, 2023).

## Improved Service Delivery

Through decentralization, there is a potential for improved service delivery in rural areas. Local government structures, when properly resourced and capacitated, can respond more effectively to the needs of the community and deliver services in a timely and appropriate manner. Decentralisation has the potential to improve the delivery of public goods by bringing decision-making closer to the people who will be impacted by it (Mawowa & Ndlovu, 2014:2) Decentralization plays a crucial role in democratic governance by empowering municipal governments to be more responsive to their communities. This empowerment allows municipal governments to become critical actors for effective local service delivery, human development, and poverty reduction (Berthin, 2018). Additionally, information is highlighted as a critical component that can enhance rural governance and service delivery by improving its availability and reliability (Kosec & Wantchekon, 2020).

## Enhanced Accountability and Transparency

The role of transparency and accountability in local governance is complex and multifaceted. Transparency, as identified by Ferry and Eckersley (2015), can increase accountability in some circumstances. However, according to Heald (2006), transparency should be valued not for its own sake but rather as a foundation for other elements of public policy, including accountability. Accountability is not always improved by transparency (O'Neill, 2006; Ferry & Eckersley, 2015). In local governance, the transparency agenda is often seen as a tool to improve organizational efficiency rather than a human right (Pickles, 2011). However, it is also viewed as a means to exercise accountability downwards from public bodies to citizens, aligning with an egalitarian worldview (Heald, 2006). The transparency agenda is considered a way to empower citizens and alternative providers to keep public authorities responsible from the ground up through the publishing of government data. (O'Neill, 2006). This aligns with the idea of "armchair auditors" exercising democratic oversight of public spending (O'Neill, 2006). However, there are challenges in achieving effective transparency and accountability in local governance. The individualist perspective, which aims to increase the use of private and volunteer providers for public services may lead to a conflict between accountability and openness. (Pickles, 2011).

While transparency and accountability are important in local governance, there are complexities and challenges in achieving their effective implementation. The nature of the information made available, the ability of citizens to interpret and analyse it, and the involvement of private sector suppliers all impact the connection between openness and responsibility in municipal government (Froud, 2003). Municipal governments are more accessible to the community, enabling better monitoring and oversight of public resources and projects. By fostering more community respect and trust in the rural government, transparency improves the efficiency of handling village money (Arth et al., 2023). By being open and honest, the rural government administration gives the community access to all available information without restrictions, enabling the community to understand how its resources and activities are managed (Suryanto and Asri, 2020; Sutrisno et al, 2023).

## Economic Development Opportunities

Decentralization can stimulate economic development in rural areas by empowering municipal governments to attract investments, promote local entrepreneurship, and develop infrastructure that supports economic activities. As noted by Chikozho and Kanyangarara (2015:2), "decentralisation can lead to economic development by promoting local entrepreneurship and investment". This can lead to job creation and improved livelihoods for rural communities. To fully harness the opportunities and overcome the challenges of rural governance in the context of decentralization, it is crucial to address the capacity gaps, ensure equitable resource allocation, promote citizen participation, and establish strong institutional frameworks that facilitate effective collaboration between different levels of governance (Kosec & Wantchekon, 2020; Berthin, 2018). Furthermore, the OECD emphasizes the importance of strategies to improve rural service delivery, highlighting that a vibrant service sector is vital for a prosperous local economy and meeting the needs of rural citizens. Inclusive local government can help engage youth, drive socio-economic development, and enhance public services.

# FINDINGS

*Table 1. Murewa District descriptive statistics on the governance system rating*

| | N | Minimum | Maximum | | Std. Deviation | Variance |
|---|---|---|---|---|---|---|
| *VR1: Empowerment of municipal governments* | | 1 | 5 | 3.34 | .808 | .653 |
| *VR2: Public services provided* | | 1 | 4 | 2.66 | .732 | .536 |
| *VR3: local policies* | | 1 | 5 | 2.76 | .744 | .553 |
| *VR4: Resource allocation* | | 1 | 3 | 1.97 | .782 | .611 |
| *VR5: Democracy* | | 2 | 5 | 3.27 | .779 | .606 |
| *VR6: Capacity building* | | 1 | 5 | 2.40 | .990 | .981 |

continued on following page

*Table 1. Continued*

| | N | Minimum | Maximum | | Std. Deviation | Variance |
|---|---|---|---|---|---|---|
| *VR7: Transparency and accountability* | | 1 | 4 | 2.22 | .903 | .815 |
| *VR8: Responsiveness to specific needs.* | | 1 | 4 | 2.50 | .985 | .971 |
| *VR9: Citizen participation* | | 1 | 5 | 2.77 | 1.096 | 1.201 |
| *VR10: Financial resources* | | 1 | 5 | 2.30 | 1.013 | 1.027 |
| *Valid N (list-wise)* | | | | | | |

**Key**: *VR – variable*

*Table 2. Mutoko District descriptive statistics on the rating of the governance system*

| | | Minimum | Maximum | | Std. Deviation | Variance |
|---|---|---|---|---|---|---|
| *VR1: Empowerment of municipal governments* | | 1 | 5 | 3.21 | .923 | .852 |
| *VR2: Public services provided* | | 1 | 5 | 2.56 | .825 | .681 |
| *VR3: local policies* | | 1 | 5 | 2.89 | .885 | .783 |
| *VR4: Resource allocation* | | 1 | 4 | 2.27 | .939 | .881 |
| *VR5: Democracy* | | 1 | 5 | 2.54 | 1.077 | 1.160 |
| *VR6: Capacity building* | | 1 | 5 | 2.10 | 1.001 | 1.001 |
| *VR7: Transparency and accountability* | | 1 | 5 | 2.34 | 1.148 | 1.317 |
| *VR8: Responsiveness to specific needs.* | | 1 | 5 | 2.44 | 1.011 | 1.022 |
| *VR9: Citizen participation* | | 1 | 4 | 2.52 | 1.001 | 1.003 |
| *VR10: Financial resources* | | 1 | 5 | 2.11 | .970 | .942 |
| *Valid N (list-wise)* | | | | | | |

· **Key**: *VR – variable*

· **Note**: The "Valid N (list-wise)" indicates the number of cases with complete data for all variables. In this case, the valid sample size is 89 for all variables.

## Empowerment and Citizen Participation

While both districts perceive decentralization as empowering municipal governments (Mutoko: VR1 = 3.21, Murewa: VR1 = 3.34), the findings suggest potential differences in citizen engagement. Mutoko residents, on average, view public participation as slightly lower (Mutoko: VR9 = 2.52) compared to Murewa, although the smaller sample size in Murewa (n = 52) necessitates caution in interpretation.

## Public Service Delivery and Resource Allocation

Both districts express moderate satisfaction with public services (Mutoko: VR2 = 2.56, Murewa: VR2 = 2.66). However, Murewa residents report significantly lower resource allocation efficiency (Murewa: VR4 = 1.97) compared to Mutoko (Mutoko: VR4 = 2.27).

## Local Policies and Needs Responsiveness

Interestingly, Murewa residents perceive local policies as addressing their needs slightly more effectively (Murewa: VR3 = 2.76) compared to Mutoko (Mutoko: VR3 = 2.89). This could be attributed to the content or communication strategies surrounding these policies in each district. Additionally, both districts report similar perceptions of local government responsiveness to specific needs (Mutoko: VR8 = 2.44, Murewa: VR8 = 2.50).

## Democracy, Transparency, and Accountability

Murewa residents perceive a slightly higher level of democracy in their local government (Murewa: VR5 = 3.27) compared to Mutoko (Mutoko: VR5 = 2.54). However, both districts hold moderate views on transparency and accountability (Mutoko: VR7 = 2.34, Murewa: VR7 = 2.22). These findings point towards the need for improvements in fostering transparent and accountable governance practices in both districts, which can be achieved through initiatives like clear communication channels, accessible grievance redressal mechanisms, and public service expenditure reports.

## Financial Resources and Capacity Building

Murewa residents hold a slightly more favourable view of available financial resources (Murewa: VR10 = 2.30) compared to Mutoko (Mutoko: VR10 = 2.11). However, both districts hold moderate views on the level of investment in capacity building (Mutoko: VR6 = 2.10, Murewa: VR6 = 2.40). Addressing these limitations through increased financial support and targeted capacity-building programs for local government officials is crucial for enhancing service delivery and governance effectiveness.

# DISCUSSION

The comparative analysis of findings from Mutoko and Murewa municipal governments provides valuable insights into the intricate relationship between democratic governance and municipal service delivery in Zimbabwean urban municipal governments. In examining the survey findings, it is evident that various aspects of democratic governance, including citizen participation, electoral competition, transparency measures, decentralization policy effectiveness, and democratic governance practices, significantly influence municipal service delivery outcomes.

## Empowerment Through Decentralization

Decentralization, as perceived by respondents in both districts, emerges as a critical aspect of democratic governance influencing local service delivery. The positive perceptions of decentralization's role in empowering municipal governments to make decisions and implement policies align with scholarly literature highlighting decentralization as a mechanism for enhancing local autonomy and responsiveness (Bardhan, 2002). Decentralization theoretically allows for better tailoring of services to local needs, increased accountability, and citizen participation (Bardhan, 2002). However, the mixed views on the quality of public services provided in Mutoko suggest that while decentralization may empower municipal governments, it does not guarantee improved service delivery outcomes without effective governance structures in place (Faguet, 2014).

## Resource Allocation and Financial Viability

Concerns about resource allocation efficiency and financial resource availability underscore the challenges faced by municipal governments in adequately funding and delivering essential services. Limited financial resources can constrain the ability of municipal governments to provide services effectively, particularly in resource-constrained environments (Smoke & Lewis, 1996). The findings from both districts highlight the need for increased financial support and improved resource allocation mechanisms to ensure equitable service delivery and meet the diverse needs of urban communities (Smoke & Lewis, 1996).

## Transparency, Accountability, and Citizen Participation

The variations in perceptions of transparency, accountability, and citizen participation reflect the complexities of democratic governance processes within municipal governments. While some respondents perceive transparency and accountability mechanisms to be adequate, others express scepticism, suggesting a need for greater transparency and accountability in local government operations. The importance of transparency and accountability in fostering public trust and confidence in municipal governments has been widely recognized in the literature (Haque, 2005). Enhanced transparency measures, such as public service expenditure reports and accessible grievance procedures, can rebuild trust between citizens and municipalities, leading to improved service delivery outcomes (Haque, 2005). Similarly, citizen participation is fundamental to democratic governance and local service delivery. The varying perspectives on citizen participation in decision-making processes highlight the importance of ensuring meaningful opportunities for public engagement and inclusion in local governance processes (Pateman, 1970). Meaningful citizen participation can enhance the legitimacy of local decisions, improve service delivery responsiveness, and promote social cohesion (Pateman, 1970).

## Electoral Competition and Democratic Governance Practices

The mixed views on electoral competition suggest differing perceptions of the fairness and credibility of local elections. Electoral competition is a central component of democratic governance, as it provides citizens with the opportunity to hold municipal governments accountable through regular, free, and fair elections (Bratton & Van de Walle, 1997). However, concerns about electoral fairness underscore the need for ongoing efforts to enhance transparency and credibility in local electoral processes (Bratton & Van de Walle, 1997). Successful Zimbabwean municipalities with demonstrably improved service delivery outcomes often employ specific democratic governance practices, such as community engagement initiatives, participatory budgeting, and transparent decision-making processes (Faguet, 2014). These practices facilitate greater citizen participation, enhance accountability, and ensure that municipal service delivery responses are tailored to community needs (Faguet, 2014).

The comparative analysis of findings from Mutoko and Murewa municipal governments highlights the multifaceted nature of democratic governance and its impact on local service delivery outcomes in Zimbabwean urban municipal governments. Empowerment through decentralization, effective resource allocation, transparency, accountability, citizen participation, and electoral competition are essential components of democratic governance that significantly influence service delivery effectiveness. Addressing challenges related to resource constraints, enhancing transparency and accountability mechanisms, promoting citizen participation, and adopting effective democratic governance practices are critical steps towards revitalizing municipal service delivery and empowering residents in Zimbabwean municipalities. These findings contribute to the broader discourse on the importance of democratic governance in promoting inclusive and sustainable development in urban communities.

# CONCLUSION

This research examined the intricate relationship between democratic governance and service delivery in Zimbabwean municipalities. The findings highlight that effective democratic governance practices are essential for empowering residents and revitalizing municipal service delivery. Decentralization, when coupled with capacity building for municipal governments, can enhance service delivery responsiveness to local needs. However, resource constraints pose a significant challenge. Increasing central government funding, implementing performance-based allocation systems, and exploring innovative financing mechanisms are crucial steps towards financial sustainability. Building trust between citizens and municipal governments requires transparency and accountability measures. Publishing public service expenditure reports, establishing accessible grievance procedures, and promoting citizen participation through public forums are key strategies. Ensuring fair and credible electoral processes through proper resource allocation, independent monitoring, and voter education is vital for democratic legitimacy. Finally, fostering democratic governance practices like participatory budgeting and collaboration with civil society organizations can leverage community expertise and resources for improved service delivery. Implementing these recommendations can strengthen local governance in Zimbabwe, leading to a more empowered citizenry, efficient service delivery, and ultimately, sustainable development in municipalities.

## RESEARCH IMPLICATIONS

The impact of democratic governance on quality service delivery by municipalities, particularly focusing on empowerment and citizen participation, carries significant practical and theoretical implications. The case study comparing Mutoko and Murewa municipal governments in Zimbabwe provides valuable insights into these implications.

Practically, the findings highlight several key areas where democratic governance influences service delivery:

### Decentralization and Empowerment

Decentralization is perceived positively by residents as empowering municipal governments. This decentralization theoretically allows for better tailoring of services to local needs, increased accountability, and citizen participation. Decentralization in democratic governance plays a crucial role in service delivery by empowering municipal governments to tailor services to local needs, enhance accountability, and promote citizen participation. While decentralization is generally viewed positively by residents, effective governance structures are essential for improved service delivery outcomes (Ahmad, Devarajan, Khemani & Shah, S., 2005; Barnett, Minis & VanSant, 1997; Smoke, 2015). Practically, this suggests the need for robust local governance mechanisms to complement decentralization efforts.

## Resource Allocation and Financial Viability

Concerns about resource allocation efficiency and financial resource availability underscore the challenges faced by municipal governments. Limited financial resources can constrain the ability of municipal governments to provide services effectively, necessitating increased financial support and improved resource allocation mechanisms. Democratic governance plays a crucial role in service delivery by ensuring equitable resource allocation and financial support for municipal governments. Recent initiatives highlight the commitment to supporting democratic processes and enhancing service delivery: The United States announced $145 million in funding, with additional private sector commitments, to support Democracy Delivers countries and advance democratic reforms.[11] Efforts to improve service delivery in municipalities emphasize citizen engagement, transparency, and accountability as key components for effective governance and enhanced service provision (Berthin, 2018). Practically, this implies the importance of securing adequate funding for municipalities to ensure equitable service delivery.

## Transparency, Accountability, and Citizen Participation

Variations in perceptions of transparency, accountability, and citizen participation reflect the complexities of democratic governance processes within municipal governments. Enhancing transparency measures, such as public service expenditure reports and accessible grievance procedures, can rebuild trust between citizens and municipalities, leading to improved service delivery outcomes. The complexities of democratic governance processes within municipal governments are closely tied to perceptions of transparency, accountability, and citizen participation. Enhancing transparency measures, such as public service expenditure reports and accessible grievance procedures, can rebuild trust between citizens and municipalities, leading to improved service delivery outcomes. [1] Democratic governance is most legitimate when it incorporates principles like transparency, pluralism, citizen involvement in decision-making, representation, and accountability. Civil society, the media, and the private sector play crucial roles alongside the government in ensuring accountable governance practices (Carothers & Brenchenmacher, 2014). This highlights the need for transparent and accountable governance practices to foster public trust and confidence.

## Electoral Competition and Democratic Governance Practices

The mixed views on electoral competition suggest differing perceptions of the fairness and credibility of local elections. Electoral competition provides citizens with the opportunity to hold municipal governments accountable. Democratic governance plays a crucial role in service delivery by ensuring accountability and transparency in local electoral processes. Electoral competition, as a cornerstone of democracy, provides citizens with the means to hold municipal governments accountable (Stephen, Charron & Justesen, 2023). The quality of local government is closely tied to an engaged citizenry and cooperation between political leaders and their constituents (Cleary, 2007). Concerns about electoral fairness highlight the ongoing need to enhance transparency and credibility in local elections, emphasizing the importance of fair and credible elections in promoting democratic governance and effective service delivery (Claire, 2015)[REMOVED HYPERLINK FIELD]. However, concerns about electoral fairness underscore the need for ongoing efforts to enhance transparency and credibility in local electoral processes. Practically, this emphasizes the importance of fair and credible elections in promoting democratic governance and effective service delivery.

Theoretically, these findings contribute to the broader discourse on democratic governance and service delivery:

## Democratic Governance and Service Delivery

The study demonstrates the intricate relationship between democratic governance and service delivery outcomes. Effective democratic governance practices, including decentralization, transparency, accountability, and citizen participation, are crucial for improving service delivery effectiveness. The relationship between democratic governance and service delivery is crucial for effective governance and citizen satisfaction. Democratic governance practices like decentralization, transparency, accountability, and citizen participation play a significant role in improving service delivery outcomes (Idea, 2015; Bjuremalm, Gibaja & Molleda, 2015). Democratic Accountability in Service Delivery. A practical guide to identifying improvements through assessment. IDEA Int, 23–24 November 2015, Pretoria, South Africa). Theoretical frameworks on democratic governance can inform policy interventions aimed at enhancing service delivery in municipalities.

## Citizen Participation and Empowerment

Citizen participation is fundamental to democratic governance and municipal service delivery. Meaningful opportunities for public engagement and inclusion in local governance processes are essential for enhancing service delivery responsiveness and promoting social cohesion. Citizen participation is crucial for democratic governance and service delivery. It empowers residents, ensures their voices are heard, and enhances service responsiveness. Meaningful engagement in local governance processes is essential for promoting social cohesion and effective service delivery. Citizens provide the authority to govern and expect effective governance and public services in return.[1] In the context of citizen participation, politicians derive legitimacy from citizens' acceptance of their authority, while public officials implement strategic directions and deliver services to citizens.[1] Theoretical perspectives on citizen participation highlight its role in empowering residents and ensuring their voices are heard in decision-making processes.

## Resource Allocation and Financial Management

The study underscores the importance of adequate financial resources and efficient resource allocation mechanisms for effective service delivery. Democratic governance plays a crucial role in service delivery by emphasizing the importance of adequate financial resources and efficient resource allocation mechanisms. The study highlights that in municipal governments, service delivery involves multiple actors like central and municipal governments, NGOs, and civil society organizations (Berthin, 2018). To enhance service provision, strong citizen engagement mechanisms are essential to ensure meaningful contributions from all segments of society (Berthin, 2018). Theoretical discussions on resource management within democratic governance contexts can inform strategies for improving financial viability and resource allocation in municipalities. For instance, e-governance initiatives play a significant role in improving data flow and decision-making processes within municipal governments, enhancing efficiency and transparency.[1] Additionally, institutional restructuring and corporatization are effective approaches to transforming government entities into professional organizations that are more accountable and efficient in service delivery.[1]

## Transparency, Accountability, and Electoral Processes

The findings highlight the significance of transparency, accountability, and credible electoral processes in democratic governance. Theoretical frameworks on transparency, accountability, and electoral integrity can guide efforts to strengthen governance mechanisms and promote public trust in municipal governments. Democratic governance plays a crucial role in service delivery, with transparency, accountability, and credible electoral processes being key components. Theoretical frameworks emphasize the significance of these elements in strengthening governance mechanisms and fostering public trust in municipal governments. Transparency in electoral governance involves openness about rules, procedures, outcomes, and decision-making processes by electoral authorities. It is believed to enhance public trust, improve policy-making, and facilitate accountability (Norris & Nai, Eds). However, the actual impact of transparency on accountability remains complex and context-dependent (Norris & Nai, Eds). Electoral integrity is essential for democratic norms and standards. It encompasses fairness, inclusivity, and transparency in elections to prevent activities that could erode trust in democracy (Hilbert College, 2023). Achieving electoral integrity involves promoting voter literacy, enhancing accessibility, mitigating electoral violence, and building confidence in electoral outcomes (Hilbert College, 2023).

The impact of democratic governance on quality service delivery by municipalities has both practical and theoretical implications. Addressing challenges related to resource constraints, enhancing transparency and accountability mechanisms, promoting citizen participation, and adopting effective democratic governance practices are critical for revitalizing local service delivery and empowering residents in urban communities. These findings contribute to advancing our understanding of the importance of democratic governance in promoting inclusive and sustainable development in municipalities.

## RECOMMENDATIONS

### Decentralization and Empowerment

**Policy Recommendation:** Strengthening local governance structures to complement decentralization efforts is crucial.

**Implementation Strategy:** This involves providing training and capacity-building programs for municipal government officials to enhance their ability to manage resources effectively and make informed decisions. Additionally, fostering collaboration between central and municipal governments is essential to ensure the alignment of policies and resources with local needs. By empowering municipal governments with the necessary skills and support, decentralization can lead to more responsive and effective service delivery tailored to the specific requirements of each community.

## Resource Allocation and Financial Viability

**Policy Recommendation:** Increasing financial support and improving resource allocation mechanisms for municipal governments is imperative.

**Implementation Strategy:** Allocating additional funding to municipalities, particularly focusing on addressing infrastructure deficits and improving service delivery in underserved areas, is necessary. Implementing transparent and equitable resource allocation frameworks will ensure fair distribution of financial resources among municipal governments. By enhancing financial support and resource allocation mechanisms, municipalities can overcome budget constraints and deliver essential services more efficiently to their constituents.

## Transparency, Accountability, and Citizen Participation

**Policy Recommendation:** Enhancing transparency and accountability mechanisms to rebuild trust between citizens and municipalities is critical.

**Implementation Strategy:** Mandating the publication of public service expenditure reports will provide transparency on resource utilization. Establishing accessible grievance procedures will enable residents to voice concerns and hold municipal governments accountable. Moreover, promoting citizen participation through community forums, participatory budgeting, and regular consultations will ensure that local decisions reflect community priorities. By fostering transparency, accountability, and citizen participation, municipalities can improve governance effectiveness and enhance public trust in their institutions.

## Electoral Competition and Democratic Governance Practices

**Policy Recommendation:** Strengthening electoral processes to enhance credibility and fairness is essential.

**Implementation Strategy:** Implementing reforms to improve the transparency and integrity of local elections is necessary. Measures should be taken to prevent electoral fraud and ensure equal access to electoral processes for all citizens. Providing training and support for electoral officials to uphold democratic principles and standards during elections will contribute to enhancing electoral credibility. By ensuring fair and credible elections, municipalities can reinforce democratic governance practices and promote citizen trust in the electoral process.

## Cross-Cutting Strategies

**Policy Recommendation:** Establishing a monitoring and evaluation framework to track progress and assess the impact of policy interventions on service delivery outcomes is essential.

**Implementation Strategy:** Prioritizing investments in technology and innovation, such as e-governance initiatives and digital platforms for citizen engagement, will improve the efficiency and effectiveness of service delivery processes. Additionally, promoting partnerships between government, civil society organizations, and the private sector will leverage resources and expertise in addressing service delivery challenges. By adopting cross-cutting strategies, municipalities can enhance their capacity to deliver quality services and foster inclusive and sustainable development in their communities.

## REFERENCES

Agrawal, A. (2001). Common Property Institutions and Sustainable Governance of Resources. *World Development*, 29(10), 1649–1672. 10.1016/S0305-750X(01)00063-8

Agrawal, A., & Ribot, J. C. (1999). Accountability in decentralization: A framework with South Asian and West African cases. *Journal of Developing Areas*, 33(4), 473–502.

Ahmad, J., & Devarajan, S. (2005). *Decentralisation and Service Delivery*. (World Bank Policy Research Working Paper 3603). World Bank. https://documents1.worldbank.org/curated/en/606871468139500265/pdf/wps3603.pdf

Arta, D. N. C., Leuhery, F., Abubakar, H., Yusuf, M., & Cakranegara, P. A. (2023). Literature Review: Analisis Hubungan Antara Pelatihan dan Kinerja Karyawan di Sebuah Perusahaan. [MSEJ]. *Management Studies and Entrepreneurship Journal*, 4(1), 162–168.

Bardhan, P. (2002). Decentralization of governance and development. *The Journal of Economic Perspectives*, 16(4), 185–205. 10.1257/089533002320951037

Bardhan, P., & Mookherjee, D. (2006). *Decentralization and Local Governance in Developing Countries: A Comparative Perspective*. The MIT Press. https://EconPapers.repec.org/RePEc:mtp:titles:0262524546

Barnett, C. C., Minis, H. P., & VanSant, J. (1997). *Democratic Decentralization*. Research Triangle Institute. https://pdf.usaid.gov/pdf_docs/pnada635.pdf

Berthin, G. (2018). *Service Delivery in Municipal governments: Some Lessons*. 4Democraticgovernance. https://4democraticgovernance.com/2018/03/31/service-delivery-in-local-governments-some-lessons/

Bjuremalm, H., Gibaja, A. F., & Molleda, J. V. (2015). *Democratic Accountability in Service Delivery. A practical guide to identify improvements through assessment*. IDEA Int, 23–24 November 2015, Pretoria, South Africa. https://www.idea.int/sites/default/files/publications/democratic-accountability-in-service-delivery.pdf

Bradley, A. (2017) *Strengthening local democracy: Empowering municipal governments*. International IDEA. https://www.idea.int/news/strengthening-local-democracy-empowering-local-authorities

Bratton, M., & Van de Walle, N. (1997). *Democratic Experiments in Africa: Regime Transitions and the Consequences of Elections*. Cambridge University Press. 10.1017/CBO9781139174657

Brinkerhoff, D., & Goldsmith, A. (2002). *Clientelism, Patrimonialism and Democratic Governance: An Overview and Framework for Assessment and Programming*.

Carothers, T., & Brenchenmacher, S. (2014). *Accountability, Transparency, Participation, and Inclusion: A New Development Consensus?* Carnegie Endowment for International Peace. https://carnegieendowment.org/2014/10/20/accountability-transparency-participation-and-inclusion-new-development-consensus-pub-56968

Chakunda, V., & Chakaipa, S. (2015). Local Government Capacity Building and Development: Lessons, Challenges and Opportunities. Journal of Political Sciences and Public Affairs. *Review Article*, 3(1).

Chikozho, C., & Kanyangarara, M. (2015). Decentralisation and service delivery in Zimbabwe: The case of education. *Journal of Public Administration and Governance*, 5(1), 1–12.

Claire, M. (2015). The Politics of What Works in Service Delivery in S. Hickey, K. Sen, & B. Bukenya (eds), *The Politics of Inclusive Development: Interrogating the Evidence*. Oxford Press. https://doi.org/10.1093/acprof:oso/9780198722564.003.0005

Cleary, M. R. (2007). Electoral Competition, Participation, and Government Responsiveness in Mexico. *American Journal of Political Science*, 51(2), 283–299. https://www.jstor.org/stable/4620066. 10.1111/j.1540-5907.2007.00251.x

CLGF (Commonwealth Local Government Forum). (2005). *Good governance and local government*. CLGF.

Conyers, D. (2003). Decentralisation in Zimbabwe: A Local Perspective. *Public Administration and Development*, 23(1), 115–124. 10.1002/pad.265

Crook, R. C., & Manor, J. (1998). *Democracy and Decentralisation in South Asia and West Africa: Participation, Accountability and Performance*. Cambridge University Press. 10.1017/9780511607899

Dahl, R. (1971). *Polyarchy. Participation and Opposition*. Yale University Press.

Faguet, J. P. (2014). Decentralization and Governance. *World Development*, 53, 2–13. 10.1016/j.worlddev.2013.01.002

Ferry, L., Eckersley, P., & Zakaria, Z. (2015). Accountability and transparency in English local government: Moving from "matching parts" to "awkward couple"? *Financial Accountability & Management*, 31(3), 345–361. 10.1111/faam.12060

Froud, J. (2003). The Private Finance Initiative: Risk, Uncertainty and the State. *Accounting, Organizations and Society*, 28(6), 567–589. 10.1016/S0361-3682(02)00011-9

Government of Zimbabwe. (1998). Rural District Councils Act [Printflow / Government Printers.]. *Pub.*, L(29), 13.

Government of Zimbabwe. (2009). Public Finance and Management Act [Printflow / Government Printers.]. *Pub.*, L(22), 19.

Government of Zimbabwe. (2013). Constitution of Zimbabwe Amendment 20 of 2013, Printflow / Government Printers, Harare Government of Zimbabwe. (1998). *Traditional Leaders Act Chapter 29:17*. Harare.

Government of Zimbabwe. (2020). Devolution and Decentralisation Policy of 2020. In *Government Gazzette*. Printflow, Harare.

Haque, M. S. (2005). Corrupt Organizations. *Journal of Economic Behavior & Organization*, 57(4), 473–495.

Hilbert College. (2023). *Electoral Integrity: Challenges, Goals and Resources*. Hilbert College. https://online.hilbert.edu/blog/electoral-integrity/

International Idea. (2015). Democracy and Service Delivery. *International IDEA Policy Dialogue*. IDEA. https://www.idea.int/sites/default/files/publications/democracy-and-service-delivery.pdf

Kooiman, J. (2003). Governing as governance. *Sage (Atlanta, Ga.)*.

Kosec, K., & Wantchekon, L. (2020). Can information improve rural governance and service delivery? *World Development*, 125, 104376. 10.1016/j.worlddev.2018.07.017

Kurebwa, J. (2015). Decentralisation and central government control: Experiences from the local government reform in Zimbabwe. *African Journal of Governance and Development*, 9(2), 73–84.

Madzimure, T. (2021). A Case for Decentralization in Zimbabwe's Local Government System: Challenges and Opportunities. *Archives of Business Research*, 9(2), 1–21. 10.14738/abr.92.9580

Main Street America. (2023). *The Mainstreet Approach.*Main Street America. https://www.mainstreet.org/ourwork/theapproach

Mansuri, G., & Rao, V. (2013). *Accountability, transparency, participation, and inclusion: A new development consensus?* Carnegie Endowment for International Peace. https://carnegieendowment.org/files/development_consensus_brief.pdf

Marks, G. (1993). Structural policy and multi-level governance in the EC. In Sbragia, A. (Ed.), *Euro-politics: Institutions and policymaking in the "new" European Community* (pp. 391–410). Brookings Institution Press.

Martin, C. (2023). *Municipalities embrace the phased design build delivery method.* Burns McDonnell. https://blog.burnsmcd.com/municipalities-embrace-the-phased-design-build-delivery-method

Mawonde, C. (2021). Citizen participation in decision-making in Zimbabwe: The case of rural district councils. *Journal of Public Administration and Policy Research*, 13(1), 12–25.

Moyo, P., & Ncube, C. (2014). Devolution of power in Zimbabwe's new constitutional order: Opportunities and potential constraints. *Journal of Public Administration*, 49(1), 1–14. http://www.scielo.org.za/scielo.php?script=sci_arttext&pid=S2077-49072014000100014

Moyo, S., Mhlanga, N., & Mavhura, E. (2019). Decentralisation and development: A case study of rural municipal governments in Zimbabwe. *International Journal of Public Administration and Management Research*, 7(1), 1–12.

Mukoyi, J. (2021). Local Governance as a Creature of the Statute: Decentralization and Local Governance in Zimbabwe. *International Journal of Scientific and Research Publications*, 11(3), 66–72. Advance online publication. 10.29322/IJSRP.11.03.2021.p11109

Norris, P., & Nai, A. (Eds.). *Election watchdogs: transparency, accountability and integrity.* Electoral Integrity Project. https://www.electoralintegrityproject.com/election-watchdogs

Nussbaum, M. C. (2011). *Creating Capabilities: The Human Development Approach.* Belknap Press. 10.4159/harvard.9780674061200

Nyikadzino, M. (2019). Zimbabwe's transition to a devolved system of government: Critical factors for success. *Africa's Public Service Delivery & Performance Review,* 7(3), 154-173. https://journals.co.za/doi/abs/10.4102/apsdpr.v10i1.604

O'Neill, O. (2006). Transparency and the Ethics of Communication. *Ratio Juris*, 19(2), 173–193.

OECD. (2010). *OECD Rural Policy Reviews*. OECD. 10.1787/9789264082151-

Olowu, D., & Wunsch, J. S. (2004). *Local Governance in Africa: The Challenges of Democratic Decentralisation.* Lynne Rienner Publishers.

Pateman, C. (1970). *Participation and Democratic Theory*. Cambridge University Press. 10.1017/CBO9780511720444

Pekkola, S., Ylinen, M. and Mavengere, N. (2022). Consortium of Municipalities Co-tailoring a Governmental e-Service Platform: What could go wrong? *Digital Government: Research and Practice, 3*(6) 1–16. 10.1145/3511889

Pickles, J. (2011). Transparency and Accountability in Local Government. *Local Government Studies*, 37(4), 427–447.

Ribot, J. C. (2004). *Rural Governance and Decentralization: Evidence from Southeast Asia.* Agricultural Decentralization & Rural Institutions.

Schmitter, P. C. (2004). Decentralization and the future of democracy. *Studies in Comparative International Development*, 39(1), 14–31.

Shongwe, B. R., & Meyer, D. F. (2023). Service Delivery Challenges within Rural Communities. The Case of the Nkomazi Local Municipal Area. *Administratio Publica, 31*(4). https://journals.co.za/doi/abs/10.10520/ejc-adminpub_v31_n2_a8

Smoke, P. (2015). Accountability and service delivery in decentralising environments: Understanding context and strategically advancing reform. *A Governance Practitioner's Notebook: Alternative Ideas and Approaches*. OECD.

Smoke, P., & Lewis, B. D. (1996). *Fiscal Decentralization in Developing Countries: Issues, Challenges, and the Search for Solutions*. Urban Institute Press.

Stephen, S., Charron, N., & Justesen, M. K. (2023). Electoral competition, political parties and clientelism: Evidence from local elections in South Africa. *Democratization*, 30(3), 479–500. 10.1080/13510347.2022.2155143

Suryanto, S., & Asri, A. R. F. (2020). Analysis of Money Market Mutual Fund Performance and Its Influencing Factors. *Journal of Finance and Banking Studies*, 10(1), 1–16.

Sutrisno, P. (2023). Literature review: Risk Mitigation and Rescue Procedures in the People's Credit System Literature Review: Mitigasi Resiko Dan Prosedur. *COSTING: Journal of Economic, Business and Accounting, 6*(2).

Uddin, N. (2019). Empowerment through participation in local governance: the case of Union Parishad in Bangladesh. *Public Administration and Policy: An Asia-Pacific Journal, 22*(1). https://www.emerald.com/insight/content/doi/10.1108/PAP-10-2018-0002/full/html

Vila Pouca de Aguiar, Portugal (2023). *Good democratic governance as tool to challenge desertification and promote attractivity of rural communities*. Council of Europe. https://www.coe.int/en/web/good-governance/-/good-democratic-governance-as-tool-to-challenge-desertification-and-promote-attractivity-of-rural-communities

Zinyama, T. (2021). Local Government, Decentralisation, Devolution, and Service Delivery in Zimbabwe. In *Encyclopedia of Information Science and Technology.* IGI Global. 10.4018/978-1-7998-3479-3.ch109

# Chapter 3
# Examining Challenges Impacting the Implementation of an Integrated Development Plan in Selected Townships of Nelson Mandela Metropolitan Municipality

**Nandiswa Mpolweni**
https://orcid.org/0000-0002-4511-4998
*Durban University of Technology, South Africa*

**Martin Mulunda Kabange**
*Durban University of Technology, South Africa*

## ABSTRACT

*The South African Integrated Development Plans (IDPs) were established to strategically coordinate development efforts, allocate resources effectively, and improve service delivery across municipalities in the country. Nevertheless, despite adhering to legal obligations, municipalities face persistent challenges that impede the realisation of their strategic goals and the effective execution of their plans. This study explores the barriers obstructing the Nelson Mandela Metropolitan Municipality's (NMMM) efficient implementation of its IDPs, notwithstanding its compliance with*

DOI: 10.4018/979-8-3693-3617-5.ch003

*legislation. Through qualitative methods, including document review and stakeholder interviews, the study identifies critical challenges such as limited community participation, insufficient budget allocation, human resource constraints, and strained intergovernmental relations. These challenges intersect and impact the municipality's capacity to deliver services effectively and achieve its strategic goals.*

## INTRODUCTION

The Nelson Mandela Metropolitan Municipality (NMMM) is situated in the Eastern Cape province of South Africa. It provides services to a heterogeneous populace exceeding 1.19 million individuals, distributed among six local municipalities (Nelson Mandela Metropolitan Municipality IDP, 2022/2023). NMMM is one of the most sizeable urban centres nationwide and is confronted with substantial demands for public services and development. As with all municipalities, NMMM is obligated by law to employ Integrated Development Plans (IDPs) to strategically coordinate service delivery initiatives, budget allocation, and capital projects to enhance living standards throughout its jurisdiction. Despite the NMMM's continuous efforts to develop five-year IDPs in pursuit of its developmental objectives for more than two decades, it continues to face enduring obstacles in the execution phase. The challenges mentioned in research conducted by Mamokhere & Meyer (2023) and Munzhedzi & Makwembere (2019) include insufficient financial and human resource allocation, inadequate community participation, and poor coordination among governmental spheres.

In the context of the NMMM, significant obstacles to effective IDP project implementation and service provision have been identified as fraught intergovernmental relations, limited public participation, budgetary limitations, and skill deficiencies (Mehlape, 2022; Mamokhere & Meyer, 2023). It is imperative to tackle these obstacles in the NMMM townships of Walmer and Motherwell. Doing so will enable the IDP to fully realise its capacity as a mechanism for advancing sustainable and inclusive development, thereby improving the standard of living and welfare of rural inhabitants. Although previous research has provided insights into the obstacles municipalities encounter in urban regions, there is a significant knowledge vacuum regarding in-depth examinations of how these challenges materialise in rural settings.

This study follows a structured format comprising a literature review, theoretical framework, methodology, results, and conclusion.

## LITERATURE REVIEW ON MAPPING THE EVOLUTION OF INTEGRATED DEVELOPMENT PLANNING: HISTORICAL CONTEXT, POLICY DYNAMICS, AND KEY INFLUENCES

Scholars have examined the relationship between IDPs and the transition towards democratic, inclusive local governance in South Africa during the early 1990s (Thabethe, 2023; Zantsi, 2020). The Constitution of the Republic of South Africa 1996 mandated this transition to address the spatial and socio-economic inequalities after apartheid (La Foy, 2020; Padayachee & Van Niekerk, 2019). It has been argued that the inadequacies of previous local governments in meeting the demands of the community have made comprehensive, locally-specific strategic planning essential (Rice, Long & Levenda, 2022; Lalu, 2022; Maela, Matloga & Zitha, 2024). IDPs were introduced to facilitate inclusive and participatory frameworks for strategic management to achieve sustainable development and fulfil the revised responsibilities of local governance (Makalela, 2019; Joseph, 2022).

Scholars have also emphasised the importance of several policy documents issued after apartheid, which established IDPs as the primary local planning framework in South Africa (Ouwencamp, 2023; Matlhoahela, 2022). One of the most influential documents was the Reconstruction and Development Programme (RDP) White Paper 1994. This paper emphasised area-based, participatory, and equitable transformation, prioritising social justice and access to basic services (Vivek, 2024; Mpya, 2020). The RDP laid the foundation for collaborative governance among various spheres, stakeholders, and communities to facilitate integrated solutions, which were subsequently incorporated into IDPs.

The 1995 White Paper on Local Government further reinforced the developmental mandate of municipalities and the importance of long-term strategic planning, which was in line with the nascent IDP concept (Mathebula & Sebola, 2019; Mehlape, 2022). At the same time, municipalities were granted formal authority over local development decisions through the Municipal Systems Act of 2000, which allowed them to use IDP processes as strategic planning instruments (Rulashe & Ijeoma, 2022; Munzhedzi, 2021; Mkhabela, 2022). Pilot IDP programs during the late 1990s were crucial in guiding standardisation and refining procedures, providing valuable insights into implementation strategy, stakeholder involvement, and development alignment with community requirements (Rogerson, 2018; Kusters et al., 2018). Finally, the Municipal Systems Act of 2000 officially recognised the significance of IDPs in achieving transformation objectives (Masilo & Gershwin, 2020). These policy developments and refinements solidified IDPs as crucial tools for rectifying historical inequities and promoting equitable, sustainable development at the local level in post-apartheid South Africa.

## Conceptual Foundations of IDPS

Integrated Development Planning (IDP) is a multi-faceted approach that emphasises two fundamental principles: participatory planning and integration. Its overarching objective is to achieve sustainable development by acknowledging the complex interrelationships among social, economic, and environmental determinants and holistically tackling them. The fundamental tenet of this methodology is integration, which underscores the need to harmonise efforts across various sectors, departments, and governmental bodies to comprehensively address intricate societal challenges (Cejudo & Michel, 2021). By pooling resources and aligning objectives, IDP maximises its developmental impact, reduces redundancy, and fosters synergies.

In addition to integration, participatory planning is another crucial pillar of IDP. This principle emphasises the participation of stakeholders and communities in the decision-making process (Eikelenboom & Long, 2023). Through inclusive discourse and participation, IDP improves the credibility, applicability, and efficacy of development endeavors, ensuring that the concerns and preferences of a wide range of stakeholders are considered (Kusters et al., 2020). This methodology recognises past disparities and seeks to enable disadvantaged communities to engage meaningfully in society by providing a forum (Makalela, Masenya & Mokoele, 2021).

IDPs also prioritise sustainable development by ensuring that current requirements are balanced with future generations (Goba, 2018). This requires development planning to incorporate environmental factors, advance social equity, and guarantee economic sustainability (Ahmad & Islam, 2024). IDP aims to foster economic growth, mitigate adverse environmental effects, and resolve social disparities to cultivate resilient communities and improve overall welfare (Kiefer & Ranganathan, 2020).

To summarise, IDPs in South Africa represent a commitment to sustainable development objectives, participatory planning processes, and integrated development principles (Eidelman, 2021). IDP aims to foster inclusive, equitable, and sustainable development outcomes while tackling complex societal issues. This concept is illustrated in Figure 1. Using collaborative efforts, active community participation, and an emphasis on enduring viability, IDP endeavours to actualise its aspiration for a society that is equitable, prosperous, and robust (Schiller & Kenworthy, 2017).

*Figure 1. IDP: Integrating for societal challenge*

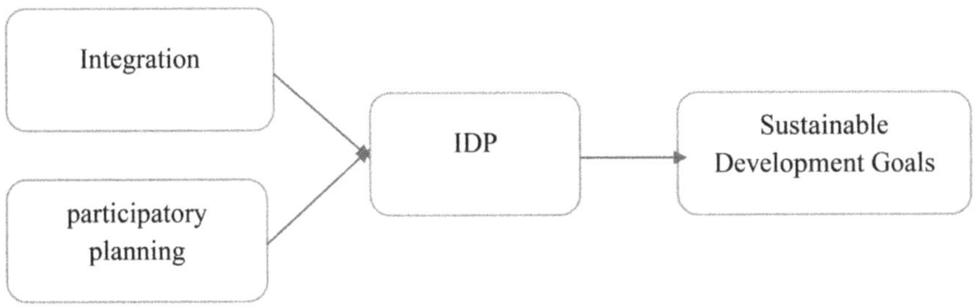


*Authors' conceptualisation*

## Challenges Facing IDP Implementation In South Africa

Implementing integrated development plans faces numerous obstacles that hinder the achievement of developmental objectives in South Africa. This section highlights several challenges relevant to this study's primary objective. These challenges include inadequate community participation, limited human resource capacities and skills, insufficient financial resource allocation and budget constraints, and other obstacles.

- *Insufficient Allocation of Financial Resources and Budget Constraints:*

One of the major hurdles to successfully implementing IDP is the inadequate commitment to allocating financial resources and budgetary restrictions. Funding constraints limit the capacity of municipalities to execute critical initiatives and fulfil the objectives outlined in their IDPs. Budget deficits pose a significant obstacle to implementing socio-economic programs and community initiatives. Budgetary limitations are compounded by the reliance on equitable share grants, which impedes the implementation of IDPs (Munzhedzi, 2020; CoGTA, 2022).

- *Limited Human Resource Capacities and Skills:*

Limited human resource capabilities and skills also present profound impediments to the realisation of development goals. Municipalities' effectiveness in IDP implementation is hindered by staff turnover, insufficient training opportunities, and challenges in recruiting and retaining qualified personnel. Due to deficiencies, capacity building is essential to facilitate critical developmental objectives in technical and specialised domains, including economic development and planning (Rogerson, 2019; Ouwencamp, 2023). Therefore, municipalities need to address these human resource challenges to facilitate IDPs' sustainable growth and development and achieve their developmental goals.

- *Inadequate Community Participation:*

Inadequate community involvement is another significant obstacle to the effective execution of IDP camps. Effective engagement is hindered by historical inequalities that stem from the lasting effects of segregation. Marginalised communities, for instance, may face obstacles such as restricted access to information and inadequate infrastructure. Furthermore, insufficient involvement of the general public diminishes the significance of IDPs, leading to development initiatives that lack alignment with the genuine requirements of the local populace. Resolving these challenges requires collective efforts to promote substantial citizen engagement (Mamokhere & Meyer, 2023; Sullivan, 2019).

- *Additional Challenges*

In addition to the above challenges, several other obstacles may impede IDP implementation, including political instability, inefficiencies within the bureaucracy, and a lack of coordination between government departments and stakeholders. Bureaucratic red tape and political interference may result in project delays and obstruction in decision-making processes. Furthermore, compartmentalised mentalities and fragmented approaches within government departments can lead to redundant endeavours and suboptimal resource distribution. In order to ensure sustainable development outcomes and effective IDP implementation, these obstacles require streamlined processes, interdepartmental collaborations, and political stability.

## Theoretical Framework

Institutional theory examines how the municipality's structural setup, processes, and entrenched culture influence IDP implementation. It emphasises the significance of formal structures, such as departmental divisions and budgeting systems, and informal norms, like resistance to change and lack of accountability. Scholars such as Woulfin & Allen (2022) and Hassenforder & Barone (2018) contribute to understanding how these institutional arrangements shape behaviour and decision-making processes, either facilitating or hindering IDP implementation.

Moreover, institutional theory emphasises the influence of external pressures on the municipality's operations. Scholars like Nyawo and Mubangizi (2021) and Mubangizi (2019) highlight the importance of external pressures from funders, communities, and other levels of government on municipalities. These pressures affect the municipality's ability to execute city-wide strategies outlined in the IDP as they determine resource allocation, priorities, and decision-making processes. In Walmer and Motherwell, within the NMMM, external pressures can look different due to distinct socio-economic dynamics and resource limitations. These regions face multiple challenges like, restricted infrastructure accessibility, inadequate economic development, and a scarcity of employment opportunities. Community resilience, environmental preservation, and agriculture often become the focal points of these townships. Therefore, addressing external pressures in this context requires tailored approaches that are sustainable and contextually appropriate.

Stakeholder Theory complements Institutional Theory by examining the interrelationships among the diverse stakeholders involved in the IDP process. It highlights the importance of involving business, government, and community stakeholders to foster collaboration and ensure that interests align with overarching developmental goals. Scholars like Masilo & Gershwin (2020) and Makalela (2019) examine the responsibilities of government stakeholders, while Abiddin, Ibrahim & Abdul Aziz (2022) emphasise the importance of community stakeholders. Stakeholder Theory emphasises the promotion of efficient governance frameworks and decision-making procedures to guarantee stakeholder alignment and coordination. In Walmer and Motherwell, traditional institutions like local councils and community elders often influence community affairs and decision-making. Community dynamics like solid interpersonal connections and shared principles could impact stakeholders' engagement and collaboration. Limited access to resources such as electricity, water, and transportation infrastructure may also impede the active participation of stakeholders in development processes.

Lastly, Public Policy Theory provides a structured approach to understanding policymaking, particularly concerning the challenges encountered during the implementation IDPs. Scholars like Ngqwala (2019) and Mangwanya & Shava (2023) examine issues related to coordination and collaboration among governmental departments and propose structural modifications to enhance integration. Herbert (2021) examines the difficulties associated with limited financial resources and suggests alternative financing frameworks in addition to involving external funding channels. As highlighted by authors like Mamokhere and Meyer (2022), community engagement and participation are essential, while Masuku and Jili (2019) stress the importance of stable leadership and political will in maintaining IDP implementation throughout political cycles. Public Policy Theory helps us identify challenges like inadequate infrastructure, limited resources, and community dynamics, enabling policymakers and stakeholders to develop customised approaches for successful rural development.

## RESEARCH APPROACH

A qualitative research approach was used for its ability to delve deeply into complex human behaviours and systems, offering richer insights compared to quantitative methods (Nardi, 2018; Lawani, 2021). Semi-structured interviews, employing open-ended questions, were utilised to gather data from 100 participants, including five municipal officials (MO1-MO5) and five ward councillors (WC1 – WC5) from Walmer and Motherwell townships. This method allowed participants to provide detailed perspectives while guiding the conversation around relevant topics, fostering active engagement and meaningful contributions to knowledge generation (Baker et al., 2018). Ethical clearance was obtained from the Institutional Research Ethics Committee (IREC) of the Duban University of Technology (DUT) (Ethical Clearance number IREC 301/21 issued on 1 June 2022), ensuring the protection of participants' rights and confidentiality. All participants provided written consent before the interviews, and their responses were treated anonymously. Thematic analysis was employed to identify common themes and patterns in the data, extracting meaning and insights from the perspectives shared by participants (Roberts et al., 2019).

## FINDINGS AND DISCUSSIONS

The findings of the study are categorised into two main themes. The first theme focuses on the impact of the IDP on service delivery, while the second theme explores potential challenges that impact the municipalities' Integrated Development Plan (IDP).

### Theme One: The IDP Impact on Service Delivery

Findings reveal that IDP is a vital document that serves as a roadmap for guiding and prioritising service delivery projects and initiatives planned by the municipality, aligning them with the needs and aspirations of the community. However, any hindrance to the IDP, including challenges related to lack of stakeholder engagement or budget limitations, can negatively impact the successful implementation of the service delivery projects outlined in the IDP. This is the view of most participants, such as:

- *Budget limitations play a role in terms of how much is allocated for each area in the NMB.*
- *As the municipality, we use IDP to guide us towards the direction of community desires, so IDP affects service delivery in a positive way.*
- *IDP informs service delivery. If it's not done properly in engagement with relevant stakeholders, it will have a negative impact on service delivery.*

The findings emphasise the significant role of the IDP in shaping service delivery within the municipality. One key finding is that budget limitations impact resource allocation to different areas in the municipality, and the IDP serves as a guiding document in this process. The IDP helps prioritise and allocate resources based on the community's needs and aspirations, ensuring that service delivery efforts align with the community's direction. This finding highlights the positive impact of the IDP on service delivery by aligning it with the desires of the community. The implication of this result for Walmer and Motherwell is significant. With the IDP as a guiding framework for resource allocation, the selected townships can benefit from more targeted and responsive service delivery efforts. Also, in aligning service delivery initiatives with the specific needs and aspirations of the communities in Walmer and Motherwell, the municipality can optimise the impact of limited resources. This approach ensures that essential services and infrastructure projects are prioritised based on the community's direction, ultimately leading to improved quality of life and socio-economic development in these townships.

Another important finding is the importance of proper stakeholder engagement in the IDP process. The study reveals that if the IDP is not implemented in a manner that involves key stakeholders, it can have a negative impact on service delivery. Inclusive and meaningful engagement with stakeholders such as community members, government officials, and local organisations is essential to ensure that the IDP accurately reflects the specific challenges and aspirations of residents in Walmer and Motherwell. By involving stakeholders in the decision-making process, the municipality can better address the nuanced requirements of these communities, leading to more effective service delivery initiatives and sustainable development outcomes.

In support of the above findings, several studies found that the IDP is vital in guiding and prioritising service delivery projects and initiatives within the municipality. The IDP is a roadmap for aligning resource allocation and delivery efforts with community needs and aspirations (Thwala, 2022; Sethu, 2021; Motshabi, 2023). By outlining service delivery priorities based on public input, the IDP helps to optimise the impact of limited resources and ensure that services target the most pressing issues identified by residents (Munwana, 2020; Makalela, 2019). As Masipa (2021) and Mofokeng (2019) found, the IDP informs both the selection of projects and budget allocation to different sectors. When adequately developed through stakeholder engagement, the IDP aligns plans with "the nuanced requirements" of communities (Mamokhere, 2022).

However, specific challenges can negatively impact the IDP process and subsequent service delivery implementation. Budget constraints, in particular, influence how much is allocated for each area and affect the municipality's ability to fully realise IDP goals (Makalela, 2019; Masilo & Gershwin, 2020). The findings also emphasise that a lack of proper stakeholder engagement throughout the IDP process can compromise service delivery outcomes (Mamokhere & Meyer, 2022; Mamokhere & Meyer, 2023). Involving communities is key to ensuring the IDP accurately reflects their specific challenges and aspirations (Mamokhere & Meyer, 2023).

Overall, these findings underscore the crucial role of the IDP in guiding and prioritising service delivery. The IDP is a roadmap that aligns resource allocation and service delivery efforts with the community's desires. However, the findings also highlight the importance of proper stakeholder engagement throughout the IDP process to avoid any negative impact on service delivery. By incorporating the perspectives and input of various stakeholders, the municipality can ensure that the IDP accurately represents the needs of the community, leading to more effective and targeted service delivery outcomes.

## Theme 2: Potential challenges impacting the municipalities' IDP

The findings reveal several potential challenges impacting the municipality's Integrated Development Plan. These challenges encompass political influences, coalition governance, budget allocation, public participation, and the qualifications of officials, as illustrated in the excerpts below. Understanding and addressing these challenges are crucial for effective IDP implementation and ensuring the plan aligns with the needs and aspirations of the community.

- *Particularly during election periods, these IDP/Budget review processes are politicised and some of the meetings [are] disrupted.*
- *We are in a very delicate political situation as the municipality and that has impacted our IDP more especially this year, the instability because of the fact that we have coalition government.... By its very nature, coalition is something new in the municipalities of the country and as a result, there's still no strategy in place to deal with it.*
- *Budget allocation [and] public participation are the challenges impacting our IDP. They affect it in the manner that if funds are inadequate, service delivery will be lacking. As well as participation by the public, if they don't engage in the IDP sessions the municipality gets in trouble.*
- *Yes, challenges are always there; for example, the issue of political instability within the municipality, the longer time that is taken to appoint the municipal managers and those are key positions that hinder decision making when it comes to approving and adopting IDP and budgeting for service delivery purpose.*

- *Some officials are not qualified and therefore do not have necessary experience on municipal planning and service delivery, also participation of community in the matters of local government. All of these do have an impact on the municipal IDP.*

The findings reveal that the IDP and budget review processes are susceptible to politicisation, particularly during elections. This politicisation leads to disruptions in meetings and compromises the decision-making process. Instead of prioritising the community's actual needs, political considerations often take precedence. These findings underscore the importance of depoliticising the IDP process to ensure its integrity and effectiveness. By removing political influences, the municipality can ensure that the IDP focuses on the genuine needs and aspirations of the community. More specifically, the depoliticisation of the IDP process in Walmer and Motherwell can lead to a more equitable distribution of resources, enhanced community participation, and improved resident development outcomes.

Another significant challenge identified in the findings is a coalition government within the municipality. The study highlights that coalition governance is a relatively new phenomenon in the country's municipalities and lacks clear strategies for effective management. This dearth of guidelines can create instability and hinder the implementation of the IDP. To address this challenge, it is essential to develop comprehensive strategies that tackle the unique challenges of coalition governance. The municipality can ensure smoother IDP implementation by establishing clear guidelines and fostering effective collaboration among coalition partners.

Budget allocation and public participation are two additional challenges highlighted by the findings. Inadequate funds directly impact service delivery, resulting in a gap between the planned initiatives in the IDP and the actual services provided to the community. The findings also reveal that low public engagement and participation in IDP sessions further exacerbate these challenges. Without active involvement from the community, there is a risk of the IDP failing to address the actual needs and aspirations of the local population of Walmer and Motherwell townships. Therefore, enhancing budget allocation mechanisms and promoting robust public participation initiatives is crucial. The municipality can bridge the gap between planned initiatives and actual service delivery by allocating sufficient funds and actively involving the community in the IDP process. This ensures that the IDP reflects the selected townships' priorities.

The study findings also draw attention to the issue of political instability within the municipality and the delays in appointing municipal managers. These challenges hamper the decision-making processes related to the approval and adoption of the IDP and budget allocation for service delivery. The findings emphasise the importance of stable governance structures and timely key personnel appointments. The municipality can facilitate efficient decision-making and overcome these challenges by streamlining administrative processes and ensuring swift appointments, thereby supporting effective IDP implementation.

Lastly, the qualifications and experience of officials emerge as a significant factor influencing the municipal IDP. The findings reveal that some officials lack the necessary expertise in municipal planning and service delivery, which can hinder the quality and effectiveness of the IDP. To address this challenge, investing in the professional development of officials becomes imperative. By providing training and ensuring that officials possess the required qualifications and skills, the municipality can enhance the overall quality and outcomes of the IDP.

In support of the above findings, several studies reveal numerous challenges that can influence the effectiveness of the municipality's Integrated Development Plan. One such challenge is the politicisation of the IDP and budget review processes, particularly during election periods. This politicisation leads to disruptions in meetings and compromises decision-making (Mboneni, 2023; Zweni, 2022). Another issue identified is the complexity of coalition governance structures within the municipality. As Bormann (2019) found, the lack of clear strategies for navigating political coalitions can create instability and tensions around resource allocation.

Financial barriers, such as inadequate budgeting, were also highlighted. Insufficient funds directly impact service delivery by widening the gap between planned initiatives and actual community services (Osborne, 2020; Makalela, 2019). Additionally, low levels of public participation in the IDP process present a challenge (Mamokhere & Meyer, 2023; Ndou, 2019). Without robust citizen involvement, there is a risk that the IDP may fail to address residents' needs. Administrative hurdles further inhibit IDP implementation. Unstable leadership, delays in key appointments, and underqualified officials hinder efficient decision-making and planning quality (Mamokhere & Meyer, 2022; Ndou, 2019). Addressing these multi-faceted obstacles through initiatives like specialised coalition training and expanded public engagement is thus imperative.

In conclusion, the findings emphasise the multi-faceted nature of challenges that impact the municipality's IDP. Addressing these challenges requires concerted efforts to depoliticise the process, develop strategies for effective coalition governance, improve budget allocation mechanisms, enhance public participation, and invest in the qualifications and expertise of officials. By addressing these challenges, municipalities can foster sustainable development, ensure effective service delivery, and meet the needs of the community. The findings provide valuable insights for policymakers and local government authorities to enhance the efficacy of the IDP framework and drive meaningful change in their communities.

## CONCLUSION

In conclusion, this study sheds light on the challenges affecting the implementation of the IDP in the NMMM. The findings highlight the interconnected nature of these challenges and their manifestation within the local context. Limited community participation, inadequate resource allocation, deficits in technical skills, and strained relations with other levels of government are identified as key challenges.

Insufficient public involvement in the planning process hampers effective implementation, calling for improved mechanisms for community engagement. Inadequate financial and human resource allocation restricts project implementation and service delivery, necessitating strategic resource planning and exploring alternative funding sources. Deficits in technical skills hinder IDP implementation, emphasising the need for training and professional development. Strained relations with other levels of government require collaborative governance and effective coordination.

Addressing these challenges requires a multi-faceted approach involving collaboration among stakeholders. Depoliticising the IDP process, establishing guidelines for effective coalition governance, enhancing budget allocation mechanisms, promoting robust public participation, and investing in officials' qualifications are essential. By overcoming these challenges, the municipality can improve service delivery, bridge the gap between planned initiatives and outcomes, and meet the developmental needs of the community.

Overall, this study contributes to a deeper understanding of the impact of the IDP on service delivery and the challenges municipalities face in its implementation. By recognising these challenges and implementing targeted strategies, the NMMM can improve the implementation of its IDP, meet its constitutional service obligations, and contribute to sustainable development and community well-being.

## REFERENCES


Abiddin, N. Z., Ibrahim, I., & Abdul Aziz, S. A. (2022). Non-governmental organisations (NGOs) and their part towards sustainable community development. *Sustainability (Basel)*, 14(8), 4386. 10.3390/su14084386

Ahmad, I., & Islam, M. R. (2024). Empowerment and Participation: Key Strategies for Inclusive Development. In *Building Strong Communities: Ethical Approaches to Inclusive Development* (pp. 47-68). Emerald Publishing Limited.

Baker, L., Cristancho, S., Kennedy, T. J., & Lingard, L. 2018. Qualitative research in medical education: methodologies and methods. *Understanding medical education: Evidence, theory, and practice*. Wiley.

Bormann, N. C. (2019). Uncertainty, cleavages, and ethnic coalitions. *The Journal of Politics*, 81(2), 471–486. 10.1086/701633

Cejudo, G. M., & Michel, C. L. (2021). Instruments for policy integration: How policy mixes work together. *SAGE Open*, 11(3), 21582440211032161. 10.1177/21582440211032161

Eidelman, T. A. 2021. *Reclaiming Cape Town: Spatial Justice and the (Post) Apartheid City* [Doctoral dissertation, Vanderbilt University].

Eikelenboom, M., & Long, T. B. (2023). Breaking the cycle of marginalisation: How to involve local communities in multi-stakeholder initiatives? *Journal of Business Ethics*, 186(1), 31–62. 10.1007/s10551-022-05252-5

Goba, N. S. (2018). *The architecture of non-grievability: a critical race spatial analysis of the continuance of apartheid spatial planning into (post) apartheid South Africa*. University of Pretoria.

Hassenforder, E., & Barone, S. (2018). Institutional arrangements for water governance. *International Journal of Water Resources Development*.

Herbert, M. M. 2021. *An Analysis of the Integrated Development Planning Process in Blouberg Local Municipality* [Master's thesis, University of Pretoria (South Africa)].

Joseph, J. E. (2022). Unequal, undiversified and underrepresented: Women on the backburner in local decision making in South Africa's local government. *ScienceRise*, (3 (80)), 24–37. 10.21303/2313-8416.2022.002533

Kiefer, K., & Ranganathan, M. (2020). The politics of participation in cape Town's slum upgrading: The role of productive tension. *Journal of Planning Education and Research*, 40(3), 263–277. 10.1177/0739456X18761119

Kusters, K., Buck, L., de Graaf, M., Minang, P., van Oosten, C., & Zagt, R. (2018). Participatory planning, monitoring and evaluation of multi-stakeholder platforms in integrated landscape initiatives. *Environmental Management*, 62(1), 170–181. 10.1007/s00267-017-0847-y28324144

Kusters, K., De Graaf, M., Buck, L., Galido, K., Maindo, A., Mendoza, H., Nghi, T. H., Purwanto, E., & Zagt, R. (2020). Inclusive landscape governance for sustainable development: Assessment methodology and lessons for civil society organisations. *Land (Basel)*, 9(4), 128. 10.3390/land9040128

La Foy, G. B. (2020). *Local government in the constitutional dispensation: defining the limits of local government's legislative and executive authority* [Doctoral dissertation].

Lalu, P. (2022). *Undoing apartheid.* John Wiley & Sons.

Maela, K. D., Matloga, S. T., & Zitha, H. E. (2024). Nurturing Development Administration in South African Local Government. *International Journal of Social Science Research and Review*, 7(3), 170–188. 10.47814/ijssrr.v7i3.1987

Makalela, K. I. 2019. *The efficacy of integrated development plan in enhancing service delivery in Lepelle-Nkumpi Local Municipality, Limpopo Province* [Doctoral dissertation].

Makalela, K. I., Masenya, M. J., & Mokoele, N. J. (2021). Women in South Africa's development trajectory: Disjuncture between Voice, Participation and integrated Development Planning. *European Journal of Economics*, 5(3).

Mamokhere, J. (2022). Leaving no one behind in a participative integrated development planning process in South Africa. *International Journal of Research in Business and Social Science (2147-4478), 11*(10), 277-291.

Mamokhere, J., & Meyer, D. F. (2022). Comprehending stakeholders' involvement in the integrated development planning process as a tool for improved community participation. *EUREKA: Social and Humanities*, (4), 18–32.

Mamokhere, J., & Meyer, D. F. (2023). The Integrated Development Planning Process's Impact as a Tool for Increasing Community Participation in South Africa. *African Journal of Development Studies*, 13(2), 7–34. 10.31920/2634-3649/2023/v13n2a1

Mangwanya, M. G., & Shava, E. (2023). Intergovernmental relations as an accelerator for the local government planning in South Africa. *Journal of Southwest Jiaotong University*, 58(2).

Masilo, T., & Gershwin, G. (2020). *The Perceived Impact Of Integrated Development Planning (Idp).* On The Social And Economic Development Of Local Communities Of Magareng Local Municipality, Northern Cape Province.

Masipa, M. H. (2021). *An analysis of the Integrated Development Planning (IDP) process in Blouberg Local Municipality* [Doctoral dissertation, University of Pretoria].

Masuku, M. M., & Jili, N. N. (2019). Public service delivery in South Africa: The political influence at local government level. *Journal of Public Affairs*, 19(4), e1935. 10.1002/pa.1935

Mathebula, N.E. & Sebola, M.P. (2019). Evaluating the Integrated Development Plan for Service Delivery within the Auspices of the South African Municipalities. *African Renaissance (1744-2532), 16*(4).

Matlhoahela, R. K. (2022). *Public participation in the Integrated Development Planning process at local government sphere in South Africa: a literature study* [Doctoral dissertation, North-West University (South Africa)].

Mboneni, A. (2023). *Political instability affects service delivery: an assessment of Dr Beyers Naude Local Municipality from 1994-2017* [Doctoral dissertation, Stellenbosch: Stellenbosch University].

Mehlape, M. M. (2022). *Community participation in the Integrated Development Planning processes as a means of improving local governance: a case of Polokwane Municipality* [Doctoral dissertation].

Mofokeng, W. N. (2019). *Assessment of budget allocation and funding of community food security projects in Emfuleni Local Municipality* [Doctoral dissertation, North-West University (South Africa)].

Motshabi, P. T. 2023. *Exploring bulk water services delivery challenges in the Dr. Ruth Segomotsi Mompati district municipality in the North West Province* [Doctoral dissertation, North-West University (South Africa)].

Mpya, M. I. 2020. *The implementation of the National Development plan and its impact on the Provision of Sustainable Human Settlements: the case of Gauteng Province* [Doctoral dissertation, Doctoral dissertation].

Mubangizi, B. C. (2019). Monitoring and evaluation processes critical to service provision in South Africa's rural-based municipalities. *Journal of Reviews on Global Economics*, 8, 555–565. 10.6000/1929-7092.2019.08.48

Munwana, P. (2020). *The effectiveness of the Integrated Development Planning (IDP) on service delivery: a case of Kagiso Township in Mogale City Local Municipality*. University of Johannesburg.

Munzhedzi, P. H. (2020). Evaluating the efficacy of municipal policy implementation in South Africa: Challenges and prospects. *African Journal of Governance and Development*, 9(1), 89–105.

Munzhedzi, P. H. (2021). An evaluation of the application of the new public management principles in the South African municipalities. *Journal of Public Affairs*, 21(1), e2132. 10.1002/pa.2132

Munzhedzi, P.H. and Makwembere, S., 2019. Good governance as a solution to local economic development challenges in South African municipalities. *Journal of Public Administration, 54*(4-1), 659-676.

Nardi, P. M. (2018). *Doing survey research: A guide to quantitative methods*. Routledge. 10.4324/9781315172231

Ndevu, Z. J., & Muller, K. (2018). Operationalising performance management in local government: The use of the balanced scorecard. *SA Journal of Human Resource Management*, 16(1), 1–11. 10.4102/sajhrm.v16i0.977

Nelson Mandela Metropolitan Municipality. (2022). *Integrated Development Plan 2022/2023*. Nelson Mandela Metropolitan Municipality.

Ngqwala, N. S. (2019). *Leadership imperatives for local government service delivery: case of a selected local municipality inthe Eastern Cape, South Africa* [Doctoral dissertation, Cape Peninsula University of Technology].

Nyawo, J. C., & Mubangizi, B. C. (2021). An exploration of government administrative processes in supporting agro-smallholders' access to municipal markets in eThekwini Municipality, KwaZulu-Natal Province. *Africa's Public Service Delivery & Performance Review*, 9(1), 12. 10.4102/apsdpr.v9i1.528

Ouwencamp, S. (2023). *Fostering public participation in integrated development planning: the case of the City of Matlosana* [Doctoral dissertation, North-West University (South Africa)].

Padayachee, V., & Van Niekerk, R. (2019). *Shadow of Liberation: contestation and compromise in the economic and social policy of the African National Congress, 1943-1996*. Wits University Press.

Rice, L. (2022). Against climate apartheid: Confronting the persistent legacies of expendability for climate justice. *Environment and Planning. E, Nature and Space*, 5(2), 625–645. 10.1177/2514848621999286

Roberts, K., Dowell, A., & Nie, J. B. (2019). Attempting rigour and replicability in thematic analysis of qualitative research data; a case study of codebook development. *BMC Medical Research Methodology*, 19(1), 1–8. 10.1186/s12874-019-0707-y30922220

Rogerson, C. M. (2018). Towards pro-poor local economic development: the case for sectoral targeting in South Africa. In *Local Economic Development in the Changing World* (pp. 75–100). Routledge.

Rulashe, T., & Ijeoma, E. O. (2022). An exploration of public accountability and service delivery at the Buffalo City Metropolitan Municipality in the Eastern Cape province, South Africa. *Africa's Public Service Delivery and Performance Review*, 10(1), 535. 10.4102/apsdpr.v10i1.535

Schiller, P. L., & Kenworthy, J. (2017). *An introduction to sustainable transportation: Policy, planning and implementation*. Routledge. 10.4324/9781315644486

Sethu, M. J. (2021). *The role of performance, monitoring and evaluation within municipal service delivery: A case study of Capricorn District Municipality, Limpopo Province* [Doctoral dissertation].

Sullivan, L. (2019). Conservation in context: Toward a systems framing of decentralised governance and public participation in wildlife management. *The Review of Policy Research*, 36(2), 242–261. 10.1111/ropr.12326

Thabethe, L. R. 2023. *The efficacy of integrated development plan implementation towards the enhancement of basic service delivery: case of Mpakeni Village, Mbombela Local Municipality, South Africa* [Doctoral dissertation].

Thwala, S. 2022. *The role of municipal budget in service delivery for Local Economic Development: the case of Ekurhuleni* [Doctoral dissertation, University of Johannesburg].

Tirivanhu, P. (2022). A framework for facilitating holistic interventions for building community resilience to climate change for sustainable community development. In *Sustainable Rural Development Perspective and Global Challenges*. IntechOpen.

Vivek, N. D. (2024). Transformation Deferred: Disparate Development in Post-Apartheid South Africa (1994-2004). [PJGD]. *PanAfrican Journal of Governance and Development*, 5(1), 128–155. 10.46404/panjogov.v5i1.5364

Woulfin, S.L. & Allen, C.D. (2022). The institution of schooling. *The Foundational Handbook on Improvement Research in Education, 67.*

Zantsi, L. K. 2020. *The approach of the African National Congress to dealing with participatory spaces in post-apartheid South African local government* [Doctoral dissertation, Keele University].

Zweni, A. G. (2022). *Critical evaluation of service delivery in selected South African municipalities: the role of budget management* [Doctoral dissertation, Cape Peninsula University of Technology].

# Chapter 4
# Local Economic Development as a Catalyst for Agricultural Growth and Poverty Relief Strategy:
## A Rural Eastern Cape Perspective

**Tando Rulashe**
*Nelson Mandela University, South Africa*

**Kutu Ramolobe**
*Nelson Mandela University, South Africa*

## ABSTRACT

*In rural South Africa, the enduring legacies of apartheid, including poverty and limited opportunities, persist. This chapter delves into how agriculture can drive local economic growth and development, despite challenges like resource scarcity and inadequate infrastructure. It explores how leveraging agriculture can alleviate poverty. Drawing on theories like systems theory and community-based development, it examines interventions to uplift rural communities. Using a mixed-method approach with an interpretive paradigm and an exploratory design, the chapter conducts a systematic review of secondary data sources, including scholarly publications and official government documents. Despite persistent challenges, findings indicate governmental efforts to support informal and smallholder farmers in enhancing their livelihoods and contributing to LED. Government support for small farmers is acknowledged, but obstacles remain. The chapter emphasizes stakeholder*

DOI: 10.4018/979-8-3693-3617-5.ch004

*collaboration to enhance skills, infrastructure, and community empowerment for sustainable development.*

## INTRODUCTION AND BACKGROUND

Many South Africans still reside in marginalized poor areas that bear the brunt of the past underdevelopment legacies, which were a result of the separate development ideologies of apartheid. These areas are characterized by high unemployment, poverty, and huge backlogs in basic service delivery. In 1994 the Reconstruction and Development Programme (RDP) was initiated as a national framework that would deal with poverty and inequality issues of the past. "A decade after the demise of apartheid, it appears that very little concrete change in rural people's livelihoods has taken place" (UNDP South Africa, 2003). This has translated to rural areas in South Africa being underdeveloped and faced with serious problems of infrastructure, unemployment and lack of basic services.

Unemployment continues to pose significant challenges: it has reached 24.3%, and youth unemployment was 49% at the end of 2014. This increased to 34.4% in the second quarter of 2021 and youth unemployment to a staggering 63.3%. While during the 1st quarter of 2023, slight decreases were seen where an overall unemployment rate of 32.9% and youth unemployment at 46.5%, (Statistics SA, 2023). The service sector has grown in contrast with the manufacturing sector, despite the government's industrialisation plans to combat unemployment. Skills shortages continue to act as a constraint on growth. The outlook for growth is better for financial services and for agriculture, forestry and fisheries sectors. The National Development Plan, which aims to eliminate poverty and reduce inequality by 2030, focuses on creating jobs and improving education", (Kumo, Omilola and Minsat, 2015). In South Africa rural development programmes are more focused on agriculture and scattered around villages with no directly defined linkage to a town, despite the existence of rural small towns for each rural community. Nevertheless, they are not considered for rural development of their surrounding hinterland therefore leaving no defined economic role for the town center. Government policies such as Local Economic Development framework (LED), Integrated Sustainable Rural Development Programme (ISRDP) and Integrated Development Plans (IDPs) are sector-based with no emphasis on localities such as small towns, (Hemson et al, 2004). Previous research reveals that there are dramatic economic and social changes taking place in small towns, which result in changing roles of small towns. Some of these changes are caused by or result in declining economic growth, and ageing community members as the economically active population is leaving for urban cities, Xuza (2005). These patterns somehow portray a picture of local economic development and the rural development dilemma when one considers the historical and current role of small towns with respect to the economic development of their rural hinterland.

In efforts to improve living conditions and empower the local communities Amathole District Municipality initiated a development agency APSIRE in 2005 to focus on rural development through projects that will uplift and help the citizens find sustainable ways that will develop them socially and economically. One of the downfalls of development in the province of the Eastern Cape especially in the small rural towns and areas is the inability to make use of the available resources and skills in its capacity. Rural development is understood to be multi-dimensional encompassing local economic development and social development.

The enhancement of service provision predicated on socio-economic infrastructure, coupled with the active engagement of local communities in developmental endeavours, constituted a pivotal aspect of rectified development paradigms (ISRDS, 2000). While some scholars persist in construing rural development solely within the confines of agriculture, others posit that its scope transcends agricultural pursuits (Makhura, 2009). In addition to challenges stemming from infrastructural deficits and resource scarcities, many smallholder farmers grapple with marketing and distribution impediments impeding their income generation, often exacerbated by geographical isolation or informational deficits, compounded by inadequate governmental and stakeholder support, among other factors. Notably, the marketing landscape for agricultural commodities underwent significant transformations from the mid-nineteenth century to 1990 in the Eastern Cape (Fraser, 1991). As the republic underwent legislative changes impacting commercial farming practices, numerous small-scale farmers, particularly in rural locales, encountered hurdles transitioning to contemporary methodologies. This transition was hindered by a dearth of requisite information, training, financial resources, discriminatory practices, high transactional costs, and technological barriers, all of which undermined the ability of smallholder farmers to produce goods meeting formal market standards (Magingxa, and Kamara, 2003). This chapter will primarily underscore the economic facets of rural development, while also considering ancillary dimensions such as infrastructural concerns, policy frameworks, community involvement, and participation.

## EASTERN CAPE RURAL DEVELOPMENT: POST-1994.

The Eastern Cape is one of five provinces where more than 60% of its population lives in rural areas serviced by small towns. The Eastern Cape Province has a legacy of endemic rural poverty and is characterized by the historical neglect of rural areas. The Eastern Cape still suffers from large outflows of people to other provinces and to the two main cities of Buffalo City Metropolitan Municipality former *(East*

*London)* and The Nelson Mandela Bay Municipality former *(Port Elizabeth)*, to find places of employment rather than staying in small towns ECSECC (2006). For the past few years, much focus of the province has been on agricultural development to curb rural underdevelopment.

Intercity migration from rural towns to larger cities in the Eastern Cape, South Africa, reflects a complex interplay of socio-economic factors influencing individual decision-making processes. Such migration patterns are often driven by aspirations for improved livelihood opportunities, better access to education and healthcare, and the allure of urban amenities. Scholars have highlighted the role of structural transformation, including shifts in the agrarian economy and the expansion of urban industries, as pivotal drivers of rural-to-urban migration (Crush, 2000). Additionally, infrastructural disparities between rural and urban areas, such as inadequate access to basic services and employment opportunities, further incentivize migration to urban centres (Ojo, 2012). Despite the potential benefits associated with urban migration, challenges persist, including housing shortages, unemployment, and social exclusion, particularly among migrant populations (Green, 2015). Understanding the dynamics of intercity migration is essential for policymakers to formulate targeted interventions aimed at addressing the needs of both rural and urban populations, fostering inclusive development strategies that mitigate the adverse impacts of migration on sending communities while maximizing the potential benefits for migrants and destination cities alike (Crush et al., 2017). Therefore, interdisciplinary research integrating perspectives from economics, sociology, and urban studies is crucial for comprehensively analyzing and addressing the complexities of intercity migration in the Eastern Cape, South Africa.

This is not a unique case, in his budget speech of 2015, the then Finance Minister Nhlanhla Nene stated, "government will continue to strengthen support for agricultural development and trade, under Minister Zokwana. The projected conditional allocation to provinces over the medium term is R7 billion. Access to finance by emerging farmers will be expanded, in collaboration with the Land Bank. Since the inception of the recapitalisation and development programme in 2008, 1 459 farms have been supported, and 4.3 million hectares have been acquired for redistribution. A further 1.2 million hectares will be acquired over the next three years, and R4.7 billion is allocated for recapitalisation and development of farms" (The Presidency: Budget speech, 2015).

According to former Finance minister who has been reinstated again Minister P Gordhan, "Increasing agriculture output, raising rural incomes, supporting small-scale farmers and investing in rural roads are key objectives of [the] government's rural development strategy" (The Presidency: Budget speech, 2011). The challenges for implementation of strategies and programmes normally focus on isolated projects, which were spread throughout the province, including the lack of a coordination strategy or linkage for the renewal of the entire town or economic corridor to feed and support other programmes in these areas.

Financial resource allocation to rural development and agriculture in the Eastern Cape is a multifaceted endeavour, reflective of broader developmental priorities and policy frameworks. Historically, the Eastern Cape has received varying degrees of financial support from the government and other stakeholders to bolster rural development initiatives and agricultural endeavours. However, disparities in resource allocation persist, with rural areas often receiving inadequate funding compared to their urban counterparts. For instance, studies have indicated that government spending on agricultural development in the Eastern Cape may not sufficiently address the diverse needs of rural communities (Du Toit et al., 2018). Moreover, budgetary constraints and competing priorities within the agricultural sector have led to challenges in effectively targeting resources to enhance productivity, sustainability, and resilience among rural farmers (Ngcobo et al., 2019). In recent years, efforts have been made to improve the efficiency and effectiveness of resource allocation through initiatives such as participatory budgeting and strategic planning processes (Bahiigwa et al., 2017). Nevertheless, a more concerted and coordinated approach is required to ensure equitable resource distribution and maximize the impact of investments in rural development and agriculture in the Eastern Cape.

## THE CONCEPT AND NATURE OF POVERTY IN SOUTH AFRICA

In 1994 after the first democratic election, the ANC took to power and the realities of the inequalities in necessities such as education, housing, healthcare, and infrastructure among others started to surface. Klasen (1997) writes, "This shows that the country was disfigured by widespread of poverty, with almost half of the South African population being categorized as poor in terms of the national poverty line". With many of the societal problems in South Africa being similar to those faced by many other countries in the world the difference in the South African situation was that the problems were an amalgamation of decades of separate development legislations during the apartheid era, (May, 2008). It is in this regard that poverty is generally acknowledged as one of the most serious problems facing post-apartheid government. The concept and nature of poverty in South Africa are deeply rooted in historical and structural factors, manifesting in multidimensional forms across various socio-economic indicators. Despite significant progress since the end of apartheid, poverty remains a pervasive challenge, disproportionately affecting marginalized communities, particularly in rural areas and informal settlements.

The persistence of poverty is intricately linked to enduring inequalities in access to education, healthcare, employment opportunities, and basic services, perpetuated by historical legacies of discrimination and systemic marginalization (Leibbrandt et al., 2019). According to recent statistics, approximately 55.5% of South Africans live below the national poverty line, with poverty rates significantly higher among black Africans, women, and rural populations (Stats SA, 2020). Moreover, the COVID-19 pandemic has exacerbated existing vulnerabilities, widening the poverty gap and exacerbating socioeconomic disparities (McCarthy et al., 2020). Understanding the complex dynamics of poverty in South Africa requires a holistic approach that considers not only income levels but also factors such as social exclusion, spatial segregation, and intergenerational transmission of disadvantage (Seekings & Nattrass, 2015). Addressing poverty effectively necessitates comprehensive policy interventions aimed at promoting inclusive growth, equitable distribution of resources, and targeted social protection programs tailored to the needs of the most vulnerable segments of society.

The biggest challenge facing South African localities today is their ability to cope with the alarmingly high levels of unemployment and lack of public infrastructure that are negatively affecting economic growth and poverty alleviation programmes, (Loots, 1998). In certain areas, such as within the former homelands, for example, the Eastern Cape Province and in some of the informal settlements, statistics have shown a level of unemployment rising as high as 65% and even in some cases growing into the 80-percentile bracket, (Nel & Hill, 2006). These few former homelands, which the district municipality is made up of, had limited or no development taking place over several years. This has translated into it experiencing high levels of poverty across the District, IDP review (2009-2010). According to the Census report (2001), the district has a population, which is predominantly rural and living in low socio-economic conditions with high poverty, illiteracy, and unemployment rates. For those in employment, the income earning is very low, and a very large proportion of the jobs are in the low-pay and low-semi-skilled sectors (www.cogta.gov.za). These high levels of poverty have led to a high percentage rate of households living on hand-outs.

## AGRICULTURE AND POVERTY REDUCTION.

"Work in various forms by 7.3 billion people has contributed to this progress. Nearly a billion people who work in agriculture and more than 500 million family farms produce more than 80% of the world's food, improving nutrition and health" (Human Development Report, 2015). Around the world, according to Roser (2016), just over 1.1bn people continue to live in absolute poverty during 2012. Simbi

(1998) estimated that 16 million South Africans are living in poverty. Contra to that an article in the Daily Maverick stats drawn from a 2011 Stats SA census indicate that 12 million people in South Africa live in extreme poverty, (https://www.dailymaverick.co.za/article/2015-02-03). With this alarming rate of poverty, the need for well-developed agricultural productivity becomes more and more of a necessity than a mere want in the fight against poverty and food security. In studies by ITDG (2005), it was concluded that "agriculture is the backbone, largest contributor to Gross Domestic Income, the biggest source of foreign exchange and the main generator of savings and tax revenues of most African economies. Therefore, agricultural growth, particularly through improved productivity, will be one of the principal routes to reducing poverty in most developing countries".

The marriage of agricultural productivity and poverty alleviation is not a recent concept but one that has been studied since the early 1950s. Thirtle et al (2003) used the data collected between 1985 and 1993 in 48 developing countries to show that for every 1% increase in recorded agricultural productivity, there was a corresponding fall of between 0.6 and 1.2% in the number of people living below US$ 1 a day. Piesse et al (2005) concluded that "agricultural productivity growth is the most effective way of reducing poverty in the short run in communal areas". Studies by Rodrik (1998) on the role of trade and market access have shown that agriculture can be more attractive with noteworthy gains accruing to farmers if systems and procedures for the marketing of surplus produce are improved. "Long-term investments into the agricultural sector would generate jobs, foreign exchange, serve as a market for industrial products and contribute to rural and urban poverty alleviation", Eicher (1999). It is evident that since the dawn of time present-day agriculture has played a vital role in uplifting the livelihood of the citizens as well as growing the economy. President Jacob Zuma in his 2016 State of the Nation Address highlighted a nine-point plan which is aimed at growing the sluggish economy of the country and point (a) of the plan was "The revitalisation of the agriculture and agro-processing value-chain".

"Currently, South African markets are characterized by inadequate property rights and high transaction costs", (Eicher, 1999). Makhura and Mokoena (2003) state that, "the South African government has initiated trade liberalization and market deregulation processes to harmonize agriculture with the rest of the world". Trade liberalization has done more harm than good to the smallholder farmers, as they cannot compete with the world's standards of quality, quantity, and prices; and their production mechanisms are characterized by high transaction costs. The FAO (2006) made a comparison of small-scale farmers' characteristics with the requirements of the liberal market economy institutions being introduced; it was concluded that these institutions are unable to solve the coordination problems that arise.

## GOVERNMENT AS AN AGENT OF DEVELOPMENT

The primary reason, that defines, the existence of government is its ability to improve the human condition while exercising its power within defined geographical confinements that outline its administrative jurisdiction. To do this, the government must untangle itself from the clutches of underdevelopment flowing from the dependency perpetuated by "trade relations that take place in highly monopolised international markets", (Seligson and Passe-Smith, 1998). Dependence, according to Seligson and Passe-Smith (1998) "describes a situation in which the economies of certain countries are conditioned by the development and expansion of another economy." Dependency makes the economy of a country vulnerable to changes outside its economic environment. Miggels and Rulashe (2022), advocate for a paradigm shift in the organization design and development of state entities especially at local government level.

In South Africa, the government serves as a crucial agent of development, wielding considerable influence through policy formulation, implementation, and resource allocation. Since the end of apartheid, successive administrations have pursued various strategies aimed at fostering inclusive economic growth, reducing inequality, and addressing historical injustices. Through initiatives such as the Reconstruction and Development Programme (RDP) and the National Development Plan (NDP), the government has sought to create an enabling environment for sustainable development, emphasizing infrastructure development, education, healthcare, and social welfare (ANC, 1994; NDP, 2012). Government expenditure plays a pivotal role in driving development efforts, with substantial investments directed towards infrastructure projects, social assistance programs, and public services. For instance, in the 2020/2021 fiscal year, the South African government allocated approximately 25.1% of its total budget towards education and 20.1% towards social protection, reflecting a commitment to human capital development and poverty alleviation (National Treasury, 2020).

Furthermore, the government plays a crucial role in facilitating private sector participation through regulatory frameworks, incentives, and public-private partnerships (PPP), aiming to stimulate investment, create employment opportunities, and spur economic growth (South African Government, 2020). However, challenges such as corruption, inefficiency, and policy uncertainty have hampered the government's effectiveness as an agent of development, necessitating ongoing reforms and enhanced governance mechanisms to ensure optimal utilization of resources and attainment of developmental objectives (Pillay & Bass, 2015). Economic indicators show that the economy of South Africa shrank by 6.4% in the first quarter of 2009; mining shrank by 33% in the final quarter of 2008 (www.amandlapublishers.co .za) when one of its trading partners America experienced a recession. People lost their jobs because American Multinational corporations that have infiltrated and have come to dominate the South African economy started retrenching people to supplement their own economy. South Africa must respond to the pressures of the global economy for its own survival.

As mentioned in the introduction the Eastern Cape-based Amathole District Municipality initiated a development vision through ASPIRE in 2005 to fulfil its obligation of improving people's lives. ASPIRE is the Amathole District Municipality's (ADM) Local Economic Development (LED) Agency. As such, its role is to support the objectives of the District Municipality in transforming the economy of the district. ASPIRE envisages itself as a leader in rural economic development. This is done to ensure that the rural communities of the ADM are self-sufficient to reverse the negative effects of outward of people migration from the district thereby implementing projects which have the potential to create jobs and increase household disposable income, by focusing primarily on rural economic development, to address the significant unemployment in the region. In order to promote the maximisation of resources and stimulate synergies between development partners, ASPIRE has signed a Memorandum of Understanding (MoU) with the Amahlathi, Great Kei, Nkonkobe Ngqushwa and Nxuba local municipalities, while negotiations of the draft agreements are underway with the balance of the municipalities in the district.

In addition, partnership agreements have been signed with Enterprise Ilembe, the Eastern Cape Development Corporation and the National Agricultural Marketing Council, stipulating areas of collaboration thereby avoiding duplication of work (ASPIRE Annual report 2013-2014). More recent initiatives to boost the agricultural sector in the country and province came with the launch of the Institute for Development Assistance Management (IDAM). The IDAM is aimed to equip Department of Agriculture, Forestry and Fisheries (Daff) officers and agricultural scientists with skills for development aid related to food production and agricultural economics starting from June. The institute came about as a result of a $10m (R153m) agreement signed by the South African government with the United Nation's Food and Agricultural Organisation (FAO) eight years ago. These are some of the many efforts of government to ensure a boost in rural development as well as the agricultural sector (http://www.thenewage.co.za/fort-hare-tackles-food-crisis/).

## LOCAL ECONOMIC DEVELOPMENT STRATEGIES

Blakely (1994) stated Local Economic Development "…is essentially a process by which local government and/or community-based groups manage their existing resources and enter into new partnership arrangements with the private sector, or with each other, to create new jobs and stimulate economic activity in a well-defined economic zone". During his reign as the President of the Republic of South Africa, Nelson Mandela believed that by mobilising the resources of urban communities, the government and the private sector would make cities the centre of opportunity for all South Africans and be competitive within the world economy. Local Economic Development (LED) strategies in South Africa are integral to fostering sustainable growth, reducing unemployment, and promoting social inclusion at the grassroots level. Municipalities play a central role in spearheading LED initiatives, leveraging their unique assets and partnerships to stimulate economic activity and enhance the well-being of local communities. Key elements of LED strategies include infrastructure development, business support services, skills development, and entrepreneurship promotion (RSA, 1998).

Through targeted interventions such as Special Economic Zones (SEZs), Industrial Development Zones (IDZs), and enterprise development programs, municipalities aim to attract investment, create jobs, and build vibrant local economies (DBSA, 2020). According to statistics, as of 2019, there were 11 operational SEZs in South Africa, generating over R16.8 billion in private investments and creating approximately 15,967 direct jobs (SEZs, 2019). Moreover, LED strategies often emphasize inclusivity and community participation, with municipalities engaging stakeholders through consultative processes to ensure that development initiatives are aligned with local needs and priorities (RSA, 1998). However, challenges such as limited financial resources, capacity constraints, and bureaucratic red tape pose significant hurdles to effective LED implementation (Bhorat et al., 2019). Addressing these challenges requires a coordinated approach involving all spheres of government, private sector actors, civil society organizations, and local communities, to unlock the full potential of LED as a catalyst for inclusive and sustainable development (DBSA, 2020). The LED Policy Paper: Refocusing Development on the Poor (2002) identifies six strategic interventions that municipalities can adopt in the strive to realize developmental targets of eradicating poverty, creating jobs and redistributing wealth:

*Table 1. Local economic development strategies*

| STRATEGY | FOCUS |
|---|---|
| *Development and Maintenance of Services and Infrastructure* | The strategy focuses on the development and maintenance of services and infrastructure and is the key component of municipal service delivery, in most cases, it addresses past imbalances by rendering basic services to the people. It is also a key component of ensuring that existing infrastructure is taken care of. |
| *Retention and Expansion of Existing Businesses (Business Support Services)* | The Policy Paper on Local Economic Development (2002) requires municipalities to give attention to retaining and expanding existing businesses of a municipality. This would primarily assist local businesses to improve their productivity, increase market share and graduate to higher value-added levels in the production chain. In terms of retention, the municipality is required to devise measures, which would ensure firms within the area do not relocate, but rather stay and expand. |
| *Small, Medium and Macro Enterprises Development (Promoting & Supporting Entrepreneurship)* | SMME development is regarded as a key strategy for the promotion of Local Economic Development in that, it generates both jobs and empowers historically disadvantaged individuals. Blakley (1994:33) agrees with the assertion and states that "this is the sector that has shown great employment potential in South Africa over the past few years. Municipalities are, therefore, expected to provide professional advice and assistance to small businesses in the areas of management, marketing, accounting, financing, sourcing resources and problem-solving". |
| *Community-Based Economic Development (Enterprise Development)* | As mandated by the RDP, supporting institutions like community development trusts and enterprises is crucial for fostering community self-reliance. This approach aims to alleviate poverty, enhance the capabilities of marginalized groups, and create sustainable livelihoods (Department of Provincial and Local Government, 2003). Reddy et al. (2003: 23) emphasize that community-based economic development focuses on combining employment, training, mentoring, and enterprise development to achieve self-sufficiency for disadvantaged communities. |
| *Industrial Recruitment and Place Marketing/ Special Economic Zones (SEZs) and Industrial Development Zones (IDZs)* | This strategy involves attracting new industries to the municipality and promoting the area as desirable for residents, businesses, and investors. Various factors influence this decision, including the cost of living, proximity to markets and suppliers, access to research institutions, transport networks, and quality of infrastructure (Reddy et al., 2003: 27). Municipalities play a crucial role in creating favourable environments to meet these criteria, which also affects the retention of existing businesses and attraction of new ones, placing significant pressure on them. |
| *Plugging the "leaks" in the Local Economy* | Reddy et al. (2003: 28) suggest a strategy of "plugging leaks" by identifying and addressing the outflow of money from local areas. This involves encouraging local purchasing, supporting periodic markets and festivals, utilizing local labour and materials for infrastructure projects, and promoting employee training and networking within the community (LED Policy Paper, 2002). In essence, the aim is to ensure that money circulates within the local economy. |
| *Human Capital Development (Skills Development)* | Ensuring that LED brings social and economic benefits often requires investing in human capital through skills development, education and health. The skilling of local people is significant because it can promote higher living wages. "There are explicit linkages between the promotion of living wages, human capital development and economic development since a well-paid, healthy and well-educated workforce would be more productive than otherwise", (Reddy et al, 2003: 33). |
| *Linking of Profitable Growth to Redistributive Development* | When utilizing this strategy for Local Economic Development, municipalities are advised to mandate that development planning or zoning permission in lucrative areas is contingent upon investment commitments in impoverished neighbourhoods. For instance, if a financial institution establishes a branch in an affluent area, it should also consider doing so in a low-income neighbourhood and allocate a portion of its turnover to support local small and medium-sized enterprises (Local Economic Development Policy Paper, 2002). It is essential to recognize that these strategies can be tailored to local conditions, considering factors such as geographical circumstances, economic structure, population demographics, labour market dynamics, and social considerations such as community safety and HIV/AIDS prevalence. |
| Local Economic Development (LED) provides support in the following areas:<br>• Development and review of national policy, strategy, and guidelines on LED.<br>• Providing direct and hands-on support to provincial and local government.<br>• Management of the Local Economic Development Fund.<br>• Management and Technical Support to Nodal Economic Development Planning.<br>• Facilitating coordinating and monitoring donor programmes, and<br>• Assisting with LED capacity-building processes. | |

## A GLOBAL PERSPECTIVE ON LOCAL ECONOMIC DEVELOPMENT.

While many factors encourage and inform the emergence of local economic development in South Africa, the phenomena are not unique to this global south country but is of imperative in the continent and across the western, eastern and northern global countries. This has seen the concept and its practice evolve and being adapted across different contexts and to the suitability of the countries that have adopted LED. According to the World Bank (2001), globally, LED has undergone three phases since the 1960s.

*Figure 1. Evolution of local economic development*

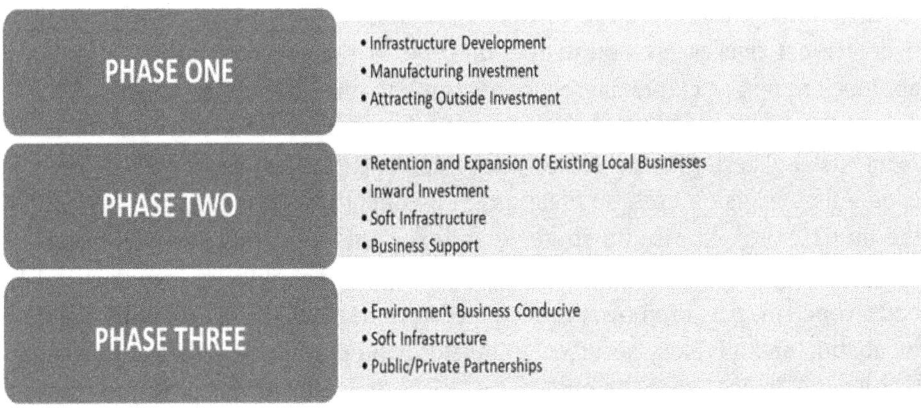


*Adapted from the World Bank, 2001*

During the first phase, that is, 1960 – 1980, LED focused on mobile manufacturing investment, attracting outside investment. Infrastructure development was at the centre of the development of local economies. Moreover, the focus was also on building or improving access to roads, airports, railways for passengers and goods and services, industrial sites, and buildings. The strategies that were used to attract investors or to achieve LED objectives during this time included providing grants, subsidised loans and tax concessions and making use of expensive industrial recruitment techniques (World Bank, 2001). Such investments assured businesses and prospective businesses that the government had a vested interest in assuring business success and creating support by investing in infrastructure. The growth would later be evident in the decrease in unemployment.

During the second phase, from the 1980s to the mid-1990s, the focus shifted towards the retention and expansion of existing local businesses and inward investment. This would ensure that direct stakeholders would have a direct interest in LED through investment. This was achieved through direct payments to individual businesses, business incubators, advisory and training services, technical and business start-up support, as well as the provision of hard and soft infrastructure (World Bank, 2001). The third phase shows that since the mid-1990s, however, the emphasis has moved away from direct financial assistance towards a focus on making the entire business environment conducive to business by concentrating on soft infrastructure, public/ private partnerships(PPPs), networking, as well as the leveraging of private-sector investments and highly-targeted inward investment through the development of a holistic strategy aimed at growing local firms, providing a competitive local investment climate, supporting and encouraging networking and the formation of business clusters, as well as the development and education of the workforce to encourage entrepreneurship (World Bank, 2001).

In summary, the evolution of Local Economic Development (LED) strategies over distinct phases, as outlined from 1960 to the present, reflects a dynamic approach aimed at catalyzing economic growth and alleviating poverty. Initially, during the 1960s to 1980s, LED initiatives focused on attracting external investment and bolstering infrastructure development, thus laying the foundation for economic expansion and job creation. Subsequent phases, spanning the 1980s to the mid-1990s, witnessed a strategic shift towards nurturing existing businesses and fostering inward investment, ensuring direct stakeholder engagement in LED endeavors. This period emphasized targeted support mechanisms, including business incubation and advisory services, to bolster local entrepreneurship and economic resilience. Finally, since the mid-1990s, LED strategies have evolved to prioritize the creation of an enabling business environment through investments in soft infrastructure, public-private partnerships, and workforce development initiatives. This comprehensive approach underscores a commitment to fostering sustainable economic growth, fostering local competitiveness, and empowering communities to thrive in the global economy (World Bank, 2001)

## THEORETICAL AND CONCEPTUAL UNDERPINNINGS FOR ENHANCED LOCAL ECONOMIC DEVELOPMENT

- **Systems Theory**

The history and evolution of systems theory can be traced back to the mid-20th century, with seminal contributions from interdisciplinary scholars such as Ludwig von Bertalanffy and Norbert Wiener. Bertalanffy's General Systems Theory (GST), introduced in the 1940s, aimed to establish a unified framework for understanding complex systems across disciplines. GST emphasized the holistic view of systems, focusing on their structure, behaviour, and interrelationships rather than reducing them to their constituent parts (Bertalanffy, 1950). Concurrently, Wiener's Cybernetics, proposed in the same era, explored the principles of control and communication in both natural and artificial systems. These foundational works laid the groundwork for systems theory, highlighting the importance of feedback mechanisms, emergence, and hierarchical organization in complex systems (Wiener, 1948).

Over the decades, systems theory has undergone significant development and diversification, extending its influence across various fields such as biology, ecology, sociology, and management. In biology, systems biology emerged as a holistic approach to studying biological phenomena, integrating molecular, cellular, and organismal levels of organization (Kitano, 2002). Ecological systems theory applies systems thinking to the study of ecosystems, emphasizing the interdependence of organisms and their environments (Odum, 1983). In sociology, systems theory provides insights into social organization, communication patterns, and institutional dynamics (Luhmann, 1995). Moreover, systems thinking has been applied in management and organizational studies to understand the complexities of decision-making, innovation, and change within diverse organizational contexts. Despite challenges in its application and integration with traditional disciplinary frameworks, systems theory continues to evolve as a powerful tool for analyzing and addressing complex phenomena in science, technology, and society.

In the context of Local Economic Development (LED) as a catalyst for agricultural growth and poverty relief in rural areas of the Eastern Cape, the systems theory offers valuable insights into understanding the interconnectedness and complexity of various factors at play. Systems theory posits that economic development in rural areas is influenced by a multitude of interconnected elements, including social, environmental, and institutional factors. These elements interact within a dynamic system, where changes in one component can have ripple effects throughout the entire system. In the case of LED initiatives aimed at agricultural growth and poverty relief, the systems approach highlights the importance of considering not only agricultural production but also factors such as access to markets, infrastructure, education, and healthcare. For instance, improvements in agricultural productivity may lead to increased incomes for rural households, which in turn can stimulate local economic activity and alleviate poverty. Additionally, investments in infrastructure and social services can enhance the overall resilience of rural communities and create an enabling environment for sustainable development (Khan, 2008). By adopting a systems perspective, LED interventions can be designed to address the multifaceted nature of rural development challenges and leverage synergies between different sectors to achieve holistic and lasting impact (Bosch, 2013).

- **Sustainable Livelihoods Approach**

The Sustainable Livelihoods Approach (SLA) has evolved as a prominent framework for understanding and addressing poverty and development challenges, particularly in rural contexts. Originating in the early 1990s, the SLA was developed by researchers such as Robert Chambers and Gordon Conway as a response to the limitations of conventional development paradigms. Chambers and Conway's seminal work, "Sustainable rural livelihoods: Practical concepts for the 21st century" (1992), laid the foundation for the SLA by emphasizing the importance of holistic and participatory approaches to development. Building upon earlier concepts of sustainable development, the SLA emphasizes the diverse strategies and assets that individuals and communities employ to sustain their livelihoods over time (DFID, 1999).

The SLA has since gained traction in development practice and scholarship, with various organizations and researchers adopting and adapting its principles. The Department for International Development (DFID) played a significant role in promoting the SLA through its Sustainable Livelihoods Guidance Sheets (1999), which provided practical tools and methodologies for its implementation. Ellis (2000) further contributed to the evolution of the SLA by refining its conceptual framework and highlighting the importance of understanding livelihoods within the context of broader social, economic, and environmental dynamics. Today, the SLA continues to inform development interventions and policy-making efforts worldwide, offering a comprehensive and participatory approach to poverty reduction and sustainable development in diverse socio-economic and ecological contexts (Carney, 1998; Scoones, 1998). The Sustainable Livelihoods Approach (SLA) offers a comprehensive framework for analyzing and addressing challenges related to local economic development (LED), particularly in rural contexts such as the Eastern Cape.

Rooted in the concept of sustainable development, SLA emphasizes the interconnectedness of various livelihood assets, including human, social, natural, physical, and financial capital, and their role in shaping individuals' and communities' ability to sustainably generate income and improve their well-being (DFID, 1999). In the context of LED as a catalyst for agricultural growth and poverty relief, SLA underscores the importance of enhancing these livelihood assets to empower rural households to engage in productive activities, such as agriculture, while simultaneously reducing vulnerability to external shocks and stresses (Carney et al., 1999). For instance, interventions aimed at improving access to land, water, and agricultural inputs can enhance natural capital, while investments in education and skills development contribute to human capital accumulation. Additionally, social capital, in the form of community networks and support systems, plays a crucial role in facilitating access to markets, information, and resources (DFID, 1999). By adopting a Sustainable Livelihoods Approach, LED initiatives can address the multidimensional nature of poverty and promote inclusive and resilient economic development in rural areas of the Eastern Cape and South Africa.

- **Community-Based Development**

Community-based development (CBD) has emerged as a significant approach to address development challenges by empowering local communities to participate in decision-making processes and take ownership of development initiatives. Rooted in principles of participatory development and grassroots empowerment, CBD gained prominence in the 1970s and 1980s as a response to the limitations of top-down development models. Scholars such as Robert Chambers and Robert Putnam have contributed to the evolution of CBD by highlighting the importance of community participation, social capital, and local knowledge in driving sustainable development outcomes (Chambers, 1997; Putnam, 1993). The CBD approach emphasizes building partnerships between communities, governments, non-governmental organizations (NGOs), and other stakeholders to identify priorities, mobilize resources, and implement locally relevant interventions (Narayan, 1995). Through a bottom-up approach, CBD seeks to enhance the capacity of communities to address their own needs and aspirations, thereby promoting social cohesion, resilience, and sustainable development (Fowler, 2000).

In linking CBD to Local Economic Development (LED) as a catalyst for agricultural growth and poverty relief, particularly in rural Eastern Cape, South Africa, the synergies between community-based initiatives and broader economic strategies become evident. LED focuses on enhancing economic opportunities and promoting inclusive growth at the local level through targeted interventions and partnerships (Rogerson, 2012). In rural Eastern Cape, where agriculture plays a significant role in livelihoods, CBD initiatives can catalyze agricultural development by mobilizing community resources, promoting sustainable farming practices, and fostering market linkages (Swanepoel et al., 2016). By empowering local communities to participate in decision-making processes and invest in agricultural enterprises, LED efforts can contribute to poverty alleviation and food security, ultimately fostering sustainable rural development (Magau, 2017). Therefore, CBD, when integrated with LED strategies, presents a holistic approach to addressing development challenges, leveraging local assets and capacities to promote agricultural growth and alleviate poverty in rural areas.

## Key Elements of the Conceptual and Theoretical Dispositions

*Table 2. System's Theory, Sustainable Livelihoods Approach (SLA), Community-Based Development Elements (Author Construction)*

| STRATEGY | FOCUS |
|---|---|
| *Development and Maintenance of Services and Infrastructure* | The strategy focuses on the development and maintenance of services and infrastructure and is the key component of municipal service delivery, in most cases, it addresses past imbalances by rendering basic services to the people. It is also a key component of ensuring that existing infrastructure is taken care of. |
| *Retention and Expansion of Existing Businesses (Business Support Services)* | The Policy Paper on Local Economic Development (2002) requires municipalities to give attention to retaining and expanding existing businesses of a municipality. This would primarily assist local businesses to improve their productivity, increase market share and graduate to higher value-added levels in the production chain. In terms of retention, the municipality is required to devise measures, which would ensure firms within the area do not relocate, but rather stay and expand. |
| *Small, Medium and Macro Enterprises Development (Promoting & Supporting Entrepreneurship)* | SMME development is regarded as a key strategy for the promotion of Local Economic Development in that, it generates both jobs and empowers historically disadvantaged individuals. Blakley (1994:33) agrees with the assertion and states that "this is the sector that has shown great employment potential in South Africa over the past few years. Municipalities are, therefore, expected to provide professional advice and assistance to small businesses in the areas of management, marketing, accounting, financing, sourcing resources and problem-solving". |
| *Community-Based Economic Development (Enterprise Development)* | As mandated by the RDP, supporting institutions like community development trusts and enterprises is crucial for fostering community self-reliance. This approach aims to alleviate poverty, enhance the capabilities of marginalized groups, and create sustainable livelihoods (Department of Provincial and Local Government, 2003). Reddy et al. (2003: 23) emphasize that community-based economic development focuses on combining employment, training, mentoring, and enterprise development to achieve self-sufficiency for disadvantaged communities. |
| *Industrial Recruitment and Place Marketing/ Special Economic Zones (SEZs) and Industrial Development Zones (IDZs)* | This strategy involves attracting new industries to the municipality and promoting the area as desirable for residents, businesses, and investors. Various factors influence this decision, including the cost of living, proximity to markets and suppliers, access to research institutions, transport networks, and quality of infrastructure (Reddy et al., 2003: 27). Municipalities play a crucial role in creating favourable environments to meet these criteria, which also affects the retention of existing businesses and attraction of new ones, placing significant pressure on them. |
| *Plugging the "leaks" in the Local Economy* | Reddy et al. (2003: 28) suggest a strategy of "plugging leaks" by identifying and addressing the outflow of money from local areas. This involves encouraging local purchasing, supporting periodic markets and festivals, utilizing local labour and materials for infrastructure projects, and promoting employee training and networking within the community (LED Policy Paper, 2002). In essence, the aim is to ensure that money circulates within the local economy. |
| *Human Capital Development (Skills Development)* | Ensuring that LED brings social and economic benefits often requires investing in human capital through skills development, education and health. The skilling of local people is significant because it can promote higher living wages. "There are explicit linkages between the promotion of living wages, human capital development and economic development since a well-paid, healthy and well-educated workforce would be more productive than otherwise", (Reddy et al, 2003: 33). |
| *Linking of Profitable Growth to Redistributive Development* | When utilizing this strategy for Local Economic Development, municipalities are advised to mandate that development planning or zoning permission in lucrative areas is contingent upon investment commitments in impoverished neighbourhoods. For instance, if a financial institution establishes a branch in an affluent area, it should also consider doing so in a low-income neighbourhood and allocate a portion of its turnover to support local small and medium-sized enterprises (Local Economic Development Policy Paper, 2002). It is essential to recognize that these strategies can be tailored to local conditions, considering factors such as geographical circumstances, economic structure, population demographics, labour market dynamics, and social considerations such as community safety and HIV/AIDS prevalence. |
| Local Economic Development (LED) provides support in the following areas:<br>• Development and review of national policy, strategy, and guidelines on LED.<br>• Providing direct and hands-on support to provincial and local government.<br>• Management of the Local Economic Development Fund.<br>• Management and Technical Support to Nodal Economic Development Planning.<br>• Facilitating coordinating and monitoring donor programmes, and<br>• Assisting with LED capacity-building processes. | |

In examining the intersection of Systems Theory, the Livelihoods Approach, and Community-Based Development (CBD), several key elements emerge as fundamental to understanding and promoting sustainable development outcomes. Firstly, Systems Theory highlights the interconnectedness and complexity of development processes, emphasizing the need to consider the interactions between various components within a system (Bertalanffy, 1968; Folke et al., 2005). This perspective underscores the importance of adopting holistic and integrated approaches to development, recognizing that changes in one part of the system can have ripple effects throughout the entire system. Similarly, the Livelihoods Approach emphasizes the importance of considering multiple livelihood assets, including human, social, natural, physical, and financial capital, in shaping individuals' and communities' well-being and resilience (Carney et al., 1999; Scoones, 2009). By focusing on building diversified and sustainable livelihood strategies, this approach aims to enhance economic opportunities, reduce vulnerability, and improve overall livelihood outcomes for communities.

Moreover, Community-Based Development emphasizes participatory decision-making, capacity building, collaboration, sustainable livelihoods, and social inclusion as central tenets of development practice (Pretty, 1995; Chambers, 1997; Carney et al., 1999; Narayan-Parker, 2000). By actively engaging community members in decision-making processes, promoting local ownership and empowerment, and fostering partnerships between stakeholders, CBD initiatives seek to address complex development challenges in a participatory and inclusive manner. Furthermore, the emphasis on building community capacity, promoting sustainable livelihoods, and addressing social inequalities underscores the importance of adopting a systemic approach to development that recognizes the interconnectedness of social, economic, and environmental factors (DFID, 1999; Huxham & Vangen, 2005; Sen, 1999). By integrating these elements into development interventions, practitioners can work towards building resilient, inclusive, and sustainable communities that thrive within their broader social and ecological contexts.

In conclusion, the integration of Systems Theory, the Livelihoods Approach, and Community-Based Development offers a comprehensive framework for understanding and addressing development challenges, particularly in rural contexts such as the Eastern Cape. By recognizing the interconnectedness of social, economic, and environmental factors, and prioritizing participatory decision-making, capacity building, collaboration, sustainable livelihoods, and social inclusion, practitioners can foster holistic and sustainable development outcomes. Furthermore, when applied within the context of Local Economic Development (LED) as a catalyst for agricultural growth and poverty relief, these approaches can play a crucial role in empowering rural communities, enhancing economic opportunities, and improving overall well-being. By leveraging local resources, building community resilience, and promoting inclusive and sustainable development practices, LED initiatives have the potential to transform rural economies and alleviate poverty in the Eastern Cape and beyond.

## METHODOLOGY

To address the research objectives, this chapter will employ a multifaceted methodology encompassing literature review, document analysis, and qualitative inquiry (Jones et al., 2018). Operating within an interpretivist research paradigm, the chapter seeks to elucidate the subjective dimensions and contextual nuances underlying the efficacy of Local Economic Development (LED) as a catalyst for agricultural growth and poverty relief in the rural Eastern Cape region. The qualitative inquiry will adopt an exploratory research design to delve deeply into the intricacies of LED implementation within the specified context. Drawing from secondary sources including governmental reports, scholarly literature, and policy documents, data collection will be comprehensive and multi-layered. This approach will be augmented by the integration of relevant theoretical frameworks to provide analytical depth and context. Central to the data analysis process will be content analysis, allowing for systematic extraction and interpretation of themes and patterns from the gathered information. Triangulation of findings with existing literature will serve to enhance the robustness and validity of the research outcomes. To ensure the trustworthiness of the study, measures such as prolonged engagement with the data, member checking, and peer debriefing will be implemented (Lincoln & Guba, 1985). Reliability will be upheld through meticulous data coding and documentation of analytical procedures. Additionally, transparency will be maintained throughout the research process, with careful consideration given to methodological choices, potential biases, and limitations inherent in the study (Creswell & Poth, 2017).

## OBSERVATIONS & DISCUSSION

The Eastern Cape province of South Africa, characterized by its predominantly rural landscape and high levels of poverty, presents a compelling case study for examining the efficacy of LED in fostering agricultural growth and alleviating poverty. LED encompasses a range of strategies aimed at stimulating economic activity at the local level through collaboration between various stakeholders, including government agencies, businesses, community organizations, and development partners. This paper delves into the multifaceted nature of LED interventions and their impact on agricultural development and poverty alleviation in the region.

## Intersectoral Collaboration/Development Agencies

Intersectoral collaboration is integral to the success of LED initiatives in rural areas. By bringing together government agencies, NGOs, private sector entities, and community-based organizations, synergies can be leveraged to address complex challenges and exploit opportunities in the agricultural sector. Case studies such as the partnership between the Eastern Cape Department of Rural Development and Agrarian Reform and local farmer cooperatives demonstrate how collaborative efforts can enhance access to markets, technology, and financial resources for small-scale farmers (Xulu & Kirsten, 2018). Moreover, development agencies such as the Industrial Development Corporation (IDC) play a crucial role in providing financial support and technical assistance to agribusinesses, thereby facilitating their growth and sustainability (Mkhize et al., 2020).

## Infrastructure Development

Investment in infrastructure is essential for unlocking the agricultural potential of rural areas and improving the livelihoods of smallholder farmers. This includes the development of transportation networks, irrigation systems, storage facilities, and market infrastructure. For instance, the construction of rural roads and bridges can enhance farmers' access to input and output markets, reduce transportation costs, and facilitate the timely delivery of produce (Naidu & Selier, 2019). Similarly, investments in irrigation infrastructure can mitigate the impact of climate variability and increase agricultural productivity, particularly in water-stressed regions such as the Eastern Cape (Van Averbeke et al., 2017).

## Business Support and Resources

Access to business support services and resources is critical for fostering entrepreneurship and enhancing the competitiveness of agribusinesses in rural areas. This includes training and mentorship programs, access to finance, market information, and technology transfer initiatives. Case studies from the Eastern Cape highlight the role of organizations such as the Eastern Cape Development Corporation (ECDC) in providing financial assistance and capacity-building support to emerging farmers and rural enterprises (Ngcwabe & Kirsten, 2021). Furthermore, initiatives such as the Agri-Parks program, which aims to establish integrated agro-industrial hubs, provide a platform for smallholder farmers to access processing facilities, storage infrastructure, and value-added services (Holloway et al., 2018).

## COVID-19 and 4IR

The COVID-19 pandemic has presented unprecedented challenges to agricultural development and poverty alleviation efforts in rural areas, exacerbating existing vulnerabilities and disrupting value chains. However, it has also underscored the importance of leveraging digital technologies and embracing the principles of the Fourth Industrial Revolution (4IR) to build resilience and promote inclusive growth. Remote sensing technologies, mobile applications, and e-commerce platforms have emerged as valuable tools for enhancing market access, monitoring crop health, and facilitating online transactions (Majola et al., 2020). Moreover, the adoption of precision agriculture techniques and data analytics can optimize resource use, improve productivity, and mitigate environmental risks in smallholder farming systems (Munzhelele et al., 2019).

## Capacity Building

Capacity building is essential for empowering local communities and institutions to actively participate in LED initiatives and drive sustainable development outcomes. This involves providing training, skills development, and institutional strengthening support to farmers, extension workers, local government officials, and other relevant stakeholders. Successful capacity-building interventions in the Eastern Cape have focused on enhancing agricultural extension services, promoting farmer-led research and innovation, and fostering collaboration between academia, government, and civil society (Masuku & Kirsten, 2021). By investing in human capital and knowledge transfer, capacity building can enhance the adaptive capacity of rural communities and enable them to respond effectively to changing socio-economic and environmental conditions.

## Projects and Project Management

Effective project management is essential for ensuring the successful implementation of LED initiatives and maximizing their impact on agricultural growth and poverty relief. This entails setting clear objectives, mobilizing resources, establishing monitoring and evaluation mechanisms, and fostering stakeholder engagement and participation. Case studies such as the Ncora Irrigation Scheme rehabilitation project demonstrate the importance of sound project management practices in overcoming challenges such as budget constraints, technical complexity, and social resistance (Ncetezo & Kirsten, 2017). Furthermore, the adoption of participatory approaches and adaptive management techniques can enhance the resilience of LED projects and enable them to respond flexibly to evolving circumstances and stakeholder needs

(Dube & Kirsten, 2019). Lastly the systems and structures of government should always encourage oversight over the delivery of projects and other government functions, (Rulashe and Dyan, 2023).

## Challenges and Successes

While LED initiatives have the potential to catalyze agricultural growth and poverty relief in rural areas, they are also confronted with a range of challenges. These include limited access to finance, inadequate infrastructure, weak institutional capacity, and policy and regulatory constraints (Ngcwabe & Masuku, 2020). Furthermore, the COVID-19 pandemic has exacerbated food insecurity and livelihood vulnerabilities, highlighting the need for targeted interventions to build resilience and ensure inclusive recovery. However, despite these challenges, there have been notable successes in promoting LED in the Eastern Cape, including increased agricultural productivity, improved market access, and enhanced livelihoods for rural communities (Majola & Naidu, 2022). By learning from both the successes and failures of past interventions, policymakers, practitioners, and development partners can refine their strategies and enhance the effectiveness of LED initiatives in driving sustainable rural development.

Local Economic Development (LED) holds immense potential as a catalyst for agricultural growth and poverty relief in rural areas, particularly in regions like the Eastern Cape province of South Africa. By fostering intersectoral collaboration, investing in infrastructure, providing business support and resources, leveraging digital technologies, building capacity, and adopting sound project management practices, LED initiatives can stimulate economic activity, enhance food security, and improve the well-being of rural communities. However, addressing the complex challenges facing rural development requires a holistic and integrated approach, guided by principles of equity, sustainability, and social inclusion. 30 years in a democratic South Africa while many good stories exist there are still service delivery and infrastructure development backlogs, poverty and other social ills that continue to haunt ordinary citizens and communities, (Rulashe, 2022). By harnessing the lessons learned from case studies, statistical data, and scholarly research, policymakers and practitioners can design and implement more effective LED strategies that promote inclusive and sustainable rural development in the Eastern Cape and beyond.

## Policy and Legislative Articulation and Application for Local Economic Development

*Table 3. Policy and legislative articulation and application for local economic development – Authors' Construction*

| Policy/ Legislation | Relevant Section | Quote/ Outline | Articulation | Application |
|---|---|---|---|---|
| *Constitution of South Africa of 1996* | Chapter 7: Local Government | "The Constitution of South Africa, specifically Chapter 7 on Local Government, outlines the objects of the Act, which include providing for democratic and accountable local government, ensuring the provision of services to communities in a sustainable manner, and promoting social and economic development." | The Constitution of South Africa establishes the legal framework for local government in the country, setting out the objectives and principles that govern the functioning of municipalities. It emphasizes the importance of local government in promoting development, delivering services, and fostering inclusive governance at the grassroots level. | Municipalities in the Eastern Cape, including those in the Amathole District, operate within the framework provided by the Constitution. By adhering to the principles of democratic governance, service delivery, and development promotion outlined in Chapter 7, municipalities can fulfil their mandate to advance LED initiatives, including those focused on agricultural growth and poverty relief. |
| *Integrated Development Plan (IDP)* | As captured by: Municipal Systems Act, 2000 (Act No. 32 of 2000) | The Municipal Systems Act requires municipalities to develop Integrated Development Plans (IDPs) that outline the objectives, priorities, and strategies for local development. The objectives of the Act include promoting participatory governance, integrated planning, and sustainable service delivery. | The IDP is a key instrument for local governance and development planning, providing a comprehensive framework for aligning municipal priorities with the needs and aspirations of local communities. It emphasises the importance of participatory decision-making, multi-sectoral collaboration, and sustainability in guiding local development efforts. | Municipalities in the Eastern Cape, including those in the Amathole District, are mandated to develop and implement IDPs per the Municipal Systems Act. By integrating LED priorities into their IDPs, municipalities can ensure that agricultural growth and poverty relief strategies are aligned with broader development objectives and reflect the needs of local stakeholders. |
| *Local Economic Development (LED) Strategy:* | As captured by: Local Government: Municipal Systems Act, 2000 (Act No. 32 of 2000) | The Municipal Systems Act empowers municipalities to develop LED strategies to promote economic growth, job creation, and poverty reduction within their jurisdictions. The objectives of the Act include fostering local economic development, attracting investment, and enhancing the competitiveness of local businesses. | LED strategies serve as blueprints for municipalities to stimulate economic activity, create employment opportunities, and improve the quality of life for residents. They provide a roadmap for leveraging local resources, fostering stakeholder collaboration, and addressing socio-economic challenges through targeted interventions. | LED strategies guide municipalities in the Eastern Cape, such as those in the Amathole District, in formulating and implementing initiatives to support agricultural growth and poverty relief. Municipalities can drive inclusive and sustainable economic development in rural areas by aligning LED strategies with local development priorities and leveraging available resources. |
| *Agricultural Support Programs* | National Agricultural Policy, Provincial Agricultural Acts<br><br>Can be accessed at: https://www.gov.za/documents/acts | "National and provincial agricultural policies provide frameworks for supporting agricultural development, including access to markets, finance, and technical assistance for smallholder farmers. The objects of these policies include promoting food security, rural livelihoods, and inclusive economic growth." | Agricultural support programs are designed to address the unique challenges faced by smallholder farmers and promote the sustainable development of the agricultural sector. They aim to improve access to markets, finance, and technology while enhancing the resilience of farming communities to external shocks. | In the Eastern Cape, agricultural support programs implemented by national and provincial governments play a critical role in complementing LED efforts by providing resources, training, and infrastructure support to local farmers. By aligning with national and provincial agricultural policies, municipalities can leverage these programs to support agricultural growth and poverty alleviation in rural areas. |
| *Broad-Based Black Economic Empowerment (B-BBEE) Act (Act No. 53 of 2003)* | Section 2 | The B-BBEE Act outlines the objectives of the Act, which include advancing economic transformation and enhancing the participation of historically disadvantaged individuals, including black farmers, in the mainstream economy. | The B-BBEE Act aims to promote economic inclusion and address historical inequalities by providing a framework for empowering historically disadvantaged individuals, including black farmers, in the economy. It emphasizes the importance of creating opportunities for equitable participation and ownership across various sectors. | In the Eastern Cape, the B-BBEE Act provides a platform for promoting the inclusion of historically marginalized farmers in agricultural value chains. By leveraging B-BBEE policies and programs, municipalities can support the economic empowerment of black farmers and promote inclusive growth in the agricultural sector. |
| *National Development Plan (NDP) - Vision 2030:* | Chapter 6: Rural Development<br><br>Chapter 7: Economic Transformation and Chapter 8: Spatial Transformation | The National Development Plan sets out a long-term vision for South Africa's development, with specific objectives and strategies for addressing rural poverty, unlocking economic potential, and promoting spatial transformation. | The NDP provides a comprehensive roadmap for achieving inclusive and sustainable development in South Africa, with a focus on rural development, economic transformation, and spatial planning. It outlines strategies for addressing poverty, inequality, and unemployment through targeted interventions and policy reforms. | LED initiatives in the Eastern Cape should align with the objectives and priorities outlined in the NDP, particularly those related to rural development and economic transformation. By integrating LED priorities into provincial and municipal planning processes, municipalities can contribute to the realization of national development objectives and promote inclusive growth in rural areas. |
| *National Framework for Sustainable Development (NFSD)* | Not Applicable (The NFSD is a comprehensive framework rather than a legislative document) | The National Framework for Sustainable Development provides a holistic approach to development planning, emphasizing principles of sustainability, equity, and inclusivity. | The NFSD serves as a guiding framework for integrating economic, social, and environmental considerations into development planning and decision-making processes. It promotes the adoption of sustainable practices and the equitable distribution of resources to ensure long-term prosperity for all. | LED initiatives in the Eastern Cape should align with the principles and objectives outlined in the NFSD to promote sustainable development outcomes. By incorporating sustainability considerations into LED strategies and projects, municipalities can contribute to the achievement of national sustainability goals and enhance the resilience of local communities. |
| *Provincial Growth and Development Strategy (PGDS)* | Economic Development Pillar | The Provincial Growth and Development Strategy sets out a strategic framework for driving economic growth and development in the Eastern Cape province, with specific objectives and interventions aimed at promoting employment creation, poverty reduction, and inclusive economic participation | The PGDS provides a roadmap for economic development in the Eastern Cape, focusing on priority sectors such as agriculture, tourism, and manufacturing. It outlines strategies for unlocking the economic potential of the province and addressing key development challenges. | LED initiatives in the Eastern Cape should align with the priorities and strategies outlined in the PGDS, particularly those related to agricultural development and rural empowerment. By integrating LED priorities into provincial planning processes, municipalities can leverage synergies and coordinate efforts to maximize the impact of their interventions. |

## CONCLUSION

In summary, the Amathole District, located within one of South Africa's most economically disadvantaged provinces, faces multifaceted challenges hindering local economic development and agricultural growth. The municipality struggles with poor planning, limited financial management capacity, and inadequate institutional support for small-scale farmers, resulting in persistently low agricultural productivity and entrenched poverty. To address these pressing issues and catalyze meaningful change, a comprehensive approach is required. Firstly, prioritizing community engagement and capacitation initiatives can empower residents to actively participate in decision-making processes and acquire the necessary skills and knowledge to drive sustainable development outcomes. By fostering partnerships with educational institutions and leveraging media platforms for public discourse, the municipality can create a conducive environment for inclusive development.

Secondly, efforts to attract investment and expand market opportunities for local farmers must be intensified. Through targeted marketing campaigns and government facilitation, the municipality can showcase its potential as a favourable destination for business investment while supporting local farmers in accessing new markets and value-added opportunities. Strengthening linkages between farmers and businesses, as well as providing tailored support services, will be essential for fostering entrepreneurship and enhancing economic resilience. Lastly, addressing information asymmetry and improving the accessibility of market information to smallholder farmers are crucial steps towards enhancing their competitiveness and sustainability. By establishing robust communication channels and disseminating relevant information on market requirements, funding opportunities, and agricultural best practices, the municipality can empower farmers to make informed decisions and capitalize on emerging trends in the agricultural sector. In conclusion, by implementing these recommendations in a coordinated manner and fostering collaboration among various stakeholders, the Amathole District can unlock its agricultural potential and pave the way for inclusive and sustainable local economic development. Through targeted interventions and a commitment to empowerment, the municipality can chart a path towards prosperity, lifting communities out of poverty and creating a brighter future for all residents.

## REFERENCES

African National Congress (ANC). (1994). *The Reconstruction and Development Programme: A Policy Framework*. ANC.

Amathole District Municipality. (2014). *ASPIRE Annual Report 2013-2014*. East London: Amathole.

Armstrong, P. (2001). Science, enterprise, and profit: Ideology in the knowledge-driven economy. *Economy and Society*, 30(4), 524–552. 10.1080/03085140120089081

Bahiigwa, G., De Pinto, A., Birner, R., & Ball, V. (2017). Strengthening agricultural education and training in sub-Saharan Africa from an innovation systems perspective: Case studies of Kenya, Nigeria, and South Africa. *European Journal of Development Research*, 29(4), 784–808.

Bertalanffy, L. (1950). An Outline of General System Theory. *The British Journal for the Philosophy of Science*, 1(2), 134–165. 10.1093/bjps/I.2.134

Bertalanffy, L. V. (1968). *General system theory: Foundations, development, applications*. G. Braziller.

Bhorat, H., Cassim, A., & Tseng, D. (2019). Local economic development in South Africa: A review of policies and practices. *Suid-Afrikaanse Tydskrif vir Ekonomiese en Bestuurswetenskappe*, 22(1), 1–11.

Blakely, E. J. (1994). *Planning Local Economic Development: Theory and Practice*. Sage.

Bosch, O. J. H. (2013). *Systems Thinking for Local Economic Development (LED) in Developing Countries*. (LEDNA Working Paper Series). LEDNA.

Carney, D. (1998). *Sustainable Livelihoods Approaches: Progress and Possibilities for Change*. Institute of Development Studies.

Carney, D., Drinkwater, M., Rusinow, T., Neefjes, K., Wanmali, S., & Singh, N. (1999). *Livelihoods approaches compared: A brief comparison of the livelihoods approaches of the UK Department for International Development (DFID), CARE, Oxfam and the United Nations Development Programme (UNDP)*. Department for International Development (DFID).

Carney, D., Drinkwater, M., Rusinow, T., Neefjes, K., Wanmali, S., & Singh, N., 1999. *Livelihoods approaches compared: A brief comparison of the livelihoods approaches of the UK Department for International Development (DFID), CARE, Oxfam and the United Nations Development Programme (UNDP).* Department for International Development (DFID).

Chambers, R. (1997). *Whose Reality Counts? Putting the First Last.* Intermediate Technology Publications. 10.3362/9781780440453

Chambers, R., & Conway, G. (1992). *Sustainable rural livelihoods: Practical concepts for the 21st century.* (IDS Discussion Paper, 296). IDS.

Creswell, J. W., & Poth, C. N. (2017). Qualitative inquiry and research design: Choosing among five approaches. *Sage (Atlanta, Ga.).*

Crush, J. (2000). *Migration in Southern Africa: A paper prepared for the Policy Analysis and Research Programme of the Global Commission on International Migration.* Global Commission on International Migration.

Crush, J., Chikanda, A., & Tawodzera, G. (2017). South-South migration and the labour market in South Africa. *European Journal of Development Research*, 29(3), 533–548.

Department for International Development (DFID). (1999). *Sustainable Livelihoods Guidance Sheets.* DFID.

Department for International Development (DFID). (1999). *Sustainable Livelihoods Guidance Sheets.* DFID.

Department of Provincial and Local Government. (2003). *Local Economic Development.* DPLG.

Development Bank of Southern Africa (DBSA). (2020). *Integrated Urban Development Framework (IUDF): Integrated Local Economic Development (LED).* Toolkit.

DFID. (1999). *Sustainable Livelihoods Guidance Sheets.* Department for International Development.

Du Toit, A., Kirsten, J., & Mabaya, E. (2018). Public expenditure on agriculture in South Africa: A provincial analysis. *Agrekon*, 57(3), 297–313.

Dube, S., & Kirsten, J. (2019). Participatory approaches in local economic development: Lessons from LED initiatives in rural South Africa. *Development Southern Africa*, 36(6), 777–793.

ECSECC. (2006). *Annual Report 2006.* Bhisho.

Eicher, C.K. (1999). Institutions and the African farmer. *Issues in agriculture, 14*(1), 1-2.

Ellis, F. (2000). *Rural Livelihoods and Diversity in Developing Countries*. Oxford University Press. 10.1093/oso/9780198296959.001.0001

FAO. (2006). *Institutional analysis of trade liberalization and agriculture*. FAO. http://www.fao.org/documents/show_cdr.asp?url_file

Folke, C., Carpenter, S., Elmqvist, T., Gunderson, L., Holling, C. S., & Walker, B. (2005). Regime shifts, resilience, and biodiversity in ecosystem management. *Annual Review of Ecology, Evolution, and Systematics*, 35(1), 557–581. 10.1146/annurev.ecolsys.35.021103.105711

Fowler, A. (2000). NGDOs as a moment in history: Beyond aid to social entrepreneurship or civic innovation? *Third World Quarterly*, 21(4), 637–654. 10.1080/713701063

Fraser, G. C. G. (1991). *Agricultural marketing in less developed countries with special reference in Ciskei.* [Unpublished PhD thesis, University of Stellenbosch: Stellenbosch].

Green, T. (2015). *Social Exclusion in South African Cities: Urbanization, Housing and Social Cohesion*. Routledge.

Hall, S. (2003). New Labour's double-shuffle. *Soundings*, 24(24), 10–24. 10.3898/136266203820467680

Harvey, D. (2005). *A Brief History of Neoliberalism*. Oxford University Press. 10.1093/oso/9780199283262.001.0001

Holloway, G., Agapitova, N., & Chamberlain, W. (2018). Agri-Parks in South Africa: A case study of Eastern Cape Province. In Sandrey, R., & Bhorat, H. (Eds.), *State of the Nation: Poverty & Inequality: Diagnosis, Prognosis and Responses* (pp. 139–159). HSRC Press.

Huxham, C., & Vangen, S. (2005). *Managing to collaborate: The theory and practice of collaborative advantage*. Routledge.

ITDG. (2005). *Ministerial conference and expo on agricultural science and technology*. FAS. http://www.fas.usda.gov/icd/stconf/pubs/conf_fact.html

Jones, P., King, N., & Eynon, R. (2018). *Interpretative phenomenological analysis: A guide to conducting and reporting*. Routledge.

Khan, H. A. (2008). Application of systems theory in agriculture. *World Applied Sciences Journal*, 4(1), 100–106.

Kitano, H. (2002). Systems Biology: A Brief Overview. *Science*, 295(5560), 1662–1664. 10.1126/science.106949211872829

Klasen, S. (1997). Poverty, Inequality and Deprivation in South Africa: An Analysis of the 1993 SALDRU Survey. *Social Indicators Research*, 41(1/3), 64–66. 10.1023/A:1006892216864

Krieger, J. (2007). The Political Economy of New Labour: The Failure of a Success Story. *New Political Economy*, 12(3), 421–432. 10.1080/13563460701485664

Kumo, L. W., Omilola, B., & Minsat, A. (2015). *African Economic Outlook*. Oxford University Press.

Leibbrandt, M., Finn, A., Woolard, I., & Argent, J. (2019). Trends in South African income distribution and poverty since the fall of apartheid. *The World Bank Economic Review*, 33(2), 251–273.

Lincoln, Y. S., & Guba, E. G. (1985). Naturalistic inquiry. *Sage (Atlanta, Ga.)*.

Luhmann, N. (1995). *Social Systems*. Stanford University Press.

Magau, A. (2017). Understanding the implementation of local economic development (LED) programmes in the Eastern Cape, South Africa. *Journal of Economics and Behavioral Studies*, 9(2), 102–114.

Magingxa, L. L., & Kamara, A. B. 2003. *Institutional perspectives of enhancing smallholder market access in South Africa.* Contributed Paper Presented at the 41st Annual Conference of the Agricultural Economic Association of South Africa (AEASA), Pretoria, South Africa.

Majola, T., Mkhize, N., & Mwaura, F. (2020). Impact of COVID-19 on Agriculture and Food Security in Africa: Policy Responses and Opportunities for Post-Pandemic Recovery. *Journal of Agricultural and Resource Economics*, 45(3), 407–424.

Majola, T., & Naidu, S. (2022). Digital Agriculture: A Potential Catalyst for Rural Development in South Africa. In Antwi-Agyei, A., Adiku, D., Vrieling, A., & Adimassu, F. (Eds.), *Digital Agriculture: Sustainable Crop Production and Food Security* (pp. 455–475). Springer.

Makhura, M., & Mokoena, M. (2003). Market access for small-scale farmers in South Africa. In Nieuwoudt, L., & Groenewald, J. (Eds.), *The Challenges of Change: Agriculture, Land and the South African Economy*. University of Natal Press.

Makhura, M. N. (2009). *Rural Development in SA: Repetition, Revision & Rethink.* Paper presented to HSRC/Land Bank seminar. Pretoria.

Masuku, M. B., & Kirsten, J. F. (2021). Capacity development for agricultural innovation systems in South Africa: Lessons from case studies in the Eastern Cape Province. *Agrekon*, 60(2), 161–180.

McCarthy, C., van Walbeek, C., & Goldstein, S. (2020). *Estimating the impact of COVID-19 on poverty in South Africa: An analysis using the first five waves of NIDS-CRAM data.* (Stellenbosch Economic Working Papers: WP21/2020).

Miggels, A., & Rulashe, T. (2022). Organisational Change as a Tool for Transforming Governance in a Local Municipality, Nelson Mandela Bay Municipality in the Eastern Cape. *Journal of Public Administration.*, 57, 508–528.

Mkhize, N., Ngcwabe, C., & Kirsten, J. (2020). The Role of the Industrial Development Corporation in Financing Agribusiness: The Case of South Africa. *Development Southern Africa*, 37(6), 883–898.

Municipality, A. D. (2010). Integrated Development Plan (IDP) [East London: Amathole.]. *RE:view*, 2009–2010.

Munzhelele, M., Van Niekerk, A., & Mafongoya, P. (2019). The Fourth Industrial Revolution: Potential Contributions to Sustainable Agriculture in Africa. *Sustainability*, 11(13), 3533.

Naidu, S., & Selier, J. (2019). Rural infrastructure investment and agricultural productivity in South Africa: Evidence from Kwazulu-Natal and Eastern Cape provinces. *Agrekon*, 58(2), 129–147.

Narayan, D. (1995). The contribution of people's participation: Evidence from 121 rural water supply projects. *Environmentally Sustainable Development Occasional Paper Series, 1*(5).

Narayan-Parker, D. (2000). *Voices of the poor: Can anyone hear us?* World Bank Publications.

National Development Plan (NDP). (2012). *Vision for 2030: Our future – make it work.* NDP.

National Treasury. (2020). *Estimates of National Expenditure 2020.* National Treasury.

Ncetezo, N., & Kirsten, J. F. (2017). Project Management of Irrigation Schemes in South Africa: Lessons from Case Studies in Eastern Cape Province. *Water (Basel)*, 9(3), 205.

Ngcobo, N. N., Idsardi, E. F., & van Rensburg, H. C. J. (2019). Budgetary allocation and expenditure in the Eastern Cape Department of Rural Development and Agrarian Reform. *Suid-Afrikaanse Tydskrif vir Ekonomiese en Bestuurswetenskappe*, 22(1), 1–11.

Ngcwabe, C., & Kirsten, J. (2021). The Role of Public Finance Institutions in Supporting Emerging Farmers in South Africa: The Case of Eastern Cape Development Corporation. *Agrekon*, 60(3), 342–358.

Ngcwabe, C., & Masuku, M. B. (2020). Challenges of Local Economic Development in South Africa: Perspectives from Eastern Cape Province. *Africa's Public Service Delivery & Performance Review*, 8(1), 1–15.

Odum, E. P. (1983). *Systems Ecology: An Introduction*. John Wiley & Sons.

OECD. (1996). *The Knowledge-Based Economy*. Organisation for Economic Co-operation and Development.

Ojo, M. O. (2012). Rural-urban migration: A livelihood pathway for the poor: A case study of migration from Amakohia in Imo State, Nigeria to Owerri. *Journal of Sustainable Development in Africa*, 14(4), 238–256.

Piesse, J., Gouse, M., & Thirtle, C. (2005). Agricultural technology, productivity and employment: Policies for poverty reduction. *Agrekon*, 44(1), 37–59. 10.1080/03031853.2005.9523702

Pillay, D., & Bass, O. (2015). Addressing government's role in South Africa's development: A capabilities approach. *Development Southern Africa*, 32(1), 47–64.

Pretty, J. (1995). Participatory learning for sustainable agriculture. *World Development*, 23(8), 1247–1263. 10.1016/0305-750X(95)00046-F

Putnam, R. D. (1993). *Making Democracy Work: Civic Traditions in Modern Italy*. Princeton University Press.

Reddy, P. S., Sing, D., & Moodley, S. (2003). *Local Government Financing and Development in Southern Africa*. Oxford University Press.

Republic of South Africa. (2007). *Growth and Development Summit Report*. Pretoria, South Africa.

Republic of South Africa (RSA). (1998). *White Paper on Local Government*. RSA.

Rodrik, D. (1998). *Trade Policy and Economic Performance in Sub-Saharan Africa*. (NBER Working Paper Series No. 6562). National Bureau of Economic Research, Massachussets.

Rogerson, C. M. (2012). Local economic development in South Africa: The role of municipalities. *Development Southern Africa*, 29(2), 190–204.

Roser, M. (2016). *'World Poverty'. Published online at OurWorldInData.org*. Retrieved.

Rulashe, T. (2022). 'A luta continua', will it ever end? The reality of local government in South Africa. *Journal of Local Government Research and Innovation*, 3. 10.4102/jolgri.v3i0.97

Rulashe, T., & Dyan, M. (2023). A Critical Review of the Municipal Public Accounts Committee and Financial Management at Amahlathi Municipality, South Africa. *Journal of Public Administration Studies*, 8(1), 56–65. 10.21776/ub.jpas.2023.008.01.7

Sasseville, D. N. (1988). *Harvesting and handling produce: Plan now for high quality*. Guide.

Scoones, I. (1998). *Sustainable rural livelihoods: A framework for analysis*. (IDS Working Paper, 72).

Scoones, I. (2009). Livelihoods perspectives and rural development. *The Journal of Peasant Studies*, 36(1), 171–196. 10.1080/03066150902820503

Seekings, J., & Nattrass, N. (2015). *Policy, politics and poverty in South Africa*. New Africa Books. 10.1057/9781137452696

Seligson, M. A., & Passe-Smith, J. J. (1998). *Development and Underdevelopment: The political economy of global inequality*. Lynne Rienner publishers.

Sen, A. (1999). *Development as freedom*. Oxford University Press.

Simbi, T. (1998). *Agricultural policy in South Africa*. NDA. http://www.nda.agric.za/docs/policy98.htm. Accessed on 16 /05/2012

South African Government. (2020). *Economic Transformation and Inclusive Growth*. South African Government.

Special Economic Zones (SEZs). (2019). *SEZ Annual Performance Report 2019*. Government of South Africa.

Statistics South Africa (Stats SA). (2020). *Poverty trends in South Africa: An examination of absolute poverty between 2006 and 2015*. Statistics South Africa.

Swanepoel, H., Cloete, P., van Niekerk, J., & van Rooyen, J. (2016). Rural development challenges in the Eastern Cape Province, South Africa: Sustainable livelihoods in the face of social and environmental crises. *Agrekon*, 55(1-2), 104–125.

Thirtle, C., Lin, L., & Piesse, J. (2003). The impact of research-led agricultural productivity growth on poverty reduction in Africa, Asia and Latin America. *World Development*, 31(12), 1959–1976. 10.1016/j.worlddev.2003.07.001

United Nations Development Programme (UNDP). (2003). *South Africa Human Development Report 2003: the Challenge of Sustainable Development in SouthAfrica-Unlocking People's Creativity*. Oxford University Press.

Van Averbeke, W., Sigwela, A., & Groenewald, J. A. (2017). The Impact of Irrigation Infrastructure on Smallholder Farming Income: Evidence from Rural South Africa. *Water (Basel)*, 9(11), 880.

Watson, M. (2001). Embedding the 'new economy' in Europe: A study in the institutional specificities of knowledge-based growth. *Economy and Society*, 30(4), 504–523. 10.1080/03085140120089072

Wiener, N. (1948). *Cybernetics: Or Control and Communication in the Animal and the Machine*. MIT Press.

Xulu, G., & Kirsten, J. F. (2018). Enhancing Smallholder Market Access through Local Economic Development: Evidence from South Africa. *Development Southern Africa*, 35(5), 629–644.

Xuza, P. H. (2005). Renewal of small-town economies: The case of Alice, Eastern Cape Province, South Africa. *Africa Insight*, 35(4), 90–96.

# Chapter 5
# Impact of Corona-Virus on Local Economic Development in Zwelisha Community, Durban, South Africa

**Ndwakhulu Stephen Tshishonga**
*University of KwaZulu-Natal, South Africa*

**Slungile Charity Sigwebela**
*University of KwaZulu-Natal, South Africa*

## ABSTRACT

*Multifaceted impacts of the pandemic on local economies and provided insights into the strategies and policies that can foster recovery and resilience. Furthermore, the chapter used qualitative research methods, such as interviews to capture the experiences and perceptions of local businesses, entrepreneurs, government officials, and community members. The chapter's findings could contribute to understanding the complex dynamics between pandemics, local economies, and economic development. By examining the impact of COVID-19 on local economic development, this chapter found evidence-based decision-making strategies that could contribute to developing strategies that can mitigate the adverse effects of pandemics on local economies, ultimately leading to more sustainable and inclusive economic growth.*

DOI: 10.4018/979-8-3693-3617-5.ch005

## INTRODUCTORY BACKGROUND

South Africa finds itself at war, and the enemy is the novel coronavirus, which gave rise to the Covid-19 disease (Arndt et al.,2020). According to Arndt et al. (2020), the only tool to mitigate the demographic effects of Covid-19 was lockdown to reduce the spread by breaking existing social and economic forms of contact. Such measures brought about shocks on the local economic development, with immediate loss of economic activity followed by medium-term and long-term economic effects. The pandemic's impact on health and mortality; and the lockdown had severe devastating economic shocks nationwide. Accordingly, LED exists to build up the economic capacity of a local area to improve its economic future and the quality of life for all (Venot, 2017). Fine (2018) claims that the success of a community today depends upon its ability to adapt to the dynamic local, national, and international market economy. Strategically, LED is often used by communities to strengthen the local economic capacity of an area, improve the investment climate, and increase the productivity and competitiveness of local businesses, entrepreneurs, and workers (Woodhouse, 2017).

In 2020, the National Institute for Communicable Diseases in South Africa confirmed that a suspected case of Covid-19 had tested positive. The patient was a 38-year-old male who had traveled to Italy with his wife as part of a group of ten people (NICD,2020). They arrived back in South Africa on 1 March 2020. What followed on 5 March is history still fresh in people's minds. Under Section 3 of the Disaster Management Act, (Act No. 57 of 2002) the government of South Africa implemented lockdown regulations and put the country on Level 5 from 27 March to 30 April (NCID, 2020).

The level 5 lockdown regulations were gradually eased to lockdown levels 4, 3, 2 and into level 1. Specific work and operational regulations are applied to different industries under each level. According to Schutte (2020), these regulations specified the capacity at which industries could operate, how many workers they could allow onto their premises and what types of commodities they could produce. Each Level had specific restrictions on the movement of households and labourers. These regulations severely impacted the local economy, level of employment and people's ability to earn income.

The magnitude of the Covid-19 outbreak significantly impacted local economic development in many regions around the world. Lockdowns and restrictions imposed to curb the spread of the virus have led to many businesses being forced to close temporarily or even permanently (Dua et al., 2020). This resulted in widespread job losses and increased unemployment rates in many areas, impacting the livelihoods of individuals and families. According to Dua et al. (2020) the pandemic has disrupted global supply chains, leading to shortages of goods and materials in various industries. This affected local businesses that rely on these supplies, leading to production delays and increased costs.

The pandemic accelerated the shift to remote work in many industries. While this enabled business continuity, it also led to changes in the demand for commercial real estate and office spaces, potentially impacting local property markets and related industries (Zondo, 2020). The magnitude of the Covid-19 outbreak had far-reaching implications for local economic development, affecting businesses, employment, supply chains, government budgets, tourism, and the way people work (Zondo, 2020). Thus, the ability of communities to improve quality of life, create new economic opportunities and fight poverty depended on stakeholders' understanding of the processes of LED. Such understanding enables LED stakeholders to be competitive in the market economy (Jones & Muller, 2016). For LED to be competitive it should draw from good practice that entails strategic planning and implementation as well as lessons and experiences gained from the cities and programmes across the globe (Brida & Pulina, 2016). However, health concerns and ongoing restrictions interrupted footfall in the markets and reduced access to passing trade and increased immediate challenges of poverty and hunger. From the above statement, it can be argued that the Covid-19 crisis dramatically affected the progress of local economic development policy. Hence there is a need for a serious local economic development recovery plan as well as, measures to prevent this pandemic from recurring. It is against this background that this chapter aims to explore the impact of COVID-19 on local economic development in the Zwelisha community, Durban and examine what has been done to mitigate the negative impacts of COVID-19 on local economic development in Zwelisha Township. The Zwelisha township of Phoenix/Verulam is in the eThekwini Metro (north of Durban) in the province of KwaZulu-Natal. The nearest place in the area is the Ottawa suburb of Verulam and the Trenance Park suburb of Phoenix (Rajpal, 2012). It comprises a mix of residential townships and informal settlements (Rajpal, 2012). There are different communities of various ethnic groupings i.e. Zulus, Xhosas within Zwelisha. A single main road leads into the area. The area is 'littered' with poor housing, sanitation and infrastructure. A portion of the community works in neighbouring suburban areas such as Phoenix, Mount Edgecombe and Mhlanga as general hands. Very few are professionally employed, and the vast majority are unemployed. The chapter argues that COVID-19 had a negative impact which is still felt in the LED sector. A systematic literature review based on secondary data was used in this chapter. Research engines such as Google Scholar and ResearchGate were used to obtain data.

## THE GROUNDING LITERATURE OF THE CHAPTER

- **Definition of COVID-19**

Covid-19 is well-defined by Andt et al (2020) as an infectious illness caused by a novel coronavirus called SARS-CoV-2. It was first identified in December 2019 in Wuhan, Hubei province, China. The World Health Organization (WHO) declared a global pandemic on March 11, 2020, due to its rapid spread worldwide. Covid-19 primarily spreads through respiratory droplets when an infected person coughs, sneezes, talks, or breathes. It can also be transmitted by touching contaminated surfaces and then touching the face, although this is considered a less common transmission mode (Miller, 2020).

It was common scientific knowledge that the SARS-CoV-2 virus caused COVID-19, and it is indeed an infectious disease that can rapidly spread from person to person. The virus can be transmitted through respiratory droplets when an infected person coughs, sneezes, talks, or breathes. As a result, it spread worldwide, affecting numerous countries and populations (Leach et al., 2021). The initial outbreak of Covid-19 was first identified in Wuhan, Hubei Province, China, in late 2019. The exact origins of the virus are still being investigated, but it is believed to have originated in bats before potentially being transmitted to humans through an intermediate animal host, although the specific animal has not been confirmed yet (Leach et al., 2021). The interconnectedness of our world through international travel and trade facilitated the rapid spread of the virus. As infected individuals traveled across borders, they unintentionally transmitted the virus to others in different countries, leading to local outbreaks and, subsequently, the global pandemic. Once COVID-19 reached a new country, it quickly spread within that country's population through community transmission. According to Houston (2021), factors such as population density, healthcare infrastructure, public health measures, and government responses played significant roles in how the virus spread within each country.

- **Definition of Local Economic Development**

Local economic development (LED) refers to strategies and activities to promote economic growth and improve the quality of life in a particular geographic area, such as a city, town, or region (Browne, 2020). The goal of LED is to create jobs, increase income, and enhance the overall economic well-being of the community. According to Browne (2020), initiatives typically involve collaboration between local government, business leaders, community organisations, and other stakeholders to identify and leverage the unique strengths and assets of the local economy. This can include developing and promoting local businesses, attracting new investment, supporting entrepreneurship, and improving workforce skills and education. Gidden (2018), states that the specific strategies and activities used in LED may vary depending on the needs and priorities of the community, but typically involve a mix of policy interventions, infrastructure investments, and community engagement efforts. Successful LED initiatives can have positive impacts, including increased economic activity, job creation, improved public services, and a stronger sense of community pride and engagement (Hunter, 2018).

## • THEORETICAL FRAMEWORK

This chapter adopted the sustainable livelihood approach. The sustainable livelihood approach (SLA) is one of the many frameworks used in analysing and addressing the relationship between poverty and development. The SLA is a development approach that goes beyond the traditional and reductionist understanding of poverty and poverty reduction based on a monetary basis at the exclusion of other social and economic aspects of poverty—such as vulnerability and social exclusion (Krantz, 2011). This increased focus on multidimensional drivers of poverty, such as social, economic, ecological, and political factors that inhibit people's ability to have a decent life.

Based on these observations, the United Nations Development Programme (UNDP) (2017) summarises the SLA as a framework used by individuals and communities to craft ways to survive and sustain their lives, including factors that influence subsistence decisions and the interplay of these factors United Nations Development Programme, 2017. At the household level, the SLA views a livelihood as comprising assets and activities needed to fulfill a socially and economically sustainable life (Krantz, 2011). The sustainability element is underpinned by people's ability to cope and recover from stress, shocks, volatilities, and vulnerabilities and to improve capabilities for better livelihood opportunities for the future generation (Chambers & Conway, 2017); UNDP, 2017.

Various shocks such as the global economic crisis experienced in 2008 undermined the sustainable livelihood of citizens by bringing episodic poverty. For example, the increase in food prices during the 2008 financial crisis undermined the livelihood of the poor as the rural and urban poor spent 50–70% of their income on food (Hadley et al., 2017). The global financial crisis also resulted in 22 million people losing jobs (International Labour Organisation, 2020a). In this context, the stagnation in wages for unskilled labour, with the majority working in the agricultural sector, led to increasing vulnerabilities in the livelihood of the people experiencing poverty. The SLA depends on five types of capital to improve people's ability to sustain their livelihood: natural capital, economic and financial capital, human capital, physical capital, and social capital (UNDP, 2017). These types of capital are useful resources, with their combination likely to increase the capabilities of people with low income to be resilient in the face of shocks. The expected livelihood outcomes from various sources of capital are increased income, improved socio-economic well-being, reduced vulnerability, improved food security, and the sustainable use of natural resources (UNDP, 2017). The expected developmental outcomes from the sustainable livelihood framework can also be linked to the sustainable development goals, particularly focusing on ending poverty (SDG 1), zero hunger (SDG 2), good health and well-being (SDG 3) and building sustainable cities and communities (SDG 11) (UNDP, 2017). Thus, it can be argued that the sustainable development framework has a potential role in attaining sustainable development goals.

## The Impact of COVID-19 on LED in the African Context

The impact of the Covid-19 pandemic has not been different in Africa compared to the developed world. The pandemic also had a significant impact on local economic development in Africa (Anjorin, 2020). The pandemic caused disruptions in the global supply chains, reduced demand for goods and services, and led to a decline in economic activity across the continent (Anjorin, 2020). The following are some ways in which the pandemic has affected local economic development in Africa:

Reduced trade and investment: The pandemic disrupted global supply chains and reduced demand for goods and services, leading to a decline in trade and investment (Linton, 2021). This has significantly impacted African economies, which are heavily dependent on exports and foreign investment. Job losses: The pandemic led to a significant of jobs losses across Africa, particularly in sectors such as tourism, hospitality, and retail. This hurt local economies, as many people lost their source of income. Reduced government revenue: The pandemic led to a reduction in government revenue, as economic activity has slowed down and tax revenues have declined (Baker, 2021). This made it difficult for governments to fund development projects and provide social services.

Increased poverty: The pandemic pushed many people into poverty, particularly those already living in poverty before the pandemic. This had a significant impact on local economies, as people have less money to spend on goods and services (Smith, 2021). Increased debt: Many African countries had to borrow heavily to finance their response to the pandemic. This led to an increase in debt levels, which have long-term implications for local economic development. In response to these challenges, African governments and development partners implemented various measures to mitigate the impact of the pandemic on local economic development (James, 2021). These measures included providing financial support to businesses, investing in healthcare infrastructure, and promoting local production and consumption (James, 2021)

In Zimbabwe, the unprecedented grotesque and obnoxious impact of COVID-19 on developed, developing and even resource-constrained states undermined development and growth in Zimbabwe (Njaya, 2020). Industries, cities, schools, and businesses were operating below optimum efficiency. According to Zimbwa (2020), the hypoxemia induced in the economy by COVID-19 has led to the unaccounted loss of life, closure of industries, increased unemployment, poverty, and destitution. Nevertheless, the impact of Covid-19 varied from country to country owing to the development and growth of that nation. For instance, large corporates and small businesses benefited from government loans and reductions in taxation. To this end, the Zimbabwean economy was not spared, the Ministry of Youth tried to give loans to youths but only a few had access to them. The Ministry of Small and Medium Enterprises also attempts to help those in Small and Medium Enterprises (SMEs) activities, but the impact of COVID-19 remained unbearable (Zimbwa, 2020).

The government of Zimbabwe implemented several economic interventions to mitigate the impact of the pandemic on businesses and individuals (Chiwara, 2022). These interventions included a waiver on import duties on essential medical supplies, the reduction of taxes on businesses, and the establishment of a stimulus package to support small and medium-sized enterprises (SMEs) (Chiwara, 2022). Several technology-led interventions were aimed at assisting individuals and businesses affected by the pandemic. For example, the government of Zimbabwe launched a mobile money transfer platform to enable people to conduct financial transactions without physical contact, and the UNDP has implemented a chatbot to provide information and support to individuals affected by the pandemic (Mpofu, 2022).

In the case of Tanzania, strict restrictions were not enforced nationally at the onset of the pandemic in Tanzania, however, round 1 data revealed that domestic workers still experienced adverse impacts on their work. Conditions and food security within six months of the start of the pandemic (Matasi, 2021). The pandemic's obstruction of global markets and tourism impacted Tanzanians' economic activities, especially across export-oriented sectors such as tourism and manufacturing, which in turn hindered employers' ability to pay domestic workers' wages and benefits. Moreover, fear of Covid-19 often affected domestic workers' work routines (Abush & Mwita, 2021). A year later, with the overhaul of Tanzania's response to the pandemic, domestic workers were still experiencing the pandemic's negative repercussions.

Tanzania took several interventions to cope with disruptions due to Covid-19. However, it is important to note that Tanzania was criticised for its lack of transparency and disclosure of Covid-19 data. The government has also been accused of downplaying the severity of the pandemic. Here are some of the interventions that have been reported:

In March 2020, Tanzania suspended all international flights to control the spread of Covid-19. Closure of schools: In March 2020, the Tanzanian government closed all schools and universities as a way of preventing the spread of COVID-19 (Makoni, 2021). The government also carried out public education campaigns to raise awareness about COVID-19 and how to prevent its spread (Makoni, 2021). It established quarantine centres to isolate individuals who have tested positive for Covid-19 or have come into contact with someone who has tested positive. Mwale (2021) states that Tanzania enhanced screening measures at all border points to prevent the importation of Covid-19 cases. Tanzania started a vaccination campaign against Covid-19. However, the government was criticised for not disclosing which vaccines are used and the number of doses administered (Kabizwe, 2021). It is important to note that the effectiveness of these interventions was not apparent due to the lack of transparency and disclosure of COVID-19 data in Tanzania (Mwambi, 2021).

- **The Impact of COVID-19 on LED in South Africa**

The impact of COVID-19 on local economic development in South Africa has been significant. The pandemic has hurt the country's economy, which was already struggling before the outbreak. The lockdown measures and restrictions on movement implemented to curb the spread of the virus have led to a sharp decline in economic activity, resulting in job losses and reduced income for many businesses and households (Mkhize, 2020). Small and medium-sized enterprises (SMEs), which are key drivers of economic growth and job creation, have been particularly hard hit by the pandemic (Peterson, 2021). Many have been forced to close their doors permanently, while others have had to scale back operations and lay off staff. The loss of income and employment opportunities has had a ripple effect on local communities, with many households struggling to make ends meet (Peterson, 2021). However, the pandemic also highlighted the resilience of South Africa's economy and the importance of local economic development. In response to the crisis, many local businesses and communities came together to support one another and find innovative solutions to the challenges posed by the pandemic (Mkhize, 2020). This included initiatives such as community-based food gardens, online marketplaces, and digital training programs for small businesses (Mkhize, 2020).

Furthermore, the pandemic underscored the need for greater investment in healthcare, education, and social infrastructure in South Africa. These areas are critical for building a more resilient and inclusive economy that can withstand future shocks and support sustainable development (Peterson, 2021) Overall, while the pandemic has had a significant impact on local economic development in South Africa, it also provided an opportunity for communities and businesses to come together and build a more sustainable and equitable future.

## COVID-19 and Small, Medium, and Micro Enterprises

Small, medium and micro enterprises (SMMEs) have a major role to play in sustainable development. SMMEs create incomes through employment and help to reduce poverty and income inequality, and to spur economic growth (World Bank, 2020). SMMEs account for most of the private sector business in developing and developed countries. Formal SMMEs contribute about 45% of total employment and 33% of gross domestic product in developing countries (United Nations, 2020). SMMEs are expected to generate 90% of the eleven million new jobs and contribute 60–80% of the increase of the gross domestic product by 2030 (National Planning Commission 2012; Small Enterprise Development Agency, 2019; SME Landscape Report, 2019). However, the performance of SMMEs has been negatively impacted by Covid-19, a communicable respiratory disease caused by a new strain of corona-virus that causes illness in humans (Catalyst for Growth, 2020; Common Market for Eastern and Southern Africa, 2020; National Youth Development Agency, 2020). On the 5th of March 2020, the Health Minister, Dr Zweli Mkhize, confirmed the existence of the Covid-19 virus in South Africa, with the first death occurring on the 27th of March 2020.

On the 15th of March, the President of the Republic of South Africa, Cyril Ramaphosa, declared a National State of Disaster, and on the 17th of March 2020, the National Coronavirus Command Council was established. On the 23rd of March 2020 the first national lockdown was announced starting on the 27th of March 2020. On the 1st of May 2020, a phased easing of the lockdown began. The second wave of Covid-19 infections started in December 2020, and the lockdown was adjusted from level 1 to level 3 on the 29th of December 2020. The lockdown was eased from level 3 to level 1 on the 1st of March 2021. On the 28th of June 2021 the lockdown was moved back to an adjusted level four, because the Delta variant became the dominant strain in the country. On the 25th of July 2021 the lockdown was moved to an adjusted level 3 (Africa Centre for Disease Control, 2019; South African Government, 2021).

- **Challenges Faced by SMMES Because of Covid-19**

Besides the negative effect on public health, Covid-19 has also caused a major economic shock and SMMEs have been adversely affected. The results of a study by the National Youth Development Agency (2021) indicated that across a sample of SMMEs, 43% temporarily closed or stopped operation due to Covid-19. This is attributed to a low demand and employee health concerns. The percentage of SMMEs that retrenched employees was 38%, and those that kept employees had to reduce salaries. Over 80% of the respondents had instituted salary cuts. Covid-19 led to a significant reduction in sales and revenue, cash flow problems and transportation issues for SMMEs (Ncube, 2020). The findings of a study by the Common Market for Eastern and Southern Africa (2020) revealed that Covid-19 has affected SMMEs on both the supply and demand side. From the supply side, Covid-19 led to a reduction in the supply of labour, as workers become unwell or have to look after children that cannot go to school because of the lockdown. In addition, Covid-19 interrupted supply chains leading to shortages of parts and intermediate goods. On the demand side, Covid-19 led to a dramatic and sudden loss of demand and revenue for SMMEs because the lockdowns prevented customers from purchasing certain goods and services (Ncube, 2020).

The challenges faced by SMMEs include lack of operational cash flow, reduction in demand for production/services, reduction of opportunities to meet new customers, the inability of workers to return to work, challenges in logistics and shipping of products, and difficulties in obtaining the supply of raw materials that are essential for production (Ncube,2020). Compared to large firms, Covid-19 negatively impacted on SMMEs, because they are more labour-intensive and have limited liquidity reserves. According to Ncube (2020) despite the lockdowns caused by Covid-19, SMMEs had to pay fixed costs such as rent, salaries, and taxes.

- **A Reflection on the Two Years of Lockdown 2020/2021**

The two years of lockdown events, 2020 and 2021, showed some similarities and differences listed below.

Similarities: a) Lockdowns: Both years saw lockdowns being implemented in many countries around the world to control the spread of Covid-19; b) Economic impact: Both years had a significant economic impact on businesses, workers, and governments; c) Health impact: Both years had a significant impact on public health, with many people becoming infected with Covid-19 and some requiring hospitalization (Balmford et al, 2022) and d) Remote work: Both years saw a significant increase in remote work as people were forced to work from home to comply with lockdown measures (Roberts, 2022).

Differences: a) Vaccines: 2021 saw the rollout of several effective Covid-19 vaccines, which were not available in 2020, b) Variants: 2021 saw the emergence of several new Covid-19 variants, including the Delta variant, which is more transmissible and has caused a surge of cases in many countries (Roberts, 2022); c) Compliance: In 2020, compliance with lockdown measures was generally high as people were still adjusting to the new reality of the pandemic. However, in 2021, compliance with lockdown measures has been lower in some countries, with many people becoming fatigued with the ongoing restrictions (Balmford et al., 2022). Finally, mental health impact: In 2021, the mental health impact of the pandemic has become more pronounced, with many people suffering from anxiety, depression, and other mental health issues because of the ongoing uncertainty and isolation (Fourie, 2022).

According to Brown (2022), the two years of lockdown provide insights into how the experience of lockdown has evolved. For example, it can help researchers understand how people's attitudes, behaviours, and mental health have changed as lockdown measures have been implemented for extended periods. White (2022) adds that it can also help identify any changes in government policies and public health measures that may have influenced people's experiences during different periods of lockdown.

Additionally, the comparison between the two years of lockdown can provide a basis for evaluating the effectiveness of measures taken during lockdowns (Cooper, 2022). For instance, if a policy or intervention was implemented during the first year of lockdown and then modified or removed during the second year, researchers can compare the outcomes of those two periods to assess the impact of that policy or intervention (Balmford et al., 2022). Overall, the contrast between the two years of lockdown can help researchers gain a better understanding of the impact of lockdown measures and inform future policy decisions.

- **Mitigation of the Negative Impacts of Covid-19 on Local Economic Development?**

The negative impacts of COVID-19 on local economic development have been significant and widespread, and governments, businesses, and communities worldwide have taken various actions to mitigate these impacts. Here are some examples:

Many governments implemented stimulus packages to help support businesses and individuals affected by Covid-19. These packages often include measures such as loans, grants, tax relief, and wage subsidies. Governments and other organizations have also implemented a range of programs to support businesses affected by COVID-19 (Douglas et al, 2020). For example, some countries provided grants to help businesses cover fixed costs, while others established loan guarantee schemes to help businesses access finance. Many businesses implemented remote work arrangements to allow employees to work from home and reduce the risk of Covid-19 transmission (Douglas et al, 2020). This helped to maintain productivity and employment levels in some sectors.

According to Griffiths (2020), COVID-19 accelerated the shift towards digital technologies, and many businesses and organizations have invested in digital transformation initiatives to adapt to the new environment. This has included implementing e-commerce platforms, improving digital marketing capabilities, and adopting new communication technologies. Community support: Local communities have also taken action to support local businesses and workers affected by Covid-19. For example, some communities launched “buy local” campaigns to encourage residents to support local businesses, while others have established food banks and other support services for those in need (Jackson, 2020). Overall, mitigating the negative impacts of COVID-19 on local economic development requires a coordinated and multi-faceted approach involving governments, businesses, and communities working together to support each other during this challenging time.

- **Inclusive development: Informal sector and SMME facilitation and support**

The South African government started to react to the economic downfall by implementing economic recovery plans. In terms of responding to the impact of COVID-19 on local economies in metros, the first emerging theme is the promotion of economic inclusivity, supporting redistribution and growing economic participation (Hlati, 2020). Lockdown regulations in the country recognised wholesale produce markets and informal traders (trading perishables food stuff) as providers of essential services. Accordingly, under lockdown level five, metros implemented measures such as issuing temporary permits for informal traders, including spaza shops (Hlati, 2020). According to Miller (2020), the City of Durban's Economic Recovery Response Plan further incorporates measures to drop historical debts of informal street merchants as well as a 50 percent decrease, for a quarter of a year, on licenses and permits for informal road traders, which can go far in assisting informal businesses with continuing their tasks.

Some local governments went further by introducing separate local government relief funds to local Small Medium and Micro Enterprises (SMMEs) and the informal sector. According to Maziwisa (2020), the City of eThekwini is a case in point. In a survey of businesses affected by COVID-19 lockdown regulations, conducted by the City during the lockdown, it was found that 93 percent of businesses experienced decreased revenue; 72 percent had to shut down completely and 22 percent indicated they urgently required a cash injection for increased debt for overhead costs (Maziwisa,2020). Accordingly, through the City's economic recovery plan, the eThekwini Economic Recovery Fund was made available through identified savings across departments and clusters in the Metro (Mkhize, 2020). The fund aimed to prevent job losses and to help local small businesses that are at risk of shutting down in eThekwini (Mkhize, 2020).

- **Measures to Prevent the Pandemic or Similar Situation from Recurring**

The SARS-CoV-2 virus caused COVID-19, and it was difficult to completely prevent it from recurring. However, several measures can help reduce the spread of the virus and prevent future outbreaks. Getting vaccinated against Covid-19 was the most effective way to prevent the disease from recurring. Vaccines can help reduce the severity of the disease and prevent hospitalization and death. Maintaining a safe distance from others can help reduce the spread of the virus (Guner et al., 2020). This was achieved by avoiding large gatherings, working from home, and maintaining at least six feet of distance from others. Wearing masks reduced the spread of the virus. Masks should be worn in public places, especially indoors, where it is difficult to maintain a safe distance from others (Davis, 2020).

Governments recommended that individuals should regularly wash their hands with soap and water for at least 20 seconds to help reduce the spread of the virus. If soap and water are not available, use hand sanitizer with at least 60% alcohol. Regular testing and contact tracing helped identify and isolate infected individuals, preventing the spread of the virus (Davis, 2020). Improved ventilation in indoor spaces was another guideline to help reduce the spread of the virus by increasing the circulation of fresh air. It is important to note that these measures should be followed even after the pandemic ends to prevent the recurrence of COVID-19 and other infectious diseases (Clark, 2020).

- **Mitigating the Effects of Covid-19 on SMMES**

Many SMMEs had to adopt flexible working arrangements, such as working from home and using digital technologies. In addition, there was a need for an adjustment in business strategy, especially cost reduction and the introduction of new processes, products, and services (Enterprise Research Centre, 2021). This led to the introduction of new business models to meet customer and operational demands, especially the use of digital technologies. In addition, SMMEs, especially those in the tourism sector lost international customers. Government financial assistance, primarily through agencies that support SMMEs, was crucial to the survival of this sector (Moore, 2020). Also, temporary relief by the government from the payment of certain taxes provided a financial cushion for SMMEs (Common Market for Eastern and Southern Africa, 2020). Commercial banks, shopping malls, and suppliers can also assist SMMEs through temporary payment holidays to pay off loans, rent, and trade credit. SMMEs have a major role in promoting their resilience post-pandemic, through the building of their technical capacity and skills, investment in e-commerce and diversification, and the use of technology to enhance competitiveness (Ncube, 2020; Common Market for Eastern and Southern Africa, 2020; Enterprise Research Centre, 2021).

- **Recovery Plans from Covid-19 post-lockdown in South Africa**

The perceptions of recovery plans from COVID-19 post-lockdown varied depending on the specific plan and the context in which it is being implemented. Many people saw the need for recovery plans focusing on reviving the economy, particularly in the wake of widespread job losses and business closures. There was a perception that recovery plans should prioritise measures that support businesses, create jobs, and stimulate economic growth (Afrin et al, 2021). Another important perception was that recovery plans must prioritise public health and safety. This included measures like vaccine distribution, testing and contact tracing, and continued social distancing measures to prevent the spread of Covid-19. According to Afrin et al (2021) there was a growing perception that recovery plans should prioritise sustainability, including efforts to address climate change and promote environmentally friendly practices. Many people believe that recovery plans should be inclusive and prioritize the needs of marginalized communities, disproportionately affected by the pandemic (Allen, 2021).

Recovery also included plans that prioritised education, particularly addressing the learning gaps that have emerged during lockdowns and remote learning. As Covid-19 restrictions were gradually relaxed, the City of Durban's economic recovery plan prioritised facilitating employment opportunities through the implementation of capital projects, and through intensifying expanded public works employment (Clark, 2020). In terms of skills development, the city partnered with companies or institutions that offer online, free platforms to match job seekers with employment opportunities, and to provide further virtual "reskilling" technical programmes in partnership with industry (automotive, aerospace, mining, agro-processing, tourism, BPO) and TVET colleges (Maziwisa, 2020). Overall, the perceptions of recovery plans from Covid-19 post-lockdown are driven by a desire to rebuild and move forward in a way that prioritises the health and well-being of communities, while also fostering economic growth and sustainability (Wilson, 2021).

## DIRECTIONS FOR FUTURE RESEARCH

Sectoral Analysis: further research could conduct a detailed analysis of specific sectors within the local economy to understand the differential impact of Covid-19. This could include sectors such as tourism, hospitality, retail, manufacturing, and services. Examine each sector's short-term and long-term effects, recovery patterns, and policy interventions. Employment and Labor Market Dynamics: Further research is needed to investigate the changes in employment patterns, including job losses, furloughs, and work arrangements (e.g., remote work). Examine the impact on different workforce segments, such as low-skilled workers, informal workers, and self-employed individuals. Explore the effectiveness of government support programs and their role in preserving jobs and supporting recovery. Entrepreneurship and Small Businesses: Explore the challenges small businesses and start-ups face during pandemics. Investigate the survival rates, closures, and pivots in business models. Assess the effectiveness of government initiatives and support measures, such as grants, loans, and business development programs, in promoting entrepreneurship and revitalizing local economies.

## CONCLUSION AND RECOMMENDATIONS

In conclusion, this chapter shed light on the multifaceted impact of the COVID-19 pandemic on local economic development. The chapter highlighted the varying effects across different sectors and regions, underscoring the importance of understanding local contexts and dynamics. It also revealed that while the pandemic presented unprecedented challenges, it also created opportunities for innovation and resilience in local economies. The chapter showed that sectors such as tourism, hospitality, and small businesses were particularly hard-hit, experiencing significant declines in revenue and employment. On the other hand, sectors such as e-commerce, healthcare, and digital services witnessed growth and adaptation in response to the changing demands and restrictions imposed by the pandemic. These shifts in economic activity have not only influenced employment patterns but also prompted changes in consumer behaviour and business models.

The pandemic accelerated digital transformation and innovation in many sectors. Future research could explore the role of technology, digital platforms, and innovation in local economic development during and beyond the pandemic. This could involve studying successful digital adaptation strategies, assessing the digital divide across regions, and identifying opportunities for leveraging technology to promote economic growth and resilience. The Covid-19 pandemic highlighted vulnerabilities in local economies and governance structures. Further research could examine the lessons learned from the crisis and identify strategies for building resilience and preparedness for future shocks. This could involve studying the role of local institutions, emergency management practices, and community engagement in mitigating the impact of future crises.

### Recommendations

The impact of COVID-19 on local economic development has been significant, and it is crucial to learn from this experience to prevent similar crises in the future. Here are some key recommendations to consider:

Diversify the local economy: Overreliance on specific industries can make a region more vulnerable to economic shocks. Encourage diverse industries, including technology, healthcare, and manufacturing, to create a more resilient local economy.

Strengthen healthcare systems: Invest in robust healthcare infrastructure, including hospitals, medical supplies, testing facilities, and vaccine distribution networks. This will help minimise the impact of future pandemics and allow for a swift response.
Enhance digital infrastructure: Develop and improve digital infrastructure to support remote work, online education, e-commerce, and telehealth. This will enable business continuity during crises and facilitate economic activities in times of social distancing.
Support small and medium-sized enterprises (SMEs): Provide financial assistance, grants, and tax incentives to SMEs, which are often the most vulnerable during economic downturns. This support can help them maintain operations, retain employees, and recover faster.
Foster innovation and entrepreneurship: Encourage innovation, research and development, and entrepreneurship within the local community. This will stimulate economic growth, create new job opportunities, and foster resilience in the face of future challenges.
Build solid supply chains: By strengthening local supply networks, reduce dependence on global supply chains. Encourage local production of essential goods and diversify suppliers to mitigate disruptions during global crises.
Invest in education and skills development: Enhance educational systems and training programs to equip the workforce with the skills needed for future jobs. This will ensure adaptability and resilience in the face of economic disruptions.
Strengthen international collaboration: Foster cooperation and knowledge sharing to respond collectively to global crises. Collaborate with other regions and countries to exchange best practices, share resources, and coordinate responses.
Prioritize social safety nets: Strengthen social safety nets and support mechanisms to protect vulnerable populations during crises. Ensure access to healthcare, income support, unemployment benefits, and housing assistance to mitigate the negative impact on disadvantaged communities.

By implementing these recommendations, communities can be better prepared to prevent and mitigate the impact of future crises on local economic development.

## REFERENCES

Abush, C., & Mwita, A. B. (2021). COVID-19 pandemic, a war to be won: Understanding its economic implications for Africa. *Applied Health Economics and Health Policy*, 18(3), 325–328.33368032

Afrin, M., MacGregor, H., Scoones, I., & Wilkinson, A. (2021). Post-pandemic transformations: How and why COVID-19 requires us to rethink development. *World Development*, 138, 105233. 10.1016/j.worlddev.2020.10523333100478

Allen, V. (2021). Comparative analysis of international crisis management in Covid-19 pandemic. *Mednarodno inovativno poslovanje (Journal of Innovative Business and Management), 13*(2), 65-73.

Anjorin, A. A. (2020). The coronavirus disease 2019 (COVID-19) pandemic: A review and an update on cases in Africa. *Asian Pacific Journal of Tropical Medicine*, 13(5), 199. 10.4103/1995-7645.281612

Arndt, S., Chowdhury, F. J., & Rahman, M. M. (2020). COVID-19 pandemic: Rethinking strategies for resilient urban design, perceptions, and planning. *Frontiers in Sustainable Cities*, 3, 668263.

Baker, D., Crescenzi, R., Roller, E., Anguelovski, I., Datta, A., & Harrison, J. (2021). Regions in COVID-19 recovery. *Regional Studies*, 55(12), 1955–1965. 10.1080/00343404.2021.2003768

Balmford, F., Smaidi, K., Salles, M. P., Lopes Neto, A. C., Heilberg, I. P., & Glina, S. (2022). COVID-19: The impact on urolithiasis treatment in Brazil. *International Braz J Urol*, 48(1), 101–109. 10.1590/s1677-5538.ibju.2021.040534735086

Brown, J. S. (2022). *Unmasking the impact of COVID-19 on businesses: Firm level evidence from across the world*. The World Bank.

Chambers, R. B., & Conway, D. (2017). How to construct a mixed methods research design. *Kölner Zeitschrift für Soziologie und Sozialpsychologie*, 69(S2, Suppl 2), 107–131. 10.1007/s11577-017-0454-128989188

Chiwara, A. G. (2022). Assessing COVID-19's economic impact in sub-Saharan Africa: Insights from a CGE model. *COVID-19 in developing economies, 53.*

Clark, A. S. (2020). Coronavirus infections—More than just the common cold. *Journal of the American Medical Association*, 323(8), 707–709. 10.1001/jama.2020.075731971553

Douglass, T. J., Chassot, O., Chaudhary, S., Cordova, L.Jr, Cruz-Trinidad, A., & Wong, M. (2020). COVID-era policies and economic recovery plans: Are governments building back better for protected and conserved areas. *Parks*, 27(Special Issue), 5.

Dua, V., Kumar, M., Verma, A., & Pais, J. (2020). COVID-19 lockdown. *Social scientist, 48*(562-565), 67-82.

Fine, J. (2018). *Understanding local economic development*. Routledge.

Gidden, T. H. (2018). National minorities between protection and empowerment: Towards a theory of empowerment. *JEMIE*, 13, 11.

Guner, H. R., Hasanoğlu, İ., & Aktaş, F. (2020). COVID-19: Prevention and control measures in community. *Turkish Journal of Medical Sciences*, 50(9), 571–577. 10.3906/sag-2004-14632293835

Hadley, O., & Serrat, O., & Oliver, N. (2017). The sustainable livelihoods approach. *Knowledge solutions: Tools, methods, and approaches to drive organizational performance*, 21-26.

Hlati, T. (2020). *Local economic development policies*. UpJohn Research.

Houston, S., Brannan, G. D., Brannan, J. M., & Sharts-Hopko, N. C. (2021). Qua*l-itative study*. NIH.

James, J. (2021). *A simple decision analysis of a mandatory lockdown response to the COVID-19 pandemic*.

Kabizwe, A. (2021). COVID-19 pandemic–an African perspective. *Emerging Microbes & Infections*, 9(1), 1300–1308.34176429

Krantz, S. B. (2011). N of I? Issues of Validity and Reliability in. *PAACE Journal of Lifelong Learning*, 4, 51–60.

Leach, O. A., Derevianko, Y. M., Kozlov, D. V., & Mukorez, A. I. (2021). *Regional Economic Development in The Context of the COVID-19 Pandemic and the Economic Crisis*.

Linton, T. (2021). Coronavirus is proving we need more resilient supply chains. *Harvard Business Review*, 5.

Makoni, T. (2021). Africa after the covid-19 lockdowns: Economic impacts and prospects.

Matasi, A. N. (2021). *"Not a Good Time": Economic Impact of COVID-19 in Africa* (*Vol. 17*, No. 1). African Development Bank.

Maziwisa, N. T. (2020). A review of the SA's tourism recovery plans post COVID-19. *Athens Journal of Tourism*, 9(1), 9–18.

Miller, G. (2020). Mitigating the wider health effects of covid-19 pandemic response. *BMJ (Clinical Research Ed.)*, 369.32341002

Mkhize, E. M. (2020). Economic impact of COVID-19 pandemic on healthcare facilities and systems: International perspectives. *Best Practice & Research. Clinical Anaesthesiology*, 35(3), 293–306.34511220

Moore, C. (2020). The impact of COVID-19 on small business outcomes and expectations. *Proceedings of the National Academy of Sciences of the United States of America*, 117(30), 17656–17666. 10.1073/pnas.200699111732651281

Mpofu, N. (2022). *Impact of COVID-19: Nowcasting and big data to track economic activity in Sub-Saharan Africa*. International Monetary Fund.

Mwale, A. O. (2021). The impact of COVID-19 on African economies: An introduction. *African Development Review*, 33(Suppl 1), S1.34149237

Mwambi, A. (2021). COVID-19 pandemic–an African perspective. *Emerging Microbes & Infections*, 9(1), 1300–1308.34176429

Ncube, C. (2020). *Regional Economic Development in The Context of the COVID-19 Pandemic and the Economic Crisis*.

Njaya, A. O. (2020). The impact of COVID-19 on African economies: An introduction. *African Development Review*, 33(Suppl 1), S1.34149237

Peterson, Z. A. (2021). Beyond informed consent. *Bulletin of the World Health Organization*, 82, 771–777.15643799

Roberts, G. (2022). Policy responses to the COVID-19 pandemic. *International Journal of Environmental Research and Public Health*, 18(2), 559.33440841

Schutte, A. R. (2020). COVID-19: Rethinking the lockdown groupthink. *Frontiers in Public Health*, 9, 625778.33718322

Smith, I. J. (2021). Cross-country comparisons of COVID-19: Policy, politics, and the price of life. *Environmental and Resource Economics*, 76, 525–551.32836862

Venot, E. J. (2017). *Planning local economic development: Theory and practice*. SAGE publications.

Wilson, F. M. (2021). The early impacts of the COVID-19 pandemic on business sales. *Small Business Economics*, 1–12.38624577

Woodhouse, J. A. (2017). *Designing a qualitative study.* SAGE.

Zimbwa, Y. (2020). Analyzing the ultimate impact of COVID-19 in Africa. *Case Studies on Transport Policy*, 9(2), 796–804.33842205

Zondo, T. (2020). The positive impact of lockdown on containing the COVID-19 outbreak in China. *Journal of Travel Medicine*, 27.32181488

## KEY TERMS AND DEFINITIONS

**COVID-19:** Also known as coronaviruses, is a type of virus. There are many different kinds, and some cause disease. A coronavirus identified in 2019, SARS-CoV-2, caused a respiratory illness pandemic called COVID-19.

**Entrepreneurs:** This refers to people who set up businesses, taking on financial risks in the hope of profit.

**Informal Economy:** The informal economy is the diversified set of economic activities, enterprises, jobs, and workers that are not regulated or protected by the state. The concept originally applied to self-employment in small unregistered enterprises. It has been expanded to include wage employment in unprotected jobs

**Local Economic Development (LED):** This refers to strategies and activities to promote economic growth and improve the quality of life in a particular geographic area, such as a city, town, or region (Browne, 2020). The goal of LED is to create jobs, increase income, and enhance the overall economic well-being of the community.

**Sustainability:** A multi-faceted approach aiming for a balanced and enduring outcome. It considers economic, social, and environmental aspects, ensuring that development projects are inclusive, equitable, and eco-friendly.

# Chapter 6
# Sustainable Provision of Municipal Services Through Community-Led Initiatives:
## Ratepayers' Associations in South Africa

**Mpfareleni Mavis Netswera**
*University of South Africa, South Africa*

## ABSTRACT

*This chapter emphases the key role that community-led initiatives play in the absence of sustainable provision of services from the government. Through these initiatives, citizens as individuals or as a formation get involved in the provision of services to improve the quality of their lives. Through secondary data analysis, this chapter examines the prevalence and the role of ratepayers' associations in the sustainable provision of public services in South Africa. The main findings reveal that in the past few years, ratepayers' associations have been holding underperforming municipalities accountable by demanding services due to them. Whereas some took over collapsed municipal services through lawsuits and volunteerism to ensure continues delivery, others managed to address the water pollution dated back to the 1990s when overworked sewage systems were continuously used with little maintenance. The chapter recommends multi-stakeholder partnerships within a municipal area to share knowledge, expertise and support to ensure availability and sustainability of services.*

DOI: 10.4018/979-8-3693-3617-5.ch006

## INTRODUCTION

This chapter emphasises the key role that community-led initiatives play in the absence of sustainable provision of services from the government. Through these initiatives, which appear to be a genuine alternative, citizens as individuals or as a formation get involved in the provision of services to improve the quality of their lives. There has been a noticeable intensification in demand for community-led initiatives as people in under-resourced and neglected areas seek to rebuild their communities and re-establish a sense of pride in the places where they live. In essence, community-led initiatives place citizens at the heart of a process that seeks fundamental changes in the way in which their community functions (Torjman & Makhoul, 2012:3). A community-led initiative is regarded as the process of a community working together voluntary to create and achieve locally determined visions and goals. It is also noted that a community-led initiative establishes a model for what is important to a specific community and builds capacity by recognising that, only by working together can such communities capitalise on the possibilities and address the constraints that they face. Such initiatives also help channel external investment and support towards relevant local priorities and plans (Loha, 2023:4).

The major tenets of a community-led initiative are to promote community participation and empower community members to lead. Along the way, members discover and define what the change should be and how they should work towards solutions. The principal goal is to empower communities to build their capacity and take charge of their own development so that they are able respond to community needs (Attygall, 2020:4). These initiatives are being recognised in a wide range of fields, such as poverty reduction, crime prevention, child care services, job creation for some members, youth programmes and social entrepreneurship (Echessa, 2010, 12). It appears that the need for community-led initiatives arises when community members who have been marginalised and discriminated against call out for justice. It is believed that in these instances, communities are fed up with being acted upon and the only objective way forward is to change the system into one that is "Done by Us for Us". Essentially, these initiatives acknowledge the limitations of development solutions created by those who are in power (Attygall, 2020:4).

Lately, a number of ratepayer's associations have opted to withhold their municipal property rates to demonstrate their dissatisfaction with the provision of municipal services in South Africa (Ayele & May, 2010). Withholding of rates which is described as another form of community protest, has detrimental effects on the municipal revenue base, which in turn reduces the expenditure on service delivery to the community. However, the move comes with certain responsibilities. The modus operandi employed by ratepayers' associations is that property rates and, in some cases, fees for municipal services that are withheld are deposited in a trust account.

Ratepayers' associations either use the funds to deliver services themselves or pay the money back to their respective municipalities once service delivery problems have been resolved (May, 2010:97).

Municipalities are key agents of service delivery and development in South Africa, tasked with the provision of basic infrastructure services such as solid waste management, roads and stormwater management, electricity provision, water supply and sanitation. During the period 2020/2021, about 29 municipalities spread over all nine provinces, were subjected to interventions in terms of Section 139 of the Constitution of the Republic of South Africa, 1996. When a municipality cannot or does not fulfil its constitutional obligations, including service provision, Section 139 allows the relevant provincial executive to intervene by taking steps to ensure the fulfilment of that obligation (Department of Cooperative Governance, 2021:13-14). According to Crous (2002,19), "Service delivery is concerned with the provision of a product or service by a government or government body to a community that it was promised to, or which is expected by that community." Through the courts of law, ratepayers' associations are given the right to takeover some municipal services to ensure continued delivery. Obviously, something is amiss when a sphere of government has its powers and functions handed over to community groups (Everatt, 2021).

Through secondary data analysis, this chapter examines the prevalence and the role of ratepayers' associations in the sustainable provision of public services in South Africa. The main findings reveal that in the past few years, ratepayers' associations have been holding underperforming municipalities accountable by demanding services due to them. Whereas some withheld their rates, others took over collapsed municipal services through lawsuits and volunteerism to ensure continued delivery. The rest of the chapter is organised as follows: The section beneath outlines the theory behind community-led initiatives. Second, the emergence of ratepayers' associations in South Africa is explained, followed by an explanation of the role of ratepayers' associations in municipal services provision. Finally, a set of recommendations and some concluding remarks are presented.

## THEORETICAL BACKGROUND BEHIND COMMUNITY-LED INITIATIVES

Social capital theory assumes that social cohesion is critical if societies are to flourish both socially and economically while achieving sustainable development (Echessa, 2010:16). The term 'social capital' is described as a set of shared values that allows individuals to work together in a group to effectively achieve a common purpose. A society is supposed to function together as a whole through trust and shared identity, norms, values, and mutual relations. Simply put, social capital aids society as a whole through social associations and the provision of much-needed ingredients for the development of stable management. One of the primary forms of social capital is bonding, which refers to social capital created within a group with shared interests and goals. A neighbourhood association is a good example of how bonding works (Kenton, 2022).

One of the earliest definitions of social capital describes it as tangible assets that count the most in the daily lives of people, namely goodwill, fellowship, sympathy, and social intercourse among the individuals and families who make up a social unit (Tata Sustainability Group, 2018:9). Political scientist, Robert Putnam, is generally credited with spearheading the term social capital. Putnam defines social capital as features of social organisation, such as trust, norms and networks, that can improve the efficiency of society by facilitating coordinated actions (Gelderblom, 2028:4). He believes that the existence of civic associations is one of the key to sustainable development and prosperous societies. Putman's seminal work on social capital associates the greater effectiveness of regional government in the North of Italy with strong horizontal bonds of collaboration, such as informal types of social networks, including friendship groups and neighbourhood get-togethers. From this point of view, social capital also improves the functioning of state institutions, with knock-on effects on the success rate of development initiatives (Gelderblom, 2028:5).

The fundamental argument of social capital points out the value of social relations that have productive benefits (Tata Sustainability Group, 2018:9). Social capital theory is applicable in this context because it recognises the role of citizens' associations in the promotion of the welfare of their communities. Ratepayers' associations are community-led initiatives that have emerged to complement the efforts of state institutions in the provision of public services (Echessa, 2010, 10). Mapuva (2011:1) adds that through residents' associations, citizens have been able to keep local authorities in check by demanding services and accountability amidst the economic crises facing the world over the years. A study on enhancing local governance through local initiatives has revealed that residents' associations are a conduit through which local communities can demand accountability and participatory spaces in promoting good local governance (Mapuva, 2011:1).

## WHAT ARE RESIDENTS/RATEPAYERS ASSOCIATIONS?

Ratepayers' associations, also known as residents' or neighbourhood associations, are among numerous examples of community-led initiatives. A residents' association is described as a group of individuals, mostly of the same community, who come together to provide a voice for their community through the pursuit of solutions to problems that commonly affect them. They represent the collective effort of people who are facing similar problems and are consequently driven by the desire and motivation to have these problems addressed. In most cases, these are issues that are related to service delivery by local authorities, such as water supply, waste and sewage disposal, infrastructure development and maintenance, street lighting and recreational facilities (Satuku, 2020). In its *guide on how to set up and run a residents' association*, Harlow Council (2019:4) emphasises that a resident's association can carry out a range of activities from resolving local problems, organising street parties and, promoting recycling projects to campaigning for youth facilities.

There are many reasons why citizens living in an area may want to partake. Whereas some associations may want to campaign for something that would have a positive impact on their community, or to campaign against something that has a negative impact on their community, others are formed to create a better sense of community and identity. Similarly, citizens may just want to be part of a residents' association to get to know their neighbours or make new friendships (Harlow Council, 2019:5). In addition, a resident's association is expected to raise awareness and represent the views of the local community. It has to inform the community about activities, projects and any other developments that may be of interest to the local community. It is imperative that an association should influence the decisions of government, especially at the local authority level, to ensure that community voices are heard. It is as well the role an association to promote a sense of belonging to a community, along with neighbourhood spirit, and responsible citizenship (Satuku, 2020).

For associations to operate smoothly, the government must create a conducive environment in which community issues can be discussed freely. This calls for cordial working partnerships that enable associations to access funds from authorities mandated with the running of municipal activities. Well-functioning associations are those that nurture strong working alliances with local government, media, societies, business community and faith-based organisations (Echessa, 2010:14-15). Studies from Asia, Africa and Latin America highlight the necessity of the role of community-based organisations in empowering and helping people exercise their democratic rights. As such, their array of responsibilities includes maintaining social accountability, raising community voices against government inefficiency and ineffectiveness, generating more inclusive decision-making processes, ensuring increased economic security and serving as channels for organised community development (Acharya & Zafarullah, 2017:277).

As alluded to earlier, associations are a vehicle for citizen engagement in their community and in their democratic institutions. As such, they become greater participants in service provision and municipal decision-making. In some parts of the world, municipal councils have structures and policies in place that serve as a formal liaison between city bureaucracy and active neighbourhood groups. Means of support in place range from communications to financing and coordination (Phillips & Conteh, 2021:3). Some degree of autonomy is, however, critical. Irrespective of the support of government, citizens should still be allowed to identify the issues that matter most to them. Such operational autonomy not only enhances the legitimacy of government-initiated visions of neighbourhood associations but also fosters a sense of community empowerment (Phillips & Conteh, 2021:6). A study that examined the role of residents' associations in urban service delivery concluded that associations were actively involved in providing services such as garbage collection, security, and water supply and acted as lobby groups for better services. Others created jobs for some members and initiated youth programmes and channels through which they could tackle anti-social behaviour (Echessa, 2010:11-12). In answering the question as to whether neighbourhood associations can be purposive instruments of public policy, Phillips and Conteh (2021:6) state that associations play a major role in the development of a strategy to guide the actions of government. This strategy often serves as a blueprint to guide funding decisions, governance structure and outreach measures.

## OVERVIEW OF RATEPAYERS' ASSOCIATIONS IN SOUTH AFRICA

In the apartheid era, civil society–state relations tended to be racially structured with white associations having collegial relationships with the state, whereas non-white associations had relations characterised by different forms of community protest (Ayele & May, 2010:1; Monaco, 2008:13). Rates boycotts, bus boycotts, student protests and community riots were among the few effective tools available to marginalised communities to voice their dissatisfaction (Ayele & May, 2010:1). The activates of associations varied according to the socio-economic differences between the neighbourhoods at the time. For instance, in South Africa at the time, it was typical for black townships associations to work to improve housing in general. These associations were often involved in community affairs and the improvement of social infrastructure. In more affluent areas occupied by white people, associations played a huge role in the monitoring of town planning matters, such as land use and building developments (Monaco, 2008:19). But, both have been important players in local government affairs. During the period of local government transition to non-racial democracy in the early 1990s, both took part in the formal representative system by participating in local transitional councils (Monaco, 2008:18).

In post-apartheid South Africa, the principle of community participation is promoted by the Constitution of the Republic of South Africa, 1996. Section 152 of the Constitution mandates local government to provide democratic and accountable government for local communities and encourages the involvement of communities and community organizations in matters of local government. Furthermore, the Local Government: Municipal System Act 32 of 2000 requires municipalities to develop mechanisms, processes and procedures for community participation. In terms of Section 16 (1) of the Act, a municipality must encourage, and create conditions for, the local community to participate in the affairs of the municipality, including in strategic decisions relating to the provision of municipal services. Section 5(2) obliges members of the local community to pay for service fees, rates on property and other taxes, levies and duties imposed by the municipality. Section 4(2) of the Act further specifies that a municipality has "the duty to use the resources of the municipality in the best interests of the local community, to encourage the involvement of the local community in its affairs, to consult the local community about the level, quality, range and impact of municipal services provided by the municipality and to give members of the local community equitable access to the municipal services to which they are entitled".

In South Africa, community associations are often referred to as civic, ratepayers' and residents' associations. The term "ratepayer" means that the members pay property rates, thus implying that they are property owners. Residents' associations, on the other hand, are made up of all residents in an area regardless of their residential status (Monaco, 2008:19). Chapter one of the Local Government Municipal Property Rates Act 6 of 2004 defines "local community" in relation to a municipality as "that body of persons comprising the residents of the municipality, the ratepayers of the municipality, any civic organisations and non-governmental, private sector or labour organisations or bodies which are involved in local affairs within the municipality; and visitors and other people residing outside the municipality who, because of their presence in the municipality, make use of services or facilities provided by the municipality".

The Municipal Property Rates Act regulates the power of a municipality to impose rates on property and makes provision for municipalities to implement a transparent and fair system of exemptions. Property rates, which are used to fund services that benefit the community are an important source of general revenue for municipalities (Department of Cooperative Governance, 2020:4). To effectively participate in the implementation of the Municipal Property Rates Act, ratepayers are required to cultivate a culture of community participation in the affairs of the municipality. They have a responsibility to engage with their municipalities when they are invited to submit their public comments on proposed rates policies and budgets. In addition, ratepayers should comply with stipulated timeframes regarding inspections of property valuation rolls and, if necessary, lodge objections in respect of the deemed market values of their properties (Department of Cooperative Governance, 2020:4-5).

## RATEPAYERS WITHHOLDING OF MUNICIPAL RATES TO PROVIDE SERVICES

Since the early 2000s, ratepayers' associations appeared to have found many ways of holding municipalities accountable, including withholding rates. This is the practice whereby ratepayers withhold their property rates and, in certain instances, fees for services such as electricity and water on the basis that municipalities are not fulfilling their responsibilities (May, 2010:97). Once the responsibilities are fulfilled, the money withheld is supposed to be paid back to the respective municipalities (Ayele & May, 2010). The withholding of rates, however, reduces the municipal revenue base, and, in turn, this can reduce expenditure on services to the community. While there is no basis in law for withholding rates in South Africa, it is also unlawful for municipalities to charge taxes and fail to deliver services for which they are charging (Ryan, 2021).

A study conducted in 2009 on the phenomenon of rates withholding in five South African municipalities discovered that ratepayers' associations in more than 200 towns were involved in some form of dispute with their municipalities. Reasons for withholding rates varied from municipality to municipality and ranged from disputes concerning property rates tariffs to service delivery failures in respect of key services such as water and electricity (May, 2010:98). The study estimated that close to R20 million had already been paid into trust accounts at the time. It was discovered that ratepayers' associations had taken over some of the responsibilities of their municipalities to provide services due to municipalities' negligence. It was also alleged that the water supplied in some municipalities was contaminated by sewage spills that posed severe health risks to communities. Other complaints reported revolved around waste accumulation, overgrown bushes along public roads, faulty street lights, and cemeteries that had become unsafe to visit (Municipal IQ, n.d.; May & Ayele, 2010).

Nonetheless, ratepayers in the same study argued that they felt compelled to withhold rates where there was a sustained failure to fulfil basic service delivery obligations and also, where ratepayers' associations had offered to assist municipalities and to work hand-in-hand with them to find solutions to service delivery problems, but to no avail (May & Aye, 2010). This stalemate was indeed one of the early warnings of municipal dysfunctionality. By 2021, the Department of Cooperative Governance had identified a number of priority municipalities with governance problems and those requiring service delivery assistance, those with high proportion of vacancies at senior management level. There were also issues identified relating to weak budgeting capabilities, ineffective budget planning and implementation, inadequate allocations for infrastructure repairs and maintenance and low revenue collection levels (Department of Cooperative Governance, 2021:14).

Within the spirit of the local government participatory framework envisioned in the Constitution, and in the Municipal Systems Act and the Municipal Property Act alluded to earlier, a culture of community participation in the affairs of the municipality should be realised. There has to be engagement between the taxpayers and the municipality, for instance, during the Integrated Development Planning. Chapter 5 of the Systems Act obliges a municipality to undertake developmentally-oriented planning to ensure that it strives to achieve its objectives. This process is conducted in consultation with the affected community in order to register their developmental needs and priorities. Community participation is also encouraged through the Local government: Municipal Structures Act 117 of 1998. Chapter 4 of this Act provides for the establishment of ward committees for each ward in the municipality. The objective of a ward committee is to make recommendations on any matter affecting its ward to the council. The question that arises concerns why ratepayers' associations opt to withhold their rates to demonstrate their dissatisfaction instead of engaging in practically accessible forms of participation available in the local government sphere?

## SELECTED RECENT CASES

Court cases about rates withdrawal are currently underway (or are anticipated by ratepayers' associations) because of municipalities' failure to comply with their constitutional obligations. These range from the pollution of the Vaal River by sewage spills in the Emfuleni Local Municipality and the failure of the Kgetlengrivier Local Municipality to deliver water and sanitation to the alleged failure by the eThekwini Metropolitan Municipality to involve residents in the budgetary process. These and other similar cases, present classic examples of community-led initiatives that aim to empower citizens to lead and demand those in power are held accountable.

### Vaal River Sewage Problem in the Emfuleni Local Municipality

Raw sewage from Emfuleni Local Municipality's Waste Water Care and Management Works had for years been leaking into and polluting the Vaal River due to the failing wastewater treatment works in the drainage basins of the river. The Vaal River is the second-largest river in South Africa, after the Orange River, supplying bulk water to the Gauteng Province, South Africa's economic hub. Emfuleni is one of three local municipalities comprising the Sedibeng District Municipality situated in Vanderbijlpark, Gauteng Province (Mnguni, 2022:17-18). The issue of poorly maintained infrastructure dates back to the 1990s when overworked sewage systems were continuously used with little maintenance. In 2018, following complaints about raw and untreated sewage flowing on the streets and into both residents' homes and the Vaal River, the South African Human Rights Commission (SAHRC) established an investigation into the Vaal River sewage problem (SAHRC, 2021:14).

The enquiry found that the Vaal River was polluted beyond acceptable levels. During the site inspection of the municipal area, the SAHRC observed some raw sewage flowing in a small stream, burst water sewerage pipes and children swimming in, and consuming, polluted waters (SAHRC, 2021:25). As a Water Service Authority, the municipality has an obligation to protect water resources and to ensure that residents have access to clean drinking water (Mnguni, 2022:20). It is, however necessary to state that the Emfuleni Local Municipality is not the only polluter, there are also other waste-water treatment systems whose effluent is pumped into the Vaal River, from Mpumulanga to the Northern Cape (Save the Vaal Environment, 2020).

Community members and civic associations not only blame Emfuleni, but also other government stakeholders for failing to adequately address the Vaal River pollution for years (SAHRC, 2021:15). Earlier in 2023, Save the Vaal Environment and the River Property and Safety Association were granted a court order to force the Water and Sanitation Department, Finance, Environment, Cooperative Governance and Traditional Affairs departments and the Gauteng Premier to deal with raw sewage flowing into and polluting the Vaal River and its tributaries (Richards, 2023). Save the Vaal, in particular, has three aims to achieve, (i) to raise public awareness about pollution issues and the importance of preventing the pollution of the Vaal River, (ii) to identify polluters in national, provincial and local government structures, mines, industry and individuals and (iii) in cases where communication with polluters fails, to approach the high court to enforce legislation to stop the pollution (Save the Vaal Environment, 2020). The court order represented a significant victory for Save the Vaal and concerned residents after the years of litigation and pressure placed on the authorities. Media reports in heightening public awareness of sewage pollution played a large part in this successful outcome, along with the intervention of the SAHRC and the deployment of engineers and town planners, including the South African Army for upgrading the dysfunctional sewage systems (Richards, 2023).

## The Kgetlengrivier Local Municipality's Broken Water and Sewage Systems

The Kgetlengrivier Local Municipality is located in the south-eastern part of the North West Province and forms part of the Bojanala Platinum District. Key economic sectors are agriculture and mining activities related to diamonds, slate and aggregate sand (Kgetlengrivier Local Municipality, 2022:1). As a water service authority, the municipality has an obligation to provide water and sanitation within its jurisdiction. Nonetheless, in the middle of the COVID-19 pandemic, the local ratepayer's association went to court requesting that they be given authority to manage the water and sewage plants in the towns of Koster (the seat of the municipality) and Swartruggens. At the time, both towns had serious water shortages and raw sewage was flowing into the Elands and Koster rivers (South African Broadcasting Authority Digital News, 2021).

After successfully arguing in court that the municipality did not have the necessary capacity to deliver water and sanitation, the local ratepayers' association was granted the authority to take control of the area's broken water and sewage systems and to be compensated by the municipality for its efforts (Everatt, 2021). The court ruled that not only was the municipality in breach of its constitutional obligation to deliver water and sanitation, but it had also failed to prevent environmental pollution in these two areas (Ludbrook, 2021). Shortly afterwards, the residents took over the provision of water and sanitation and managed to restore the systems to working order. This organised community effort to assist with services demonstrated the power of a committed citizenry being turned into action that benefits the broader community (Ludbrook, 2021). The Court's endorsement of the residents' takeover of service provision, according to Ludbrook (2021), brings several questions to the fore:

- How sustainable is service provision by residents?
- Who takes decisions on how services are delivered?
- How accountable are ratepayers to all citizens?
- What is the role of the constitutional structures? and
- What would residents be voting for in the forthcoming local government elections?

The fight for authority for water and sanitation in the municipality seems to be far from over, yet. While it was agreed that residents would take control until the appointment of an independent water authority, the ratepayers' association took the matter back to court. They were not convinced that the municipality would maintain the plants properly, but hoped that they had raised the bar as far as water quality is concerned (South African Broadcasting Authority Digital News, 2021). Certainly, the residents of Kgetlengrivier should be applauded for their civic virtue, goodwill, dedication and skill. They have set an example of how a community-led initiative establishes a model for what is important to a specific community and builds local capacity by incorporating active citizens within the prevailing constitutional structures (Ludbrook, 2021).

## eThekwini Rate Protest Movement

Ethekwini Metropolitan Municipality is one of many areas in South Africa where rates withholding has been considered. The metropolitan municipality is located on the east coast of South Africa in the province of KwaZulu-Natal. It is the third largest metropolitan municipality in the country following Johannesburg and Cape Town. The economy of the metro is dominated by the manufacturing, finance, wholesale, transport and government sectors (eThekwini Metropolitan Municipality, 2022).

As the city prepared for the budgetary processes for the financial year 2023-2024, several civic bodies and ratepayers' associations, including those in Tongaat, Isipingo, Westville, Sydenham and Durban North, mobilised their members to withdraw rates payment (Singh, 2023). The essence of the dispute that was brought before the court by the Westville Ratepayers' Association as the applicant was that there had been little public participation in the passing of the municipal budget. Therefore, they proposed that the increases in rates should be deemed unlawful until the budget was recalculated (Comins, 2023). eThekwini ratepayers also questioned how the council could ask for higher rates when it had failed to account for fruitless and wasteful expenditure amounting to more than R350 million and losses of R50 billion, as highlighted in several Auditor-General reports over the preceding five years (Comins, 2023). Other ratepayers' demands that formed part of the dispute included:

- The setting aside of rates increases on properties where residents had filed valuation appeals.
- A review of all credit agreements and a moratorium on all interest on overdue accounts.
- A simplified bill.
- Regular accurate meter reading.
- Cessation of estimated readings.
- Writing off of arrears rates owed by people over the age of 65; and
- The establishment of an oversight board comprising ratepayers and city officials (Comins, 2023).

So far, the stand-off between the eThekwini council and the residents has transformed into the eThekwini Rate Protest Movement with the slogan "Our city matters" and the withholding of close to R1 million in municipal taxes. The Protest Movement aims to prioritise the civilian oversight of spending and immediately fix the water leaks for some residents who have had no running water for three years (Ardé, 2023). It is assumed that every week the movement gets calls from residents whose areas do not have formalised civic bodies. This protest is not only for the middle class but for every person in the metro, especially in underprivileged areas that are worst affected by backlogs in service provision (Comins, 2023a).

In Westville specifically, the metro went ahead and disconnected boycotters' services including those who are in arrears. In response, boycotters went to court to interdict the metro from disconnecting their services pending finalisation of the dispute they lodged with the municipality (Comins, 2023a). From the beginning of rates withdrawal, the mayor had been warning residents that withholding payments for rates and services was illegal and that the metro would have no choice but to implement its credit control policy to deal with revolting ratepayers (Ardé, 2023; Comins, 2023a). At the time of writing this chapter, the Durban High Court had ruled in favour of the eThekwini Metropolitan Municipality on this matter. The Westville Ratepayers Association's application was dismissed with costs, meaning that residents withholding rates as part of the boycott should resume to pay for services, including penalties, interest, including reconnection fees (eThekwini Metropolitan Municipality, 2023).

## CONCLUSION AND RECOMMENDATIONS

Putnam's theoretical background of social capital advocates for the existence of community-led initiatives such as civic associations, as key in working towards sustainable development and prosperous societies. South African cases presented demonstrate how ratepayers' associations have found ways of holding municipalities accountable, including withholding rates where services were not provided sufficiently. These are battles that are fought in a court of law. While withholding rates is against legislation, ratepayers do not necessarily avoid payments, rather opt to pay their municipal accounts into a trust account. Once municipalities fulfil their responsibilities, the monies withheld are supposed to be paid back to the respective municipalities. For municipalities to fulfil their objectives, they must forge working relationships between themselves and the residents they serve, meaning that ratepayers are indeed involved in the provision of services to improve the quality of their lives. The chapter recommends that multi-stakeholder partnerships be forged within municipal areas to share knowledge, expertise and support for the good cause of ensuring the availability and sustainability of services.

## REFERENCES

Acharya, K. K., & Zafarullah, H. (2017). Service delivery and development at the grassroots: The evolution and contribution of community-based organisations in Nepal. *Asia Pacific Journal of Public Administration*, 39(4), 276–286. 10.1080/23276665.2017.1408268

Attygall, L. (2020). *Understanding community-led approaches to community change*. Tamarack Institute.

Ayele, Z., & May, A. 2010. *Withholding rates: a new culture of non-payment*. Dullahomar Institute. https://dullahomarinstitute.org.za/multilevel-govt/local-government-bulletin/archives/volume-11-issue-2-april-may-2009/lgb-iss11-2-withholding-rates-a-culture-of-non-payment.pdf

Comins, L. (2023). *Durban rates revolt: tempers flare at meeting with mayor.* CO. https://mg.co.za/news/2023-08-14-durban-rates-revolt-tempers-flare-at-meeting-with-mayor/

Comins, L. (2023a). *Durban rates boycotters in court to stop city from cutting their water and lights*. CO. https://mg.co.za/news/2023-09-12-durban-rates-boycotters-in-court-to-stop-city-from-cutting-their-water-and-lights/

Crous, M. (2002). Service delivery in the South African public service: implementation of the Batho Pele principles by Statistics South Africa. [Thesis, University of Pretoria].

Department of Cooperative Governance. (2020). *General guidelines on the Local Government: Municipal Property Rates Act no.6 of 2004*. Department of Cooperative Governance.

Department of Cooperative Governance. (2021). *State of local government*. Department of Cooperative Governance.

Echessa, G. M. (2010). *The role of residents' associations in urban service delivery: the case of Nairobi City, Kenya*. [Thesis, Kenyatta University]. https://www.durban.gov.za/pages/government/about-ethekwini

eThekwini Metropolitan Municipality. (2023). *Court rules in favour of eThekwini in Westville rates boycott battle*. Durban. https://www.durban.gov.za/news/Court+rules+in+favour+of+eThekwini+in+Westville+rates+boycott+battle

Everatt, D. (2021). South Africans are revolting against inept local government. Why it matters. *The Conversation*.https://theconversation.com/south-africans-are-revolting-against-inept-local-government-why-it-matters-155483

Gelderblom, D. (2020). The limits to bridging social capital: Power, social context and the theory of Robert Putnam. *The Sociological Review*, 00(0), 1–16. 10.1177/0038026118765360

Kenton, W. (2022). *What Is Social Capital? Definition, Types, and Examples*. Investiopedia. https://www.investopedia.com/terms/s/socialcapital.asp

Loha, W. (2023). Community-led development: perspectives and approaches of four member organizations. *Qeios, CC-BY 4.0.*

Ludbrook, K. (2021). Local government in South Africa is broken: but giving the job to residents carries risks. *The Conversation.*https://theconversation.com/local-government-in-south-africa-is-broken-but-giving-the-job-to-residents-carries-risks-155970

Mapuva, J. (2011). Enhancing local governance through local initiatives: Residents' associations in Zimbabwe. *African Journal of History and Culture*, 3(1), 1–12.

May, A. (2010). The withholding of rates in five local municipalities. Good Governance Learning Network (GGLN).

Mnguni, E. S. (2022). Pollution of the vaal river system in South Africa: A case study. *WIT Transactions on Ecology and the Environment*, 257. 10.2495/WMEI220021

Monaco, S. (2008). Neighbourhood Politics in Transition: residents' associations and local government in post-apartheid Cape Town. [Dissertation, Uppsala University].

Phillips, C., & Conteh, C. (2021). *Neighbourhood associations and the municipality: supporting citizen engagement in the city*. (Niagara Community Observatory Working Paper).

Powell, D., May, A., & Ntliziywana, P. (2010). The withholding of rates and taxes in five local municipalities. *Local Government Bulletin*, 12(4), 9–12.

Republic of South Africa. (1996). *Constitution of the Republic of South, 1996.* Government Printer.

Republic of South Africa. (2000). *Local Government: Municipal Systems Act, (Act 32 of 2000)*. Government Printer.

Republic of South Africa. (2003). *Local Government: Municipal Finance Management Act, (Act 56 of 2003)*. Government Printer.

Republic of South Africa. (2004). *Local Government: Municipal Property Rates Act, (Act 6 of 2004)*. Government Printer.

Richards, N. (2023). *Veil of secrecy' lifted: vaal NPO has court order against Emfuleni municipality*. EWN. https://ewn.co.za/2023/06/29/veil-of-secrecy-lifted-vaal-npo-has-court-order-against-emfuleni-municipality

Ryan, C. (2021). *The revolt of the ratepayers*. MoneyWeb. https://www.moneyweb.co.za/news/south-africa/the-revolt-of-the-ratepayers/

Satuku, S. (2020). *What is a residents association?* Repobackend. https://repobackend.zimcitizenswatch.org/uploads/What_is_a_Resident_Association_156284d880.pdf

Save the Vaal Environment. (2020). *The aim of save the Vaal environment*. Save the Vaal Environment. https://www.save.org.za/about-us/

Singh, K. (2023). *Durban revolts: Civic groups launch eThekwini rates boycott in what the city calls a 'mob mentality'*. News24. https://www.news24.com/news24/southafrica/news/durban-revolts-civic-groups-launch-ethekwini-rates-boycott-in-what-the-city-calls-a-mob-mentality-20230802

South African Broadcasting Authority Digital News. (2021). *Kgetlengrivier Municipality take back charge of sewage and water plants*. SABC News. https://www.sabcnews.com/sabcnews/kgetlengrivier-municipality-take-back-charge-of-sewage-and-water-plants/

Tata Sustainability Group. (2018). *Social capital – an eclectic literature survey*. Aequitas Consulting Pvt. Ltd.

Torjman, S., & Makhoul, A. (2012). *Community-Led Development*. Caledon Institute of Social Policy.

# Chapter 7
# Enhancing Rural Governance in Zimbabwe:
## Exploring the Significance of Inter-Governmental Coordination in Facilitating Collaboration and Communication

**Tendai Kaponda**
https://orcid.org/0009-0003-3287-4335
*Central China Normal University, China*

## ABSTRACT

*Zimbabwe's rural governance involves coordination across different government levels, with distinct roles and responsibilities. The chapter highlights the historical evolution of rural governance in Zimbabwe, which has shifted towards greater decentralisation. The RDDC serves as a platform for coordination across government entities at the district level, but issues such as inadequate participation and conflicting authorities have been noted. Political dynamics, economic constraints, and social traditions influence intergovernmental coordination. Ansell and Gash's collaborative governance model offers insights for stakeholders. Intergovernmental coordination is crucial for facilitating collaboration and communication. There is a need for enhanced information sharing, clarified roles, improved leadership, adequate resources, and better communication mechanisms. Leveraging the lessons from Ansell and Gash's model can significantly contribute to promoting effective intergovernmental collaboration and improving rural governance and development outcomes in Zimbabwe.*

DOI: 10.4018/979-8-3693-3617-5.ch007

## INTRODUCTION

Zimbabwe consists of eight provinces, fifty-seven districts, and an equal number of Rural District Councils. Each district contains a minimum of one Growth Point; however, some districts may have two or more. A Growth Point is a developing urban area, typically serving as the administrative centre of a district, although this is not always the case (Zhou, 2000). Growth Points often house Rural District Councils, which serve as the local governing bodies with administrative power over the land within their respective areas. The local authorities closely collaborate and engage with the central government, which comprises Ministries and Departments with distinct roles that are somehow dependent on land administration.

Inter-governmental coordination, collaboration, and communication play a crucial role in rural governance for several reasons. Firstly, they help in coordinating rural development efforts among federal, state, and local governments, leading to more effective and efficient use of resources (Radin, 1992). Additionally, inter-governmental coordination can prevent negative externalities, harmful competition, and intergovernmental conflict, while promoting problem-solving and enhancing the reliability of intergovernmental interactions (Schnabel & Hegele, 2021). Moreover, it allows governments to tailor policies to local circumstances and preferences, as well as to engage in policy experimentation and learning (Ibid). Furthermore, inter-governmental coordination is essential for avoiding incoherencies and inconsistencies in governance, particularly in systems with multiple levels of government (Ibid). It also facilitates the sharing of perspectives and experiences among regional and subnational actors, leading to better policy alignment and decision-making (OECD, 2023). In the context of rural governance, where local needs and challenges are diverse, such coordination is vital for the effective design, implementation, and monitoring of policies and reforms (Ibid). Inter-governmental coordination, collaboration, and communication are fundamental in rural governance as they enable the effective use of resources, prevent conflicts, promote problem-solving, and ensure that policies are tailored to local needs and implemented coherently.

The purpose of the review paper is to examine the importance of inter-governmental coordination in improving rural governance in Zimbabwe. The paper aims to explore how the reform of intergovernmental planning and budgeting processes, as well as the dynamics of intergovernmental relations, can facilitate collaboration and communication among different levels of government in Zimbabwe. It also seeks to assess the efficacy of policy-making and governance structures in promoting equitable participation and social justice in rural areas. The review further intends to critically analyze Zimbabwe's water, sanitation, and hygiene (WASH) sector institutional arrangements to strengthen governance in this sector. The paper is set against the backdrop of the country's adoption of a new Constitution and the need to address challenges in rural development through improved inter-governmental coordination, as evidenced by the empowerment of Rural District Councils.

## CONCEPTUAL FRAMEWORK

The concept of inter-governmental coordination, collaboration, and communication is of paramount importance in the context of rural governance. In Zimbabwe, the effectiveness of rural development initiatives is intricately linked to the ability of government institutions to coordinate their efforts and communicate seamlessly. Intergovernmental coordination involves the harmonization of activities and policies among different levels of government, such as federal, state, and local, to achieve common goals. This is particularly significant in the Zimbabwean context, where rural development is a key priority (Schnabel & Hegele, 2021). Scholars have emphasized the role of inter-governmental coordination in Zimbabwe's rural governance. For instance, the establishment of Rural Development Councils has been identified as a mechanism to coordinate rural development efforts among various government entities (Radin, 1992). Additionally, the review of Zimbabwe's Rural Local Government System highlights the importance of inter-governmental coordination and participation in rural development (Kurebwa, 2015). Furthermore, the OECD (2023) emphasizes that inter-governmental bodies provide subnational actors with the opportunity to share perspectives and experiences, understand the needs and problems of other levels of government, and obtain help in the design, implementation, and monitoring of policies or reforms.

In the context of rural governance, collaboration and communication are also essential components of effective inter-governmental coordination. Collaborative relationships between different government levels and agencies can lead to more efficient resource utilization and prevent intergovernmental conflicts (Schnabel & Hegele, 2021). Moreover, open communication channels facilitate the sharing of experiences and perspectives, ultimately contributing to better policy alignment and decision-making (OECD, 2023).

Inter-governmental coordination, collaboration, and communication are fundamental pillars of effective rural governance in Zimbabwe. By examining the significance of these concepts, it becomes evident that their integration is essential for promoting coherent policy implementation, preventing conflicts, and ensuring that rural development efforts are tailored to local needs and challenges.

## THEORETICAL FRAMEWORK

The theoretical framework guiding the review is rooted in the concepts of collaborative governance, intergovernmental relations, and the significance of coordination in policy implementation. Collaborative governance, as discussed by Ansell and Gash (2008), emphasizes the importance of joint decision-making and shared responsibility among different levels of government and other stakeholders (Ansell & Gash, 2008). This framework is particularly relevant in the context of Zimbabwe, where the dynamics of intergovernmental relations have been influenced by a unitary system with a strong centralist ideology, as highlighted by Machingauta (2016).

The review also draws on the significance of inter-governmental bodies in facilitating communication and policy alignment, as discussed in the OECD's report on regional governance (OECD, 2023). This emphasizes the need for formal and informal mechanisms to understand the needs and problems of other levels of government, negotiate, and obtain help in the design, implementation, and monitoring of policies or reforms. Moreover, the review is informed by the work of scholars such as Bouckaert, Peters, and Raadschelders (2010), who provide a nuanced conceptualization of intergovernmental coordination, highlighting its role in avoiding negative externalities, harmful competition, and intergovernmental conflict, while promoting problem-solving and enhancing the reliability of intergovernmental interactions (Schnabel & Hegele, 2021).

This theoretical framework will guide the review in analyzing the significance of inter-governmental coordination in enhancing rural governance in Zimbabwe, with a focus on facilitating collaboration and communication among different levels of government and other stakeholders.

## ANSELL AND GASH'S COLLABORATIVE GOVERNANCE MODEL

This model emphasizes collaboration at multiple points throughout the governance process, focusing on consensus building and stakeholder engagement. It provides a framework for understanding the changing processes of governing in rural regions (Gibson, 2014). Ansell and Gash's Collaborative Governance Model, as outlined in their work, focuses on bringing public and private stakeholders together in collective forums with public agencies to engage in consensus-oriented decision-making processes. The model emphasizes critical variables that influence the success of collaborative governance, such as the history of conflict or cooperation, stakeholder incentives, power imbalances, leadership, and institutional design (Ansell & Gash, 2008). Within the collaborative process, factors like face-to-face dialogue, trust building, and the development of commitment and shared understanding are highlighted as crucial elements for successful collaboration (Ansell & Gash, 2008; Emerson, Nabatchi, & Balogh, 2012). Ansell and Gash also stress the importance of focusing on "small wins" within collaborative forums to deepen commitment and shared understanding, leading to a virtuous cycle of collaboration.

*Figure 1. Model of collaborative governance*

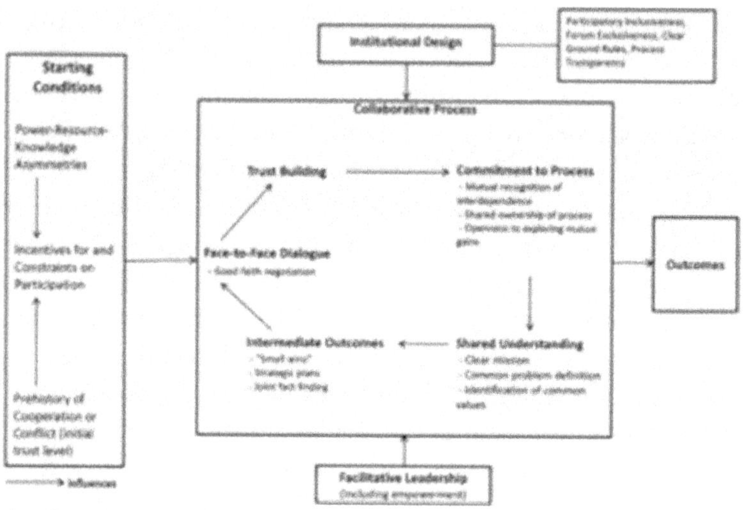


*Source: Ansell and Gash (2008), p. 550.*

The Collaborative Governance Model by Ansell and Gash is characterized by a contingency approach that aims to highlight conditions under which collaborative governance can be successful. The model was developed through a meta-analytical study of existing literature on collaborative governance, refining and elaborating over time to create a common language for analyzing collaborative governance based on real-world cases (Ansell & Gash, 2008; Bianchi, Nasi & Rivenbark, 2021). This model underscores the evolution of governance strategies towards more inclusive and consensus-driven decision-making processes involving various stakeholders from both the public and private sectors.

In summary, effective rural governance thrives on collaboration built on trust, shared goals, inclusive processes, elite participation, good communication practices, consensus decision-making, and successful models like Ansell and Gash's Collaborative Governance Model that emphasize stakeholder engagement throughout the governance process.

## Collaboration in Rural Governance

Building Trust is a cornerstone of successful collaboration in rural governance. Establishing trust among stakeholders, including government entities, organizations, businesses, and residents, is crucial for effective decision-making and implementation (Savage et al., 2023; Gibson, 2014). Rural communities often exhibit tight-knit social networks and a strong sense of shared identity. Building trust among diverse stakeholders in such settings, including government entities, NGOs, businesses, and residents, becomes paramount for effective collaboration. Here, trust acts as a social lubricant, facilitating open communication, reducing transaction costs associated with collaboration, and fostering a willingness to compromise for the greater good of the community (Putnam, 1993).[1] When stakeholders trust each other's motives, competence, and commitment to shared goals, decision-making becomes more inclusive and implementation efforts encounter less resistance. This highlights the need for rural governance models to actively cultivate trust-building mechanisms, such as fostering open communication channels, ensuring transparency in decision-making processes, and demonstrating a commitment to equitable outcomes. By prioritizing trust-building initiatives, rural governance can unlock the full potential of collaborative approaches, leading to more effective solutions for local challenges.

Collaborative efforts are strengthened when all stakeholders come together around common goals. Shared fears and aspirations can help align diverse interests towards a unified vision for rural development (Savage et al., 2023). While rural communities may possess diverse interests, fostering a sense of shared purpose can act as a powerful unifying force. When stakeholders, encompassing government agencies, local businesses, residents, and NGOs, come together around a common vision, it allows them to transcend individual agendas and work towards mutually beneficial outcomes. Shared anxieties concerning the future of their rural environment, coupled with aspirations for a prosperous and sustainable community, can create a fertile ground for collaboration. This alignment facilitates the development of a unified vision for rural development, ensuring that collaborative efforts are not scattered or inefficient. It allows stakeholders to prioritize initiatives that address the most pressing concerns for the community as a whole and leverage their diverse expertise towards achieving a common objective. Furthermore, shared goals can foster a sense of collective responsibility, promoting ownership and buy-in for the success of collaborative initiatives.

Inclusive processes that involve individuals, community-based organizations, and key stakeholders enhance the legitimacy and effectiveness of rural governance initiatives (Gibson, 2014). Traditional governance models often operate with a limited scope, neglecting the valuable perspectives and expertise of community members. However, by incorporating individuals, community-based organizations

(CBOs), and key stakeholders into the decision-making process, rural governance can unlock its full potential.

Inclusivity fosters a sense of ownership and legitimacy for governance initiatives. When individuals and CBOs directly participate in shaping policies and programs, they are more likely to feel invested in their success. This fosters a sense of shared responsibility and encourages community buy-in for implementation efforts. Furthermore, including a diverse range of stakeholders ensures that rural governance initiatives address the multifaceted needs of the community. CBOs often possess a deep understanding of local challenges and priorities, while key stakeholders from the private sector or academia can contribute valuable expertise and resources. By fostering inclusivity, rural governance can leverage the collective intelligence and social capital within the community, leading to more effective and sustainable solutions.

The involvement of elites in rural governance is highlighted as a key element for success. Leveraging the expertise, leadership, and social influence of elites can introduce new dynamics and opportunities for community development (Peng, Peng, Li, Lu & Yin, 2023). While the involvement of elites can be a source of criticism due to concerns about power imbalances and neglecting the voices of marginalized groups, their expertise, leadership, and social influence can introduce valuable dynamics and opportunities. Elites, often categorized as individuals with significant economic or social power in the community, can possess specialized knowledge and skills relevant to rural development initiatives. They may have established networks and connections that can attract investment or resources from external actors. Additionally, their leadership abilities can be instrumental in mobilizing community members and fostering a sense of collective action. Furthermore, the social influence of elites can act as a bridge between government agencies and local communities, facilitating communication and collaboration.

However, it's crucial to acknowledge the potential pitfalls associated with elite involvement. Unchecked power dynamics can lead to initiatives that prioritize the interests of elites over the broader needs of the community. To mitigate these risks, rural governance models should strive for a balanced approach. Mechanisms for ensuring inclusivity and transparency are essential, alongside fostering the participation of marginalized groups alongside elites. By harnessing the potential benefits of elite involvement while remaining vigilant against potential drawbacks, rural governance can leverage the diverse skillsets and resources within the community for successful development.

## Communication in Rural Governance

Effective communication is essential for establishing and maintaining commitment among stakeholders. It fosters trust, encourages meaningful interactions, and develops channels for open dialogue (Savage et al., 2023). Open and transparent communication acts as the lifeblood of collaboration, fostering trust, encouraging meaningful interaction, and establishing channels for ongoing dialogue. Effective communication builds trust by ensuring all stakeholders have access to relevant information and a clear understanding of decision-making processes. When stakeholders feel informed and valued, they are more likely to trust the motives and competence of other participants. Furthermore, effective communication fosters meaningful interactions, allowing stakeholders to share diverse perspectives, identify common ground, and work towards solutions collaboratively. This exchange of ideas fosters a sense of shared ownership and empowers stakeholders to contribute their expertise effectively.

Open dialogue is particularly crucial in rural governance, where information dissemination can be challenging due to geographical dispersion or limited access to technology. By establishing clear communication channels, such as community forums or regular meetings, rural governance can ensure all voices are heard and concerns are addressed. This fosters a sense of inclusivity and strengthens the commitment of stakeholders to collaborative efforts. Effective communication, therefore, acts as a vital tool for building trust, promoting meaningful interaction, and fostering a collaborative environment that is conducive to successful rural governance.

Consensus decision-making processes help in reaching agreements that reflect the collective input of stakeholders. This approach ensures that diverse perspectives are considered in governance decisions (Savage et al., 2023). Unlike top-down approaches, consensus building fosters a more inclusive environment where diverse perspectives are actively considered in governance decisions. By striving for agreements that reflect the collective input of all stakeholders, consensus decision-making fosters a sense of ownership and buy-in for implemented initiatives. When stakeholders feel their voices have been heard and their concerns addressed, they are more likely to support the chosen course of action. This collaborative approach also ensures that rural governance decisions consider the multifaceted needs of the community, encompassing the diverse viewpoints of residents, businesses, and community-based organizations.

However, it's important to acknowledge the potential challenges associated with consensus building. The process can be time-consuming, requiring patience and skilful facilitation to navigate differing opinions. Reaching consensus may necessitate compromise on all sides, which some stakeholders may find difficult. Despite these limitations, consensus decision-making offers a valuable approach to rural governance. By fostering inclusivity, ensuring diverse perspectives are considered, and promoting a sense of shared ownership, this collaborative process can lead to more effective and sustainable solutions for rural communities.

Encouraging honest and respectful feedback creates an environment where stakeholders feel their opinions are valued. This openness enhances transparency and strengthens relationships among collaborators (Savage et al., 2023). Openness to diverse viewpoints, even those that challenge the status quo, is crucial for effective collaboration. By creating a space where stakeholders feel comfortable expressing their opinions freely and respectfully, rural governance can reap significant benefits. This fosters a sense of trust and psychological safety, encouraging stakeholders to share their knowledge and concerns without fear of retribution. Honest feedback allows for the identification of potential shortcomings in proposed initiatives and facilitates course correction before implementation. This openness also enhances transparency, allowing stakeholders to hold each other accountable and ensuring decision-making processes are fair and inclusive. Furthermore, encouraging respectful dialogue strengthens relationships among collaborators. When stakeholders feel their voices are heard and valued, regardless of their position, it fosters a sense of camaraderie and collaboration. This strengthens the social fabric within the community and creates a foundation for long-term, successful partnerships in rural governance.

However, fostering such an environment requires conscious effort. Establishing clear guidelines for respectful communication and actively listening to diverse perspectives are crucial. By prioritizing open dialogue and honest feedback, rural governance can unlock the collective wisdom of the community and strengthen the collaborative spirit that is essential for addressing local challenges.

## ROLE OF COLLABORATION AND COMMUNICATION

Collaboration and communication play pivotal roles in fostering effective rural governance.

*Figure 2. Three key components to successful collaboration for rural revitalization*

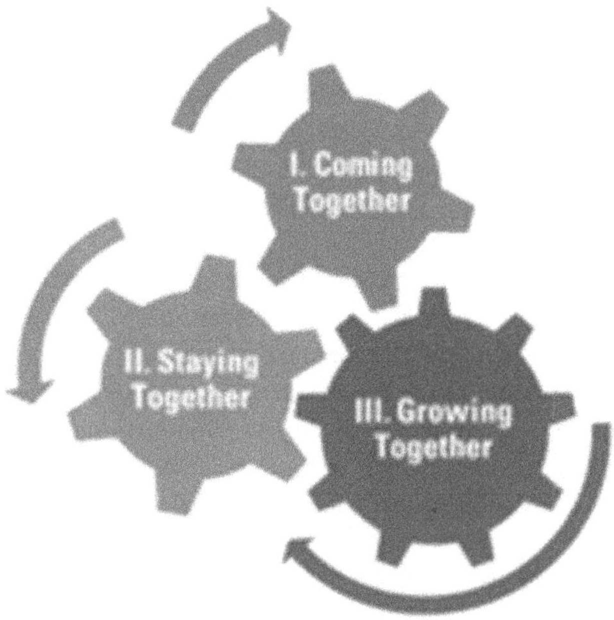


*Source: Savage et al., (2023) p. 02).*

## Collaborative Governance vs. Traditional Governance

Collaborative governance differs from traditional governance models in several key aspects. In traditional governance, stakeholders are defined based on their importance in achieving objectives and are engaged according to needs-based market research and consultation approaches. On the other hand, collaborative governance defines stakeholders by their role and influence across the system, engaging them through co-designing for shared understanding, issue identification, and painting a shared picture of success (Chaplyn, Fraser & Ryan, 2020). Traditional governance models are typically established at or before the start of a change process, while collaborative governance evolves through inclusive decision-making processes that span organizational and sectoral boundaries (Chaplyn, Fraser & Ryan, 2020; Bianchi, Nasi & Rivenbark, 2021). Additionally, collaborative governance emphasizes a multi-sectoral approach that brings diverse participants together to create relevant solutions and lasting impact for communities, focusing on outcomes at a population level and addressing underlying conditions that sustain complex problems (Chaplyn, Fraser & Ryan, 2020; Bianchi, Nasi & Rivenbark, 2021).

## Criticism of Traditional Governance Models and How Collaborative Governance Addresses Them

### Lack of Inclusivity and Stakeholder Engagement

Traditional governance models may lack inclusivity and fail to engage a diverse range of stakeholders effectively (Chaplyn, Fraser & Ryan, 2020). Collaborative governance addresses this criticism by organizing collaborations that involve stakeholders from various sectors, providing a holding environment for inclusive decision-making processes (Chaplyn, Fraser & Ryan, 2020). This can lead to policies that don't reflect the needs of the community and have lower rates of adoption. Collaborative governance offers a solution by bringing together stakeholders from various sectors, such as government agencies, community groups, and businesses. By creating a "holding environment" – a space for respectful dialogue and shared decision-making – collaborative governance fosters inclusivity and empowers stakeholders to contribute their expertise. Additionally, collaborative governance can lead to better-informed solutions and increased public trust due to a more transparent and participatory process. However, it's important to acknowledge that this approach can also be time-consuming and finding consensus with diverse viewpoints can be challenging.

### Limited Adaptability and Innovation

Traditional governance models can be rigid and struggle to adapt to changing circumstances or foster innovation (Chaplyn, Fraser & Ryan, 2020). Collaborative governance, on the other hand, promotes multi-sectoral collaboration, allowing for diverse perspectives and innovative solutions to complex issues (Chaplyn, Fraser & Ryan, 2020; Rivernbark; Waardenburg, Groenleer, de Jong & Keijser, 2019). This exchange of ideas can spark innovation, leading to more effective solutions for complex challenges. For instance, involving environmental groups in infrastructure projects can lead to more sustainable designs, while incorporating citizen input on social programs can ensure they better meet community needs. However, implementing collaborative processes for fostering innovation can be challenging. It requires effective facilitation to ensure all voices are heard and finding common ground among diverse perspectives can be time-consuming.

## Insufficient Focus on Shared Goals and Outcomes

Traditional governance models may prioritize individual organizational goals over shared community outcomes (Chaplyn, Fraser & Ryan, 2020). Collaborative governance emphasizes creating a shared understanding of community goals, and fostering collaboration towards achieving sustainable outcomes (Chaplyn, Fraser & Ryan, 2020; Bianchi, Nasi & Rivernbark). This statement highlights a key tension between traditional and collaborative governance models. Traditional models, focused on individual organizations, can operate in silos, prioritizing their own goals over the well-being of the broader community. This can lead to disjointed policies and missed opportunities for collaboration. In contrast, collaborative governance emphasizes a shared vision. By fostering communication and understanding of community needs, stakeholders can work together towards achieving sustainable outcomes that benefit everyone. This collaborative approach transcends individual organizational objectives, prioritizing the long-term health and success of the community as a whole (Chaplyn, Fraser & Ryan, 2020; Bianchi, Nasi & Rivernbark).

## Inadequate Conflict Resolution Mechanisms

Traditional governance models often lack effective mechanisms for managing conflicts that arise among stakeholders (Bianchi, Nasi & Rivernbark). Collaborative governance addresses this by providing methods to support leadership in conflict management, trust-building, and pursuing shared views to overcome challenges and achieve common goals (Chaplyn, Fraser & Ryan, 2020; Bianchi, Nasi & Rivernbark; Waardenburg, Groenleer, de Jong & Keijser, 2019). One of the significant shortcomings of traditional governance models lies in their inadequacy to manage conflicts arising amongst stakeholders (Bianchi, Nasi & Rivernbark). This often stems from a hierarchical structure that prioritizes internal decision-making processes, neglecting the diverse viewpoints and potentially conflicting interests of various stakeholders. Collaborative governance emerges as a potential solution by equipping stakeholders with the necessary tools for navigating these complexities. Through dedicated methods that support leadership in conflict management, trust-building exercises, and a focus on fostering shared visions, collaborative governance aims to bridge divides and create a space for overcoming challenges collaboratively (Chaplyn, Fraser & Ryan, 2020; Bianchi, Nasi & Rivernbark; Waardenburg, Groenleer, de Jong & Keijser, 2019). By fostering a culture of open communication and shared goals, collaborative governance empowers stakeholders to move beyond individual agendas and work towards achieving mutually beneficial outcomes.

By addressing these criticisms through its inclusive approach, emphasis on shared goals, adaptability, and conflict resolution mechanisms, collaborative governance offers a more dynamic and participatory framework for decision-making that can lead to more effective outcomes in addressing complex social issues (Chaplyn, Fraser & Ryan, 2020; Bianchi, Nasi & Rivernbark)

## HISTORICAL CONTEXT OF RURAL GOVERNANCE IN ZIMBABWE

The historical development of rural governance in Zimbabwe can be divided into three periods: the colonial era, the post-independence period, and the present. During the colonial era, rural development policies were geared towards the exploitation of natural resources and the provision of services to white settlers, with little regard for the needs of the indigenous population. The post-independence period saw the adoption of a more inclusive approach to rural development, with the establishment of Rural District Councils (RDCs) in 1980 to promote local participation and decision-making (Helmsing, 1990). However, the RDCs faced several challenges, including limited financial resources, inadequate capacity, and political interference, which hindered their effectiveness (Kurebwa, 2015).

In post-independence Zimbabwe, two main components of rural development emerged: development within communities and the resettlement of farmers from other areas to former white farms. Despite improvements in farmers' agricultural output in recent years, increasing population pressure on degraded land resources appears to be an intractable and worsening problem in many community areas. The current government still needs to address rural development issues comprehensively and nationwide. In recent years, the government has introduced several reforms aimed at enhancing rural governance, including the devolution of power to provincial and local authorities, the establishment of Rural Development Councils (RDCs), and the adoption of a new Constitution in 2013 (Masuku & Macheka, 2020). These reforms seek to promote local participation, accountability, and transparency in rural governance, as well as to address the challenges of service delivery and infrastructure development in rural areas (Masuku & Macheka, 2020). Despite these efforts, rural governance in Zimbabwe continues to face several challenges, including limited financial resources, inadequate capacity, political interference, and corruption (Masuku & Macheka, 2020). Moreover, the COVID-19 pandemic has exacerbated these challenges, highlighting the need for more effective and efficient rural governance structures and policies (Masuku & Macheka, 2020).

The historical development of rural governance in Zimbabwe has been marked by a shift from a colonial-era approach focused on resource exploitation to a more inclusive approach aimed at promoting local participation and decision-making. However, the effectiveness of rural governance structures has been hindered by several challenges, including limited financial resources, inadequate capacity, and political interference. The government's recent reforms seek to address these challenges, but more needs to be done to ensure effective and efficient rural governance in Zimbabwe.

## KEY MILESTONES, POLICIES AND CHALLENGES

### Milestones

Since gaining independence from Britain in 1980, Zimbabwe has undergone significant political and governance changes. The District Councils Act of 1980 (as amended in 1981 and 1982) applied to the Communal Lands, where it revived local government following the liberation struggle, merged the previously dispersed African Councils from having over 220 to a smaller number of 55 and democratically changed the local governance system (Mutizwa-Mangiza, 1985). In 1984, the Prime Minister's Directives, a decentralization initiative was introduced by the Prime Minister aimed at addressing historical power imbalances from the colonial era, empowering rural communities, and fostering inclusive development. The Provincial Councils and Administration Act of 1985 was also passed during this time, creating the provincial councils. The results of the instructions seem to have a connection to the essential elements of colonial control. The Rural District Councils Act passed in 1988, was the last significant decentralisation reform to be put into effect. It institutionalised the planning process as envisioned by the Prime Minister's Directives and provided a structure for the administration, management, and development of rural areas. The Rural District Councils Act was enacted in 1988 to combine district and rural councils. Due to this, the rural local government's dual system was abolished. However, it wasn't until 1993 that it went into force when 55 Rural District Councils were created by combining 45 Rural Councils with District Councils (Community Law Centre, 2010). The Rural District Councils Act and the Urban Councils Act were updated in 1997 to give local governments more autonomy and control over decision-making, including the capacity to generate revenue and manage local resources. Additionally, in 1999, the Traditional Leaders Act was passed to strengthen rural governance, giving Chiefs, Headmen, and Village Heads the authority to coordinate development, distribute land, etc.

Scholars such as Muzenda (2018) have highlighted the intensified political competition after 2000, signifying a shift in local governance reforms, particularly in urban governance. While there were indications of progress, this period also witnessed some setbacks in functional aspects. A pivotal moment came in 2013 with the introduction of a new constitution, which for the first time in Zimbabwe's post-independence history, formally recognized local government. A key principle of this constitution was the decentralization of power to local communities, reflecting a significant step towards empowering local governance structures (Muzenda, 2018).

## Policy

Decentralization has been a central policy in Zimbabwe since independence, with a focus on empowering marginalized communities and dispersing power from the central government. The Constitutional Amendment (No.20) Bill of 2013 represents a significant step in this direction, as it outlines provisions for devolving government powers and responsibilities to provincial, metropolitan councils, and local governments. Moreover, in 2020, the Government of Zimbabwe instituted the Decentralisation and Devolution Policy. This move aims to promote local governance and enhance citizen participation in decision-making processes, reflecting a continued commitment to decentralization and empowering local communities in Zimbabwe's governance structure (Muzenda, 2018).

## Challenges

The presence of parallels and overlaps in governance structures has been identified as a source of conflict in rural communities, impeding development, dividing communities, and even leading to instances of violence (Centre for Conflict Management and Transformation, 2014). Furthermore, local governance reforms post-2000, while demonstrating progress in urban governance, have also experienced functional regression characterized by legal ambiguity and the establishment of symbolic institutional structures (Muzenda, 2018). Additionally, political interference, limited resources, fragmented decision-making power, corruption, low citizen participation, and a lack of accountability have significantly hampered the governance capacity of local governments, leading to challenges in the effective functioning of the governance system (Muzenda, 2018).

## UNDERSTANDING INTERGOVERNMENTAL COORDINATION IN RURAL ZIMBABWE

A range of studies have explored different aspects of governance in Zimbabwe, shedding light on the challenges and potential solutions. Nyakurukwa (2022) emphasizes the need for state infrastructure to enhance corporate governance, which could have implications for inter-governmental coordination. Sharon (2023) highlights the difficulties faced by local authorities in service delivery, a key area where inter-governmental coordination is crucial. Such (2022) provides insights into the governance of intersectoral collaborations, which could inform the coordination of different government sectors in rural governance. Jachi (2019) suggests a positive relationship between efficient public procurement and effective public service delivery, an area that could benefit from improved inter-governmental coordination. These studies collectively underscore the importance of effective governance and coordination in rural governance in Zimbabwe.

The issue of intergovernmental coordination in rural governance in Zimbabwe is a complex one, with a history of hierarchical structures and mechanisms that have not effectively promoted integrated and coherent governance (Chigwata, 2018). This has led to tensions between local and central governments, impacting the autonomy and efficiency of local authorities (Vincent, 2017). The allocation of authority and responsibility in rural district councils has also been a challenge, with a top-down approach that does not effectively involve local communities (Mandondo, 2001). In the urban context, the Ministry of Local Government, Public Works and Urban Development plays a supervisory role, leading to a need for interdependence and balance in urban governance (Mhlahlo, 2007).

Intergovernmental coordination in Zimbabwe's rural development structure is influenced by a strong centralist ideology, political party incongruence, and the absence of political will for crucial reforms (Chakunda, 2018). This has led to a distortion of local relations and a strain on development facilitation (Chatiza, 2008). The role of governmental organizations in rural development, including agricultural field services, is crucial but faces challenges in coordination (Leach, 1982). The policy of decentralization, introduced in 1984, aimed to empower rural communities, but has been hindered by weak local structures, lack of consultation, and state and NGO interference (Malinga, 2017).

A problem seriously limiting the potential impact of development organizations in participative rural development is the lack of effective coordination and cooperation (Duvel, 1996).

## Rural District Development Committee

The RDDC is a committee of the Council where all government organisations both ministries and quasi-government entities (parastatals) meet and plan for the rural districts. The composition and impact of the Rural District Development Committee (RDDC) in Zimbabwe's rural governance have been the subject of several studies. Chiunye (2018) and Nsingo (2006) both highlight the need for improved community participation in the policy-making process, with Chiunye specifically calling for the inclusion of lower-level council structures in policy proposals.

The Rural District Development Committee (RDDC) in Zimbabwe is a crucial body established to coordinate the development of the district. The RDDC is responsible for considering Ward Development Plans, making recommendations to the council for the inclusion of matters in the annual development and other long-term plans, preparing the Annual District Development Plan for approval by the council, and assisting in the preparation of other Long-term Plans for the district (Vungu Rural District Council, 2017; Chigwata & Marumahoko, 2018). The RDDC is composed of various stakeholders, including the District Administrator, the Chairman of every other committee established by the council, the Chief Executive Officer of the council and its officers, the senior officer in the district of various forces, departments, or Ministries, and other organizations and interests as the Minister may permit (Vungu Rural District Council, 2017)

The RDDC plays a significant role in strengthening intergovernmental coordination in rural governance by providing a platform for various stakeholders to collaborate and coordinate their efforts in district development. The RDDC's composition, which includes representatives from national government departments, local authorities, traditional leaders, and other organizations and interests, ensures a diverse range of perspectives and interests are represented in the decision-making process (Vungu Rural District Council, 2017). The RDDC's functions, such as considering Ward Development Plans, making recommendations to the council, and preparing the Annual District Development Plan, require coordination and cooperation between various stakeholders. The RDDC's role in coordinating the development of the district is particularly important in the context of Zimbabwe's decentralization and devolution policies, which aim to strengthen local democracy and promote inter-governmental cooperation (Chakunda, 2018; OECD, 2016).

However, both studies note a lack of effective community participation, with Nsingo (2006) attributing this to the dominance of officials in planning processes. Mudimu (2019) further complicates this picture by highlighting the conflicting authorities in post-land reform areas, which can further hinder effective governance. Misi (2014) adds a financial dimension, noting the challenges of donor funding in sustainable rural development. These studies collectively underscore the need for improved community participation, streamlined governance procedures, and sustainable funding in the work of the RDDC. The Rural District Development Committee (RDDC) in Zimbabwe is a vital body that plays a significant role in strengthening intergovernmental coordination in rural governance. The RDDC's composition and functions provide a platform for various stakeholders to collaborate and coordinate their efforts in district development, promoting intergovernmental cooperation and strengthening local democracy.

## Factors Influencing Inter-Governmental Coordination

In Zimbabwe, inter-governmental coordination within the context of rural governance is indeed influenced by a range of political, economic, and social factors.

## Political Influences

Zimbabwe operates as a unitary nation with a three-tier government structure, consisting of the national government, provincial and metropolitan councils, and local government (Chakunda, 2018). The transition towards a devolved system of government in Zimbabwe is crucial. Devolution involves the transfer of powers and functions to local governments, which are closer to the people (Nyikadzino &Vyas-Doorgapersad, 2022). The 2013 Constitution of Zimbabwe mandates coordination among government tiers through intergovernmental planning and budgeting (Chigwata & Marumahoko, 2018). Historical transformations have shaped intergovernmental relations in Zimbabwe, reflecting varied ideological contexts and shifts in power dynamics (Chakunda, 2018; Chakunda, 2015)

## Economic Influences

The economic factors influencing inter-governmental coordination in Zimbabwean rural governance can be analyzed through the lens of fiscal decentralization, political decentralization, and administrative decentralization. The central government's fiscal commitments to decentralized institutions, such as health and education grants, have been affected by the declining economic situation, leading to a gap between rhetoric and reality in decentralization (Chakunda, 2018). The institutional development of decentralization in Zimbabwe, such as the establishment of Provincial Councils and Administration Act Chapter 29:11, has created a clear intergovernmental network from the local level to the provincial level for promoting development (Chakunda, 2018). However, there are still challenges in the coordination and cooperation between different tiers of government, with strong arguments in the literature suggesting that devolution may not necessarily guarantee positive impacts on cooperation and development (Chakunda, 2018). Under the Economic Opportunities, the U.S. Government guides U.S. businesses to leverage opportunities in Zimbabwe, indicating a potential economic influence on inter-governmental relations (US Department of State, 2022).[2] The allocation of national resources, including funding for rural development projects, is frequently decided by the national government, potentially resulting in development disparities between regions based on political priorities (Mandondo, 2000). Moreover, Zimbabwe's land reform program, initiated in 2000, has significantly influenced rural governance and agricultural productivity. The implementation of this policy has had notable political and economic implications for inter-governmental coordination (Scoones, 2010).

The competition law in Zimbabwe, introduced in 1996 through the Competition Act, Chapter 14:28, primarily prohibits restrictive and unfair business practices (Nyikadzino &Vyas-Doorgapersad, 2022). However, the involvement of very senior political and military figures in a range of cartels limits effective enforcement, leading to market distortions and an unfavourable business climate (Nyikadzino &Vyas-Doorgapersad, 2022). The mismanagement and policy inconsistencies in the implementation of Zimbabwe's land reform program, such as the $3 billion state-led Command Agriculture program, have affected the program's success (BTI, 2024). The constitutional alignment exercise, which is intended to align Zimbabwe's laws with the constitution adopted in 2013, has not been completed, and the ZANU PF government has made continued constitutional amendments instead (BTI, 2024). These economic factors have significant implications for inter-governmental coordination in Zimbabwean rural governance, highlighting the need for effective mechanisms to regulate intergovernmental relations and improve cooperation and coordination between different tiers of government.

## Social Influences

Historical debates in Zimbabwe have revolved around issues like decentralization, devolution of power, and even thoughts of secessionism or federalism. These historical divisions can impact inter-governmental coordination (Chakunda, 2015). Strengthening local democracy through inter-governmental cooperation is vital for the successful implementation of devolution in Zimbabwe (Nyikadzino &Vyas-Doorgapersad, 2022). These influences collectively shape the dynamics of inter-governmental coordination in Zimbabwe, highlighting the intricate interplay between political structures, economic considerations, and social factors within the country's governance framework. The level of community participation in rural governance is known to vary widely, influenced by local traditions, cultural practices, and levels of education, as highlighted by Mudege & Ansell (2013). This variability can significantly impact how policies are received and implemented at the local level.

Furthermore, traditional leaders, including chiefs and headmen, continue to wield substantial influence in rural governance. Their roles have been extensively discussed by scholars such as Mandaza (2005), who have emphasized that their influence can either facilitate or complicate inter-governmental coordination, depending on their relationships with national and local government authorities.

The effectiveness of inter-governmental coordination in Zimbabwe is complex and multifaceted, requiring ongoing analysis of these and other factors to understand the dynamics at play.

## DISCUSSION

The paper underscores the pivotal role of intergovernmental collaboration in Zimbabwe's rural governance. Zimbabwe's rural governance involves coordination across various government levels - national, provincial, district, and local - each with distinct roles and responsibilities. Effective coordination among these levels is crucial for rural development. The paper highlights the historical development of rural governance in Zimbabwe, which has evolved from a top-down, colonial-era approach to a more inclusive model post-independence. However, challenges such as limited resources and political interference persist. The adoption of a new constitution in 2013 mandated greater decentralization and devolution of powers to local governments. This has placed increased emphasis on intergovernmental coordination for rural governance. The Rural District Development Committee (RDDC) serves as a critical platform for coordination across different government entities at the district level. However, challenges such as inadequate community participation and conflicting authorities have been noted. Various factors, including political dynamics, economic constraints, and social traditions, influence intergovernmental coordination. The centralist political ideology and resource constraints are noted as significant challenges. The paper emphasizes the importance of overcoming barriers such as inadequate information sharing, unclear roles, leadership shortcomings, and communication gaps to enhance intergovernmental collaboration. Ansell and Gash's collaborative governance model provides a useful framework for understanding intergovernmental collaboration in Zimbabwe's rural governance. Key elements such as building trust, shared goals, inclusive processes, elite participation, communication, and consensus decision-making are highly relevant. The paper demonstrates that intergovernmental collaboration is of paramount importance for effective rural governance in Zimbabwe. It also illustrates how Ansell and Gash's collaborative governance model can be applied to Zimbabwe's context, offering valuable insights for stakeholders in rural development.

## Challenges and Gaps

The challenges faced in achieving effective inter-governmental coordination, collaboration, and communication are multifaceted, as highlighted in the provided sources.

## Lack of Information Sharing

One significant challenge is the lack of information sharing among agencies, which can hinder effective collaboration and decision-making (Hocevar, Jansen & Thomas, 2011). This lack of transparency can lead to confusion, duplication of efforts, and inefficiencies in addressing complex issues. When information remains siloed within individual organizations, it can significantly hinder effective collaboration and decision-making. This lack of transparency can breed confusion, as stakeholders operate with incomplete information. Furthermore, it can lead to duplication of efforts, as agencies unknowingly pursue similar goals without knowledge of each other's initiatives. Ultimately, this information bottleneck hinders efficient responses to complex issues that often require coordinated efforts across multiple organizations.

## Confused Inter-Organizational Relationships

Another challenge is the presence of confused inter-organizational relationships, where roles and responsibilities are not clearly defined among different agencies (Hocevar, Jansen & Thomas, 2011). This ambiguity can result in overlapping mandates, conflicting actions, and difficulties in working towards common goals. This ambiguity can lead to overlapping mandates, where multiple agencies tackle similar issues without coordination. Furthermore, conflicting actions can occur if different agencies pursue their interpretations of their roles. Without clear boundaries and a shared understanding of responsibilities, collaboration becomes difficult, hindering progress towards common goals.

## Competing Roles and Responsibilities

Competing roles and responsibilities among various government entities pose a significant challenge to effective inter-governmental coordination (Hocevar, Jansen & Thomas, 2011). When agencies have conflicting objectives or priorities, it can impede collaboration efforts and hinder progress on shared initiatives. Conflicting objectives or priorities between agencies can lead to friction and impede progress on shared initiatives. Imagine two agencies tasked with rural development: one focused on economic growth and another on environmental conservation. Without clear boundaries, their efforts might clash, hindering overall progress. This lack of clarity around roles fosters confusion, and inefficiencies, and ultimately weakens collaborative efforts in addressing complex issues that often necessitate a unified approach across multiple government entities.

## Shortcomings in Leadership

Inadequate leadership within inter-governmental collaborations can also be a barrier to effective coordination and communication (Hocevar, Jansen & Thomas, 2011). Strong leadership is essential for guiding collaborative efforts, fostering trust among partners, and ensuring alignment towards common objectives. Without strong leadership, communication can break down, priorities can diverge, and overall progress can stall. Imagine a collaborative effort to address water quality, lacking a clear leader to navigate the different perspectives of environmental agencies, agricultural departments, and local communities. In such a scenario, the absence of strong leadership can hinder effective collaboration and prevent the achievement of shared goals.

## Resource Constraints

Resource constraints within government organizations can indeed create barriers to effective collaboration and communication. Limited funding, competing budget priorities, and resource shortages can significantly impact the ability of agencies to engage in collaborative initiatives effectively. This challenge highlights the importance of adequate financial resources and budget allocations to support inter-governmental coordination efforts and ensure the successful implementation of collaborative projects (Osei-Kojo, Bawole, J. Sakyi, E., 2020).

## Inadequate Communication Mechanisms

Poor communication mechanisms between government entities can indeed hinder coordination efforts, as highlighted in the provided sources (Alon-Barkat, 2020; Blumenthal, 2016). Effective communication channels are essential for sharing information, aligning strategies, and ensuring that all stakeholders are informed and engaged in collaborative endeavours. Ineffective communication can lead to confusion, duplication of efforts, contradictory messages, missed opportunities for collaboration, and overall inefficiencies in achieving common goals. This emphasizes the critical need for clear, consistent, transparent, and engaging communication within and between government agencies to facilitate effective coordination and collaboration.

Addressing these challenges requires a concerted effort to enhance information sharing, clarify roles and responsibilities, strengthen leadership capabilities, allocate resources effectively, and improve communication mechanisms among government agencies. By overcoming these obstacles, inter-governmental coordination, collaboration, and communication can be significantly enhanced to address complex issues more efficiently and effectively.

## IMPLICATIONS FOR POLICY AND PRACTICE

The literature review on intergovernmental coordination in rural governance in Zimbabwe highlights several practical implications for policymakers, practitioners, and stakeholders:

### For Policymakers

The review underscores the need for policies that promote information sharing, clarify roles and responsibilities, strengthen leadership, allocate resources effectively, and improve communication mechanisms among government agencies. Policies should aim to address the lack of inclusivity and stakeholder engagement in traditional governance models, promote adaptability and innovation, focus on shared goals and outcomes, and provide adequate conflict resolution mechanisms.

### For Practitioners

The review suggests that collaboration and communication are essential for effective rural governance. Practitioners should focus on building trust, shared goals, inclusivity, elite participation, communication, consensus decision-making, and successful collaboration models. Practical implications include the need for improved community participation in rural governance, streamlined governance procedures, and sustainable funding.

### For Stakeholders

The review emphasizes the importance of intergovernmental coordination for avoiding negative externalities, and conflicts, and promoting problem-solving and policy alignment. Stakeholders should prioritize trust-building, shared goals, inclusive processes, elite participation, communication, and consensus decision-making in rural governance. Collaborative governance offers solutions to overcome the limitations of traditional governance models in areas such as inclusivity, adaptability, shared goals, and conflict resolution.

The review paper presents practical implications for policymakers, practitioners, and stakeholders, focusing on the importance of intergovernmental coordination, collaboration, and communication for effective rural governance.

## CONCLUSION

Both central government organisations and local governments play a crucial role in supporting the successful implementation of rural development initiatives and activities. Donors and private organisations have played a crucial role in rural development, both before and following the country's independence in 1980 (Dzvimbo, Monga & Mashizha, 2017). The significance of intergovernmental coordination in facilitating collaboration and communication in rural governance in Zimbabwe is undeniable. It enables the alignment of efforts, pooling of resources, sharing of expertise, and ensures policies are tailored to local needs. The literature review has illuminated the historical evolution of Zimbabwe's rural governance, emphasizing the shift towards greater decentralization and devolution of powers. However, challenges related to political dynamics, economic constraints, and social traditions continue to pose barriers to effective coordination. The Rural District Development Committee (RDDC) serves as a vital platform for intergovernmental coordination at the district level, yet issues such as insufficient community participation and conflicting authorities need to be addressed. The insights provided by Ansell and Gash's collaborative governance model offer valuable guidance for enhancing intergovernmental collaboration in Zimbabwe's rural governance. The model emphasizes the importance of building trust, establishing shared goals, inclusive processes, elite participation, effective communication, and consensus decision-making.

In conclusion, intergovernmental coordination plays a critical role in facilitating collaboration and communication in rural governance in Zimbabwe. To overcome existing barriers, there is a need for enhanced information sharing, clarified roles, improved leadership, adequate resources, and better communication mechanisms. Leveraging the lessons from Ansell and Gash's model can significantly contribute to promoting effective intergovernmental collaboration. This holds immense potential for improving rural governance and development outcomes in Zimbabwe.

## Gaps in the Existing Literature That Warrant Further Research

*Impact of technological advancements*: While the challenges of information sharing and communication are highlighted, how can advancements in communication technologies and data sharing platforms be leveraged to improve collaboration?

*Long-term sustainability of collaborative efforts*: Much research focuses on the initial stages of collaboration. How can inter-governmental collaborations be structured to ensure long-term sustainability and continued effectiveness?

*Measuring the success of collaboration*: Existing literature often emphasizes process-oriented metrics. How can we develop robust frameworks to measure the actual impact and success of collaborative initiatives on the community?

*Role of power dynamics*: The literature acknowledges the challenges of competing priorities and roles, but how do existing power dynamics between different government entities influence collaboration efforts? How can these dynamics be navigated to ensure equitable participation and decision-making?

*Collaboration beyond government*: The focus has primarily been on collaboration between government agencies. How can we expand the framework to explore the role of non-governmental organizations, private sector actors, and community members in successful inter-governmental collaboration?

*Context-specific challenges and solutions*: While general challenges are identified, how do these challenges and potential solutions vary depending on factors like geographical location, cultural context, or the specific issue being addressed?

By exploring these gaps, researchers can contribute to a more comprehensive understanding of inter-governmental collaboration and its potential to address complex challenges.

## REFERENCES


Alon-Barkat, S. (2020). Can Government Public Communications Elicit Undue Trust? Exploring the Interaction between Symbols and Substantive Information in Communications. *Journal of Public Administration: Research and Theory*, 30(1), 77–95. 10.1093/jopart/muz013

Ansell, C., & Gash, A. (2008). Collaborative Governance in Theory and Practice. *Journal of Public Administration Research and Theory: J-PART*, 18(4), 543–571. https://www.jstor.org/stable/25096384. 10.1093/jopart/mum032

Ansell, C., & Gash, A. (2008). Collaborative Governance in Theory and Practice. *Journal of Public Administration: Research and Theory*, 18(4), 543–571. 10.1093/jopart/mum032

Bianchi, C., Nasi, G., & Rivenbark, W. C. (2021). Implementing collaborative governance: Models, experiences, and challenges. *Public Management Review*, 23(11), 1581–1589. 10.1080/14719037.2021.1878777

BTI. (2024). *Zimbabwe Country Report 2024*. BTI Transformation Index, Country Dashboard Zimbabwe. https://bti-project.org/en/reports/country-report/ZWE

Chakunda, E. (2018). Local governance in Zimbabwe: A review of literature. *Journal of Public Administration and Governance*, 8(2), 14–26.

Chakunda, V. (2018). *A Critical Analysis of The Dynamics of Intergovernmental Relations in Zimbabwe*. 10.4172/2332-0761.1000326

Chatiza, K. (2008). *Opportunities and challenges in institutionalising participatory development: the case of rural Zimbabwe.*

Chigwata, T. C., & Marumahoko, S. (2018). Intergovernmental planning and budgeting in Zimbabwe: learning the lessons of the past. *Commonwealth Journal of Local Governance, 20.* http://dx.doi.org/cjlg.v0i20.6140

Chigwata, T. C., & Marumahoko, S. 2018. Intergovernmental planning and budgeting in Zimbabwe: learning the lessons of the past. *Commonwealth Journal of Local Governance, 20,* 1-15. http://dx.doi.org/cjlg.v0i20.6140

Chigwata, T. C., & Marumahoko, S. (2018). *Intergovernmental planning and budgeting in Zimbabwe: learning the lessons of the past.* Commonwealth Journal of Local Governance. 10.5130/cjlg.v0i20.6140

Chiunye, T. M. (2018). *An Impact- assessment of the Rural District Council's Capacity Building Programme (RDCCBP) on organisational performance: the case of Chaminuka Rural District Council*. Shamva Administrative District.

Duvel, G. (1996). Institutional Linkages for Effective Coordination and Cooperation In Participative Rural Development. *Journal of International Agricultural and Extension Education*, 3(2), 3. 10.5191/jiaee.1996.03204

Dzvimbo, M. A., Monga, M., & Mashizha, T. M. (2017). The Link between Rural Institutions and Rural Development: Reflections on Smallholder Farmers and Donors in Zimbabwe. *IOSR Journal of Humanities and Social Science*, 22(6), 46–53. 10.9790/0837-2206064653

Emerson, K., Nabatchi, T., & Balogh, S. (2012). An Integrative Framework for Collaborative Governance. *Journal of Public Administration: Research and Theory*, 22(1), 1–29. https://www.jstor.org/stable/41342607. 10.1093/jopart/mur011

Helmsing, A. H. J. (1990). Transforming Rural Local Government: Zimbabwe's Postindependence Experience. *Environment and Planning. C, Government & Policy*, 8(1), 87–110. 10.1068/c080087

Hocevar, S. P., Jansen, E., & Thomas, G. F. (2011). Inter-Organizational Collaboration: Addressing the Challenge. *Homeland Security Affairs, 7*.https://www.hsaj.org/articles/64

Jachi, M., Makumbe, M., & Mandongwe, L. (2019). Public Procurement and Public Service Delivery in Zimbabwe Local Authorities. A Non-systematic Review. *Public Policy and Administration Research*. 10.7176/PPAR/9-12-05

Malinga, W., Moyo, P. M., Sikhosana, N., & Moyo, M. (2017). Decentralisation and Rural Development: Is it a Policy of Empowering or Disempowering Rural Communities in Zimbabwe? *International Journal of Innovative Research and Development*, 6(4). 10.24940/ijird/2017/v6/i4/APR17061

Mandaza, B. (2005). The State and the Crisis of Zimbabwean Nationalism. In Raftopoulos, B., & Muzondidya, A. (Eds.), *Becoming Zimbabwe: A History from the Pre-colonial Period to 2009* (pp. 277–292). Weaver Press.

Mandondo, A. (2000). Environmental policy and law in Zimbabwe: Issues and challenges. In Moyo, S., & Rosalie, P. S. (Eds.), *Zimbabwe's environment: Issues and policies* (pp. 95–110). University of Zimbabwe Publications.

Mandondo, A. (2001). Allocation of governmental authority and responsibility in Tiered governance regimes: The case of the Chivi Rural District Council land use planning and conservation by-laws. *African Studies Quarterly*, 5, 41–56.

Misi, J. (2014). *Donor Funding and Sustainable Rural Development and its Challenges in Zimbabwe; A Case Study of Mudzi District: 2000-2012*. Semantic Scholar.

Mudege, N. N., & Ansell, N. (2013). Women's representation in rural councils in Zimbabwe: The significance of local government structures. *Journal of International Women's Studies*, 14(2), 202–218.

Mudimu, G.T., Ting, Z., & Nalwimba, N. (2019). *Contested Terrain: Local Governance and Development in Post-Land Reform Zimbabwe.*

Nsingo, S. (2006). Assessing the performance of public sector institutions in Zimbabwe: a case study approach.

Nyakurukwa, K., & Seetharam, Y. (2022). *Corporate governance in a weak legal environment: a systematic review focusing on Zimbabwe*. Qualitative Research in Financial Markets.

Nyikadzino, T., & Vyas-Doorgapersad, S. (2022). Zimbabwe's transition to a devolved system of government: Critical factors for success. *Africa's Public Service Delivery and Performance Review*, 10(1), a604. 10.4102/apsdpr.v10i1.604

OECD. (2023). *Multi-level governance tools: Enabling sound regional governance*. OECD. https://www.oecd-ilibrary.org/sites/df3fa2fe-en/index.html?itemId=%2Fcontent%2Fcomponent%2Fdf3fa2fe-en# 3310.1007/s11115-019-00452-6

Peng, Y., Peng, X., Li, X., Lu, M., & Yin, M. (2023). Effectiveness in Rural Governance: Influencing Factors and Driving Pathways—Based on 20 Typical Cases of Rural Governance in China. *Land (Basel)*, 12(7), 1452. 10.3390/land12071452

Phillimore, J. (2013). Understanding Intergovernmental Relations: Key Features and Trends. *Australian Journal of Public Administration*, 72(3), 228–238. 10.1111/1467-8500.12025

Radin, B. A. (1992). Rural Development Councils: An Intergovernmental Coordination Experiment. *Publius*, 22(3), 111–127. https://www.jstor.org/stable/3330255

Raftopoulos, B., & Mhute, E. (2009). The Politics of Local Government in Zimbabwe. In Raftopoulos, B., & Muzondidya, A. (Eds.), *Reflections on Zimbabwe's Liberation War: Politics, economics and society* (pp. 243–268). Weaver Press.

Savage, A., Brune, S., Hovis, M., Spenser, S. E., Dinan, M., & Seekamp, E. (2023). *Working Together: A Guide to Collaboration in Rural Revitalization.* North Carolina State University. https://content.ces.ncsu.edu/show_ep3_pdf/1710596944/24402/

Schnabel, J., & Hegele, Y. (2021, June 15). Explaining Intergovernmental Coordination during the COVID-19 Pandemic: Responses in Australia, Canada, Germany, and Switzerland. *Publius*, 51(4), pjab011. 10.1093/publius/pjab011

Scoones, I. (2010). *Zimbabwe's land reform: Myths and realities*. James Currey.

Sharon, C., Faitira, M., & Zororo, M. (2023). *Local Authorities' Performance in Zimbabwe Systematic Review of Related Literature*. International Journal of Research in Commerce and Management Studies., 10.38193/IJRCMS.2023.5204

Such, E., Smith, K., Woods, H. B., & Meier, P. (2022). Governance of Intersectoral Collaborations for Population Health and to Reduce Health Inequalities in High-Income Countries: A Complexity-Informed Systematic Review. *International Journal of Health Policy and Management*, 11, 2780–2792. 10.34172/ijhpm.2022.655035219286

UCLG and OECD. (2016). *Zimbabwe Unitary Country*. OECD. https://www.oecd.org/regional/regional-policy/profile-Zimbabwe.pdf

US Department of State. (2022). *U.S. Relations With Zimbabwe. Bilateral Relations Fact Sheet, Bureau of African Affairs*. US DoS. https://www.state.gov/u-s-relations-with-zimbabwe/

Vincent, C. (2015). The Context of Inter-Governmental Relations in Zimbabwe. Reflections from the Constitution of Zimbabwe Amendment Number 20 Of 2013. *IOSR Journal of Humanities and Social Science (IOSR-JHSS), 20*(1), 37-41.

Vincent, C. (2017). *Central-local Government Relations*. Implications on the Autonomy and Discretion of Zimbabwe's Local Government.

Vungu Rural District Council. (2017). *About*. Rural District Development Committee (RDDC). http://www.vungurdc.org.zw/RDDC.html

Waardenburg, M., Groenleer, M., de Jong, J., & Keijser, B. (2020). Paradoxes of collaborative governance: Investigating the real-life dynamics of multi-agency collaborations using a quasi-experimental action-research approach. *Public Management Review*, 22(3), 386–407. 10.1080/14719037.2019.1599056

Zhou, S. (2000). *Understanding The Inter-Relationships for The Creation of a Local Land Information System: The Zimbabwean Local Government Experience at Growth Points*. University of Kwa-Zulu-Natal.

## ENDNOTES

1 Refer to the social capital by Putman 1993.

2 For more information relating to the U.S. Government and the Zimbabwean Economy, see the United States of America ZiDERA Act of 2001 on https://www.congress.gov/107/plaws/publ99/PLAW-107publ99.pdf?_gl=1*1j6hggf*_gcl_au*MTE5MTcxODIxLjE3MTA1OTU0NDY. It is the policy of the United States to support the people of Zimbabwe in their struggle to effect peaceful, democratic change, achieve broad-based and equitable economic growth, and restore the rule of law.

# Chapter 8
# Leveraging Spatial Data Infrastructure for Enhanced Municipal Planning: A Case Study of Pakistan

**Munir Ahmad**
https://orcid.org/0000-0003-4836-6151
*Survey of Pakistan, Pakistan*

**Asmat Ali**
https://orcid.org/0000-0002-8804-2285
*Survey of Pakistan, Pakistan*

**Hammad Hussain**
https://orcid.org/0009-0009-0552-2549
*COMSATS University Islamabad, Wah, Pakistan*

## ABSTRACT

*The significance of spatial data infrastructure (SDI) in municipal planning in Pakistan cannot be overstated, as it can plays a central role in reshaping urban development endeavors. By amalgamating a variety of geospatial datasets and fostering cooperation among government bodies and stakeholders, SDI can facilitate well-informed decision-making, streamlined resource allocation, and heightened citizen involvement. In grappling with obstacles such as procedural delays, insufficient coordination, and limited resources, SDI emerges as a comprehensive framework that tackles the multifaceted challenges of urbanization, transportation, and environmental sustainability. Furthermore, through its emphasis on transparency,*

DOI: 10.4018/979-8-3693-3617-5.ch008

*accountability, and citizen empowerment, SDI can ensure that planning endeavors are inclusive and attuned to the diverse needs of the populace.*

## INTRODUCTION

Pakistan's cities are growing fast, mirroring a global trend. Current planning solutions for Pakistan's cities are proving to be ineffective. ul Hussnain et al. (2020) argued that there is a need for a new process fusion of scenario planning and traditional planning, as 83% of urban settlements in Pakistan are growing without a spatial plan and require immediate attention. Pakistani cities have failed to develop and manage public transport systems for mobility, equity, and environmental sustainability, highlighting the importance of governance, capacity building, and urban planning (Imran, 2009). Lack of planning policies for small and medium agricultural industries in secondary cities, fiscal reliance on central government, and reliance on foreign aid are weaknesses in the Pakistani five-year plans for agricultural-based industrial development as noted by Kalwar et al. (2019). Implementation of peri-urban structure plans in Pakistan often leads to further urban sprawl, making it crucial to revise city master plans and identify zones for infill/high-density development (Nadeem et al., 2020).

Urbanization, especially in low- and middle-income countries of the global south, is leading to deteriorating urban centers and increased health issues. Explicit consideration of urban health in urban planning is crucial to address these challenges (Safwan, 2020). City planning can reduce non-communicable diseases and road trauma by encouraging walking, cycling, and public transport use while reducing private motor vehicle use (Giles-Corti et al., 2016). For example, urban planning in Lahore, Pakistan, contributes to increasing levels of urban segregation and inequality, reinforcing inequalities of access and exclusions (Cermeño, 2021). Some growth strategies in Lahore, Pakistan, were based on ground realities but could not be fully implemented due to administrative, fiscal, and enforcement issues, leading to inadvertent land use conversion and urban sprawl (Hussain & Nadeem, 2021). (Anwar (2014) explored the complexities of urban planning and community building in Karachi, Pakistan's largest city, focusing on its periphery, a previously rural area now being absorbed into the city.

Geographic Information Systems (GIS) significantly enhance municipal planning by providing a comprehensive platform for spatial analysis, data management, and decision-making. Through GIS, planners can integrate diverse datasets such as land use, infrastructure, demographics, and environmental factors, enabling them to visualize and understand complex spatial relationships. In developing countries, GIS can significantly improve spatial planning and decision-making processes

(Kucukpehlivan et al., 2023; Raihan, 2024; Waheeb et al., 2023). Similarly, Butt et al. (2016) proposed a web-based system using GIS to improve transparency in housing schemes in Lahore, Pakistan. The system allows people to access information about the legal status of housing schemes through a web interface.

Spatial Data Infrastructure (SDI) complements GIS by providing the infrastructure and standards for organizing, sharing, and accessing spatial data across different organizations and sectors. In the context of municipal planning, SDI facilitates data interoperability and collaboration among government agencies, private organizations, and the public. For example, the Fortaleza Municipal Finance Department (SEFIN) implemented an SDI with a tax focus between 2019 and 2020 to improve data sharing with other municipal entities. The SDI, based on INDE and ET-EDGV 3.0 and built on GeoServer, has led to benefits like improved data quality, accessibility, and decision-making, and SEFIN plans to further develop it as a model for other municipalities (Gimenes et al., 2024). Similarly, Poirier et al. (2024) argued that building data infrastructure for planning documents can improve transparency, public engagement, policy oversight, and local coordination by allowing users to search terms across plans, track policy adoption, identify best practices, and compare plans for effectiveness.

SDI stands as a pivotal framework globally, facilitating both e-governance and g-governance across a spectrum of government sectors. The advent of emerging technologies has sparked a revolution in SDI implementation (Ahmad, 2023; Ahmad, Ali, Nawaz, et al., 2024; Ahmad, Ali, Tin, et al., 2024; Ahmad et al., 2023; Ahmad & Ali, 2023b), amplifying its capacity to address the myriad challenges surrounding information governance (Ahmad, Ali, Mobo, et al., 2024). Notably, Pakistan is currently underway with national-level SDI implementation (Ahmad et al., 2022; Ahmad & Ali, 2023a; Ali et al., 2024), underscoring the relevance of testing SDI's applicability within the realm of municipal planning in the context of Pakistan. Against this backdrop, this study delineates its primary objectives as follows:

i. To scrutinize the implementation landscape of SDI in Pakistan.
ii. To delve into the ramifications of SDI on municipal planning within the Pakistani context.

In pursuit of these objectives, the chapter is structured as follows: Section 2 elucidates the conceptual framework of SDI and municipal planning. Subsequently, Section 3 illuminates the current state of SDI implementation in Pakistan. Section 4 delves into the pivotal role of SDI in shaping municipal planning in Pakistan. Lastly, the chapter concludes with a synthesis of key findings and recommendations tailored for policymakers and stakeholders.

## LITERATURE REVIEW

This section provides an overview of the key concepts involved in the chapter such as spatial data infrastructure and municipal planning.

### Spatial Data Infrastructure

The Spatial Data Infrastructure (SDI) is a comprehensive framework comprising institutional arrangements, policies, and technologies designed to enhance the accessibility and availability of spatial data and information (Diaz et al., 2012). It can be conceptualized as a collaborative endeavor aimed at facilitating easier access, wider dissemination, and more efficient utilization of spatial data for the collective benefit of society (Cetl et al., 2009). Furthermore, SDI promotes interoperability not only among different regions but also between provinces, states, and countries, serving as a conduit linking socioeconomic, environmental, and institutional databases (Coleman & Nebert, 1998). This interconnectedness is vital for establishing a national spatial data infrastructure, ensuring smoother access to information resources and services for organizations, government bodies, and the public.

As SDI has progressed, it has transitioned from being a second-generation service-oriented system to a third-generation user-centric system, with a focal point on facilitating geospatial data exchange and access within its information architecture (Granell et al., 2011). This evolution aligns with the objective of facilitating and coordinating the flow of spatial data across stakeholders in the spatial data community, thus supporting decision-making processes across various governmental jurisdictions (Rajabifard et al., 2002, 2006). According to (Nedović-Budić et al., 2011), SDIs are pivotal in addressing challenges related to data policy, technological standards, and integration. By enhancing the affordability, accessibility, and interoperability of spatial data, SDI plays a crucial role in overcoming barriers within the spatial data industry. Consequently, the sharing of spatial data remains the central narrative focus for spatial data infrastructures (Crompvoets et al., 2018; Masser, 2019).

### Benefits of SDI

SDI facilitates access to accurate and up-to-date spatial data, thereby enhancing decision-making processes significantly. Across various domains such as education, public health, disaster management, agriculture, and land management, SDI aids decision-makers in making informed assessments (Manfré et al., 2012). SDI enables decision-makers to discern connections and patterns that might otherwise go unnoticed, as illustrated by Boerboom (2010). For instance, in the event of a natural disaster like an earthquake, SDI can swiftly and accurately inform policymakers about affected areas, enabling them to make informed decisions that enhance response and recovery efforts (Manfré et al., 2012).

Organizations can realize substantial savings through the adoption of SDI, as it eliminates redundant activities and resources associated with data collection, maintenance, and dissemination, leading to significant cost reductions (Bishop et al., 2000). Web-based portals and services that share spatial datasets contribute to cost savings by reducing expenses related to data acquisition and maintenance, as well as the management of multiple data sources (Borzacchiello & Craglia, 2013). These cost savings free up resources for other activities such as data analysis and decision-making, providing additional benefits to organizations leveraging SDI.

SDI also enhances efficiency by streamlining data management and sharing processes, thereby reducing administrative burdens and facilitating faster and improved data processing (Borzacchiello & Craglia, 2013). Through the adoption of standardized data models and metadata, SDI automates tasks such as data discovery, validation, and integration, resulting in significant time and energy savings in spatial data management (Crompvoets et al., 2011). This enhances organizational efficiency and enables prompt responses to market changes.

Moreover, SDI can foster cooperation among various entities, including public-private sector corporations, government agencies, and the general public. Beyond facilitating public engagement and interaction processes, SDI promotes accountability and transparency through a shared platform for information exchange and collaboration (Bishop et al., 2000; Crompvoets et al., 2011). For example, through participatory mapping techniques and crowdsourcing, SDIs empower citizens to actively participate in the collection and analysis of geographic information necessary for the policymaking process or decision support systems.

## Municipal Planning

Municipal planning refers to the process of designing, regulating, and managing the physical, social, and economic development of a municipality or local government area. It involves making decisions about land use, transportation, infrastructure, zoning regulations, housing, environmental protection, and other aspects of urban and regional development. Municipal strategic planning can be a public policy instrument for local and regional development, influenced by factors such as financial resources, citizens' demands, and political dynamics (Guamba, 2016). The primary goal of municipal planning is to ensure that communities are developed and managed in a sustainable and equitable manner, taking into account the needs and aspirations of residents, businesses, and other stakeholders. This typically involves comprehensive analysis, community engagement, and collaboration between various government agencies, private sector entities, and community groups.

Municipal planning as a strategic tool can improve integration practices by strengthening administrative and political foundations, involving more partners, and addressing issues like lack of intersectoral collaboration and employee engagement (Busengdal, 2022). Delmastro et al. (2016) noted that key constraints in urban underground planning include land use constraints, infrastructure limitations, and the need for suitable local conditions for building. Similarly, Guyadeen et al. (2023) noted that municipal strategic plans in Ontario, Canada lack in many areas including a comprehensive fact base, clear goals, and provisions for monitoring and evaluation. Dring et al. (2023) argued that municipal governments in British Columbia, Canada can create separate agricultural plans to complement their official community plans.

Abubakari et al. (2023) highlighted that inner-city development in Germany offers valuable lessons for developing countries aiming for sustainable urban growth. The authors emphasized Germany's success in revitalizing its inner cities and highlighted strong commitment, comprehensive planning, and contextual sensitivity as key factors for achieving this. They argued that this approach can inform planning strategies in developing countries facing the challenge of accommodating a growing urban population. Similarly, Morato (2022) illustrated the intricate interplay between municipal planning, metropolitan governance, and the development of high-rise neighborhoods in Greater London, revealing both opportunities and challenges in shaping urban landscapes. The author argued that municipal planning in London faces challenges in addressing the housing crisis and shaping high-rise neighborhoods, revealing the limitations of local government in metropolitan governance. The role of municipal planning in delivering a built environment supportive of residents' quality of life is explored, along with the influence of structural and strategic issues of metropolitan governance.

Moreover, Amlaev & Karabakhtsyan (2022) examined how city planning, focusing on the design of built environments and the sustainable use of resources, can be used to create healthier cities for residents. Reinar & Lundberg (2023) noted that Norwegian municipalities translate SDGs into local action plans through a process involving planners, government officials, and sometimes politicians. They focus on SDGs where they can make a difference, often aligning them with existing policies, and prioritize health, education, and cities/communities. Similarly, Wester (2022), tested a new decision-making tool for municipalities to address climate change adaptation by embracing uncertainty, incorporating bottom-up approaches, and designing adaptive measures. They argued that challenges emerged including potential burden on staff, limitations in interdepartmental collaboration, and political resistance due to short-term priorities. Even well-designed tools may not be valuable if not used by decision-makers, so tailoring approaches to specific municipal contexts is crucial.

## METHODOLOGY

This chapter utilizes the qualitative case study approach as a means to examine and analyze the intricate National Spatial Data Infrastructure (NSDI) system in Pakistan. Employing the case study approach allows researchers to delve deeply into the complexities of the NSDI and gain a thorough understanding of its functioning within a specific context (Tasci et al., 2020). By focusing on individual cases, this approach provides valuable insights into particular situations. In this chapter, the application of the case study approach facilitates an in-depth exploration of the implementation of SDI in Pakistan at the national level. Furthermore, it seeks to examine the role of SDI in municipal planning within the Pakistani context.

## STATUS OF SDI IN PAKISTAN

This section delves into the present state of affairs regarding the establishment of the National Spatial Data Infrastructure (NSDI) in Pakistan, outlining several ongoing activities elaborated upon in subsequent paragraphs.

Currently, a feasibility study is underway to lay the groundwork for the establishment of a National Spatial Data Infrastructure in Pakistan. The primary aim of this feasibility study is to assess and document the available financial, legal, technical, and human resources necessary for the project's realization. Additionally, the feasibility study tackles issues concerning governance structure, management frameworks, financial and business models, as well as the design of the NSDI secretariat. Data for numerous analyses within the feasibility study have been derived from research conducted through workshops, surveys, and meetings. For instance, a workshop convened at COMSATS University Islamabad explored various aspects of the Pakistan National Spatial Data Infrastructure.

It is anticipated that the benefits derived from the National Spatial Data Infrastructure will extend beyond mere upgrades to cadastral systems. This is particularly significant in the realm of effective agricultural policy-making, as emphasized by Ali & Imran (2021). Notably, the PULSE (Punjab Urban Land Systems Enhancement) Project initiated by PLRA Punjab Pakistan aims to enhance and regulate land management in the Province of Punjab. A pivotal component of this project involves the development of a provincial SDI with land administration and management at its core.

The active involvement of stakeholders is integral to the success of any Spatial Data Infrastructure. To foster collaboration among various stakeholders in guiding the implementation of Pakistan's NSDI, a coordination committee has been established by the Survey of Pakistan. This committee is currently tasked with spearheading the creation and development of the country's NSDI.

## CHALLENGES OF MUNICIPAL PLANNING IN PAKISTAN

This section explores the various challenges of municipal planning in Pakistan. This section reviews the relevant literature to identify various challenges. These challenges are summarized in Figure 1.

Rizwan & Obaidullah (2006) studies various master plans related to Lahore Pakistan such as "Master Plan for Greater Lahore – 1966", "Lahore Urban Development and Traffic Study –1980" and "Integrated Master Plan for Lahore–2021 " and noted challenges in implementing urban master plans such as significant delays in planning and approval processes, an ineffective institutional framework, inadequate interdepartmental coordination within the government, constrained financial resources, legal shortcomings, inadequate distribution of plans, and lack of political commitment. Javed & Farhan (2020) identified a lack of a well-equipped governance system with expertise in various sectors, poor legislative arrangements to clarify the division of power between provincial and local governments, and inadequacy of public sector services to respond to the requirements of a fast-expanding urban economy as the main challenges of urban planning in Pakistan.

Ahmed (2008) asserted that Karachi's strategic development plan 2020 poses challenges to city planners due to a lack of planning guidelines in the development of large-scale real estate projects, mega transportation projects, major initiatives for landscape development, and rapid conversion or demolition of heritage sites. The authors argued that nearly all projects are announced spontaneously without consideration for existing or historical urban planning principles. Urban planners in Pakistan face challenges in coordinating with various planning departments and addressing issues related to housing, transportation, and sustainable development as argued by Nawaz & Tahir (2022). Whereas, Hussnain et al. (2020) argued that digital planning tools can enhance peri-urban spatial planning in Pakistan, but very low familiarity of urban planners with the digital planning tools and user acceptance are the main barriers. Similarly, inconsistent legal and regulatory frameworks, as well as institutional capacities of local planning agencies in Pakistan, affect the implementation of development plans as noted by Ahmad & Anjum (2012). Shaukat et al. (2019) argued that mismanaged solid municipal waste is a challenge and the main cause of environmental pollution in Pakistan and proposed an IoT-based model for efficient and intelligent management of municipal solid waste. Moreover, the poor state of municipal services and infrastructure in Pakistan is due to a checkered history of local government initiatives and urbanization pressure as noted by (Haider & Badami, 2010).

Barriers to effective implementation of water planning, governance, and management in Karachi and Lahore, Pakistan, continue to impose significant costs on these cities. Despite facing water scarcity, poor quality, and rising demand, Lahore and Karachi can improve their water security through better data collection, stronger governance, water conservation measures, improved infrastructure, and wastewater treatment as asserted by Syvrud et al. (2021). Whereas, Khan et al. (2023) elaborated that investments in water systems within South Asian megacities like Lahore and Karachi are prompted by the perceived gap between water supply and demand. Yet, assessments of water demand in these cities frequently overlook local socioeconomic and demographic factors and fail to consider seasonal fluctuations. Similarly, Irfan et al. (2018) noted that Karachi faces a severe water scarcity problem due to rapid urbanization, climate change, and population growth, requiring a comprehensive city development master plan to address water sector challenges.

Pakistan lacks inclusive and resilient land-use planning policies to protect inhabitants and ecosystems from climatic hazards. Rayan et al. (2021) identified several sustainable urban green infrastructure planning indicators with an increased percentage of green surface, planting higher concentration of trees, optimizing green energy saving techniques, and reducing the risk of flood damages, being the most important indicators. Whereas, Abbas et al. (2023) asserted that lack of institutional capacity, coordination, outdated rules, poorly perceived implementation of motorization policy, and knee-jerk approaches for transportation planning are challenges to sustainable transportation in Lahore, Pakistan.

Challenges of municipal planning in Pakistan include a lack of integrated urban development policies, unchecked urban growth, overlapping jurisdictions of land governing authorities, and ineffective building control (Rana & Bhatti, 2018). Green spaces in Gujrat city face challenges such as infrastructure development, lack of planning, and budget, but their addition is essential for improved urban growth, economy, and environmental engagement (Anwar et al., 2021). Waste collection inefficiency is a major problem in low-income countries like Pakistan. Waste management can improve a country's economy by reducing reliance on foreign oil and fertilizer. Community involvement and education are key to successful waste management (Iqbal et al., 2022). The authors proposed a new model for waste management to improve service delivery and material recovery facilities.

Pakistan's urbanization is haphazard and informal, with cities lacking adequate basic infrastructure and existing policies unable to cope with growing challenges (Javed et al., 2020). Demand-side information about household preferences and priorities can provide valuable input into municipal planning in Pakistan (Altaf, 1994). Efficient solid waste management systems, informed by the waste amount and characterization studies, are essential for sustainable infrastructure planning in intermediate cities of Pakistan. K. Nadeem et al. (2023) argued that more than 80% of valuable materials are salvaged by the informal sector during waste transfer. Non-scientific waste disposal methods currently result in significant GHG emissions, which could be mitigated by implementing the proposed MSF and composting practices. Nawaz et al. (2021) highlighted the need for stakeholders, including residents, municipalities, and waste pickers, to collaborate under clear regulations to create a trusting and efficient waste management system. The authors asserted that waste management in Pakistan is a complex issue requiring better integration, recognition of the informal sector, and continued research to find lasting solutions.

*Figure 1. Challenges of municipal planning in Pakistan*

## ROLE OF SDI FOR MUNICIPAL PLANNING

Spatial Data Infrastructure for municipal planning in Pakistan holds immense potential for transforming urban development processes. By integrating diverse geospatial datasets and facilitating collaboration among government agencies and stakeholders, SDI can enable informed decision-making, efficient resource management, and enhanced citizen engagement. Through access to up-to-date spatial information, urban planners can identify areas of priority, optimize infrastructure development, and address pressing challenges such as urbanization, transportation, and environmental sustainability. Moreover, SDI can enhance transparency and accountability in governance by empowering citizens to participate in planning processes and contribute valuable data. Based on the identified challenges in the previous section, Table 1 shows how SDI can particularly address these challenges.

*Table 1. Role of SDI for municipal planning in Pakistan*

| Challenges in Municipal Planning | How SDI Address these Challenges |
|---|---|
| Delays in planning and approval processes | SDI can facilitate data sharing and collaboration among departments, speeding up the planning process and reducing bureaucratic hurdles. |
| Ineffective institutional framework | SDI can promote better coordination and communication among institutions, leading to more streamlined decision-making and implementation. |
| Inadequate interdepartmental coordination | SDI can provide a common platform for sharing spatial data, fostering better coordination and integration of efforts across departments. |
| Constrained financial resources | SDI can enable more efficient resource allocation by providing data-driven insights into infrastructure needs and investment priorities. |
| Poor legislative arrangement | SDI can support evidence-based policy-making by providing spatial analysis to inform legislative reforms and improve regulatory frameworks. |
| Inadequate distribution of plans | SDI can facilitate the dissemination of planning documents and maps, ensuring wider access and transparency in the planning process. |
| Lack of political commitment | SDI can increase accountability by providing transparent data on planning decisions, encouraging greater political engagement and commitment. |
| Lack of well-equipped governance system | SDI can strengthen governance by providing tools for better management of spatial data, improving decision-making processes and outcomes. |
| Inadequate public sector services | SDI can enhance public sector services by enabling better planning and optimization of service delivery through spatial analysis and visualization. |
| Lack of planning guidelines | SDI can help develop comprehensive planning guidelines by providing data-driven insights into land use, zoning, and infrastructure needs. |
| Spontaneous project announcements | SDI can promote informed decision-making by providing data on existing infrastructure and development plans, reducing ad-hoc project announcements. |
| Low familiarity of Digital Planning Tools | SDI training programs can improve the skills of planners in using digital tools, enhancing their effectiveness and efficiency in planning processes. |
| Overlooked local factors in assessments | SDI can ensure comprehensive data collection and analysis, including local factors, leading to more accurate and context-specific planning assessments. |
| Lack of capacity | SDI can build capacity by providing training and technical support in spatial data management and analysis, empowering planners to make better decisions. |

continued on following page

*Table 1. Continued*

| Challenges in Municipal Planning | How SDI Address these Challenges |
|---|---|
| Outdated rules and implementation | SDI can support policy reform and implementation by providing data to identify gaps and inefficiencies in existing regulations and enforcement practices. |
| Lack of integrated policies | SDI can promote integrated planning by providing a holistic view of spatial data, facilitating coordination among sectors and alignment of policies. |
| Unchecked urban growth | SDI can enable better monitoring and management of urban growth by providing data on population trends, land use changes, and infrastructure development. |
| Overlapping jurisdictions | SDI can promote coordination among jurisdictions by providing a common platform for sharing spatial data and facilitating joint planning efforts. |
| Lack of community involvement | SDI can enhance community involvement by providing tools for public participation, such as interactive maps and online forums, in the planning process. |

From the Table, it is clear that SDI can play a crucial role in addressing various challenges in municipal planning by providing data-driven insights, facilitating collaboration and coordination, and promoting transparency and accountability in decision-making processes such as prioritizing infrastructure projects, allocating resources efficiently, supporting emergency response planning or helping environmental impact assessments.

## CONCLUSION

The role of Spatial Data Infrastructure for municipal planning in Pakistan is pivotal in transforming urban development processes. Through the integration of diverse geospatial datasets and the facilitation of collaboration among government agencies and stakeholders, SDI can enable informed decision-making, efficient resource management, and enhanced citizen engagement. By addressing challenges such as delays in planning processes, inadequate coordination, and constrained resources, SDI can offer a comprehensive solution framework for addressing the complexities of urbanization, transportation, and environmental sustainability. Moreover, by promoting transparency and accountability in governance and empowering citizen participation, SDI can ensure that planning processes are inclusive and responsive to the needs of the community.

Future work in the implementation of Spatial Data Infrastructure in Pakistan's municipal planning should can focus on several key areas. Firstly, there is a need for ongoing research and development to enhance the technical capabilities of SDI platforms, including improving data quality, interoperability, and accessibility. Secondly, efforts should be made to expand the scope of SDI beyond traditional planning domains to address emerging challenges such as climate change adaptation, disaster risk management, and smart city initiatives. Additionally, there is a need for capacity-building initiatives to ensure that planners and decision-makers have the necessary skills and knowledge to effectively utilize SDI tools and technologies. Furthermore, fostering collaboration and partnerships among government agencies, academic institutions, and the private sector will be essential to leverage resources and expertise for SDI implementation and innovation.

## REFERENCES


Abbas, Z., Aziz, A., & Hameed, R. (2023). *Toward Sustainable Urban Transportation: Examining the Potential of Transport Departments in Lahore, Pakistan*. SAE Technical Papers. 10.4271/2023-01-5074

Abubakari, M., Hussain, J., Arhin, P., Paul, B. N., & Uwayisenga, V. (2023). Inner-city development experiences of Germany: Lessons for Pakistan, Ghana, Kenya, and Rwanda in urban development. In *Cogent Social Sciences, 9*(2). 10.1080/23311886.2023.2282487

Ahmad, M. (2023). Leveraging Blockchain for Spatial Data Infrastructure: Challenges and Opportunities. *Supporting Technologies and the Impact of Blockchain on Organizations and Society*, 177–194. 10.4018/978-1-6684-5747-4.ch011

Ahmad, M., & Ali, A. (2023a). A Review of Governance Frameworks for National Spatial Data Infrastructure. In Correia, A., & Agua, P. B. (Eds.), *Innovation, Strategy, and Transformation Frameworks for the Modern Enterprise* (pp. 186–207). IGI Global. 10.4018/979-8-3693-0458-7.ch008

Ahmad, M., & Ali, A. (2023b). Integrated Geospatial Information Management in the World of Metaverse. In Lekhi, P., & Kaur, G. (Eds.), *Concepts, Technologies, Challenges, and the Future of Web 3* (pp. 248–270). IGI Global. 10.4018/978-1-6684-9919-1.ch013

Ahmad, M., Ali, A., & Khiyal, M. S. H. (2023). Fog Computing for Spatial Data Infrastructure: Challenges and Opportunities. In D. P. Acharjya & K. Ahmed P. (Eds.), *Multi-Disciplinary Applications of Fog Computing: Responsiveness in Real-Time* (pp. 152–178). IGI Global. 10.4018/978-1-6684-4466-5.ch008

Ahmad, M., Ali, A., Mobo, F. D., & Hussain, H. (2024). *Spatial Data Infrastructure for Information Governance: The Case Study From Pakistan*. Research Gate. https://doi.org/10.4018/979-8-3693-0472-3.ch011

Ahmad, M., Ali, A., Nawaz, H., Arslan, M., & Kumar, N. (2024). Optimizing Integrated Spatial Data Management Through Fog Computing: A Comprehensive Overview. In Prakasha, G. S., Lapina, M., Balakrishnan, D., & Sajid, M. (Eds.), *Digital Technologies in Modeling and Management: Insights in Education and Industry* (pp. 263–283). IGI Global. doi.org/10.4018/978-1-6684-9576-6.ch013

Ahmad, M., Ali, A., Tin, T. T., & Ali, A. (2024). Harnessing the Power of Geospatial Data: The Convergence of SDI, Big Data, and Cloud Computing. In Darwish, D. (Ed.), *Emerging Trends in Cloud Computing Analytics, Scalability, and Service Models* (pp. 312–330). IGI Global. 10.4018/979-8-3693-0900-1.ch016

Ahmad, M., Khayal, M. S. H., & Tahir, A. (2022). Analysis of Factors Affecting Adoption of Volunteered Geographic Information in the Context of National Spatial Data Infrastructure. *ISPRS International Journal of Geo-Information*, 11(2), 120. 10.3390/ijgi11020120

Ahmad, N., & Anjum, G. A. (2012). Legal and institutional perplexities hampering the implementation of urban development plans in Pakistan. *Cities (London, England)*, 29(4), 271–277. 10.1016/j.cities.2011.07.006

Ahmed, N. (2008). Karachi in 2020: Approaching planning as a project. *Proceedings of the Institution of Civil Engineers. Urban Design and Planning*, 161(3), 123–129. 10.1680/udap.2008.161.3.123

Ali, A., Ahmad, M., Nawaz, M., & Sattar, F. (2024). Spatial data infrastructure as the means to assemble geographic information necessary for effective agricultural policies in Pakistan. *Information Development*, 02666669241244503, 02666669241244503. 10.1177/02666669241244503

Ali, A., & Imran, M. (2021). National Spatial Data Infrastructure vs. Cadastre System for Economic Development: Evidence from Pakistan. *Land (Basel)*, 10(2), 188. 10.3390/land10020188

Altaf, M. A. (1994). Household demand for improved water and sanitation in a large secondary city. Findings from a study in Gujranwala, Pakistan. *Habitat International*, 18(1), 45–55. 10.1016/0197-3975(94)90038-8

Amlaev, K. R., & Karabakhtsyan, G. A. (2022). The municipal planning for the benefit of health. *Problemy Sotsial'noi Gigieny. Problemy Sotsial'Noi Gigieny i Istoriia Meditsiny*, 30(2). 10.32687/0869-866X-2022-30-2-244-24635439383

Anwar, M. M., Fayyaz, F., Aziz, A., & Mahmood, M. R. (2021). Socio-Ecological and Ethical Economic Demand of Urban Parks in Gujrat City, Punjab, Pakistan. *Arid Ecosystems*, 11(2), 141–148. 10.1134/S2079096121020037

Anwar, N. H. (2014). Urban transformations: Brokers, collaborative governance and community building in Karachi's periphery. *South Asian History and Culture*, 5(1), 75–92. 10.1080/19472498.2013.863011

Bishop, I. D., Escobar, F. J., Karuppannan, S., Williamson, I. P., Yates, P. M., Suwarnarat, K., & Yaqub, H. W. (2000). Spatial data infrastructures for cities in developing countries. Lessons from the Bangkok experience. *Cities (London, England)*, 17(2), 85–96. 10.1016/S0264-2751(00)00004-4

Boerboom, I. (2010). Integrating spatial planning and decision support system infrastructure and spatial data infrastructure. *GSDI 12 World Conference Singapore*. http://www.gsdi.org/gsdiconf/gsdi12/papers/82.pdf

Borzacchiello, M. T., & Craglia, M. (2013). Estimating benefits of spatial data infrastructures: A case study on e-Cadastres. *Computers, Environment and Urban Systems*, 41, 276–288. 10.1016/j.compenvurbsys.2012.05.004

Busengdal, E. (2022). Prioritising Integration of Refugees in Municipal Planning at a Local Political Level. *Scandinavian Journal of Public Administration*, 26(4), 3–17. 10.58235/sjpa.v26i4.10576

Butt, M. A., Li, S., & Javed, N. (2016). Towards Co-PPGIS—a collaborative public participatory GIS-based measure for transparency in housing schemes: A case of Lahore, Pakistan. *Applied Geomatics*, 8(1), 27–40. 10.1007/s12518-015-0160-5

Cermeño, H. (2021). Living and planning on the edge: Unravelling conflict and claim-making in peri-urban lahore, pakistan. *Urban Planning*, 6(2), 189–201. 10.17645/up.v6i2.3858

Cetl, V., Ivić, S. M., & Tomić, H. (2009). Improvement of national spatial data infrastructure as a public project of permanent character. *Kartografija i Geoinformacije, 8*(11).

Coleman, D. J., & Nebert, D. D. (1998). Building a North American Spatial Data Infrastructure. *Cartography and Geographic Information Systems*, 25(3), 151–160. 10.1559/152304098782383098

Crompvoets, J., Vancauwenberghe, G., Bouckaert, G., & Vandenbroucke, D. (2011). Practices to develop spatial data infrastructures: Exploring the contribution to e-government. In *Practical Studies in E-Government*. Best Practices from Around the World. 10.1007/978-1-4419-7533-1_13

Crompvoets, J., Vancauwenberghe, G., Ho, S., Masser, I., & Timo De Vries, W. (2018). Governance of national spatial data infrastructures in Europe. *International Journal of Spatial Data Infrastructures Research*, 13, 253–285.

Delmastro, C., Lavagno, E., & Schranz, L. (2016). Underground urbanism: Master Plans and Sectorial Plans. *Tunnelling and Underground Space Technology*, 55, 103–111. 10.1016/j.tust.2016.01.001

Diaz, L., Remke, A., Kauppinen, T., Degbelo, A., Foerster, T., Stasch, C., Rieke, M., Schaeffer, B., Baranski, B., Bröring, A., & Wytzisk, A. (2012). Future SDI - Impulses from Geoinformatics research and IT trends. *International Journal of Spatial Data Infrastructures Research*, 7. 10.2902/1725-0463.2012.07.art18

Dring, C. C., Newman, L., & Wittman, H. (2023). Assessing governability of agricultural systems: Municipal agricultural planning in Metro Vancouver, Canada. *Frontiers in Sustainable Food Systems*, 6, 855684. 10.3389/fsufs.2022.855684

Giles-Corti, B., Vernez-Moudon, A., Reis, R., Turrell, G., Dannenberg, A. L., Badland, H., Foster, S., Lowe, M., Sallis, J. F., Stevenson, M., & Owen, N. (2016). City planning and population health: a global challenge. In *The Lancet* (Vol. 388, Issue 10062). 10.1016/S0140-6736(16)30066-6

Gimenes, F. de S. F., De Oliveira, A. A. F., Noberto, L. V. V., Sabino, C. W. C., & Cavalcante, J. R. V. (2024). The experience of the Municipal Finance Department of Fortaleza in implementing spatial data infrastructure as an integrated management tool for the real estate registry. *CONTRIBUCIONES A LAS CIENCIAS SOCIALES, 17*(2). 10.55905/revconv.17n.2-055

Granell, C., Schade, S., & Hobona, G. (2011). Linked Data: Connecting Spatial Data Infrastructures and Volunteered Geographic Information. In *Geospatial Web Services: Advances in Information Interoperability*.

Guamba, J. M. E. (2016). Municipal Management in a Systemic Perspective. *International Journal of Management*. 10.18535/ijmei/v2i9.03

Guyadeen, D., Henstra, D., Kaup, S., & Wright, G. (2023). Evaluating the quality of municipal strategic plans. *Evaluation and Program Planning*, 96, 102186. 10.1016/j.evalprogplan.2022.10218636410094

Haider, M., & Badami, M. G. (2010). Urbanization and Local Governance Challenges in Pakistan. *Environment & Urbanization Asia*, 1(1), 81–96. 10.1177/097542530900100107

Hussain, Z., & Nadeem, O. (2021). The nexus between growth strategies of master plans and spatial dynamics of a metropolitan city: The case of Lahore, Pakistan. *Land Use Policy*, 109, 105609. 10.1016/j.landusepol.2021.105609

Hussnain, M. Q., Waheed, A., Anjum, G. A., Naeem, M. A., Hussain, E., Wakil, K., & Pettit, C. J. (2020). A framework to bridge digital planning tools' utilization gap in peri-urban spatial planning; lessons from Pakistan. *Computers, Environment and Urban Systems*, 80, 101451. 10.1016/j.compenvurbsys.2019.101451

Imran, M. (2009). Public transport in Pakistan: A critical overview. *Journal of Public Transportation*, 12(2), 53–83. 10.5038/2375-0901.12.2.4

Iqbal, A., Yasar, A., Nizami, A. S., Haider, R., Sharif, F., Sultan, I. A., Tabinda, A. B., Kedwaii, A. A., & Chaudhary, M. M. (2022). Municipal Solid Waste Collection and Haulage Modeling Design for Lahore, Pakistan: Transition toward Sustainability and Circular Economy. *Sustainability (Basel)*, 14(23), 16234. 10.3390/su142316234

Irfan, M., Kazmi, S. J. H., & Arsalan, M. H. (2018). Sustainable harnessing of the surface water resources for Karachi: A geographic review. *Arabian Journal of Geosciences*, 11(2), 24. 10.1007/s12517-017-3365-6

Javed, N., & Farhan, K. (2020). Access to urban services for political and social inclusion in Pakistan. In *Advances in 21st Century Human Settlements*. Springer. 10.1007/978-981-15-2973-3_10

Javed, N., Hasan, R., & Qureshi, N. N. (2020). Developing a National Urban Policy: A Case Study of Pakistan. In *Developing National Urban Policies*. Springer. 10.1007/978-981-15-3738-7_5

Kalwar, S., Sahito, N., Memon, I. A., Hwang, J., Mangi, M. Y., & Lashari, Z. A. (2019). National Planning Strategies for Agro-based Industrial Development in Secondary Cities of Sindh Province, Pakistan. *Sustainability (Basel)*, 11(24), 7066. 10.3390/su11247066

Khan, H. F., Arif, M. A., Intikhab, S., & Arshad, S. A. (2023). Quantifying Household Water Use and Its Determinants in Low-Income, Water-Scarce Households in Karachi. *Water (Basel)*, 15(19), 3400. 10.3390/w15193400

Kucukpehlivan, T., Cetin, M., Aksoy, T., Senyel Kurkcuoglu, M. A., Cabuk, S. N., Isik Pekkan, O., Dabanli, A., & Cabuk, A. (2023). Determination of the impacts of urban-planning of the urban land area using GIS hotspot analysis. *Computers and Electronics in Agriculture*, 210, 107935. 10.1016/j.compag.2023.107935

Manfré, L., Hirata, E., Silva, J. B., Shinohara, E. J., Giannotti, M., Larocca, A. P. C., & Quintanilha, J. (2012). An Analysis of Geospatial Technologies for Risk and Natural Disaster Management. *ISPRS International Journal of Geo-Information*, 1(2), 166–185. 10.3390/ijgi1020166

Masser, I. (2019). Geographic Information Systems to Spatial Data Infrastructure. In *Geographic Information Systems to Spatial Data Infrastructure*. Taylor & Francis. 10.1201/9780429505904

Morato, L. C. (2022). Opportunities and Challenges of Municipal Planning in Shaping Vertical Neighbourhoods in Greater London. *Urban Planning*, 7(4). 10.17645/up.v7i4.5757

Nadeem, K., Shahzad, S., Hassan, A., Usman Younus, M., Asad Ali Gillani, S., & Farhan, K. (2023). Municipal solid waste generation and its compositional assessment for efficient and sustainable infrastructure planning in an intermediate city of Pakistan. *Environmental Technology*, 44(21), 3196–3214. Advance online publication. 10.1080/09593330.2022.205437035302920

Nadeem, O., Hameed, R., & Afzal, M. (2020). Is peri-urban structure plan likely to be a viable approach to manage development in urban peripheries?–Case studies from Punjab, Pakistan. *Pakistan Journal of Engineering and Applied Sciences.*

Nawaz, M., & Tahir, Z. (2022). Roles and Responsibilities of Urban Planners to Address the Issues of Built-up areas in Pakistan. *Global Sociological Review*, VII(I), 9–15. 10.31703/gsr.2022(VII-I).02

Nawaz, M., Yousafzai, M. T., Khan, S., Ahmad, W., Salman, M., Han, H., Ariza-Montes, A., & Vega-Muñoz, A. (2021). Assessing the formal and informal waste recycling business processes through a stakeholders lens in Pakistan. *Sustainability (Basel)*, 13(21), 11717. 10.3390/su132111717

Nedović-Budić, Z., Crompvoets, J., & Georgiadou, Y. (2011). Spatial data infrastructures in context: North and South. In *Spatial Data Infrastructures in Context*. North and South. 10.1201/b10857

Poirier, L., Antonio, D., Dettmann, M., Eng, T., Ganata, J., Ghosh, S., Lopez, M., Karma, R., Natekal, A., & Brinkley, C. (2024). Making plans findable, accessible, interoperable, and reusable with data infrastructure: A search engine for constructing, analyzing, and visualizing planning documents. *Environment and Planning. B, Urban Analytics and City Science*, 23998083241227471. 10.1177/23998083241227471

Raihan, A. (2024). A Systematic Review of Geographic Information Systems (GIS) in Agriculture for Evidence-Based Decision Making and Sustainability. *Global Sustainability Research*, 3(1), 1–24. Advance online publication. 10.56556/gssr.v3i1.636

Rajabifard, A., Binns, A., Masser, I., & Williamson, I. (2006). The role of sub-national government and the private sector in future spatial data infrastructures. *International Journal of Geographical Information Science*, 20(7), 727–741. 10.1080/13658810500432224

Rajabifard, A., Feeney, M. E. F., & Williamson, I. P. (2002). Future directions for SDI development. *International Journal of Applied Earth Observation and Geoinformation*, 4(1), 11–22. 10.1016/S0303-2434(02)00002-8

Rana, I. A., & Bhatti, S. S. (2018). Lahore, Pakistan – Urbanization challenges and opportunities. *Cities (London, England)*, 72, 348–355. 10.1016/j.cities.2017.09.014

Rayan, M., Gruehn, D., & Khayyam, U. (2021). Green infrastructure indicators to plan resilient urban settlements in Pakistan: Local stakeholder's perspective. *Urban Climate*, 38, 100899. 10.1016/j.uclim.2021.100899

Reinar, M. B., & Lundberg, A. K. (2023). Goals à la carte: Selective translation of the Sustainable Development Goals in strategic municipal planning in Norway. *Journal of Environmental Planning and Management*, 1–17. 10.1080/09640568.2023.2191816

Rizwan, H., & Obaidullah, N. (2006). Challenges of Implementing Urban Master Plans: The Lahore Experience. *World Academy of Science, 24: 101, 108.*

Safwan, M. (2020). *Building healthy cities in the global south: A case study of the City of Lahore*. University of Waterloo.

Shaukat, N., Ullah, Z., Khan, B., Ali, S. M., & Waseem, A. (2019). An Information-Based Waste Management Approach for Pakistan. *1st International Conference on Electrical, Communication and Computer Engineering, ICECCE 2019*. IEEE. 10.1109/ICECCE47252.2019.8940796

Syvrud, A., Pohlner, H., Punthakey, J. F., Grant, M., & Green, T. (2021). Advancing urban water security in the indus basin, pakistan—Priority actions for karachi and lahore. *Water (Basel)*, 13(23), 3399. 10.3390/w13233399

Tasci, A. D. A., Wei, W., & Milman, A. (2020). Uses and misuses of the case study method. *Annals of Tourism Research*, 82, 102815. 10.1016/j.annals.2019.102815

ul Hussnain, M. Q., Waheed, A., Wakil, K., Pettit, C. J., Hussain, E., Naeem, M. A., & Anjum, G. A. (2020). Shaping up the future spatial plans for urban areas in Pakistan. *Sustainability (Switzerland), 12*(10). 10.3390/su12104216

Waheeb, S. A., Zerouali, B., Elbeltagi, A., Alwetaishi, M., Wong, Y. J., Bailek, N., AlSaggaf, A. A., Abd Elrahman, S. I. M., Santos, C. A. G., & Majrashi, A. A. (2023). Enhancing Sustainable Urban Planning through GIS and Multiple-Criteria Decision Analysis: A Case Study of Green Space Infrastructure in Taif Province, Saudi Arabia. *Water (Basel)*, 15(17), 3031. 10.3390/w15173031

Wester, M. (2022). Robust municipal decision making? A pilot study of applying robust decision making in three Swedish municipalities. *Journal of Environmental Planning and Management*, 65(4), 745–758. 10.1080/09640568.2021.1914560

# Chapter 9
# District Development Model and Service Delivery in South Africa:
## Reality or Misnomer?

**Sanah Tebogo Matloga**
https://orcid.org/0000-0001-6309-2561
*University of Venda, South Africa*

**Mahlodi Joyce Sethu**
https://orcid.org/0000-0001-9873-2215
*University of Venda, South Africa*

## ABSTRACT

*The chapter aimed to provide a critical overview of the district development model (DDM) and service delivery challenges in South Africa. South African planning has been characterised by fragmented planning, impacting service delivery. To resolve this, the cabinet adopted the DDM as an innovation to improve integrated planning and service delivery across all spheres of government. The main objective of the model was to solve the silo problem. The study employed the desktop method. Critical theory was adopted to review DDM and service delivery challenges. The findings revealed that DDM is expected to develop, support, and promote entrepreneurs by prioritising service procurement. Government should ensure stakeholders' involvement in the planning and implementation process. Spheres of government should stop working in silos and fight the triple challenges for DDM to become a reality rather than a misnomer. Government must develop mechanisms for accountability across municipalities for the implementation of DDM.*

DOI: 10.4018/979-8-3693-3617-5.ch009

## INTRODUCTION AND BACKGROUND

The South African government created the District Development Model (DDM) as a framework to improve local development planning, coordination, and execution. It seeks to address service delivery difficulties and promote socioeconomic development in certain districts. The concept promotes collaboration across several levels of government (national, provincial, and local) and other stakeholders to create integrated and successful development results (Mamokhere & Kgobe, 2023). This chapter will critically review the District Development Model (DDM) and service delivery difficulties in South Africa. The District Development Model (DDM) is a strategy implemented by the government to address deep-rooted silos and triple issues across all levels of government (DPME, 2019). The State of the Nation Address (SONA) (2019) cited the silos' style of operation as a concern, resulting in a lack of cohesion in the planning and execution of government programmes. The local government failed to enhance its production efficiency during the first decade of the National Development Plan. Thus, the South African government implemented the DDM to boost municipalities' ability to offer services (Khambule, 2021). The DDM is an operational paradigm for strengthening cooperative governance to create a competent, ethical, and developmental state (CoGTA, 2023). The SONA (2019) also advocated for a new integrated district-based strategy to resolving service delivery difficulties, localised procurement, and job creation that promotes and supports local enterprises while involving communities.

The DDM is a whole-of-government method to improve integrated planning and service delivery across all three levels of government (Khambule, 2021). The concept aims to address service delivery issues and triple difficulties by enabling all levels of government to collaborate more effectively. The concept aims to expedite, coordinate, and consolidate service delivery through a single development plan (CoGTA, 2019). The DDM guarantees that planning and expenditure across the three levels of government are integrated and in line with community interests and input (Lodi, 2020). The government must abandon the silo mindset and collaborate as a team to overcome the triple concerns of poverty, unemployment, and inequality (SONA, 2019). The DDM's aims are to coordinate the government's response to poverty, unemployment, and inequality, particularly among women, youth, and persons with disabilities (Munungufala, 2019). Munungufala (2019) goes on to say that, guided by the National Development Plan (NDP), the Integrated Urban Development Framework (IUDF), and other government policies, the DDM strives for maximum coordination and collaboration across all three branches of government. Each district and metro must create a long-term strategy to unravel the developmental concerns of growth and development to support local economic development (LED) in resolving service delivery difficulties. (CoGTA, 2023).

As a result, DDM is an operational paradigm for increasing service delivery by establishing a competent, ethical developmental state in which all government domains begin working together rather than in silos (CoGTA, 2023). The model represents a strategy in which state organisations collaborate in an impactful way to increase performance and responsibility for consistent service delivery and development results (Munungufala, 2019).

## CONCEPTUALISATION OF DISTRICT DEVELOPMENT MODEL AND SERVICE DELIVERY

The District Development Model (DDM) is a strategy framework for improving socioeconomic development at the district level via the integration and decentralisation of governance, resource allocation, and service delivery. It focuses on local empowerment, participatory planning, and multi-sectoral cooperation to ensure that development activities reflect the unique requirements of communities. According to DPME (2019), the District Development Model (DDM) is a new integrated district-based strategy to tackle service delivery difficulties through localised procurement and job creation that promotes and supports local companies while incorporating communities.

According to Sausi *et al.,* (2023), a single DDM plan transforms government planning procedures by requiring all sectors to have the same vision for a single location. In light of this, if properly executed, the plan becomes the most effective tool for alleviating the triple burden of poverty, unemployment, and inequality. It pushes the government to fulfil its mission to reduce district poverty and disparities. The DDM offers community consultation processes that the One Plan guides. As a result, an accountability framework and specific action plans are effectively implemented. As a result, the DDM will develop a strategy that focuses on one goal at a time, progressing from national to provincial to district levels.

When reviewing literature regarding DDM, it is important to focus on its critical components outlined by CoGTA (CoGTA, 2023);

- **Integrated Planning and Implementation:**

The DDM seeks to integrate planning, budgeting, and implementation efforts across all levels of government to ensure that resources are allocated efficiently, and projects are implemented effectively.

- **Collaboration, Coordination, and Coherence**

The DDM encourages collaborative governance by bringing together diverse levels of government, civil society, business, and communities to cooperate towards common development goals (Mamokhere & Kgobe, 2023). The Intergovernmental Relations Act of 2005 (Act 13 of 2005) is the legislative framework that governs collaboration, coordination, and coherence in DDM. To ensure the efficient implementation of DDM, government organisations must work with the highest expectations about programme delivery. The fact is that there is a lack of collaboration, coordination, and coherence across national, provincial, and municipal governments as envisioned by the Constitution (CoGTA, 2019).

- **Inclusive Governance**

The National Development Plan 2030 states that "meeting our transformation agenda requires a much higher and more focused intergovernmental commitment towards functional municipalities and capable machinery at a local level that can create safe and healthy and economically sustainable areas where citizens and people can work, live and socialise". Chapter 4 of the Constitution promotes cooperative governance concepts, including the requirement for "all spheres and all organs of state" to enable inclusive government (RSA, 1996). The DDM intends to increase local authorities' competencies, allowing them to be more active in driving district development.

Inequalities must be addressed in order to implement DDM schemes, as discussed above successfully. Thus, it is advised that monitoring and assessment be used as useful instruments. By enabling more efficient and coordinated collaboration across all levels of government—from local municipalities to the federal government—the DDM is intended to alleviate issues with service delivery (Mamokhere & Kgobe, 2023). According to SONA (2024), the DDM would assist municipalities in better project and programme planning, budgeting, and execution. Additionally, it will guarantee that municipal work is overseen and managed to stay on course.

## LEGISLATIVE FRAMEWORK ON DISTRICT DEVELOPMENT MODEL AND SERVICE DELIVERY

The DDM was accepted as an operational model for developing Cooperative Governance, which includes boosting and upgrading local government to create a competent and moral developmental state (CoGTA, 2019). If put into practice, laws in South Africa may help achieve the objectives of the District Development Model. The 1997 Constitution of the Republic of South Africa, the 1998 Local Government Municipal Structures Act (117 of 1998), the 2000 Local Government Municipal Systems Act (32 of 2000), the 2003 Local Government Municipal Finance Management Act (56 of 2003), the 1998 White Paper on Local Government, and the 2005 Intergovernmental Relations Framework Act (IGRFA) Act No. 13 of 2005, which lays out guidelines and procedures for collaborative governance amongst various branches of government, are some of the laws governing local government functions.

Although several DDM-regulating laws and ideas, such as those mentioned above, were examined and consulted, it is unclear whose legal framework oversees and manages the DDM's implementation in South Africa. The Intergovernmental Relation Framework Act, 2005 (Act 13 of 2005), which aims to "establish a framework for the national government, provincial government, and local government to promote and facilitate intergovernmental relations," can be taken to be the foundation for the establishment of DDM, nevertheless (Republic of South Africa, 2005). DDM, according to Sausi *et al.,* (2023), is an intergovernmental relations mechanism that aims to provide districts and metropolitan regions with a single, strategically oriented "One Plan" and "One Budget" to solve socioeconomic and service delivery concerns.

Sections 38, 39, and 41 of the Local Government: Municipal Systems Act, 2000 (Act No. 32 of 2000) provide guidance on creating and implementing a performance management system in municipalities. It becomes relevant that DDM monitors municipal performance. Section 40 of the Local Government: Municipal Systems Act, 2000 (Act No. 32 of 2000) provides greater detail on monitoring and assessing performance management systems. It specifies that a municipality must set up processes to monitor and assess its performance management system, resulting in the DDM. Other sections of the Local Government: Municipal Systems Act, 2000 (Act No. 32 of 2000) outline important sectors such as:

- Section 41- core components;
- Section 42- community involvement;
- Section 43- general key performance indicators;
- Section 44- notification of key performance indicators and performance targets; and
- Section 45- audit of performance measurements.

The above legislation does not exclude the Local Government: Municipal Structures Act of 1998 (Act 117 of 1998) and the White Paper on Local Government, 1998, which emphasise the need to develop appropriate mechanisms, such as an integrated development plan (IDP) and a district development model, to facilitate public participation, collaboration, and coordination among different stakeholders and ultimately resolve service delivery backlogs and a lack of coherence in planning and implementation (Mamokhere & Kgobe, 2023).

As a result, South Africa's District Development Plan is believed to be governed by the legislation mentioned above. As a result, the Local Government: Municipal Finance Management Act, 2003 (Act No. 56 of 2003) mandates local governments to create, monitor, and assess DDM; engage communities; define Key Performance Areas (KPAs); and publish annual performance reports (National Treasury, 2004). As a result, it may be claimed that local government focuses more on issues such as leadership, risk management, the environment, and providing basic services to communities through programs/projects. Section 95 (a) of the Local Government: Municipal Finance Management Act, 2003 (Act No. 56 of 2003) provides that the Accounting Officer is responsible for administering the municipality's financial administration and ensuring that resources are spent properly. Furthermore, the White Paper on Local Government, 1998, proposes a new developmental local government system and identifies tools such as performance management for achieving a developmental local government. Section B (1) of the White Paper on Local Government, 1998 defines developmental local government as one that collaborates with residents and community groups.

However, it is important to highlight that South Africa's legal environment may change, and new laws or regulations may be required to provide norms and procedures for DDM implementation (Mamokhere & Kgobe, 2023). Despite the enabling legislative structure and policies, significant work has to be done to achieve the government's commitment to adopting the model, despite the numerous problems that South African local government faces. The absence of strategic coordination among government areas has hampered service delivery due to job duplication and a lack of clear leadership (Khambule, 2021). Section 24 of the Local Government Municipal Systems Act (32 of 2000) establishes mechanisms for developmentally oriented planning that implements local government objectives in accordance with the Constitution of the Republic of South Africa, 1996. Despite the existing enabling frameworks, significant effort has to be made to achieve the DDM's relevance and potential contributions to localisation (Lodi, 2020).

Section 19 of the Local Government Municipal Structures Act 117 of 1998 requires municipalities to achieve the objectives outlined in Section 152 of the Constitution to provide sustainable services to communities. The DDM was launched with noble intentions, but execution remains difficult since most municipalities continue to underperform and fail to meet their objectives (Khambule, 2021). Municipalities require a transformation and turnaround plan for local government capacity building and local economic development (LED) for service delivery (Meyer & Venter, 2014). All spheres of government are largely responsible for guaranteeing interdependence in the optimal government operation. Local governments are well-positioned to implement LED programmes in their integrated development plans. In this situation, adequate consideration is given to formulating the essential rules and policies to promote LED deployment and forming partnerships with important stakeholders (Masuku *et al.,* 2015).

Municipalities connect diverse stakeholders in LED efforts to foster positive relationships for successful service delivery and to establish initiatives to attract investors to their community. These measures are often implemented to create a favourable business climate (Masuku *et al.,* 2015). Part of the municipality's responsibility is coordinating and mobilising local resources to tackle local problems in a participatory way that benefits everyone. This is made possible by the Local Government: Municipal Systems Act, 2000 (Act 32 of 2000), which requires municipalities to support socioeconomic growth within their jurisdiction.

## THEORETICAL FRAMEWORK ON DISTRICT DEVELOPMENT MODEL AND SERVICE DELIVERY

This section presents the theoretical framework of the DDM and service delivery. Critical theory is one of the theories underpinning DDM, which this study focuses on. For this study, the implementation approach of DDM focused on how well a project, programme, or policy is being executed, and it often links the implementation to a unit of responsibility. This approach, however, does not provide policymakers, managers, and stakeholders with an understanding of the success or failure of a specific project, in this instance, the DDM. In contemporary DDM and service delivery, the new focus is on "results-based systems" to address the "so what" question. The new tick-box type questions include:

- So, what about the fact that outputs have generated results?
- So, what about activities that have taken place?
- So, what about the outputs from activities that have been counted? (Sanders, 2018).

One may argue that a results-based approach offers input on the real results and objectives of government initiatives; that is, it addresses the critical topic of results and the analysis of results and impacts, which Kusek & Rist (2004) refer to as the "so what" question. According to the authors, service delivery has shifted from traditional implementation-based techniques to a new results-based approach in DDM; the latter helps to address the "so what" dilemma. Thus, projects or policies may be successfully implemented by the government or executive authorities. Still, unanswered concerns remain: Have they yielded the desired outcomes? Have districts and executive branches of government fulfilled their commitments to stakeholders? What is the impact of programmes against previous results? (Sanders, 2018).

## The Critical Theory

The study adopted critical theory to critically review the District Development Model and service delivery challenges in South Africa. Critical theory historically relates to three leading critical theorists of the original Frankfurt School (Asghar, 2013). Critical theory seeks human emancipation to liberate human beings from the circumstances that enslave them. Critical theory examines, evaluates, and critiques binary societal power dynamics, taking a Marxist perspective (Dimock, 2021). The theory helps us understand how communication is used to oppress and provides ways to foster positive social change, looking at alternatives to those forms of oppression (Foss & Fay, 1975). Dimock (2021) further indicates that critical theory exposes and challenges the communication of dominant social, economic, and political structures and other social movements. The graph below gives the definition, emphasis, view of power, and goals of critical theory.

*Figure 1. Critical theory*

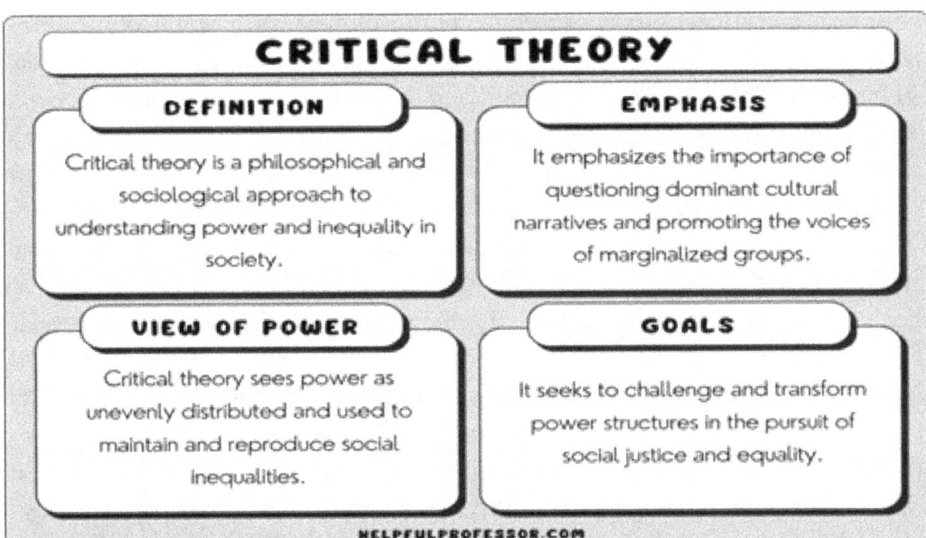


**Source**: *(Foss & Fay, 1975)*

Critical theory aids in understanding how communication is used to oppress and offers strategies for promoting good social change by examining alternatives to oppression (Foss & Fay, 1975). The praxis of critical theory combines theory with activity. According to Dimock (2021), critical theory exposes and criticises dominant social, economic, and political systems and other social movements. The theory is significant because it examines present power structures and challenges the existing order while identifying regulations, laws, and ideologies ingrained in a specific society. Critical theory holds that reality is formed over time by structures such as social, political, cultural, economic, ethnic, and gender conceptions (Paradis *et al.*, 2020).

## CRITICAL OVERVIEW OF THE DISTRICT DEVELOPMENT MODEL

The DDM was created to counter the culture of local government acting independently of other levels of government (DPME, 2020). Municipalities have been plagued by service delivery issues, dysfunctional governments, council and administrative instability, financial mismanagement, service delivery protests, and ageing municipal infrastructure (Scheba, 2022; Kanyane, 2014). Most municipalities are in financial trouble as a result of people's inability to pay for services and corruption, resulting in poor service delivery (Auditor General of South Africa (AGSA) (2021). Lack of coherence in development planning and implementation to increase the coherence and effect of social and economic development services (CoGTA,2020). However, given municipalities' rising capacity to provide key services to their constituents, the DDM is critical in responding to South Africa's government's issues. The lack of commitment by national and provincial sector departments is a major issue, and municipalities have responsibility for inadequate service delivery (Nkuna & Nemutanzhela, 2012).

Assuming that the problems that DDM attempts to address exist, the government's strategic action plans are made possible by aligning national, provincial, and local goals throughout execution. Synergy is essential for efficient service delivery and a long-term strategic foundation for steady, consistent development. As a result, the National Development Plan (NDP) may be implemented thanks to the DDM. As a result, the NDP collaborates with the DDM's Medium-Term Strategic Framework (MTSF), the Integrated Urban Development Framework (IUDF), and the National Spatial Development Framework (NSDF). In light of this, the triple concerns of unemployment, inequality, and poverty are addressed in a location that is both responsive and targeted in terms of space. The DDM is connected to the NDP, MTSF, and NSDF to improve the system by aligning national, provincial, and local goals in the district and metro areas (COGTA, 2023).

In terms of service delivery, local government is under more pressure than ever to reclaim South Africans' faith in key services like water and sanitation, power, and roads (AGSA, 2022). Sausi *et al.,* (2023) urge that the government guarantee that the model's direct beneficiaries are district residents rather than government officials. According to AGSA (2021), just seven municipalities in South Africa have received clean audit views for at least four years, with some going back even further. This demonstrates failure, given how few South African towns have obtained a clean audit opinion and how many still struggle to compile credible financial accounts.

## DISTRICT DEVELOPMENT MODEL AS A BLUEPRINT FOR SERVICE DELIVERY

The District Development Model is a practical approach to strengthening cooperative governance to create a competent, ethical, and developmental state (CoGTA, 2020). The DDM, as a blueprint/photographic representation of service delivery, aims to reorganise the economy and improve people's quality of life through cooperative governance (Munungufala, 2019). The DDM is viewed as a new integrated district-based method to address service delivery difficulties through localised procurement and employment development involving local communities (Munungufala, 2019). The DDM was implemented to enhance the institutional coherence, coordination, and effect of service delivery, economic growth, and job creation across all levels of government (Khambule, 2021). As a result, effective communication methods and approaches must be used to educate and mobilise people to raise awareness of DDM and NDP and how they might help South Africa overcome its socioeconomic difficulties. The Auditor-General of South Africa (AGSA, 2022) has urged all local government stakeholders to work tirelessly to ensure government expenditure accountability while enhancing service delivery and quality of life for South Africans. Municipal infrastructure plays an important role in supporting service delivery, and a lack of infrastructure to offer basic services has a detrimental influence on service delivery. The DDM tackles service delivery issues across all government sectors (CoGTA, 2023). According to Khambule (2021), a state cannot be called competent if the domain of government in charge of service delivery fails.

The primary objective for local government was to collaborate with communities to address their needs and provide badly needed water, sanitation, power, and road infrastructure (Nel & Minnie, 2022). However, reality has diverged significantly from the goals of the first democratic administration elected in 1994. The DDM establishes a framework for collaborative governance to accelerate integrated service delivery in human settlements, water, tourism, land, and other municipal sectors (Munungufala, 2019). Municipalities should employ information technology systems to provide efficient and effective services to their citizens (CoGTA,2023). As a result, improved communication methods and tactics will be developed to educate and activate communities so that they are informed of the services they will get, when and how. Service delivery must be organised in accordance with community demands, as well as available funds and resources (AGSA, 2020). Municipalities should support the national government's measures to improve service delivery, such as Municipal Service Partnerships (MSPs) (Zerihun & Mashingo, 2022). This will position DDM as a game changer for increasing the coherence and effect of government service delivery and economic growth, including job creation (Khambule, 2021).

## CRITICAL OVERVIEW OF DISTRICT DEVELOPMENT MODEL AND SERVICE DELIVERY CHALLENGES

Poor service delivery has been a problem for South African municipalities, and many areas lack access to essential services, including garbage disposal, power, clean water, and sanitation (Mamokhere, 2022). The local level of government is essential for fundamental infrastructure and services to be delivered effectively. South African local governments have used IDP to improve basic services within their purview (Aklilu & Makalela, 2020). According to Mokhutso, Marumo, and Motswaledi (2023), Red-flag occurrences have been reported recently in South Africa, suggesting that the nation is facing political instability and a crisis in service delivery. According to Section 152 of the Republic of South Africa's 1996 Constitution, local governments are responsible for supporting community services. According to Zerihun and Mashingo (2022), municipalities should select the appropriate delivery method for their community after considering its specific demands. According to Beyers (2016), municipalities should decide on service delivery alternatives, while municipal councils must create systems for interacting with communities to determine service needs and priorities. In this sense, municipalities should be led by rules and regulations that regulate local governance. However, many municipalities find service delivery difficult due to corruption, political favouritism, and skills shortages (Zerihun & Mashingo, 2022). According to Asha and Makalela (2020), local municipalities in South Africa are struggling to properly execute Integrated Development Plans (IDPs) and provide basic services to their residents. To improve service delivery, municipalities must develop efficient IDP implementation methods. While the DDM has considerable promise for enhancing service delivery, there are certain obstacles to consider, including:

### Lack of Capacity Building

Local governments have the resources and expertise to implement the DDM properly. Capacity building focuses on human resource development (people), institutional development (local government systems), and the overall policy environment in which local governments (as public service organisations) operate and interact (Naal *et al.,* 2020). Capacity development efforts include strengthening individuals' knowledge, talents, skills, and behaviour and improving institutional structures and procedures to accomplish the organisation's mission and goals in the long run (Vincent & Stephen, 2015).

## Poor Resource Allocation

Adequate funds and resources are required to support the implementation of development initiatives and programmes. Insufficient infrastructure, such as dependable transport or utilities, stifles company growth and job creation, resulting in high unemployment rates. (Ngcamu,2019). Poor-quality education and insufficient healthcare stifle human capital development, leaving individuals unprepared to find competent jobs (Mamokhere & Kgobe, 2023). According to Mamokhere and Kgobe (2023), DDM makes it easier to allocate resources based on a thorough understanding of the needs of a specific district area, ensuring that funds, personnel, and infrastructure are directed where they are most needed, reducing waste and maximising impact.

## Lack of Political Will and Commitment

The DDM's success depends on sustained political will and commitment at all levels of government. Lack of political will and support in South African municipalities to implement Local Economic Development (LED) initiatives and other public policies is frequently caused by a combination of factors, such as competing priorities, limited resources, and insufficient alignment with political agendas (Ramodula & Govender, 2021). As a result, numerous initiatives may go unfunded, restricting and impeding the overall growth of the local economy.

## Lack of Monitoring and Evaluation

Strong monitoring and evaluation procedures are required to track progress and modify appropriately. According to Dipela and Mohapi (2021), monitoring and assessment are critical for ensuring good governance, including openness, accountability, effectiveness, and efficiency within government departments. Improved monitoring and evaluation methods lead to better planning quality and proper execution of community poverty alleviation programmes (Arcilla *et al.*, 2011).

The DDM was adopted to assist in developing a cohesive state that promotes inclusive economic growth, spatial change, strategic infrastructure investment, and dependable service delivery for everyone (South African Academy of Science, 2022). The DDM is a new, integrated planning approach for cooperative government. It intended to promote an integrated district-based delivery system that would accelerate service delivery while ensuring that municipalities were appropriately supported and resourced to carry out their mandate. However, issues with service delivery impede DDM's success.

## CHALLENGES OF DDM ON MUNICIPAL SERVICE DELIVERY

It has proven challenging to adopt DDM in government service delivery. Kambuwa and Wallis (2002) also acknowledge this truth. Managers should be aware of possible hurdles that require proper action to overcome. According to Luthuli (2005), policy design has been more effective in South Africa than policy implementation. A performance measurement and management system are also thought to boost the performance of public sector enterprises. However, to improve service delivery, particularly in municipalities, constant monitoring of the DDM is essential.

Maila (2006) contributes to our understanding of how performance management adopted in municipalities might improve service delivery. It is a public institution within the national government, albeit the services it offers differ from those offered by municipalities. The adoption of DDM has put immense pressure on local governments to improve service delivery. According to the National Treasury (2005), numerous metrics provided by local governments do not match the assigned budget. When such an act is in effect, local governments cannot perform their statutory and constitutional tasks. Therefore, the following problems:

- The unsuccessful implementation of DDM in local government wherein the systems are often centralised and follow a top-down approach. This results in programme managers perceiving DDM as a way for the government to control the tasks performed by managers, causing the implementation to fail. If DDM could be given the latitude to allow a bottom-up approach, the ongoing service delivery protests would stop or be minimised. The DDM information seeks to influence decision-making and informs future planning by learning from past experiences, but this rarely happens.
- Lack of stakeholders' relationship with the analysed financial, human and related skills information. People don't expect to make or complete any development-related duties, especially when considering stakeholders' viewpoints, and instead see DDM as the exclusive duty of the municipal practitioner. A centralised approach to DDM might lead to staff members and stakeholders carrying out their duties to satisfy the national mandate instead of carrying out specific responsibilities to enhance project execution for efficient service delivery.

- The DDM in local government is not recognised as a model of effective implementation of programmes as outlined in the IDP. Often, misconceptions of DDM results hinder any system from becoming fully operational.
- No systematic evaluation of DDM in local government.
- Lack of capacity building: Project staff and stakeholders do not understand the reports provided by personnel and often complain that reports are too long, unclear and often come too late for implementation. Project managers perceive DDM as a threat and are sometimes reluctant to compile and submit progress reports of their projects and use evaluation recommendations to improve their performance.

The study points out that DDM challenges have arisen from a lack of understanding of what DDM entails, which limits people's understanding of their tasks. The South African government has encountered several challenges when implementing the DDM, ensuring it is a mechanism for change initiatives and management.

## FACTORS AFFECTING MUNICIPAL SERVICE DELIVERY

Local governments play a vital role in community development and service delivery to the individuals who live within their territories. South Africa has had difficulty delivering basic services in recent years, resulting in community demonstrations over unfulfilled demands. This section discusses budgetary restrictions, a lack of accountability, inadequate leadership, ineffective human resources, and a lack of community involvement.

### Financial Constraints

According to Goldsmith (2014), budgetary limits are one of the issues that local governments face while providing services. Limited budgets, high financial risks, and regulatory failures reinforce the claim that financial limits make providing services difficult. Several revenue streams include service fees, government taxes, energy, water, and sanitation subsidies. However, funding for these services is minimal (Wadesango *et al.,* 2018). Many towns rely on municipal rates as an income source to provide services, which has proven ineffective (Nyoni, 2017). This implies that towns gain revenue from citizens' rates and taxes, which allows them to provide services. As a result, the government's capacity to carry out its mandate and impact service delivery

## Lack of Accountability

According to Khalo (2013), accountability entails the obligation to expose, clarify, and justify one's actions. The local government is responsible for ensuring that municipal services are available and that residents benefit from them. Policy-makers should guarantee the law is high quality since it influences service delivery capability. This means deficient municipal service supply is linked to a lack of accountability, demonstrating that municipal officials can redirect public revenues for personal gain (Odaro, 2012). In addition, disagreements among community voters and philosophical perspectives may contribute to service failures.

Decentralisation is one of the tactics used to improve transparency and community involvement in municipal service delivery. Rural regions benefit from improved services such as water and sanitation due to decentralisation, which recognises people's demands and fosters local responsibility (Wadesango *et al.*, 2018). Decentralisation, on the other hand, presents several obstacles, including low-income local governments' limited tax revenue in rural regions and a lack of practical work and government competency (Odaro, 2012; Munzhedzi, 2020). The government's initiatives must prioritise public accountability. Local governments carry out certain legislative responsibilities and implement policies and government structures (Goldsmith, 2014).

## Poor Leadership

Leadership is crucial because it permits regulations to be controlled and updated to reflect new changes. According to this study, leadership has a role in DDM and municipal service delivery by ensuring it is effectively implemented in their municipalities. Wadesango *et al.*, (2018) identify two types of municipal leaders: political and administrative. It is difficult for leaders to practise their skills in a political environment in municipalities, so there is a need for collaboration between political and administrative leaders who play diverse roles in the administration of municipalities (Lee *et al.*, 2015). To effectively carry out their mandate for the local communities under their authority, municipal officials must possess strong leadership qualities. The local government's leadership impacts the management of municipal services since they can interact with the community and recognise its demands.

Maserumule (2017) states that political leaders may generate fresh ideas, support, and financing. Therefore, they have a bigger effect on motivating policy implementers in local government to deliver services adequately. Unfortunately, Wadesango *et al.*, (2018) state that the representatives chosen to oversee the smooth operation of the local municipality lack the skills required to carry out their political mandate in a way that will enable services to be provided to the public. Furthermore, lacking leadership makes unethical hiring practices, power abuse, resource theft, and corruption possible (Nefale, 2018). This is a sign of bad leadership, and leaders must set a positive example for people under them to carry out their mandate successfully.

### Lack of Community Participation

According to Lachapelle and Austin (2014), community participation is the physical engagement of a group of people who make decisions. According to Kalonda and Govender (2021), a community comprises people with a common geography, values, beliefs, and interests. Meetings, decision-making, and outcomes are all direct aspects of participation. Community engagement may be utilised to discover and resolve issues. Municipal authorities are required to invite locals to community meetings so that they can hear their perspectives on current issues. This suggests that only via the community will the local municipality be able to determine which demands of the people to meet are not static but rather constantly changing. Leadership has a vital role in developing mechanisms for community members to interact and express issues. Leadership enhances good governance by encouraging openness, accountability, cooperation, involvement, and responsibility in service delivery (Kalonda & Govender, 2021). As a result, municipal officials with strong leadership abilities promote good governance by being held accountable for their actions.

## GOVERNMENT'S COMMITMENT TO THE DISTRICT DEVELOPMENT MODEL

To achieve inclusive growth, combat triple problems, and enhance service delivery, all three levels of government must collaborate in integrated development strategies by mobilising government resources and enterprises (Masiya *et al.*, 2019). The Department of Cooperative Governance and Traditional Affairs (CoGTA) (2020) confirms that the DDM governance system promotes integrated planning and service delivery across all three levels of government. According to CoGTA (2020), the government implemented the Intergovernmental Relations (IGR) planning, budgeting, and implementation model to achieve long-term DDM results. The approach is based on the White Paper on Local Government (1998), which aims to strengthen and restructure local government to play a developmental role.

In the process of DDM implementation, the COVID-19 pandemic emerges and negatively affects government plans (Slater, 2021). The COVID-19 epidemic destroyed the country's economy, as well as the health and livelihoods of its population (DPME,2020). Many firms closed due to the pandemic, resulting in a smaller commercial rate base and decreased food and non-food production (Khambule,

2021). The government's commitment to the DDM is critical, particularly in local government, which directly interacts with local communities and is at the forefront of service delivery (CoGTA, 2019). As part of the Integrated Development Plan (IDP) development process, municipalities must consult with communities about the kind of basic services that they provide, such as roads, power, water, sanitation, and health (Masiya *et al.,* 2019). In order to provide the people of South Africa with fair socioeconomic services, the local government mostly carries out the country's developmental strategy (Khambule, 2021). However, in order to make it a reality, the DDM aims to guarantee the greatest amount of coordination and collaboration across all three branches of government, as guided by the National Development Plan (NDP) and the Integrated Urban Development Framework (IUDF) through Inter-governmental Relations (IGR). The DDM action plan is created collaboratively with key partners, communities, and the commercial sector. The model identifies service delivery issues and potential for growth and development in each location (CoGTA, 2023).

Adopting the 2030 Agenda for Sustainable Development marks a significant shift in the government's development strategy (CoGTA, 2020). This is done to identify the roles of local governments in poverty reduction, such as guaranteeing access to water and sanitation, health, education, economic growth, and resistance to climate change (Zerihun & Mashingo, 2022). According to Khambule (2021), in its commitment to the DDM, the South African government works to abolish poverty by all methods, including establishing cooperatives to reduce poverty, unemployment, and inequality. According to the National Planning Commission (NPC) (2019), the government's commitment to the DDM includes continued investments in Science, Technology, and Innovation (STI). This achieves the Fourth Industrial Revolution's (4IR) aim and vision. Despite the introduction of the DDM in South Africa, the country continues to face serious issues such as high unemployment, poverty, and inequality.

As part of its obligations under the DDM, the government established partnerships and collaborations for the implementation of District Development with the Public-Private Growth Initiative (PPGI), the Water Research Commission (WRC), the United Nations (UN), the Council for Scientific and Industrial Research (CSIR), and the National Business Institute (NBI) (CoGTA, 2021). This was carried out to facilitate the formulation, execution, and investment in One Plan's technological assistance, opening doors for job creation and economic growth. DDM's main goal is to address problems with governance, economic growth, and service delivery by encouraging cooperation across departments, stakeholders, and different governmental levels (Mamokhere & Kgobe, 2023).

## CONTEXTUALISATION AND IMPLEMENTATION OF DISTRICT DEVELOPMENT MODEL FRAMEWORK 2020

The DDM offers a framework for South African municipalities to address service delivery issues (SONA, 2023). The framework intends to provide a consistent strategy for executing the DDM to strengthen the government's capacity to support municipalities (Lodi, 2020). However, according to Sausi *et al.* (2023), the most important rationale for establishing DDM was to reduce the government's inclination to function in silos.

The DDM Implementation Framework (DDMIF) is designed to facilitate implementation by localising objectives, targets, and directives that meet triple problems (CoGTA, 2020). As a result, substantial engagement with all stakeholders is required to achieve thorough awareness and commitment to executing the DDM in accordance with the methodology and plan provided in DDMIF. As a result, the model should not be a one-size-fits-all approach to successful service delivery but rather be implemented differently in different provinces to address societal concerns (CoGTA, 2023). Consequently, the DDM is a useful Intergovernmental Relations (IGR) tool that allows all three government branches to collaborate with the general public and other stakeholders. According to Munungufala (2021), the model offers a cooperative governance structure that expedites integrated service delivery in human settlements and several other municipal sectors.

Masiya et al. (2019) state that municipalities offer services to the people while also fulfilling the purposes of local government as outlined in Section 152 of the Republic of South Africa's 1996 Constitution. Although all towns are constitutionally required to provide long-term and effective services, this is not always simple. Various components must be incorporated before municipalities may succeed. Communication methods and tactics should be used to educate and mobilise all segments of society to become more aware of the DDM and its power to create employment while eliminating poverty and inequality.

## METHODOLOGY

The study used the desktop approach, emphasising reviewing relevant material, such as pertinent reports, government policies, laws, and published and unpublished academic work. This is done to better understand the DDM as a framework for improving service delivery, investigate the problems, and offer ways for overcoming those challenges. The study used critical theory to examine the realities of the District Development Model and service delivery issues. Understanding the power dynamics, socioeconomic inequities, and underlying structures that affect DDM governance processes is important.

## NATIONAL AND INTERNATIONAL CASE STUDIES OF THE DISTRICT DEVELOPMENT MODEL

The District Development Model (DDM) has been tested in several South African districts, exhibiting a variety of approaches and outcomes in tackling local development concerns. These case studies show how the DDM impacts service delivery, economic growth, and community empowerment. Here are a few thorough examples:

### O.R. Tambo District in the Eastern Cape Province

The O.R. Tambo District Municipality represents one of the six district municipalities in the Eastern Cape province (Teti *et al.*, 2024). Despite having enormous potential for the maritime economy, tourism, and agriculture, the O.R. Tambo District municipality is thought to be the most economically challenged area in the Eastern Cape (Currie, 2021). Teti et al. (2024) said that the O.R. Tambo District Municipality's DDM implementation was unsuccessful because some government stakeholders did not fully comprehend the program's implementation obstacles. Sausi *et al.* (2023) state that the O.R. Tambo District admits to having governance issues concerning public infrastructure and service delivery. Nevertheless, despite the DDM's shortcomings in the O.R. Tambo District Municipality. In order to prepare for the changes, the DDM initiative would bring to IDP and other municipal procedures, Teti *et al.* (2024) advise that workers of municipalities and other stakeholders get training on the initiative and its implementation.

### eThekwini Metropolitan, KwaZulu-Natal

The DDM has also prioritised the eThekwini Metropolitan, which contains the city of Durban. This case study showcases initiatives aimed at improving service delivery and tackling issues related to urbanisation. Under the DDM framework, the metro has implemented many integrated initiatives, including infrastructure construction and better housing in informal settlements (Gwala,2023). The significance of intergovernmental collaboration and integrating different sectoral programmes to attain holistic development objectives is an important lesson to be learned from this area. The DDM's ability to improve the effectiveness of governmental programmes and reduce procedures is demonstrated by the eThekwini Metropolitan instance.

## Waterberg District, Limpopo

The DDM has promoted economic growth in the Waterberg District of Limpopo, especially in rural areas. The concept has aided initiatives like expanding agriculture and enhancing infrastructure. Creating agribusiness centres, which aim to strengthen local economies and give communities sustainable means of subsistence, is a noteworthy undertaking (Sausi *et al.*, 2023). Improved stakeholder coordination and ensuring that initiatives align with more general developmental objectives, including reducing poverty and promoting economic inclusion, are among the district's challenges (Academy of Science of South Africa, 2022).

## International Perspective of the District Development Model

## Germany

Regional policy and structural development are given a lot of weight in Germany's district development strategy (Böcher, 2008). In Integrated Rural Development, Germany employs initiatives such as LEADER (Liaison Entre Actions de Développement de l'Économie Rurale), a component of the EU's rural development policy (Chatzichristos & Perimenis, 2022). In order to create and carry out local development strategies, the policy encourages local stakeholders to organise into Local Action Groups (LAGs). Koetter, Sikder, and Weiss (2021) assert that economic development is encouraged to increase competitiveness and innovation.

## Italy

In order to meet the unique demands of both urban and rural regions, Italy uses Integrated Territorial Investment (ITI) to promote development at the district level (Cotella & Brovarone, 2020). The goals of Integrated Territorial Investment include environmental sustainability, economic growth, and social inclusion. According to Vendemmia, Pucci, and Beria (2021), Italy created the National Strategy for Inner Communities, emphasising methods for enhancing the socioeconomic redevelopment of isolated and underprivileged communities through improved infrastructure and services.

## Poland

District development in Poland is strongly related to the country's National Cohesion Strategy, which is in line with the cohesion policy of the European Union (EU) (Dąbrowski, 2014). Poland's Regional Operational Programmes are intended to accommodate the unique demands of regions, fostering balanced development and minimising regional imbalances, according to Cotella and Dąbrowski (2021). Through targeted investments in infrastructure, social services, and economic diversification, urban and rural renewal projects aim to revitalise urban areas and promote rural growth (Prota *et al.,* 2020).

## Uganda

Based on subsidiarity and integration without subordination, Uganda's local government system is multitiered, consisting of districts, local governments, and councils (Andama, 2020). Lakuma et al. (2017) state that District Development Plans, which span five years and include funding frameworks and strategies that delineate the primary sources of revenue, are utilised by Uganda. Uganda has implemented a decentralised approach to development planning, prioritising community input and local government authority (Lubuulwa, 2021). According to Lubuulwa (2021), Uganda's local government system also gives local authorities the authority to manage resources and carry out development initiatives that meet their requirements. Focusing on local-level coordination and participatory planning aligns with the DDM's emphasis on improving service delivery and addressing regional inequities.

## China

Like the DDM, China has effectively adopted regional development policies emphasising local empowerment and integrated planning (Lu, 2024). One noteworthy example is the creation of Special Economic Zones (SEZs), which have changed areas via targeted economic policies and infrastructural investment. Naeem, Waheed, and Khan (2020) assert that the integrated strategy used by SEZs in China, which entails collaboration between national, provincial, and local administrations and large expenditures in infrastructure and education, is primarily responsible for their success.

## Brazil

Momm and Jöns (2020) state that participatory governance and integrated territorial planning are key to Brazil's regional development strategy. In order to promote sustainable development and lessen inequality, Brazil has launched several initiatives under its National Policy for Regional Development (Randolph, 2019). Like the DDM, these programmes improve coordination between governmental branches and interested parties to guarantee well-thought-out project planning and efficient execution. Brazil's experience emphasises how crucial it is to match local needs and capacities with regional development programmes to ensure equitable and sustainable development.

These case studies highlight the DDM's promise and its implementation challenges. The model provides a potential foundation for integrated and comprehensive development, but it will only function if there is strong governance, sufficient money, and engaged community involvement.

## Challenges and Lessons Learnt

In South Africa, the District Development Model (DDM) seeks to improve the efficacy and efficiency of public services using integrated and coordinated planning and execution. Despite its potential, the DDM has challenges, and lessons are being learnt.

Bibri, Krogstie and Kärrholm (2020) identify the challenges as follows;

- **Resource Constraints**: The efficient execution of development plans may be hampered by the local level's lack of funding and personnel.
- **Coordination Complexities**: It can be difficult to ensure cooperation amongst many sectors and players, which requires strong governance frameworks.
- **Measuring Impact**: Assessing the effects of district-level development initiatives may be difficult, particularly when working on varied and complicated projects.

In order to promote sustainable and equitable development across the continent by addressing each district's particular needs and challenges, the Development Model demonstrates a commitment to fostering regional and local development through decentralised governance, integrated planning, and inclusive growth (Gargano, 2021). The District Development Model (DDM) has offered a useful framework for comprehending the intricacies of integrated development planning and execution at the district level, according to the lesson learned. This encompasses the insights gained from the DDM encounter, highlighting achievements and enhancement opportunities. The value of cross-level government-integrated planning is one of the most important lessons to be learned from the DDM. National, provincial, and local governments must collaborate to ensure that development efforts are coherent and avoid fragmentation. Integrating several sectors' plans delivers more comprehensive development results by optimising resource utilisation and avoiding redundancy. However, the active participation and support of all stakeholders, including local businesses, government agencies, and communities, is critical to the DDM's success. The successful execution of the DDM is dependent on the effective coordination of various sectoral plans and governmental levels.

## DISCUSSION AND DDM POLICY IMPLICATIONS

The District Development Model (DDM) in South Africa is a revolutionary strategy for improving service delivery and promoting sustainable development via localised, integrated planning and implementation. It brings together government agencies, stakeholders, and communities to address socioeconomic concerns and promote inclusive growth. Based on the DDM's goals of improving the coherence and impact of government service delivery to serve as economic development and job creation hubs, it was discovered that a lack of inter-governmental relations between the three spheres of government causes a delay in implementing the District Development Model. Effective implementation of the DDM requires significant investment in capacity building at the district level. Policies should focus on training and skills development for local government officials, community leaders, and other stakeholders to improve their ability to plan, implement, and monitor development projects.

This may be accomplished by monitoring and evaluating the current project. Policies should incorporate environmental issues into DDMs, encouraging sustainable development planning and implementation techniques. This involves using green technology, conserving natural resources, minimising the effects of climate change, and emphasising environmental sustainability to ensure that development projects do not harm the ecosystem but contribute to long-term ecological balance and resilience. This chapter contributed to key objectives of DDM to coordinate a government response to challenges of poverty, unemployment, and inequality, particularly among women, youth, and people living with disabilities; to ensure inclusivity by gender budgeting based on the needs and aspirations of our people and communities at a local level; and to foster a practical intergovernmental relations mechanism to plan, budget, and implement jointly in order to provide a coherent government.

According to COGTA (2021), the DDM, as a new way of working and doing things, will play an important role in increasing the execution of programmes and initiatives that promote and improve service delivery within municipalities. The DDM, with the introduction of the One Plan, is on track to make this a reality. Furthermore, the DDM argues for the same involvement across all three levels of government, namely the recent nomination of political district champions at the national level, which cascades to provinces and districts to complement one another. The DDM thus adopts a district-wide strategy. COGTA (2021) concludes that complementarity may be shown in that the DDM provides a more focused and regional stance within a district, i.e. cities and towns. This could also imply that DDM interventions in cities and towns will be critical for providing a district-wide perspective, particularly in integrated urban planning and management, integrated sustainable human settlement, integrated urban infrastructure, efficient land governance and management, inclusive economic development, and so on. As a result, the emphasis is on individuals, the economy, and locations to invest in the necessities of increasing quality of life.

As a result, the DDM did not replace or replicate the work of other models, such as the Integrated Urban Development Framework. However, the two should be viewed as complimentary. It is a fallacy that the DDM is the new sheriff in town, replacing the IUDF. As a result, improved communication tactics and approaches must be used to educate and mobilise people to raise awareness of the two programmes and their potential to alleviate socioeconomic difficulties. The tagline "One District, One Budget, and One Plan" articulates the DDM's goal, strongly related to the IUDF's aim of reaping the urban dividend (COGTA, 2021). The successful implementation of the District Development Model necessitates extensive policy support that covers all aspects of governance, planning, participation, resource management, and sustainability. These policies must empower local governments, promote inclusivity, and guarantee that development projects are well-coordinated and efficiently meet the unique requirements of each district in South Africa.

The DDM aims to strengthen and supplement many previous reform initiatives, including Project Consolidate, the Integrated Sustainable Rural Development Programme (ISRDP), the Urban Renewal Programme (URP), District-level Planning and Implementation Management Support Centres, the Local Government Turnaround Strategy (LGTAS), and Back to Basics. All of these efforts were targeted at increasing residents' quality of life by establishing institutional changes that strengthen the capacity of local administrations and councils to provide integrated services. Recent budgeting changes, such as Built Environment Performance Plans (BEPPS) and alignment with the Integrated Urban Development Framework (IUDF), have aimed to promote more spatialisation of government operations and prioritisations that require public expenditure.

## CONCLUSION AND WAY FORWARD

The objective of this chapter was to present a critical review of South Africa's service delivery difficulties and the District Development Model (DDM). Through the prism of critical theory, pertinent material, including reports and official regulations, was reviewed using the desktop approach. If the government wants the model to be a reality rather than just a name, it must overcome its triple obstacles and cease operating in silos. The concept may foster social and economic growth and enhance local government performance. For the DDM to be successful and regarded seriously, legislation is required. All stakeholders should be included in the planning and execution process according to government policy. For the model to become a reality rather than a misnomer, the spheres of government must cease functioning in silos and confront the triple difficulties. The strategy can help local governments function better and promote social and economic growth. However, DDM must be implemented to handle the local government's key issues, including energy, housing, road infrastructure, water, and sanitation. The Department of Planning, Monitoring, and Evaluation should oversee all DDM procedures across all levels of government to ensure responsibility and commitment to the initiative. Most towns in South Africa continue to struggle to deliver basic amenities such as water, sanitation, power, and roads (Stats SA, 2022). The government must identify constraints that prevent municipalities from fully adopting the DDM to improve service delivery.

To achieve the developmental goals outlined in the National Development Plan (NDP) 2030, it is proposed that the District Development Model and service delivery framework be built at the district and national levels. These may help address municipal service delivery difficulties. The government must provide a clear framework for DDM and guarantee that all stakeholders participate in the planning and implementation stages. For the District Development Model to become a reality rather than a misnomer, all levels of government must cease operating in silos and address the triple difficulties. The DDM ought to put more emphasis on local governments that are capable of developing in order to eradicate poverty and lessen inequality in South Africa. At the district level, the District Development Model is a strategic method for enhancing service delivery and encouraging sustainable development. The DDM seeks to improve communities' well-being and quality of life in selected districts by promoting integrated planning, coordination, and efficient resource allocation. This will eventually aid in the achievement of more general socio-economic development objectives.

## REFERENCES

Academy of Science of South Africa. (2022). *The District Development Model as a platform for innovation for inclusivity*. Academy of Science of South Africa.

Andama, F. A. (2020). Decentralisation and Public Policy implementation in Uganda: the case Of West Nile Sub-Region [Doctoral dissertation, North-West University, South Africa].

Arcilla, G. R., Co, F. F., & Occampo, R. S. (2011). Correlates of poverty: Evidence from the community-based-monitoring system (CBMS) data. *DLSU Business & Economics Review*, 20(2), 33–43. 10.3860/ber.v20i2.1912

Asghar, J. (2013). Critical paradigm: A preamble for novice researchers. *Life Science Journal*, 10(4), 3121–3127.

Asha, A. A., & Makalela, K. I. (2020). Challenges in the implementation of the integrated development plan and service delivery in Lepelle-Nkumbi Municipality, Limpopo province. *International Journal of Economics and Finance Studies*, 12(1), 1–15. 10.34109/ijefs.202012101

Auditor General of South Africa (AGSA). (2021). *Municipal Finance Management Act (MFMA) Consolidated General Report on Local Government Audit Outcomes 2019–2020*. AGSA. https://www.agsa.co.za/Portals/0/Reports/MFMA/201920

Auditor General South Africa (AGSA). (2022). *Auditor-General calls on municipal leaders to transform local government to improve people's lives—media release*. AGSA. https://www.agsa.co.za/Portals

Beyers, L. J. E. (2016). Service Delivery challenges facing municipalities: A case study of Fetakgomo Local Municipality in Sekhukhune District Municipality, Limpopo Province. *Bangladesh e-Journal of Sociology*, 13(2), 167–178.

Bibri, S. E., Krogstie, J., & Kärrholm, M. (2020). Compact city planning and development: Emerging practices and strategies for achieving the goals of sustainability. Developments in the built environment, 4, 100021.

Böcher, M. (2008). Regional governance and rural development in Germany: the implementation of LEADER+. *Sociologia Ruralis, 48*(4), 372-388.

Chatzichristos, G., & Perimenis, A. (2022). Evaluating the social added value of LEADER: Evidence from a marginalised rural region. *Journal of Rural Studies*, 94, 366–374. 10.1016/j.jrurstud.2022.07.016

Cotella, G., & Brovarone, E. V. (2020). The Italian National Strategy for Inner Areas: A Place-based approach to Regional Development. In *Dilemmas of regional and local development* (pp. 50-71). Routledge.

Cotella, G., & Dąbrowski, M. (2021). EU Cohesion Policy as a driver of Europeanisation: A comparative analysis. In *EU Cohesion Policy and Spatial Governance* (pp. 48–65). Edward Elgar Publishing. 10.4337/9781839103582.00013

Dąbrowski, M. (2014). Towards place-based regional and local development strategies in Central and Eastern Europe? EU cohesion policy and strategic planning capacity at the sub-national level. *Local Economy*, 29(4-5), 378–393. 10.1177/0269094214535715

Department of Cooperative Governance and Traditional Affairs (CoGTA). (2019). *Coordinated Service Delivery Model, President Coordinating Council.* CoGTA. https://www.thepresidency.gov.za

Department of Cooperative Governance and Traditional Affairs (CoGTA). (2020). *Implementation Framework of DDM*. CoGTA. www.cogta.gov.za/ddm/index

Department of Cooperative Governance and Traditional Affairs (CoGTA). (2021). *How is the DDM Aligned to the IUDF?* CoGTA. www.cogta.gov.za/ddm/index

Department of Cooperative Governance and Traditional Affairs (CoGTA). (2023). *Implementation of DDM*. CoGTA. https://www.cogta.gov.za/cgta

Department of National Treasury. (2004). *Annual Report: 2004-2005*. Government Printers.

Department of National Treasury. (2015). *Local Government Revenue and Expenditure*. Cape Town: Press Release.

Department of Planning, Monitoring and Evaluation (DPME) (2020). *The Impact of COVID-19 on South African Municipalities Survey Results*. DPME.

Department of Planning, Monitoring, and Evaluation. (DPME) (2019). *Presidential launch of DDM*. DPME. https://www.dpme.gov.za/news

Dimock, J. P. (2021). The Critical Paradigm. In *Understanding Communication Research Methods* (pp. 35–47). Routledge. 10.4324/9781003109129-5

Dipela, M. P., & Mohapi, B. J. (2021). Barriers affecting effective monitoring and evaluation of poverty alleviation projects within Waterberg District. *Social Work*, 57(3), 287–301.

Foss, D. J., & Fay, D. (1975). Linguistic theory and performance models. *Testing linguistic hypotheses*, 65–91.

Gargano, G. (2021). The bottom-up development model as a governance instrument for the rural areas. The cases of four local action groups (LAGs) in the United Kingdom and in Italy. *Sustainability (Basel)*, 13(16), 9123. 10.3390/su13169123

Goldsmith, J. (2014). *Government outsourcing: a practical guide for safe and local governments*. India: School of public and environmental affairs Press.

Gwala, S. N. (2023). *Municipal planning in dense rural settlements: a case of Mzinyathi in eThekwini Metropolitan Municipality* [Doctoral dissertation, Durban University of Technology]. DUT Library.

Kalonda, J. K., & Govender, K. (2021). 'Factors Affecting Municipal Service Delivery: A Case Study Of Katima Mulilo Town Council, Namibia'. *African Journal of Public Affairs*, 12(2), 1–26.

Kambuwa, M., & Wallis, M. (2002). *Public Management*. University of Durban-Westville.

Kanyane, M. (2014). Exploring challenges of municipal service delivery in South Africa (1994-2013). *Africa's Public Service Delivery & Performance Review*, 2(1), 90–110. 10.4102/apsdpr.v2i1.45

Khalo, T. (2013). Accountability and Oversight in Municipal Financial Management: The Role of Municipal Public Accounts Committees. *Journal of Public Administration*, 48(4), 589–501.

Khambule, I. (2021). The DDM: Towards a Capable Local Development State in South Africa. The University of KwaZulu-Natal. *Journal of Public Administration*, 56(3), 507–523.

Koetter, T., Sikder, S. K., & Weiss, D. (2021). The cooperative urban land development model in Germany-An effective instrument to support affordable housing. *Land Use Policy*, 107, 105481. 10.1016/j.landusepol.2021.105481

Kusek, J. Z., & Rist, R. C. (2004). *Ten steps to a Result-Based Monitoring and Evaluation. A Handbook for Developing Practitioners*. D.C. The World Bank. 10.1596/0-8213-5823-5

Lachapelle, P. R., & Austin, E. K. (2014). *Community Participation: Encyclopaedia of Quality of Life and Well-Being Research*. Springer: Dordrecht publisher. 10.1007/978-94-007-0753-5_471

Lakuma, C. P., Katunze, M., Nagawa, M., Mawejje, J., Lwanga, M., Mbowa, S., & Shinyekwa, I. (2017). *Country reviews of capacity development: The case of Uganda.*

Lee, A., Martin, R., Thomas, G., Guilaume, Y., & Maio, G. R. (2015). Conceptualiz2ing leadership perceptions as attitudes: Using attitude theory to further understand the leadership process. *The Leadership Quarterly*, 26(6), 28–31. 10.1016/j.leaqua.2015.10.003

Lodi, J. D. (2020). *Implementation of the DDM. Department of Cooperative Governance and Traditional Affairs.* CoGTA. http://www.cogta.gov.za

Lu, D. (2024). *Regional development and its spatial structure.* Springer. 10.1007/978-981-99-7683-6

Lubuulwa, K. B. (2021). *Putting decentralisation policy into practice in Uganda: a participatory action research study of local government empowerment for local economic development.*

Luthuli, T. B. (2005). *Performance Measurement as a Public Policy Implementation Tool in the South African Public Service.* University of Pretoria.

Maila, H. M. (2006). *Public Management and Service Delivery in the Department of Water Affairs and Forestry.* [Unpublished MTech Dissertation. UNISA].

Mamokhere, J. (2022). Understanding the Complex Interplay of Governance, Systematic, and Structural Factors Affecting Service Delivery in South African Municipalities. *Commonwealth Youth & Development, 20*(2).

Mamokhere, J., & Kgobe, F. K. L. (2023). One District, One Approach, One Budget, One Plan: Understanding District Development Model as an Initiative for Improving Service Delivery and Socio-economic Development in South Africa. *IAHRW International Journal of Social Sciences Review*, 11(3), 362–370.

Maserumule, M. H. (2017). 'Editorial: Just a thought'. *Journal of Public Administration*, 52(2), 308–502.

Masiya, T., Davids, Y. D., & Mangai, M. S. (2019). Assessing Service Delivery: Public Perception of Municipal Service Delivery in South Africa. *Theoretical and Empirical Research in Urban Management*, 14(2), 20–40.

Masuku, M. M., Jili, N. N., & Selepe, B. M. (2015). The implementation of Local Economic Development initiatives towards poverty alleviation in Big 5 False Bay Local Municipality. *African Journal of Hospitality, Tourism and Leisure*, 5(4), •••.

Meyer, D. F., & Venter, A. (2014). An analysis of the effectiveness of the Local Government Turnaround Strategy (LGTAS): The case of the Fezile Dabi District Municipality, *South Africa.African Journal of Public Affairs*, 7(1), 80–93.

Mokhutso, J., Marumo, P. O., & Motswaledi, T. R. (2023). Ubuntu: An Antidote to Service Delivery Crisis and Political Instability in South Africa. *Journal of Nation-building &. Policy Studies*, 7(2).

Munungufala, T. (2019). *Overview of the DDM – A Framework for Co-operative Service Delivery*. South African Parliament Research Unit. www.parliament.gov.za

Naal, H., El Koussa, M., El Hamouch, M., Hneiny, L., & Saleh, S. (2020). Evaluation of global health capacity building initiatives in low-and middle-income countries: A systematic review. *Journal of Global Health*, 10(2), 020412. 10.7189/jogh.10.02041233110574

Naeem, S., Waheed, A., & Khan, M. N. (2020). Drivers and barriers for successful special economic zones (SEZs): Case of SEZs under China Pakistan economic corridor. *Sustainability (Basel)*, 12(11), 4675. 10.3390/su12114675

National Planning Commission (NPC). (2019). *Our future - make it work National Development Plan*. NPC. (www.gov.za)

Nefale, M. D. (2018). *An investigation into Citizens' trust in service delivery in Makhado Municipality, Limpopo province, South Africa*. [Unpublished Thesis, University of Limpopo].

Ngcamu, B. S. (2019). Exploring service delivery protests in post-apartheid South African municipalities: A literature review. The Journal for Transdisciplinary Research in Southern Africa, 15(1), Nkuna N.W., Nemutanzhela T.L. (2012). Locating the role of service delivery within powers and functions of local government in South Africa. *Journal of Public Administration*, 47(si-1), 355–368.

Nyoni, V. G. (2017). *An investigation on the role played by Local Authorities in service delivery: A case of Kadoma City Council*. [Unpublished Thesis, Midlands State University].

Odaro, E. D. (2012). 'Causes of Poor Service Delivery in Africa and Their Impact on Development'. Consilience. *Journal of Sustainable Development*, 7(1), 34–45.

Paradis, E., Nimmon, L., Wondimagegn, D., & Whitehead, C. R. (2020). Critical theory: Broadening our thinking to explore the structural factors at play in health professions education. *Academic Medicine*, 95(6), 842–845. 10.1097/ACM.000000000000310831809292

Prota, F., Viesti, G., & Bux, M. (2020). 10. The Contribution of European Cohesion Policy to Public Investment. *A European Public Investment Outlook*, 175.

Ramodula, T. M., & Govender, K. K. (2021). Developmental local government: A framework for implementation. *Africa Journal of Public Sector Development and Governance*, 4(1), 45–72. 10.55390/ajpsdg.2021.4.1.3

Randolph, R. (2019). Regional development policies and the challenge to reduce spatial inequalities in Brazil. *Area Development and Policy*, 4(3), 271–283. 10.1080/23792949.2019.1570824

Republic of South Africa. (1996). *Constitution of the Republic of South Africa, 1996*. Government Printers.

Republic of South Africa. (1998). *Local Government: Municipal Structures Act, 1998 (Act No. 117 of 1998)*. Government Printers.

Republic of South Africa. (1998). *White Paper on Local Government (Notice 423 of 1998)*. Pretoria: Government Printers.

Republic of South Africa. (1998). *White Paper on Local Government.* Pretoria: Government Printers.

Republic of South Africa. (2000). *Local Government: Municipal Systems Act, 2000 (Act No. 32 of 2000)*. Government Printers.

Republic of South Africa. (2003). *Municipal Finance Management Act, 2001 (Act No. 56 of 2003)*. Government Printers.

Republic of South Africa. (2005). *Intergovernmental Relations Framework Act, 2005 (Act No. 13 of 2005)*. Government Printers.

Sanders, A. (2018). *Different types of assessment and what you need to know about them*. Edulastic.

Sausi, K., Kanyane, M., Gumede, N., Mchunu, N., Davids, D., Zondi, T., Houston, G., Ngqwala, N., Bohler-Muller, N., & Cosser, M. (2023). Implementation of the DDM in South Africa.https://repository.hsrc.ac.za/bitstream/handle/20.500.11910/20128/9812719

Scheba, S. (2022). Viewpoint–The South African Water Sector: Municipal Dysfunction, Resistance and Future Pathways. *Water Alternatives*, 15(3), 632–649.

Shongwe, B. R., & Meyer, D. F. (2023). Service Delivery Challenges within Rural Communities. The Case of the Nkomazi Local Municipal Area. Johannesburg. University of Johannesburg, School of Public Management, Governance and Public Policy.

Slater, D. (2021). DDM to improve planning, implementation as South Africa Embarks on economic recovery: African News. https://www.polity.org.za/article/district-development-model

*State of Nation Address*. (2024). South African Government. https://www.gov.za/SONA2024#

*State of the Nation Address*. (2019). South African Government. https://www.stateofthenation.gov.za/

*State of the Nation Address*. (2023). South African Government. https://www.stateofthenation.gov.za/

Statistics South Africa. (2022). https://www.statssa.gov.za/wp-content/uploads/

Vendemmia, B., Pucci, P., & Beria, P. (2021). An institutional periphery in discussion. Rethinking the inner areas in Italy. *Applied Geography (Sevenoaks, England)*, 135, 102537. 10.1016/j.apgeog.2021.102537

Vincent, C., & Stephen, C. (2015). Local government capacity building and development: Lessons, challenges and opportunities. *Journal of Political Sciences & Public Affairs*, 3(1), 1–5. 10.4172/2332-0761.1000149

Wadesango, N., Mhaka, C., Chikomo, T., & Wadesango, V. O. (2018). 'Causes of Poor Service Delivery and the Feasibility of Outsourcing to Improve Services in Local Authorities'. *Journal of Economics and Behavioral Studies*, 10(2), 88–198.

Zerihun, M.F., & Mashingo M.P. (2022). The quest for service delivery: The case of a rural district municipality in the Mpumalanga province of South Africa. *Africa's Public Service Delivery and Performance Review 10*(1), a512. (1). 10.4102/apsdpr.v10i1.512

# Chapter 10
# A Critical Appraisal on the Impact Maximization of Integrated Service Delivery Through District Development Model

**Ndwakhulu Stephen Tshishonga**
*University of KwaZulu-Natal, South Africa*

**Bernard Karabo Sebake**
*Nelson Mandela University, South Africa*

## ABSTRACT

*This chapter assesses the impact of the district development model (DDM) 's impact in maximizing integrated service delivery in South Africa. This chapter argues that the maximization of service delivery could only occur through proper alignment of resources, closing gaps between the people and the government. The chapter uses DDM objectives to evaluate the potential and challenges in enhancing integrated service delivery and intergovernmental relations at the local government level. DDM objectives are as follows: a) to promote cooperation instead of functioning in silos; b) to attenuate the disassociation between government and people; c) to ensure the delivery of consolidated services. OR Tambo District Municipality, eThekwini Metropolitan Municipality, and Waterberg District Municipality were used as case studies to reflect on the operation of the piloted DDM in South Africa.*

DOI: 10.4018/979-8-3693-3617-5.ch010

# INTRODUCTION

The democratically elected South African government has faced multiple challenges since the dawn of democracy. At the national level, these challenges include governance and public leadership, with inequality, poverty, and unemployment being at the center of citizens' dissatisfaction and disgruntlement (Schwella, 2017). Central to the provision of services is the state's capacity to develop and translate policies into tangible projects and programmes for the benefit of the public (Muriu, 2014). It is within the executive and legislative mandate of government, especially local government to provide sustainable services to the general public and the communities (Mdlalose, 2016). The main objective of municipalities, highlighted in sections 152 and Chapter 2 of the 1996 Republic of South African Constitution, is to render essential services. The notion of service delivery signifies the capacity of the developmental local government to work with citizens to comprehend the essence of government and comfort the needs of ordinary citizens (Sebake & Mukonza, 2020).

The study conducted by Kanyane (2014) extrapolates that poor service delivery exposes the local government to a lack of capacity to resolve municipalities' systemic challenges, from financial obligations to poor governance, planning, monitoring, and evaluation. This phenomenon exposed the long-fragmented models of local government where service delivery of the metros is better than that of the rural municipalities (Mokoele, 2022), exacerbating the dilemma for planning and management of service delivery. This chapter, therefore, interrogates the impact of the District Development Model introduced by President Ramaphosa in terms of maximizing integrated service delivery at the district level. The chapter laid the service delivery profile based on its conceptual meaning and scope of local government, approaches, and models that have evolved over the past decades. The theorisation of IGI follows this as a framework to conceptualise the chapter. The District Development Model is traced within the existing legislative frameworks and programmes at the local government sphere.

# SERVICE DELIVERY PROFILE IN SOUTH AFRICA

- **Service Delivery and Historic Evolution**

The post-1994 local government is based on the efforts to reform and dismantle the fragmented system that was not inspiring to consolidate service delivery that recognises the role of citizens (Reddy, 2016). This historical account first improved local government planning systems to respond to citizens' agency and that local government must inspire democratic systems. In this context, infusing public participation in planning through the consolidation of the Integrated Development Plan (IDP) planning system, the idea was to drive local governance as a key factor of political management (Reddy, 2016). The historical account notes that democratic government must be reconstructed from the grassroots level with an effort to build blocks for people-centered service delivery. While the historical evolution of local government predicated the necessary efforts to improve service delivery performance of a fragmented municipal landscape in South Africa (Brinkerhoff & Wetterberg, 2013), we argue that the DDM approach is foregrounded to accelerate service delivery through intergovernmental relation approaches that close the existing gap that resulted in silos and uncoordinated service delivery. From a global perspective, the DDM in India is initiated systematically to address consolidation and improve the socio-economic development through planning and impetus of the policy effectiveness (Goswami, Tripathi, Jain, Pathak & Seth, 2019).

Tsheola (2012) opines that the service delivery profile in the South African context lacks value for money where the integration of the multi-stakeholder role is not clearly defined from the planning approach, execution, and impact toward the public good. Hence, it is arguable that the DDM is directed at refining fragmented service delivery where local government had been in the spotlight for failing to meet the objectives of developmental local government. In this context, an effective and efficient implementation of DDM could be instrumental in eliminating wasteful expenditure and further consolidating integrated and intergovernmental approach to service delivery in South Africa.

- **State of Service Delivery: Rural and City Fragmentation**

Municipalities in the rural demarcated areas are confronted with the incapacity to better the lives of citizens given the scope and backlogs of provision of services that comfort human lives. Hence, local government is viewed as a non-responsive institution of a major concern in the 21st century (Mamokhere, 2019). For instance, Managa (2012) argues that over two decades in democratic South Africa, there is a growing concern about the capacity of local government to deliver public services to the citizens. Communities in rural municipalities are served less by the local government, clearly demonstrated by simply looking at communities still living without clean water (Masiya, Davids & Mangai, 2019).

Chikulo (2013) suggests that metropolis in South Africa are historically spaces where socio-economic development must be at the cutting edge of inspiring confidence in reducing the unemployment rate and poverty among citizens. This is mainly based on the metropolis being designed to enhance the quality of life, where service delivery must attract strategic and viable economic drivers through state-of-the-art infrastructure to support the economy. In this context, we argue that the local government has been operating through a fracture for more than two decades. This argument is now laid down in the next sub-sections below.

- *Provision of Clean Water and Constitutional Obligation*

McGraw (2011) notes that in 2010, there were approximately 122 countries that conceded that water and sanitation by international law standards are fundamental human rights. This notion is predicated by a global debate within the global water movement advocating for a move toward human rights to water (Mirosa & Harris, 2012). Additionally, Khorommbi (2019) states that human need requires the provision of water, and this part is ringfenced by the Constitution of the Republic of South Africa, 1996 (hereinafter referred to as the Constitution (1996) under the "Bill of Rights" and ignites the Water Services Act no108 of 1997. This provides no escape route for developmental local government to work with all stakeholders in supplying water as part of a constitutional obligation. Moriarty, Smits, Butterworth & Franceys (2013) assert that local government has been distressed and inundated with pressure to supply clean water in rural areas due to incapacity to manage water infrastructural development and water management systems for decades. This failure has made the local government not fulfill its constitutional obligations and, therefore, was found to violate people's rights to access services as stipulated in the Constitution (1996). In this context, the DDM is a strategic response to ignite multi-layers of government and interdepartmental efforts to tackle the challenge of this violation of human rights through which the government cannot meet its basic constitutional obligations.

The urban areas are also finding it not easy to supply clean and quality water to its citizens, and other metropolis are threatened to hit day zero of water supply. Turok and Borel-Saladin (2014) argue that water supply is becoming crisis in urban areas and cities even though urbanisation signifies a move towards prosperity and quality enhanced life. Perhaps the collapsing water supply in cities might be partly due to urban migration where the demand for clean water is overstretching the capacity to supply (Cole, Bailey, Cullis & New, 2018). In this context, the envisaged developmental local government is experiencing an incapacity to comprehend service delivery.

- *Rural & Urban Local Economic Development*

The concept of Local Economic Development (LED) serves to cultivate economic responsiveness by local government and its institutions. Rogerson (2014) explains that LED has been an important embodiment of local government planning to address inequalities, poverty and unemployment through creating a community's self-organisation and reliance. The long-standing challenges of LED has been that it requires a spatial intervention to attract massive industrial infrastructure. On the other hand, massive infrastructure in the Central Business Districts (CBD's) in the cities is dilapidating to the state of collapse hence, most investors are moving out or failing to occupy the infrastructure for business. In this context, LED in cities remains at the crossroads and represents a pipedream. Additionally, conceptualising a thriving urban economy, LED is a strategy to refine the role localities play as both sites and agents of economic development (Harvey, 1989; Nel & Rogerson, 2016). Rural citizens in South Africa are caught in a web of deprivations that undermine their potential to live a decent life. Most of their challenges and deprivations are attributed to the apartheid policies which relegated millions of black South Africans into overcrowded and impoverished reserves, homelands and townships (Tshishonga, 2021). Without basic infrastructure, arable land and skills to make land productive, without financial resources for rural citizens to secure services, rural life remains bleak. Chamber's (1983) deprivation trap could be used to understand the conditions and marginalization under which rural citizens are exposed. In this context, exclusion and marginalization of rural dwellers take place in forms such as isolation, powerlessness, vulnerability, poverty, and physical weakness. These life dimensions are further compounded by health, educational capacity constraints, budget deficit, skills deficit, income poverty, slow rural transformation, and land degradation (Cebekhulu, 2018). Developmental services include water & sanitation, electricity, refuse removal, public housing, roads, public safety, etc. (Reddy, 2026; Mbatha, 2022). This chapter argues that there is an intrinsic connection between rural elements of the deprivation trap. Isolation, powerlessness, and physical weakness render people to be vulnerable and poverty-stricken. Poverty renders the poor voiceless and powerless. Their powerlessness is exacerbated by physical weakness. Thus, Local Economic Development (LED) and Independent Development Plan (IDP) are among some of the existing strategies designed to close the rural-urban gap in South Africa. These frameworks enable developmental local government to execute legislative and executive mandates as the closest to the people through human, financial, material, and technological resources (Kanyane & Koma, 2014). LED constitutes a convergence improvement of human development and socio-economic conditions for the greater good (Rogerson, 2018). Rogerson (2018) argues that even in the quest to examine a pro-poor LED, municipalities must deliver services that enable the pro-poor economy to thrive, such as construction and maintenance of infrastructural support. This notion predicts the state of LED in South African Local Government as being constrained by the spatial development support that is not responsive to the needs of LED as a point of convergence. It is in this context that DDM is expected to close the silo approach to the infrastructural development for the improvement of LED as an approach towards realising the mandate of developmental local government.

## THEORISING INTERGOVERNMENTAL RELATIONS

The concept of Intergovernmental relations signifies a breaking ground for integrating and redeeming emerging conflicts of the role through the harmonization of government policy frameworks to respond to the mounting needs of citizens (Keating, 2012). This strategy of governance consolidates government strength and coordinates all capabilities towards building a responsive government that positions service delivery at the center of promoting quality lives of ordinary citizens. In this context, Burke (2014) argues that intergovernmental relations is a governance of convergence for the greater public good. A capable state is defined by its ability to integrate systems to address pitfalls of service delivery and enhance democratic governance. Additionally, the DDM is an embodiment of such efforts to break silos of government spheres and enhance interdependence. Auel (2014) notes that intergovernmental relations promote dynamic working connectivity from national, provincial, and local governments. This predicates that no sphere of governance in a democratic state can exist in isolation, but co-exist in promoting symbiotic relations in governance ideal.

South Africa has an intergovernmental system based on cooperation among the three levels of government: local, provincial, and national. While certain functions are assigned to a particular sphere, many other operations are shared among the three domains (Purfield, 2016). The Constitution (1996) provides the functions administered by these organs. The Intergovernmental Relations Framework Act, 2005 (Act 13 of 2005) defines intergovernmental relations as "relationships that arise among different governments or among organs of state from different governments in the conduct of their affairs" (Malan, 2012; Makoti & Odeku, 2018). Hence, intergovernmental relations aim to encourage and enable cooperative decision-making and ensure that policies and practices in all spheres of government promote service delivery and effectively meet the needs of citizens. Krane, & Wright (2018) further emphasise that intergovernmental relations are not one-time, sporadic occurrences formally laid out in agreements or rigidly framed by statutes or court decisions, but rather a constant pattern of contacts, sharing of knowledge by public officials, and information exchange.

The challenge of intergovernmental relations is that officials and politicians serving on spheres and in charge of intergovernmental relations fail to create a 'mindset' of cooperation and information-sharing and show a genuine commitment to implementing the principles of collaborative government (Munzhedzi, 2022). Challenges are often the result of the tension between national directive where the national government defines the roles of provincial and local government, while provincial and local governments determines their preferred choices within their area of jurisdiction (Homsy, Liu, & Warner, 2019). Despite the constitution's existence to guide and promote intergovernmental relations, complex problems of interdepartmental and intergovernmental coordination emerge as the three branches of government seek to integrate and implement a working government by ensuring that citizens' basic needs are met. In this context, the challenges of intergovernmental relations are a breeding ground for poor national barometers in monitoring all functions of other spheres.

## EMERGENCE OF DISTRICT DEVELOPMENT MODEL

District Development Models should be understood within the municipal categories A, B, and C. Shared local authority was established for the territories outside of category A municipal areas even though category A was a self-standing municipality (metropolitan areas). A category B municipality shares municipal executive and legislative responsibility in its jurisdiction with a category C municipality, whose area it falls into, according to Section I 55(I) (b) of the Municipal Structures Act (1998). As a result, a Category B municipality and a Category C municipality share the authority and responsibilities outlined in Parts B of Schedules 4 and 5. A municipality with municipal executive and legislative responsibility over a region that includes other municipalities is considered a category C municipality. Integrating these categories under the local sphere of government is key in advancing the District Development Model as spearheaded by President Ramaphosa during the State of Nation Address (SONA) (2019).

Local municipalities and district municipalities are the terms used in subsequent legislation for category B and category C municipalities, respectively (Bowden & Liddle, 2017). Thus, a district municipality is made up of various local municipalities. Sotarauta *et al.* (2017) claim that the constitution defers to parliament when deciding how much power to give to category B and C municipalities. When a region contains both category B and category C municipalities, Section 155(3)(c) of the Municipal Structures Act (1998) mandates that national legislation provide for an adequate division of responsibilities and functions amongst municipalities. To ensure that proper separation of powers and functions is in place, three sets of criteria are offered. First, a set of guidelines for the division of budgetary authorities are provided in Section 229 of the Constitution (1996), which is subject to this division (Wolman & Spitzley, 2022). The national legislation must consider the requirement to provide municipal services in an equitable and sustainable way, according to Section 155(4) of the Constitution. Third, the division need not be uniform; the powers of B municipalities inside a C municipality can differ.

The introduction of DDM was aimed at maximizing integrated service delivery through the district-based approach in addressing service delivery challenges and localise procurement and job creation. The District Development Model (DDM) was introduced by the President of the Republic of South Africa and approved by the Cabinet in August 2019 to express and actualize the intergovernmental relations framework as outlined in the Constitution (1996) (Academy of Science of South Africa, 2022). The approval of DDM meant that there will be a new approach to strengthening and synchronizing planning across all levels of government, as well as increasing citizen, business, and civil society participation in municipal districts and metros. The DDM aims to facilitate integrated planning, service, and monitoring of the government's development programs through the establishment of national technical capacity as well as district hubs that will drive program implementation (Khambule, 2021). DDM approach will not only hasten local economic development, urbanization, and economic activity, but it will also hasten the provision of basic services (Cooperative Governance and Traditional Affairs, 2020). It is in this regard that responding to service delivery challenges, DDM is a practical intergovernmental relations (IGR) method that aims to create an integrated and single strategic approach "One Plan" and "One Budget" for each of the 44 districts and eight metropolitan geographic regions.

Effective and efficient implementation of the DDM could advance inter-departmental and sphere cooperation and further avert spheres of government and departments operating in silos. Thus, according to Khambule (2020), the DDM is mandated to improve the working of intergovernmental relations in a coordinated and integrated manner at the district level. Through DDM, all 44 district municipalities and 8 metropolitans across the country are delegated to plan and implement an integrated and single development plan for each district municipality (Gumede, 2022). Considering the fragmented planning and implementation of municipality plans, DDM helps mobilize all spheres of government towards streamlining human and financial resources for the development of the local constituencies. The working of DDM depends strictly on the IGR processes are predominantly multi-layered in coordinating the activities of government (Bergström, Kuhlmann, Laffinand & Wayenberg, 2022). Introspectively, the championing of DDM questions a decentralised system and its effectiveness in discharging the mandated functions of local government in particular. DDM is mandated ; a) to promote cooperation instead of functioning in silos, b) to attenuate the disassociation between government and people, c) to ensure the delivery of consolidated services; d) to maximize the impact of community development projects and properly align resources and encourage long-term strategic planning, and e) to strengthen the systems of the Local government and state capacity to gauge the feasibility of this Model in expediting integrated service delivery. The actualization of these objectives could render the principles of good and participatory democracy, such as cooperation, accountability, and transparency (Madlala, 2020). Bergström et al. (2022) argue that IGR structures should provide vertical pathways with the capacity for subnational governments to execute their mandate and resolve arising conflicts among the spheres of government.

The District Development Model (DDM) intends to link service delivery with the integrated development plan to achieve the developmental state. The DDM essentially draws on the existing policy structures that guide local and district municipalities' intergovernmental planning coordination functions (Department of Planning, Monitoring and Evaluation, 2019). The DDM encourages economic development, growth, and inclusion through a bottom-up approach by creating a favourable environment and providing regulatory certainty in municipalities. Cooperative Governance and Traditional Affairs (2020) further ascertain that DDM allows the government to work together by focusing on municipal districts and metropolitan areas as impact areas for joint planning, budgeting, and implementation. As the DDM focuses on long-term infrastructure management activity at the district level, its emphasis is on building technical capacity and inter-governmental coordination to facilitate associated planning, implementation, and monitoring for effective service delivery (Sausi et al. 2022; Nel & Minnie, 2022).

The District Development Model (DDM) is grounded on existing legislative frameworks such as the RSA Constitutions (1996), the White Paper on Local Government (1998), and The National Development Plan (2011). DDM is reflective of the above-stated legislation. Hence, this model should not be understood as new but as a critique and enjoiner of other amalgamated policies. In this context, DDM contributes to the evolution of local government knowledge and strategy for institutional enhancement.

## OPERATION OF DDM IN SELECTED DIDTRICT MUCIPLAITIES

- **Profile of DDM in OR Tambo**

In OR Tambo, the District Development Model is an operational model for improving Cooperative Governance to establish a capable and ethical government. It is an all-of-government and-society approach that employs a method in which all three branches of government and state entities collaborate impact-oriented (Zabala, *et al.*, 2020). It is altering the way the government operates. The OR Tambo District Municipality is categorized as a category C2 municipality, indicating that it has a largely rural character, a low rate of urban development, and limited municipal staff and budget capacity (Ngcinela, *et al.* 2019). All local municipalities, with the exception of King Sabata Dalindyebo Local Municipality, are classified as category B4 rural, reflecting limited institutional capacity and areas characterized by small centers, limited market opportunities, reliance on public support, and local economic development activities (Sausi, *et al.* 2022) The district has adopted a long term DDM which the district integrated as a way to bolster service delivery. The DDP has five key targets under its vision. These are district bodies repositioned to drive inclusive economic development, transformed land ownership and land management, agricultural revitalization, and inclusive socio-economic development (Taruvinga et al., 2022).

- **Profile of DDM in eThekwini**

The geographic location of the eThekwini district maps it as a strategic consideration in the national space economy, playing an essential role in regional spatial and economic integration (Brand & Drewes, 2020). As a result, eThekwini is regarded as a national asset, with its infrastructure and growth protected and harnessed in the national interest and for the benefit of the people occupying it. As a result, eThekwini was selected as one of three DDM pilot sites to break down "silos" and improve service delivery and development outcomes through better horizontal and vertical government coordination (Kunene, Mashau & Nyawo, 2022). The eThekwini One Plan is essentially an implementation tool for the National Development Plan (NDP), as it localizes national targets and goals and synergizes the priorities of all three spheres of government, including the city's participatory Integrated Development Plan in order to fundamentally alter the fortunes of eThekwini residents by addressing the underlying causes of structural and systemic deprivation, unemployment, and inequality Currie, 2021; and Academy of Science of South Africa, 2022).

- **Profile of DDM in Waterberg**

Waterberg District is one of the three DDM pilots launched in 2019. Mining and agriculture are key economic drivers of the district (Mazzucato, Qobo & Kattel, 2022). Game farming, livestock farming, and irrigated agriculture contribute immensely to the economic development of the district and province (Nel & Minnie, 2022). With the aforementioned resources, the DDM is being used by the government to institutionalize an integrated, district-based development strategy aimed at accelerating service delivery and ensuring that municipalities collaborate and are adequately supported and resourced to carry out their mandate (Msemburi, 2020; Mazzucato, Qobo & Kattel, 2022). Therefore, the DDM Waterberg district is a vehicle for refocusing service delivery and strengthening implementation through a well-coordinated and coherent national plan of action. In this regard, the implementing officials will contribute to the implementation of key interventions and this plan will go a long way towards eliminating inefficiencies and duplications caused by government departments operating in silos (Mazzucato, Kattel & Ryan-Collins, 2020).

## FINDINGS AND ANALYSIS

- **DDM's Enhancement of Co-ordinated Service Delivery Strategy**

It is worth noting that DDM has not been thoroughly researched in the South African context as a service delivery model. The model is based on development theory that consolidates state capacity through collaborative mechanisms. In this context, the idea of state capacity to deliver services in a complimentary manner is promoted as part of a reformed local government response strategy (Mazzucato, Qobo & Kattel, 2022). The art of improving service delivery by developmental local government is an essential part of a state that prioritises reforms that are an embodiment of enhancement of democratic governance. It is in this regard that the coordination of local government is not a static phenomenon but an essential part of institutional growth and development (Mamokhere, Musitha & Netshidzivhani, 2022). The concept of DDM is assumed to be a strategy for institutional collective enhancement and promoting state institutional shared vision that demonstrates improved service provision. DDM is a center for developing knowledge of redefining government spheres as an interdependent and interrelated set of one government concerned about its citizens' welfare. The government's success is based on the state of infrastructure, enabling an environment for reducing poverty and unemployment, in which DDM is a fundamental management tool for enhanced service delivery (Mazele & Amoah, 2022). In this context, DDM influences the organizational culture of good performance (Gasela, 2022), which promotes a developmental local government that works with citizens to improve people-centred service delivery.

- **DDM and Intergovernmental Participatory Local Government**

The existence of DDM is assumed in this chapter as a mechanism of strengthening Intergovernmental Relations and interdepartmental corporations amongst the state organs and institutions. From the historical context, the concept of intergovernmental relations can be traced from United State in the 1930s (Munzhedzi, 2022). It is in this context that we argue that DDM is established to crystalise a concept that is old. This notion demonstrates that DDM is rather not new but a reformed and integrated strategy that addresses cooperation amongst the institutions charged with the responsibilities of fashioning service delivery. Shopola (2022) states that the global context of service delivery is largely a fundamental component of collaborative efforts between municipalities at local levels and their established districts through coordinated plans and budgeting systems. Therefore, the chapter moves from the premise that DDM promotes financial stewardship and assists in defining collaborative roles of government at all levels toward a coordinated service delivery.

Local government is an institution established in terms of the wishes of citizens. The fragmented competition between District Municipalities and their local municipalities posed a threat to South African developmental local government. Rulashe and Ijeoma (2022) note that a constant account of service delivery in local government is sending a shocking wave despite national frameworks promoting public participation. Arguably, DDM gives both levels of government a mandate in shaping the course of democratic localized government and jostling out the previous competition.

## RECOMMENDATIONS FOR FUTURE RESEARCH

The DDM aims to embed the culture of an integrated service delivery model. Arguably, this model should be piloted to integrate the provincial administration so that the national government can become closer to service delivery. Additionally, the DDM is the epitome of a strategy to cultivate participatory service delivery while improving transparency and accountability and maximise the impact on service delivery (Pfahl, O'Gorman & Fischer, 2017). There is a need for comprehensive research on how the DDM model could be used as a springboard for the future reformed model of governance in South Africa.

## CONCLUSION

DDM is a contemporary in the South African local government context. This chapter laid a basis to introspect conceptual strategies that developmental local government. The DDM was presented as a solution driven by the mounting challenges that developmental local government is confronted with, such as a lack of clear ownership of service delivery that ignited competition and silos by government institutions. These challenges depend on local government's capacity to meet citizens' interests, and it crystalized a new democratic system of intergovernmental relations. The reformed local government is now enjoying the single coordinated planning and execution of service delivery that ensures stewardship of financial duplications and wastage to the government institutions. In this context, the profile of DDM in the piloted districts in three provinces of South African local government must be strengthened to serve as a case in point of an improved service delivery that promotes Intergovernmental Relations in which developmental local government can gain much-needed experience for strengthening institutions of localized democracy.

## REFERENCES

Academy of Science of South Africa. (2022). The District Development Model as a platform for inclusive innovation and innovative districts. Academy of Science of South Africa. [http://hdl.handle.net/20.500.11911/240]. Accessed on. [07 February 2023]

Auel, K. (2014). Intergovernmental relations in German federalism: Cooperative federalism, party politics and territorial conflicts. *Comparative European Politics*, 12(4), 422–443. 10.1057/cep.2014.13

Bergström, T., Kuhlmann, S., Laffin, M., & Wayenberg, E. (2022). Special issue on comparative intergovernmental relations and the pandemic: How European devolved governments responded to a public health crisis. *Local Government Studies*, 48(2), 179–190. 10.1080/03003930.2022.2039636

Brand, A., & Drewes, E. (2020). Structuring South Africa's national economic space: A regional corridor network model approach. *Town and Regional Planning*, 77, 120–135.

Breakfast, N., Bradshaw, G., & Nomarwayi, T. (2019). Violent service delivery protests in post-apartheid South Africa, 1994–2017-a conflict resolution perspective. *African Journal of Public Affairs*, 11(1), 106–126.

Brinkerhoff, D. W., & Wetterberg, A. (2013). Performance-based public management reforms: Experience and emerging lessons from service delivery improvement in Indonesia. *International Review of Administrative Sciences*, 79(3), 433–457. 10.1177/0020852313491059

Burke, B. F. (2014). Understanding intergovernmental relations, twenty-five years hence. *State & Local Government Review*, 46(1), 63–76. 10.1177/0160323X13520461

Cebekhulu, E. (2018). *Umhlaba Uyahlaba! The World is Thorny. Wandsbeck.* Reach Publishers.

Chikulo, B. C. (2013). Developmental local governance and service delivery in South Africa: Progress, achievements and challenges. *Journal of Social Development in Africa*, 28(1), 35.

Cole, M. J., Bailey, R. M., Cullis, J. D., & New, M. G. (2018). Spatial inequality in water access and water use in South Africa. *Water Policy*, 20(1), 37–52. 10.2166/wp.2017.111

Cooperative Governance and Traditional Affairs. (2020). *District development model progress*. Pretoria: COGTA. Republic of South Africa.

Cooperative Governance and Traditional Affairs. (2020). *Update on the roll-out of the DDM approach. Presentation at the dialogue on the institutionalisation of the District Development Model.* Pretoria: COGTA. RSA.

Currie, A. (2021). Industry engagement on DDM implementation. *IMIESA*, 46(2), 20–21.

De Vries, M. S. (2016). *Understanding Public Administration.* Palgrave Macmillan. 10.1007/978-1-137-57546-3

Department of Planning, Monitoring and Evaluation. (2019). *Khawuleza District Development Model.* Pretoria: DPME. RSA.

Gasela, M. M. (2022). The influence of organizational culture on performance in public entities of South Africa. *Africa's Public Service Delivery and Performance Review*, 10(1), 563. 10.4102/apsdpr.v10i1.563

Goswami, D., Tripathi, S. B., Jain, S., Pathak, S., & Seth, A. 2019. Towards building a district development model for India using census data. In *Proceedings of the 2nd ACM SIGCAS Conference on Computing and Sustainable Societies* (pp. 259-271). ACM. 10.1145/3314344.3332491

Gumede, V. (2022). *South Africa Sate & Development. Soshanguve & Pretoria: SAAPAM & Unisa Press.* RSA.

Harvey, D. (1989). From managerialism to entrepreneurialism: The transformation of urban governance in late capitalism. *Geografiska Annaler. Series B, Human Geography*, 71B(1), 3–17. 10.1080/04353684.1989.11879583

Homsy, G. C., Liu, Z., & Warner, M. E. (2019). Multilevel governance: Framing the integration of top-down and bottom-up policymaking. *International Journal of Public Administration*, 42(7), 572–582. 10.1080/01900692.2018.1491597

Kanyane, M. (2014). Exploring challenges of municipal service delivery in South Africa (1994-2013). *Africa's Public Service Delivery & Performance Review*, 2(1), 90–110. 10.4102/apsdpr.v2i1.45

Kanyane, M., & Koma, S. (2014). *Developmental Local Government in South Africa: Issues for Considerations. Wandsbeck.* Reach Publishers.

Keating, M. (2012). Intergovernmental relations and innovation: From co-operative to competitive welfare federalism in the UK. *British Journal of Politics and International Relations*, 14(2), 214–230. 10.1111/j.1467-856X.2011.00484.x

Khambule, I. (2021). The District Development Model: Towards a Capable Local Developmental State in South Africa. *Journal of Public Administration*, 56(3), 507–523.

Khorommbi, K. C. 2019. *The establishment of catchment management agencies in South Africa: an organisational design perspective* [Doctoral dissertation, North-West University, South Africa].

Krane, D., & Wright, D. S. (2018). Intergovernmental relations. In *Defining public administration* (pp. 83–101). Routledge. 10.4324/9780429501074-8

Kunene, B., Mashau, P., & Nyawo, J. (2022). Ascertaining The Challenges Faced By Women Entrepreneurs in Ethekwini Municipality, KwaZulu-Natal Province. *Gender & Behaviour*, 20(1), 19060–19083.

Madlala, S. (2020). Reconceptualizing Public Participation in Local Government: The District Development Model. Kariuki and Reddy, 2020 (Ed). *The Covid-19 Pandemic in South Africa: A Review of Selected Local Governance and Policy Responses, 2,* 81-100.

Makoti, M. Z., & Odeku, O. K. (2018). Critical perspective on the complexity and functionality of intergovernmental relations between provincial and local governments in South Africa. *African Journal of Public Affairs*, 10(1), 98–112.

Malan, L. P. (2012). *Intergovernmental relations in South Africa: a revised policy approach to co-operative government*. University of Pretoria.

Mamokhere, J. (2019). An exploration of reasons behind service delivery protests in South Africa: A case of Bolobedu South at the Greater Tzaneen Municipality. *International Conference on Public Administration and Development Alternatives (IPADA)*. IEEE.

Mamokhere, J., Musitha, M. E., & Netshidzivhani, V. M. (2022). The implementation of the basic values and principles governing public administration and service delivery in South Africa. *Journal of Public Affairs*, 22(4), e2627. 10.1002/pa.2627

Managa, A. (2012). Unfulfilled promises and their consequences: A reflection on local government performance and the critical issue of poor service delivery in South Africa. Africa Institute of South Africa. AISA. *Policy Brief*, 76, 1–8.

Manungufala, T. (2020). Overview of the District Development Model – A framework for co-Operative service delivery. Parliament, Research Unit: 9. [https://www.parliament.gov.za/storage/app/media/Pages/2020/september/02-09-2020_National_Council_of_Provinces_Local_Government_Week/docs/Overview_of_the_district_development_model_a_framework_for_co-operative_service_delivery.pdf]

Masiya, T., Davids, Y. D., & Mangai, M. S. (2019). Assessing service delivery. *Theoretical and Empirical Researches in Urban Management*, 14(2), 20–40.

Mazele, O., & Amoah, C. (2022). The causes of poor infrastructure management and maintenance in South African municipalities. *Property Management*, 40(2), 192–206. 10.1108/PM-06-2021-0042

Mazzucato, M., Kattel, R., & Ryan-Collins, J. (2020). Challenge-driven innovation policy: Towards a new policy toolkit. *Journal of Industry, Competition and Trade*, 20(2), 421–437. 10.1007/s10842-019-00329-w

Mazzucato, M., Qobo, M., & Kattel, R. (2022). Building state capacities and dynamic capabilities to drive social and economic development: The case of South Africa. In *The Future of the South African Political Economy Post-COVID 19* (pp. 43–74). Springer International Publishing. Midtown Manhattan. New York. 10.1007/978-3-031-10576-0_3

Mbatha, S. (2022). *Informal Transactions of Low-Income Houses in South Africa: A Case Study of eThekwini Municipality*. [Doctoral Thesis, Habitat International]. V26/ transcript.

McGraw, G. S. (2011). MINIMUM CORE: LEGAL CONSTRUCTION AND THE ROLE OF NATIONAL JURISPRUDENCE. *Loyola University Chicago International Law Review*, 8(2), 127–204.

Mirosa, O., & Harris, L. M. (2012). Human right to water: Contemporary challenges and contours of a global debate. *Antipode*, 44(3), 932–949. 10.1111/j.1467-8330.2011.00929.x

Modisha, N. J. (2013). *The role of rural-based municipalities to promote socio-economic development: The case of Molemole and Blouberg Municipalities in Limpopo province* [Doctoral dissertation, University of Limpopo].

Mokoele, N. J. (2022). Fragmented Governance in South African Cities: The Dilemmas of Planning and Management. *African Renaissance*, 19(2), 13–30.

Moriarty, P., Smits, S., Butterworth, J., & Franceys, R. (2013). Trends in rural water supply: Towards a service delivery approach. *Water Alternatives*, 6(3), 329.

Msemburi, W. T. (2020). *A Subnational Analysis of Burden of Disease in South Africa: Mortality Levels, Causes of Death and Their Forecasts*. University of Washington.

Munzhedzi, P. H. (2022). The top-down approach in intergovernmental relations in South Africa: Challenges and prospects. *Journal of Public Affairs*, 22(2), e2431.

Munzhedzi, P. H. (2022). The top-down approach in intergovernmental relations in South Africa: Challenges and prospects. *Journal of Public Affairs*, 22(2), e2431.

Ndevu, Z., & Muller, K. (2017). A conceptual framework for improving service delivery at local government in South Africa. *African Journal of Public Affairs*, 9(7), 13–24.

Nel, E., & Rogerson, C. M. (2016). The contested trajectory of applied local economic development in South Africa. *Local Economy*, 31(1-2), 109–123. 10.1177/0269094215623729

Nel, V., & Minnie, S. (2022). Can the district development model deliver development in South African local governments? *Rozwój Regionalny i Polityka Regionalna, 15*(60), 39-53.

Ngcinela, S., Mushunje, A., Taruvinga, A., Ngarava, S., & Mutengwa, C. S. (2019). Determinants of genetically modified (GM) maize adoption and the intensity of adoption in OR Tambo District Municipality, Eastern Cape Province, South Africa. *GM Crops and Food: Biotechnology in Agriculture and the Food Chain*, 10(1), 1–11. 10.1080/21645698.2019.158012730913974

Purfield, C. (2016). *Developing an Intergovernmental Fiscal Framework. Making It Happen, 13*. The World Bank.

Reddy, P. S. (2016). The politics of service delivery in South Africa: The local government sphere in context. *TD: The Journal for Transdisciplinary Research in Southern Africa*, 12(1), 1–8. 10.4102/td.v12i1.337

Rogerson, C. M. (2014). Reframing place-based economic development in South Africa: The example of local economic development. *Bulletin of Geography. Socio-Economic Series*, 24(24), 203–218. 10.2478/bog-2014-0023

Rogerson, C. M. (2018). Pro-poor local economic development in South Africa: the application of public procurement. In *Local economic development in the developing world* (pp. 101–130). Routledge.

Rulashe, T., & Ijeoma, E. O. (2022). An exploration of public accountability and service delivery at the Buffalo City Metropolitan Municipality in the Eastern Cape province, South Africa. *Africa's Public Service Delivery and Performance Review*, 10(1), 535. 10.4102/apsdpr.v10i1.535

Sausi, K., Kanyane, M., Davids, Y. D., Gumede, N., Houston, G., Mchunu, N., & Bohler-Muller, N. (2022). *Evaluating the District Development Model: a review, with case studies. Developmental, capable & ethical state research division human sciences research council.* Human Sciences Research Council.

Schwella, E. (2017). *South African Governance*. Oxford University Press Southern Africa. RSA.

Sebake, B. K., & Mukonza, R. M. (2020). Integrated Development Plan, Monitoring and Evaluation in the City of Tshwane: A confluence question for optimising service delivery. *Journal of Public Administration*, 55(3), 342–352.

Shopola, A.M., 2022. Management of District-Local Relations through the District Intergovernmental Forum in Mopani District Municipality, South Africa. *African Journal of Governance & Development, 11*(1.1), 25-46.

Taruvinga, A., Kambanje, A., Mushunje, A., & Mukarumbwa, P. (2022). Determinants of livestock species ownership at household level: Evidence from rural OR Tambo District Municipality, South Africa. *Pastoralism*, 12(1), 8. 10.1186/s13570-021-00220-6

Tsheola, J. P. (2012). Theorising a democratic developmental state: Issues of public service delivery planning and violent protests in South Africa. *Journal of Public Administration*, 47(1), 161–179.

Turok, I., & Borel-Saladin, J. (2014). Is urbanisation in South Africa on a sustainable trajectory? *Development Southern Africa*, 31(5), 675–691. 10.1080/0376835X.2014.937524

Zabala, L., Febres, J., Sterling, R., López, S., & Keane, M. (2020). Virtual testbed for model predictive control development in district cooling systems. *Renewable & Sustainable Energy Reviews*, 129, 109920. 10.1016/j.rser.2020.109920

## KEY TERMS AND DEFINITIONS

**District Development Model:** The DDM is a model designed to address problems with service delivery by allowing all spheres of government, from local municipalities to national government, to work together in a more effective and coordinated way. This will help municipalities to better plan, budget and implement projects and programmes.

**District Municipality:** A district municipality or Category C municipality is a municipality that executes some of the functions of local government for a district. The district municipality will, in turn, comprise several local municipalities, with which it shares local government functions.

**Integrated Service Delivery:** This is a service delivery model that brings together all service delivery stakeholders to provide services, support, and interventions in an integrated manner to the general public.

**Intergovernmental Relations:** is a concept that refers to the relationships between different governments within a single country. Intergovernmental relations also recognizes relationships among various units and sectors within the three spheres of government and focus on public officials acting in an inter-jurisdictional context.

# Chapter 11
# Analysis of the Significance of Good Governance in Municipal Planning and Implementation

**Emmanuel Maemu**
*University of Venda, South Africa*

## ABSTRACT

*This chapter focuses on the significance of good governance in municipal planning and implementation to develop changeable activities that may foster good governance during municipal planning and implementation. This chapter will seek to assess the obstacles that cause developmental projects to fail in South African municipalities. Municipal planning means the control and regulation of land use at a municipal level whereas implementation entails the requirement that all municipalities in the country develop and approve such plans to adequately respond to the needs. Good governance means the capacity of city councils and their partners to formulate and implement sound policies and systems that reflect the interests of local citizens, and to do so in a way that is transparent and inclusive of those with the least power and resources.*

DOI: 10.4018/979-8-3693-3617-5.ch011

## INTRODUCTION

The purpose of this article is to outline the significance of good governance in municipal planning and implementation in South African municipalities. Good governance is concerned about the formulation and implementation of sound policies and systems that reflect the interests of local citizens, and to be transparent and inclusive of those with the least power and resources. Municipalities set out the vision and framework for the future development of an area through local plans within the area of Jurisdiction. Planning helps the municipality to see in advance those things that can help in achieving the goals and those things that can prevent it from achieving the goals and work out what to do about them.

### Historical Background of Good Governance and Municipal Planning and Implementation

Good governance adds a normative or evaluative attribute to the process of governing. From a human rights perspective, Mutua (2017:103) indicates that it refers primarily to the process whereby public institutions conduct public affairs, manage public resources, and guarantee the realization of human rights. Poniatowicz, Dziemianowicz, and Kargol-Wasiluk (2020:80) posit that good governance is the process of measuring how public institutions conduct public affairs and manage public resources, and guarantee the realization of human rights in a manner essentially free of abuse and corruption and with due regard for the rule of law. Dellepiane-Avellaneda (2010:195) articulates that the concept of "good governance" thus emerges as a model to compare ineffective economies or political bodies with viable economies and political bodies. Dellepiane-Avellaneda (2010:195) adds that the concept centers on the responsibility of governments and governing bodies to meet the needs of the masses as opposed to select groups in society. Duarte and Ratti (2018:3) state that Town planning has been practiced for at least four thousand years. Poniatowicz *et al.* (2020:80) suggest that it would have first been practiced sometime after early groups of people had initially given up their prior nomadic way of life and settled down permanently, initially in a haphazard way, with other people where water and food were readily available or cultivatable and thereby gradually enabling increasing degrees of specialization of occupations to occur. Sorenson (2018) views that town planning was probably originally the exclusive preserve of thc priest class that emerged in the very early civilizations located in Sumer in Mesopotamia (Iraq), in the Indus Valley, and along the length of the Nile Valley (Egypt/Sudan). Wassenhoven and Wassenhoven (2019) show that later planning was practiced throughout the greater Hellenic Empire (Greece/Turkey/Persia), the Roman Empire, China, and the Olmec/Aztec/Inca Empires in Central and South America.

Today, generally only the grand-scale achievements of those early civilizations are still evident, although ongoing excavations are constantly unearthing new evidence that indicates that even the common man at the time benefited from town planning in these early ages (Orlando, 2020:190).

## LEGISLATIONS THAT REGULATE MUNICIPAL PLANNING AND IMPLEMENTATION

There is a considerable array of legislation that controls planning within the geographic boundaries of the Republic of South Africa. Some of the most important are as follows:

- **Constitution of the Republic of South Africa of 1996**- the primary role being the assigning of municipal planning responsibility to municipalities.
- **Municipal Systems Act (Act No. 32 of 2000)**- setting out in Chapter 2 the requirement, amongst others, for newly elected municipal councils to prepare and adopt an integrated development plan (IDP) for their respective areas and to provide for annual revision thereof. The IDP is required in terms of the act to include a spatial development framework (SDF) which must include the provision of basic guidelines for a land use system for the municipality.
- **Development Facilitation Act (DFA) (Act No. 67 of 1995)**- originally envisaged as interim legislation post the 1994 national elections to facilitate accelerated housing delivery by waving other legislation and giving decision-making to provincial Development Tribunals (where established), but utilized largely by the private sector for the development of amongst others, shopping centers, golf course estates, etc. DFA has since been declared unconstitutional by the Constitutional Court as it usurped the decision-making powers of municipalities and is required to be repealed or amended by June 2012. Note: Despite sections of the Act being declared unconstitutional by the court, its General Principles for Land Development, as contained in Chapter 1, Section 3 of the Act, are still deemed valid.
- **Less Formal Township Establishment Act (Act No. 113 of 1991)** – this act provides for shortened procedures for the establishment of townships, for less formal forms of residential settlement and to regulate the use of land by tribal communities for communal forms of residential settlement. This act is administered by the provinces, and it provides for the exclusion of certain laws and the suspension of servitudes and restrictive title deed conditions. Although not challenged yet in the Constitutional Court, this law is also no

doubt, like the DFA, unconstitutional as it shifts decision-making from the municipalities to the provinces.

- **Planning Acts and Ordinances in the provinces**. Most of the legislation directly controlling planning in the nine provinces is still pre-1994 legislation enacted by the original four provinces of South Africa, and they are all also generally unconstitutional in some or other aspect. Only in KwaZulu-Natal and in the Northern Cape has new planning legislation been enacted and put into effect since 1994 and even here certain aspects (relating to appeals) are challengeable. Some of the other provinces are in the process of drafting new planning legislation. As a result of the Constitutional Court ruling concerning the DFA and the tardiness of the preparation of the new legislation in some provinces, the Department of Rural Development and Land Affairs recently published the Spatial Planning and Land Use Management Bill for comment which it hopes to have enacted by June 2012.

## THE HIERARCHY OF PLANS

A suite of plans is legally required to be prepared by the municipality ranging from a very broad level strategic plan encompassing the entire municipality down to a very detailed plan to which specific land use rights are assigned to individual properties. In addition, there are other non-statutory plans which a local authority may or may not elect to prepare, based on its particular circumstances. The following plans are a likely suite of plans found with large cities in South Africa, different names may apply but intentions are largely the same to direct development from the strategic to the specific.

- **Long-Term Development Strategy (LTDS)**. A plan with a twenty-year-plus time horizon setting out the vision of the municipality in achieving its development objectives. This plan is directly linked to the integrated development plan (IDP) and gives the longer-term strategy direction for successive IDPs for the municipality that should otherwise be contained directly within the IDP. It however often common practice to see this as a standalone plan.
- **Integrated Development Plan (IDP).** It is a statutory plan required in terms of Chapter 5 of the Municipal Systems Act, 2000 encompassing all the functions undertaken by the Council within a 5-year time horizon guided by long-term objectives and strategies (see LTDS above). The IDP is required to be updated annually. This strategic plan for the development of the municipality should link, integrate, and coordinate various sector plans considering proposals for the development of the municipality, align the resources and ca-

pacity of the municipality for the implementation of the plan, form the policy framework and general basis on which annual budgets are set and in addition must be compatible with both national and provincial development plans.

- **Spatial Development Framework (SDF)** – a spatial depiction of the IDP as required in terms of Section 26 (e) of the Municipal Systems Act, 2000. It is the principal strategic planning instrument that guides and informs all planning and development, and all decisions regarding planning, management, and development in the municipality. It must include the provision of basic guidelines for a land use management system (LUMS). Note the SDF supersedes or prevails over any plan that may have been prepared under the Physical Planning Act, of 1991.
- **Scheme (variously called a town planning scheme or land use scheme)**. Normally prepared in terms of a provincial Ordinance or Act. This plan or series of plans, with its zoning maps and controls, forms the nuts and bolts of day-to-day development administration within a municipality. The scheme amongst others designates the zones and what activities may, or may not, be carried out in the respective zones whether by free entry or by (special) consent. The administration of the scheme in the main, when not initiated by the municipality, usually involves the consideration of rezoning and (special) consent applications brought by the public. The decisions can either be recommended by the administration for committee approval or approved by the administration through the process of delegation by the City Manager and relevant officials. Councils in particular Councilors must create an environment for the adjudication of planning and building applications that are free of any form of influence and to ensure that clear lines of separation between the administration and that of the political component of a Council.
- **Other non-statutory plans.** These include a Spatial Development Plan, a Sector Plan, a Local Area Plan, a Nodal Plan, a Corridor Plan, a Precinct Plan, etc. These plans would normally sit between the SDF and the Scheme. The plans at different scales, usually give a greater level of interpretation of the SDF over a specific geographic area. These plans may also be hierarchical from one to another. While giving a greater indication of acceptable land use within a certain geographical area they do NOT confer land use rights. The Scheme must be amended to reflect these higher-order plans before any land use rights may be conferred. These plans are not requirements in terms of any specific legislation but are nevertheless considered and approved by the formal resolution of the Council.

## GOOD GOVERNANCE AND ETHICAL CONDUCT IN MUNICIPAL PLANNING AND IMPLEMENTATION: THE *LINKAGE BETWEEN ETHICAL CONDUCT AND GOOD GOVERNANCE*

Oketch (2016:2) probes that as a fundamental component of successful governance, ethical governance is based on the ability to coordinate a democratic balance with efficiency and equity as guiding principles, as well as responsiveness to the needs and desires of the public. Every member of a municipal council is subject to the Code of Conduct, which is outlined in Chapter 12, Schedules 1 and 2, of the Local Government: Municipal Systems Act 2000 (32 of 2000). The Code of Conduct for Municipal Councilors is similarly outlined in Schedule 5 of the Local Government: Municipal Structures Act 1998 (Act 117 of 1998). Its goal is to foster an atmosphere rich in moral and ethical principles and behavior (SALGA, 2018). Furthermore, the Code of Ethics is necessary for South Africa's municipal governments to operate well. The municipal code of ethics aims to ensure moral leadership and openness from public servants; and to restore or foster public confidence and citizen assurance in the public administration. Hence, Bordvik (2022) advocates that creating an ethical culture requires new delivery methods, budgetary constraints, and a larger delegation of authority and discretion to public employees. Although the Local Government: Municipal Systems Act (32 of 2000) and the municipal handbook provide guidelines for councilors and municipal officials, there is no standard code of ethics for local government. The principles of cooperative government, the Bill of Rights, and intergovernmental relations are all upheld by municipal officials through the operation of the Constitution of the Republic of South Africa, 1996. It is required of public servants to be familiar with and comprehend the fundamental values and norms that they would be using on the job. Section 195 of the Constitution *of the Republic of South Africa 1996* indicates that Public Administration must be governed by democratic values and principles, such as the promotion of a high standard of professional ethics; The promotion of efficient, economic, and effective use of resources; That transparency must be fostered by providing the public with timely, accessible and accurate information; and That public administrations must be accountable. Enaifoghe (2023) contends that to effectively plan and carry out projects, there is a need to promote an ethical culture and environment in the South African municipal government. This can be achieved through the use of institutional organizations, legislative procedures, and codes of ethics. Moreover, Enaifoghe (2023) alludes that an ethically sound culture might focus on the actions of local leaders that lead to the correct decisions being made for the right reasons. With a legitimate justification for their moral autonomy and discretion in making decisions, council members and public officials can evaluate their actions against expected norms using ethical behavior and ethical codes. Ethical behavior is ingrained in organizations and repeatedly imparted to people. The democratic ideals enshrined in the Constitution of the Republic of South Africa, 1996 serve as the basis for values in South Africa. A few of the fundamental ideals and principles guiding public institutions are accountability, impartiality, development orientation, representation and participation, fairness, public accountability, effectiveness and efficiency, and professional ethics, as stated in Section 195 of the Constitution of the Republic of South Africa, 1996. Since the beginning, local government officials and political appointees have been held to a higher standard of accountability for upholding democratic norms responsively and responsibly. When serving the public, local government representatives are supposed to uphold democratic principles; the benefits can subsequently be seen in the high-quality goods and services that are provided to communities.

Ethical awareness and training as a way of effectively planning and implementing municipal projects: *Learning to do the right thing* Botes (2015:57) highlighted that the training and development of public officials should always include ethical issues. This would include training on values and the scope of ethical and moral behavior. This training will help officials to cope with the demands made by the public, as well as to improve their skills. Enaifoghe (2023) proposes that it is necessary to raise ethical awareness in the workplace, where local authorities can plan campaigns to raise awareness of ethical issues and execute training and development initiatives. To combat misconduct, corruption, and maladministration, it is crucial to provide ethical training to community members and stakeholders participating in municipal planning and implementation. Conversely, Enaifoghe (2023) moreover, added that it is possible to successfully conduct a voluntary ethical survey by asking all employees at various levels of the municipality. Hence, to guarantee that everyone in the workforce shares the same values and is equipped with the knowledge and tools to handle moral quandaries, ethics education is required at all levels of the municipality. Better outcomes can be obtained from training programs that are continuously monitored and assessed. Additionally, High standards of behavior can also be promoted in an ethical workplace by offering suitable rewards for moral behavior, such as respectable working circumstances and efficient performance evaluation. *Learningfrom failures is a crucial step towards achieving productivity, efficiency, and effectiveness. To put it briefly, ethical education and training are, therefore, necessary to establish good governance in municipal planning and implementation. In recap, good governance plays a significant role in municipal planning and implementation as it advocates for good morals towards municipal activities and project implementation. Good governance goes together with ethical conduct. Therefore, to achieve good governance in municipal project planning and implementation there is a need for ethical conduct and effective leadership. Learning is key in fostering good governance in municipal planning and implementation to achieve socio-economic development.*

## CHALLENGES ASSOCIATED WITH THE MUNICIPAL PROJECTS PLANNING AND IMPLEMENTATION: A CRITICAL ANALYSIS

Phago (2009) adds that inadequate public participation is a serious concern that inhibits the planning and implementation of the IDP in the municipality, whereby in addition He asserted that Ward consultation meetings for identification and prioritization of community needs are tending to violence and civil unrest. Beyers (2016) stresses that politics are the reason for the failure of municipal planning and implementation, wherein he suggests the separation of functionalities between politicians and administrative officials. According to Asha and Makalela (2020), the municipality's inability to provide for the severe requirements of its constituents is mostly caused by the communities' failure to pay for some municipal services (revenue collection), including water, property taxes, and trash collection. The municipality's predominately rural location, as opposed to urban municipalities where residents are able and ready to pay for services, is the primary cause of the non-payment of such services. Additionally, Asha and Makalela (2020) said that the municipalities had some sort of managerial issue when it came to finishing a project. Fraud and a lack of funding to complete the projects are the primary causes of the municipality's numerous project abandonments, which result in a lot of white elephant projects or projects that are futile in communities. Consequently, Kanyane (2014) adds that direct consequences or manifestations of municipal capacity constraints, financial viability problems, service delivery protests, convoluted political processes, and corruption are the challenges faced by municipalities in the planning and implementation of the projects. *This paper suggests or proposes the problems that are associated with municipalities when planning and implementing the projects. These challenges include poor community-stakeholder involvement, power hunger, political battles, working for money instead of working for people to promote their value and serving the needs of the community, greed and selfish traditional leaders who seek self-development, uneducated municipal officials, failure to practice merit appointment personnel system, too much power that is vested on politicians than administrators, hunger and poor capacity building to cater the socio-economic development. In a nutshell, illiteracy is the reason for the failure of the municipal projects planning and implementation*

## MEASURES FOR PROMOTING GOOD GOVERNANCE IN MUNICIPAL PLANNING AND IMPLEMENTATION

This paper argues that public institutions in South Africa must select law-abiding, morally honest, transparent, and accountable public servants. Moreover, Integrity, openness, and independent supervision should be regarded as the three components that comprise accountability and enforce good governance in municipal planning and implementation. Ubisi (2018) quoted in Kgobe *and* Mamokhere (2021:3) add that accountability is about accepting responsibility for your actions, dealing with the fallout, and growing as a result of them. One mechanism that supports global good governance for sustainable development is accountability, which is mandated by the Constitution. Similarly, accountability is implied by the Council of Europe (2022) to mean that all decision-makers, whether individual or collective, must be accountable for their actions. According to Banerjee (2020), having integrity in ethics means carrying out one's actions with honesty, truthfulness, or accuracy. Integrity is the discipline of telling the truth and exhibiting an unflinching commitment to high moral and ethical standards in the service of effective government. Thus, to properly design and carry out municipal projects, public officials must serve the public interest by carrying out their official duties in an honest, fair, and consistent manner with the soundness of moral values. In the public sector, transparency is an essential concept, especially when it comes to municipal planning and implementation. As a result, it ought to be supported and carried out by the Constitution of the Republic of South Africa 1996. Transparency, according to Alma'arif & Wargadinata (2022:23), is the process of ensuring that people have the freedom to learn about policies at every stage of development and assessment. Transparency is added by Alma'Arif *et al.* (2022) and Da Cruz *et al.* (2016) as part of government initiatives to improve community engagement in the formulation of public policy, particularly in the area of development planning. Furthermore, according to Chiyamwaka (2007), transparency is the process of making sure that data is accessible so that it can be used to assess how well the government is performing and to prevent any abuses of power. Oversight agencies must operate independently of others and on a professional basis to uphold public confidence in the government and advance good governance (United Nations Department of Economic and Social Affairs, 2019).

Promoting the independence of regulatory bodies like Anti-corruption strategy and the Auditor General is one of the frequently employed tactics. These institutions are frequently thought of as systems that guarantee responsibility, as Kgobe et al. (2021) have shown. The Auditor-General's responsibility is to ensure that the government is held accountable for its financial actions. The Constitution of the Republic of South Africa 1996 ensures the democratic norms and principles needed to guide governmental administration in that country. In terms of section 195 (1) (b), a public administrator should utilize government resources in an efficient, effective, and economic manner (Mamokhere, Musitha, & Netshiedzivhani, 2021:5). To facilitate good governance municipalities need to ensure effective planning and implementation of the projects. To enhance efficacy within municipalities, partnerships with business associations, non-governmental organizations, and communities are recommended to foster good governance during project plan and implementation. Thus, cooperation is also the principle that deals with effectiveness. Residents should have access to government services, support, and information to ensure that no one is left behind in municipal planning, according to IASIA (2022) and the United Nations Department of Economics and Social Affairs (2021). Ensuring the inclusion of marginalized groups in public governance is vital, especially in areas such as planning, decision-making, service delivery, and sustainable development. Additionally, it is critical to grant these populations the authority and dignity required to engage in these processes appropriately. According to the Constitution of the Republic of South Africa 1996, public engagement ought to be strengthened and encouraged in South African municipalities as a way of promoting good governance.

## RECOMMENDATIONS AND CONCLUSION

For this paper, the Chapter 9 Institutions must be effectively fostered in all municipalities as a way of fighting maladministration towards municipal planning and implementation. Moreover, public-private partnerships should be advocated in municipal planning and implementation. The paper also suggests a crucial punishment in terms of misconduct in the sense that people tend to do misconduct knowing very well that they will be arrested and later come back. The case of former president Jacob Zuma demonstrates that wrongdoing is not taken seriously, and as a result, to establish a penalty that works, the Chapter 9 institution needs to be reviewed and updated, hence productivity continues to be the primary focus as the report recommends excellent governance, highlighted by the Chapter Institutions, as a strategy to effectively target the wrongdoing in municipal planning and implementation. The report also recommends that to combat maladministration and release residents from their mandated service delivery, more research be done on the promotion of good governance in municipal planning and implementation. In recap, good governance is paramount in the municipal planning and implementation. In concluding remarks good governance is responsible for effective municipal planning and implementation, but only if the principles of good governance are promoted and enforced by the Chapter Institutions.

The paper was about the significance of good governance in municipal planning and implementation to develop changeable activities that may foster good governance during municipal planning and implementation. Public participation, accountability, collaboration, monitoring and evaluation, inspection, and inter alia serve as important measures for promoting good governance. The E-governance system is vital for municipal service planning and implementation however, data will remain the challenges to communities, therefore education and training should also be emphasized.

## REFERENCES


Alma'arif, A.A. & Wargadinata, E.L. (2022). Adopting Open Government in Local Development Planning. *Jurnal Kebijakan dan Administrasi Publik, 26*(1), 18-26.

Asha, A. A., & Makalela, K. I. (2020). *Challenges in the implementation of integrated development plan and service delivery in Lepelle Nkumphi Municipality*. Limpopo Province. 10.34109/ijefs.202012101

Banerjee, C. (2020). *Guidelines on Integrity and Transparency in Governance and Responsible Code of Conduct.* New Delhi, India: Confederation of Indian Industry (CII). https://www2.deloitte.com/content/dam/Deloitte/in/Documents/risk/inrisk-cii-guidelines-on-integrity-transparency-in-governance-and-responsible-code-of-conduct-noexp.pdf.

Beyers, L. J. E. (2016). Service delivery challenges facing municipalities: A case study of Fetakgomo Local Municipality in Sekhukhune District Municipality, Limpopo Province. *Bangladesh e-Journal of Sociology*, 13(2), 167–178.

Bordvik, M. B. (2022). *Ethical Code of Conduct and its impact on decision making among managers in local government in Zimbabwe*. Walden University.

Bouckaert, G., Chawdhry, U., Fraser-Moleketi, G., Meuleman, L., & Pizani, M. (2018). *Effective Governance for Sustainable Development: 11 Principles to Put in Practice*. International Institute for Sustainable Development.

Chiyamwaka, B. (2007). *The role of the media in fostering good governance, transparency, and accountability*. Media Council of Malawi.

Council of Europe. (2022). *Twelve Principles of Good Governance*. Strasbourg Cedex, France: Council of Europe. https://www.coe.int/en/web/good-governance/12-principles

Da Cruz, N. F., Tavares, A. F., Marques, R. C., Jorge, S., & De Sousa, L. (2016). Measuring local government transparency. *Public Management Review*, 18(6), 866–893. 10.1080/14719037.2015.1051572

Dellepiane-Avellaneda, S. (2010). Good governance, institutions, and economic development: Beyond the conventional wisdom. *British Journal of Political Science*, 40(1), 195–224. 10.1017/S0007123409990287

Duarte, F., & Ratti, C. (2018). The impact of autonomous vehicles on cities: A review. *Journal of Urban Technology*, 25(4), 3–18. 10.1080/10630732.2018.1493883

Enaifoghe, A. (2023). The Role of Ethical Behavior and Public Value Creation in the Local Government System in South Africa. *International Journal of Social Science Research and Review*, 6(1), 471–483.

Kanyane, M. (2014) Exploring Challenges of Municipal Service Delivery in South Africa (1994-2013). *Africa's public service delivery and performance review*, *2*(1), 90-110.

Kgobe, F. K. L., & Mamokhere, J. (2021). Interrogating The Effectiveness Of Public Accountability Mechanisms In South Africa: Can Good Governance Be Realized? *International Journal of Entrepreneurship*, 25(2), 1–12.

Mamokhere, J., Musitha, M. E., & Netshidzivhani, V. M. (2021). The implementation of the basic values and principles governing public administration and service delivery in South Africa. *Journal of Public Affairs*, 22(1), 26–27.

Mutua, M. W. (2017). The ideology of human rights. In *International Law of Human Rights* (pp. 103–172). Routledge. 10.4324/9781315092492-6

Orlando, L. (2020). Ancient genomes reveal unexpected horse domestication and management dynamics. *BioEssays*, 42(1), 1–8. 10.1002/bies.20190016431808562

Phago, K. (2009). An integrated development plan in South African local government: The case of the City of Tshwane Metropolitan Municipality. *Journal of Public Administration*, 44(3), 483–491.

Poniatowicz, M., Dziemianowicz, R., & Kargol-Wasiluk, A. (2020). Good governance and institutional quality of public sector. *Theoretical and empirical implications, 23*(2), 529-556.

Rawat, F., & Dobie, K. (2021). *The local government Ethics Committee Guidebook*. The Ethics Institute, Canada.

Ubisi, S. V. (2018). Accountability as one of the basic values and principles governing public administration in South Africa. *International Conference on Public Administration and Development Alternatives (IPADA)*. Research Gate.

United Nations Department of Economic and Social Affairs. (2019). *Principles of Effective Governance for Sustainable Development*. New York: United Nations Department of Economic and Social Affairs.

Wassenhoven, L. C., & Wassenhoven, L. C. (2019). Introduction, Historical Periods, and Examples. *The Ancestry of Regional Spatial Planning: A Planner's Look at History*. Research Gate.

# Chapter 12
# Management of Municipal Transport System in South Africa

**Maijane Mashamaite**
https://orcid.org/0000-0002-3846-8296
*University of South Africa, South Africa*

## ABSTRACT

*Travelling to and from work is the second most popular cause for household travel in South Africa, trailing only educational travels. South Africa's municipal transport system also suffers from fluctuating ridership, with some workers compelled to drive owing to a lack of safe and reliable transport options, while others frequently have little choice but to use public transport, despite the obstacles and unreliability. This chapter explores the current issues confronting the Southern African municipal transport systems and suggests a potential way to address them. The chapter outlined difficulties encountered in municipalities for which a universal solution may be implemented. These difficulties were determined to be primarily the result of government initiatives. The chapter concludes that social outcomes must be better integrated into South African municipal transport system at the strategic, tactical, and operational levels.*

## INTRODUCTION

Transport is vitally imperative and apex priority of any country ensuring movement from point A to point B. This is essential in a quest for social inclusion which subsequently could be attributed to the ability for members of the public to connect to bigger cities for economic and job opportunities and services such as schools,

DOI: 10.4018/979-8-3693-3617-5.ch012

healthcare, sporting, leisure, and social activities. Dariusz, Kinga and Ewa (2021) assert that in most cases, Municipal Transport is deemed to be the most cost effective, faster, and most reliable mode of transport for commuter to travel to work, social activities, day to day commuting and other desired destinations. Maintaining the apt standard of Municipal Transport is essential as it could be seen as an instrument for the development of members of the public thus – benefiting communities on socioeconomic ventures and enhance social cohesion.

Access to efficient municipal transport systems facilitates interaction between communities and individuals, contributing to the overall fabric of society. It may then be deduced that municipal transport could be seen as a vital social institution which, if maintained and developed accordingly could benefit communities through enhanced social cohesion. This chapter begins with a brief explanation of South African municipal transport system, then contextualise the municipal transport system; infrastructure overview; municipal transport planning; integrated transport plan; Challenges of municipal transport and finally the remedial actions in addressing municipal transport challenges.

## BACKGROUND OF MANAGEMENT OF MUNICIPAL TRANSPORT SYSTEM

In South Africa, the management of municipal transport systems plays a crucial role in ensuring the effective and efficient movement of people in cities and municipalities. The country has a versatile transport network consisting of buses, taxis, trains and various non-motorized transport vehicles (Dariusz, Kinga & Ewa 2021). Managing these systems is important for promoting economic development, reducing congestion and improving the overall quality of life for residents (Netshisaulu 2021). Managing South Africa's municipal transport systems has been a significant challenge over the years due to a number of factors including aging infrastructure, funding constraints and increasing urbanization. Effective and efficient management of transport systems is crucial for the economic and social development of a country (City of Cape Town 2023).

One of the main challenges in the management of South Africa's municipal transport systems is the legacy of apartheid-era spatial planning, which resulted in many municipalities located far from economic centres (Walters 2014). This has led to long commute times for residents, especially those on low incomes. To address this challenge, the government has implemented several initiatives to improve public transport infrastructure and accessibility.

South Africa's most important public transport systems are bus rapid transit systems (BRT). According to Soto, Orozco-Fontalvo and Useche (2022) BRT systems are designed to provide residents with fast, reliable and affordable transportation services, especially in underserved areas. They have helped reduce travel times, improve road safety and promote the use of public transport as a viable alternative to private cars. In addition to BRT systems, the country also has a large number of minibuses, which are the main means of transport for many South Africans. However, the informal nature of the taxi industry presented challenges to the regulation and management of these services (City of Polokwane 2020). Problems such as overcrowding, safety violations and competition between operators have hindered efforts to improve the quality and efficiency of taxi services.

To address these challenges, the South African government has introduced various policies and regulations aimed at improving the management of urban transport systems. For example, the Land Transport Act 2009 provides a legal framework for the planning, regulation and financing of public transport services. It also creates municipal-level transport authorities that coordinate the operation of public transport and the development of infrastructure. In addition, the government prioritized investments in public transport infrastructure, including expanding BRT systems, improving train services and building integrated transport hubs (City of Polokwane 2020). These initiatives aim to promote sustainable urban development, reduce carbon dioxide emissions and improve the overall quality of life for residents.

The management of urban transport systems in South Africa is a complex and multifaceted problem that requires a coordinated approach involving several stakeholders. Although significant progress has been made in recent years, challenges remain to ensure the efficient and sustainable provision of public transport services. By implementing sound policies, investing in infrastructure and encouraging collaboration between stakeholders, South Africa can continue to improve its municipal transport systems and increase the mobility of its citizens.

## RESEARCH METHODOLOGY

Desktop research method was used to gather information without conducting interviews, surveys, or experiments by analysing existing data, reports, and articles online. This method was used because it is found to be cost-effective and time-efficient, allowing access to a wide range of information without expensive surveys. Furthermore, the method provides access to diverse sources like academic journals, government publications, and news articles, allowing for a comprehensive understanding of a topic. However, Saunders, Lewis, and Thornhill (2019) urge the researchers to critically evaluate sources to ensure accuracy and reliability, especially in the age of misinformation on the internet. By verifying authors' credentials, checking publication dates, and cross-referencing information, researchers can ensure the validity of their findings. Flick (2018) asserts that desktop research is a valuable tool for efficiently collecting information and gaining a comprehensive understanding of a subject matter.

## THEORETICAL FRAMEWORK UNDERPINNING TRANSPORT MANAGEMENT

The management of transport systems is crucial to ensure the efficient movement of people and goods from one place to another. As urbanisation and population growth increase in many cities around the world, it has become necessary to develop effective strategies to manage transport systems to reduce congestion, pollution, and other negative environmental and economic impacts (Banister 2008). One widely accepted theory in the management of transport systems is the concept of sustainable transport (Enoch & Potter 2006). The goal of sustainable transport is to find a balance between social, economic and environmental goals by promoting the use of public transport, walking, cycling and other environmentally friendly modes of transport (ibid). This theory emphasizes the need to reduce dependence on private vehicles and promote the use of alternative modes of transportation to minimize carbon dioxide emissions and other harmful pollutants.

Cities can benefit from sustainable traffic practices by improving air quality, reducing congestion, promoting physical activity, and enhancing life quality. Integrated transport planning is crucial for effective management (Enoch & Potter 2006). Integrated transport planning involves the coordination of different modes of transport such as road, rail, air and water to create a smooth and efficient transport network. Nijkamp, and Pepping (2003) believe that combining different modes of transport, cities can optimize the use of existing infrastructure, reduce travel times and improve connections between different regions. This theory also emphasizes the importance of cooperation between various stakeholders such as government agencies, transport companies and community organizations to develop a comprehensive and coordinated transport plan.

In addition to sustainable traffic and comprehensive planning, the concept of intelligent traffic systems has emerged in recent years. Intelligent transport systems use technology and data solutions to improve the efficiency, safety and reliability of transportation networks. Using sensors, GPS systems and other technologies, cities can collect real-time data on traffic patterns, transit services and infrastructure conditions to make informed decisions and respond to transport challenges (Rodriguez 2019). According to Wang (2018) intelligent transport systems offer opportunities for innovations such as autonomous vehicles, ride-sharing services, and on-demand transportation options that can further improve the overall efficiency of transportation systems.

In short, the management of transport systems requires a comprehensive and multidisciplinary approach that takes into account the social, economic and environmental effects of transport on society. By adopting theories such as sustainable transport, integrated planning, and intelligent transport systems, cities can create more efficient, sustainable, and sustainable transport networks that meet the needs of residents and support long-term economic growth.

## SOUTH AFRICAN MUNICIPAL TRANSPORT SYSTEM OVERVIEW

Municipal Transport is mode of transport established by municipalities especially in big cities as means to reduce the use of private vehicles which is subsequently aimed at reducing traffic congestions into the cities (Netshisaulu 2021). Not only so but also to provide transport for commuters travelling to cities on a day-to-day bases for mostly work, this mode of transport is predominantly buses which are subsidised by municipalities. Apartheid in South Africa left a legacy of social segregation and a severely distorted isolation of individuals from both their places of employment and most social services essential to live a productive life (Walters 2014). As a result, this chapter notes that the post-apartheid issue has been to restructure these geographies of exclusion and inequality while also providing a more functional municipal transport system. Thirty years into democracy, South Africa's desire for efficient, affordable, and integrated transport systems have yet to be met. This chapter asserts that current issues arise from years of poorly delivered, yet heavily funded systems and networks, as well as spatial segregation and other causes of unequal infrastructure supply (Mthimkhulu 2017). Municipal transport systems are inevitably complex and require high level of reliability and safety while ensuring quality and should be cost effective.

Within the South African context, the Bus Rapid Transport (BRT) was initiated in the Department of Transport's Public Transport Strategy Action Plans of 2007 (Thomas 2016). Unlike the Gautrain the project connects the townships and the main city by providing buses with dedicated bus lanes and stations that are accessible to individuals. The BRT system connects people residing in townships to the core of big cities and does a much better job in connecting people from historically segregated areas to their places of work (Thomas 2016). It is also much less expensive than the Gautrain and the project has been cost efficient to meeting the needs of the people.

According to McKay (2020) South Africa has no centralised bus operators, with various companies operating inside each municipality based on city size or population density. McKay (2020) states that despite the overabundance of bus services in the country, the number of households using a bus to get to work, or school has decreased significantly. Buses in South Africa are a moderately cheaper alternative to taxis, but at the expense of safety and reliability; buses are frequently late and do not follow to precise timetables if they ever arrive. BRT in cities is infinitely safer than many other modes of transport because to the additional safety and surveillance cameras installed on most buses; however, these features are not standard across the remainder of the country's bus operations (Gajbhiye, Maaz, Gedam, & Patil 2023).

South African government is working hard to develop an equitable public bus system that addresses poverty, access, and inequality, the pace of change is painfully slow and fails to address the needs of individuals who do not have access to such services.

The taxi sector remains the most significant component of South Africa's transport system. Taxis are the preferred mode of transport. With over 200 000 cabs on the road, the sector earns R40 billion annually and employs almost 300,000 people, including drivers, marshals, and administrative support (Fobisi 2023). The Department of Transport has committed to eliminating 63 000 taxis by 2024 as part of the Revised Taxi Recapitalisation Programme, which is critical to the government's attempts to reform public transport. According to Stats SA's GHS for 2019, around 37.8% of South African households had at least one member who used a minibus taxi in the week preceding the survey.

## CONTEXTUALISING MUNICIPAL TRANSPORT

Transport is an integral part of economic growth and has been recognized by the development community. Most countries are driven by rapid economic growth and population migration to large cities in search of such economic opportunities, which is inevitably a major challenge for urban transport planners (Dariusz, Kinga and Ewa 2021). Therefore, traffic congestion and deterioration of public transport has become a major problem for more and more cities. As a result, several cities have created municipal transportation systems in an attempt to deal with this global phenomenon.

Within the South African context, with the emergence from apartheid, as a nation South Africa has been struggling to address the imbalances of the past caused by immense socio-economic inequalities because of the apartheid regime. Focusing on transport systems and services, much progress has been enumerated in transport policy reform which begun in the mid-1990s with the development of the *White*

*Paper on National Transport policy* 1996. Walters (2012) suggests public transport policy in South Africa provides a useful overview of what has transpired in the policy arena. From the *White Paper on National Transport Policy*, 1996 there was an explicit emphasis on prioritising the needs of public transport and non-motorised users. The public transport strategy document produced by National Department of Transport in 2006 is indicative of the amount of work that has occurred in this area, and the recent improvements in public transport infrastructure and services can arguably be attributed to this effort.

South Africa adopted the Bus Rapid Transport (BRT) Programme which is the road-based component of the BRT Public Transport Strategy that was approved by Cabinet.

Bickford (2013) provides perspective on public transport and mobility in South African cities as identified by the South African Cities Network (SACN). Subsequently, SACN has identified transport as a critical area in the future of South African cities. With the devolution of transport functions to the local government sphere, the future of South African transport systems will hinge on the ability of local governments to respond effectively to the increased transport responsibility.

## OVERVIEW OF MUNICIPAL ROAD INFRASTRUCTURE

An adequate transport infrastructure is essential for a successful transport system. Large expenditures in transport infrastructure are required, as well as frequent maintenance, to ensure that it is safe for drivers to use. The high expense of paved road building often limits most significant road improvements to the public sector (Porter 2007). The road infrastructure has deteriorated at an alarming rate, with roads getting narrower and potholes injuring vehicles and raising maintenance costs for road users. There is a difference in rural and urban transport infrastructure. Rural road infrastructure is less advanced than urban infrastructure, making public transport difficult to access. Another difficulty that infrastructure poses is its availability.

The current road transport environment is comprised of both positive and negative elements. On the positive side, South Africa continues to have a relatively robust, extensive, and functional road infrastructure network when compared with neighbouring countries. The road transport network contributes much towards economic and social development goals. On the negative side, there are problems manifesting in certain challenges that emanate from financial, institutional, physical, and human frailties. The Department of Transport (2020) indicates that the review of the roads environment in SA indicated the following:

- Although the national road network is in a satisfactory condition, the overall road maintenance backlog, including provinces and municipalities, is increasing.
- Government has limited funds from the national fiscus to meet the road maintenance burden, as well as the increased road network demand due to increased number of vehicles and new, rapidly expanding towns and cities. This is contributing to increased and sometimes severe congestion in South African cities.
- As part of a strategic vision to promote sustainable forms of transport, government has also embarked on a drive to introduce integrated rapid public transport networks (IRPTNs) in all major towns and cities in SA. The implementation of these IRPTNs is also placing significant demand on the national fiscus.
- It is reported the bulk of all freight is conveyed by road. The prominent use of road infrastructure for freight transport is contributing to poor road safety and compounding the road maintenance backlog. Overloading control is still not sufficient to enforce allowed freight limits and is not able to arrest the negative impact of overloaded vehicles on the road network.
- The poor standard of many provincial and local roads is a concern, and the backlog is growing every year. This is further compounded by limited funds as well as a reduced focus on maintenance and limited skills in the public sector. Many municipalities and provinces lack the skill, capacity and funding to efficiently manage local road networks.
- Access to rural areas is limited while rural road infrastructure and corridors are neglected due to limited funds.
- In an environment of limited funds for roads construction and maintenance, the situation is further exacerbated by maladministration and corruption.
- Growth in private vehicles and freight is increasing at a rapid rate and outstripping the supply and availability of roads, leading to growing congestion in major urban areas (Dept. of Transport Roads Infrastructure Policy: Policy framework, 2014).

Most commonly the failure of paved road surfaces is cause by neglect – neglect of routine maintenance, and neglect to repair damage within a reasonable time frame. The lack of maintenance of surface damage, mostly potholes or of cracking which may have been caused heavy rain. Another common cause is overloading – for example, a road might, for economic reasons, be designed in the expectation that heavy traffic will be infrequent, but the use by heavy vehicles then increases significantly, with consequent damage. It is therefore imperative that municipalities allocate reasonable resources to ensure swift attendance to road damage – thus ensuring adequate and effective road infrastructure maintenance.

## MUNICIPAL TRANSPORT PLANNING IN CONTEXT

Transport planning involves preparing for the travel of both people, goods and animals, including highway system operations and traffic amenities (Ramadhan 2017). The current model views transport as a collaborative process that involves all stakeholders, including businesses, community groups, environmental organisations, travellers, freight operators, and the public. Transport planning consists of several steps. These include:

- Monitoring existing conditions.
- Forecasting future population and employment growth, including assessing projected land.
- Identifying current and projected future transportation problems and needs and analysing, through detailed planning studies, various transportation improvement strategies to address those needs.
- Developing long-range plans and short-range programs of alternative capital improvement and operational strategies for moving people and goods.
- Estimating the impact of recommended future improvements to the transportation system on environmental features, including air quality.
- Developing a financial plan for securing sufficient revenues to cover the costs of implementing strategies (U.S. Department of Transportation 2017).

Transport planning is a collective and inclusive process in which agencies, organisations, and the public consider national, provincial, regional, and local demands.

The schedule 4A of the *Constitution of the Republic of South Africa, 1996* prescribes the legislative responsibilities of the different spheres of government with regards to the provision of transport. In this regard schedule 4A states that airports, other than international and national airports are concurrent functions between the national and provincial spheres of government. The Schedule 4B of the Constitution of the Republic of South Africa, 1996 further specifies municipal airports as well a municipal public transport as solely the local government competency (The Constitution of the Republic of South Africa, 1996). There is recognition in government that there is a scarcity of planning competencies and skills, particularly at the local government level. Consequently, numerous strategies and interventions were initiated to assist municipalities bolster their capacity within this domain.

All Municipalities in South Africa are legible to receive the Public Transport Network Grant to promote accessibility, reliable and affordable integrated municipal public transport network services to members of the public. This allocation is distributed in accordance with categories of municipalities as stipulated in section 155 of the constitution on the Republic of South Africa. This is done to improve their public transport systems in the quest for the development of integrated public transport network infrastructure, inclusive of the bus rapid transit systems, conventional bus services and upgrades for pedestrian and cycling infrastructure (National Treasury 2016).

Notably, it is evident that transport planning in municipalities is a concerted effort between all spheres of government and it is not solely the responsibility of municipalities. Moreover, in the case of district municipalities they at times serve in a coordinating role to assist local municipalities.

## PREVIEW OF INTEGRATED TRANSPORT PLAN IN MUNICIPALITIES

In South Africa, municipal transport comprises of three main modes of transport: the commuter rail system, the subsidized and unsubsidized commuter bus industry, including the Bus Rapid Transit (BRT) system and a growing minibus-taxi industry. Integration in the sense of transport can refer to the coordination of three modes' planning, financing, and implementation processes. It may also refer to the physical proximity of transport facilities and the organization of those services. Finally, it could refer to the integration of transport networks and services with the communities they serve. In both the academia and the field of transport policy, the concept of integrated transport planning is generally recognized. According to Givoni and Banister (2010), an Integrated Transport Plan (ITP) is used for transport development in almost every municipality around the world. In terms of time, cost, comfort, security, accessibility, and convenience, an Integrated Transport Plan integrates different modes of transport to optimize the user's versatility and productivity (Walters 2014). Different modes of transport have different technical and organizational capabilities.

The related pieces of legislation that include the legal and policy frameworks are the South African Constitution of 1996, the National Land Transport Act, 2009 (ACT NO. 5 OF 2009 (NLTA), Paper on National Transport Policy, 1996 and the Municipal Systems Act 32 of 20005 (MSA). These legislations will not be addressed in depth in this chapter but will be referred to when appropriate. Municipalities are required to prepare an Integrated Transport Plan under section 2 of the South African National Land Transport Act, 2009 (ACT NO. 5 OF 2009). The plan must adhere to the Act's minimum requirements. Furthermore, transport planners must do additional planning as permissible by their budgets and capacities, with the aim of promoting the Act's objectives. There are three different types of Integrated Plans in South Africa, one, the Comprehensive Integrated Transport Plan (CITP), which are prepared by all metropolitan municipalities. Two, District Integrated Transport

Plan (DITP) prepared by all district municipalities. Three, the Local Integrated Transport Plan (LITP) prepared by all local municipalities.

The ITPs should incorporate yearly activity plans indicating the tasks to be carried out. Only projects for which financing is probably going to be accessible for execution should be included for the yearly activity plans. The ITP is meant to provide municipalities with a planning guide to overcome the challenges identified within the transport system. The ITP focuses on traffic and responds to the increase in volume by increasing infrastructure ability to handle the flow (Litman 2013). Thus, the integrated solution aims for long-term transport growth by concentrating on people's needs.

While modernizing transport is an important tool for achieving financial and environmental goals at the municipal level, the aim of implementing an Integrated Transport Plan is to improve the conditions under which a local community meets their transport needs. This community-based vision, according to Walker (2012), is encapsulated in eight demands that any transport system should meet, and which should be the aim of every Integrated Transport Plan., namely:

- Inclusion
- Accessibility
- More limited travel times
- Sensibly estimated admissions
- Dependability
- Adaptability
- Openness
- Quality

Since the existing traffic system faces well-realized issues such as congestion, natural impact, and public space use, the establishment of an Integrated Transport Plan is critical. Non-integrated transport systems would generally ignore the needs of communities, resulting in a reduction in ridership. South African transport faces a range of challenges, despite the numerous modes of transport available. Low ridership, a shortage of public transport in rural areas, equity imbalances, and traffic congestion are just a few of them (Jennings 2015). According to Walters (2014), the South African municipal transport system is under scrutiny because vulnerable users are subjected to risky, inefficient, and expensive systems. As a result, ensuring that public transport infrastructure is safe and accessible is critical to South Africa's socioeconomic development.

Mashamaite (2018) attests that the aim of the transport planning process is to solve problems caused by urbanization and the rapid growth of motor vehicle ownership and usage while also using the full range of available transport options. One of the critiques levied at the South African transport-planning framework in the literature is that it is vehicle-centric. This strategy largely ignores public and non-motorized modes of transport. The 1996 South African White Paper on National Transport Policy stresses the development opportunities for all modes of transport. A slew of problems plague South African transport planning. Davies et al (1995) identified the following issues in transport planning, which still exist today:

- The importance of walking is often underestimated.
- Public and private transit models do not work well together.
- Inadequate training on the part of qualified professionals.

According to Bickford (2013), transport planning was largely carried out in a business-as-usual fashion for most of the apartheid era. According to Walters (2012)'s analysis of each mode and its operations, the issue is that policy and preparation for each is done in silos, which makes system integration difficult.

## THE STATE OF BUS RAPID TRANSIT (BRT) IN SOUTH AFRICAN CITIES

Bus Rapid Transit (BRT) is a high capacity, low-cost municipal transport system that can increase urban mobility significantly. Levinson, Zimmerman, Clinger, Gast, Rutherford and Bruhn (2003) describe the BRT as a "flexible, rubber-tired type of rapid transit that integrates stations, vehicles, walking ways, and information technology aspects into an integrated system with a distinct culture." Cities all over the world are looking for solutions to their urban mobility problems, which range from traffic congestion to road safety and climate change concerns (Mashamaite 2018). BRT networks have become more viable alternative transport options in recent years. In contrast to a minibus taxi, a BRT system combines versatility and low-cost features while maintaining modernity and technology (Mfinanga & Ochieng, 2006); the benefit of a BRT system over a minibus taxi is, among other things, the operation of longer buses on dedicated bus lanes, which provides passengers with a frequent, quicker, safer, and congestion-free ride.

In comparison to other municipal transport networks, the BRT system is commuter friendly and cost effective over long distances because it runs at a flat rate. Pedestrian security, accessibility, and safe access to the facility are provided for both physically disabled and able-bodied commuters. Bannister and Esteves (2015) believe that the BRT systems, like other friendly, safe, cost-effective, and reliable transport systems, can reshape local cities and towns. This phenomenon is now known as transport-oriented development (TOD), and it consists of increased stages of development around transit stations.

Table 1 grouped the BRT system from three different points of view. One, the seven major elements of BRT are defined. Two, key performance characteristics of BRT systems and significant benefits of integrated BRT systems are described. Three, the BRT elements are linked to system performance attributes.

*Table 1. BRT elements, system performance, and system benefits*

| Major Elements of BRT | System Performance | System Benefits |
|---|---|---|
| Running Ways | Travel Time Savings | Ridership |
| Stations | Reliability | Capital Cost Effectiveness |
| Vehicles | Identity and Image | Operational Efficiency |
| Fare Collection | Safety and Security | Transit-Supportive Land |
| ITS (Intelligent Transportation Systems) | Capacity | Development |
| Service and Operations Plan | Accessibility | Environmental Quality |
| Branding Elements | | |

Source: Diaz (2009)

Each element of the BRT system has a specific impact on system efficiency. The six ways that BRT systems improve performance are also ways that transit commuters' profit from BRT implementation (Diaz 2009). In addition to shaping how the BRT system operates, BRT system features benefit the customer, the municipal transport system, and the communities in which BRT systems operate. However, since they are outside the scope of this chapter, they will not be addressed in detail.

The BRT system is both unique and tailored to the circumstances.

As previously stated, they are designed to offer bus services that are quicker, more efficient, and more convenient than those offered by private bus companies. Private bus services are often unattractive, unreliable, time-consuming, inaccessible, inconvenient, crowded, filthy, and dangerous. In this light, Levinson et al. (2002) argue that the BRT can be considered as a better version of the private bus service, rather than a separate mode of transport or a different bus service. The following are the cities and towns in South Africa that have already implemented a BRT system:

**Johannesburg: Rea Vaya:** In October 2013, the Rea Vaya bus system route in Johannesburg became operational. The path connects the CBD and runs from Soweto to Noordegesig, New Canada, Pennyville, Bosmont, Coronationville, Newclare, Westbury, Westdene, Melville, Auckland Park, and Parktown. Rea Vaya buses transported an average of 37 579 passengers per working day by June 2015 (Scorcia & Munoz-Rakin 2019).

**Cape Town: MyCiTi**: Nearly 900,000 passenger journeys have been registered since the MyCiTi N2 Express service from Mitchells Plain and Khayelitsha to the Civic Centre station in Cape Town began on July 4, 2014 (City of Cape Town 2023).

**Tshwane: Areyeng:** In 2014, the Tshwane Rapid Transit (A Re Yeng) began operation. On the trunk line, all A Re Yeng buses have free wi-fi, full air conditioning, low-floor technology that meets Euro V emission standards, vehicle stability, and a cashless integrated electronic system that is completely controlled by cameras and censors. The buses are driven by trained former taxi drivers who have been recruited from the city's numerous taxi associations.

**George: Go George:** From ten buses in December 2014, the GO GEORGE fleet has expanded to 54 daily buses (including the new MAN buses), 33 midibuses, and 35 minibuses. In the year after the launch of the GO GEORGE Smart Card in October of 2019, 22 996 cards have been purchased.

**Durban: GO! Durban:** In 2015, the GO!Durban system was launched. When the project is over, minibus vehicles will gather people from residential areas and transport them to transfer stations where they will board buses to their desired destinations. By 2027, it was planned that R20 billion set aside for the transformation of Durban's municipal transport system would link 600 000 commuters across the city to nine municipal transport corridors.

**Ekurhuleni: Harambee:** The first step of Ekurhuleni's Harambee BRT service was launched in mid-2016. Harambee is a project that aims to connect the nine Ekurhuleni towns. Harambee's 56-kilometer trunk route from Tembisa in the north to Vosloorus in the south will be constructed in stages, with the first segment connecting Tembisa and OR Tambo International Airport via Kempton Park.

**Rustenburg: Yarona:** The citizens own the Rustenburg Rapid Transport (RRT) system. Yarona, which means "It is ours" in Setswana, was introduced in 2016 but only began operating in 2021, serving 80% of Rustenburg's 3 500km$^2$ metropolitan area. The new Rustenburg Rapid Transport system would make city travel more convenient.

**Polokwane: Leeto la Polokwane:** The first phase of Leeto la Polokwane, which means the Journey of Polokwane, began in 2021. Phase one will include dedicated trunk routes from Seshego to the Central Business District, carrying an average of 15 000 passengers per weekday over the initial three years of operations. Over the next decade, all of South Africa's BRT systems will be phased out. Bus Rapid Transit systems that operate in conjunction with other existing municipal transport services have been successfully implemented in metropolitan municipalities (City of Polokwane 2020). This demonstrates that a variety of transport forms can be accommodated to account for all modes of municipal transport systems, and therefore aspire to see the same in local and district municipalities in the future.

## NON-MOTORISED TRANSPORT (NMT) AS MODE OF TRANSPORT

Non-motorised transport (NMT) refers to any mode of transport that is operated by humans or animals. Driving, cycling, and horseback riding are all examples of NMT for personal mobility. Wheelbarrows and carts pulled by donkeys, horses, or humans are also NMT modes for transporting goods. NMT can accommodate a wide range of transport requirements, including regional mobility and local connectivity. In a number of cases, whether by choice or necessity, NMT may be used as part of or for the entire journey (Todes 2009). According to Jennings (2014), the NMT infrastructure in Africa is commonly considered to be of poor quality, with NMT infrastructure levels being lower in poorer communities. Public areas, like NMT routes in road settings, are often unsociable, poorly managed, underutilized, and infiltrated with crime.

In some of the world's poorest countries, non-motorized transport (NMT) is the most accessible, but also the most inconvenient and risky, mode of transport. As a result, it is often correlated with poverty, low-tech, and non-innovative development as something that countries strive to achieve (Zimmerman & Fang 2015). ICE (2000) identified several barriers to the NMT's implementation, including private vehicle-oriented spatial and transport planning in cities. The public's perception of walking and cycling. The public sees walking and cycling as poor people's modes of transport.

According to Simões (2014), NMT serves as a vital link between a pedestrian's destination and the chosen mode of municipal transport. Simões (2014) further contends that to ensure the successful movement of pedestrians in any area, both motorized and non-motorized modes of transport must collaborate effectively to integrate the transport network. NMT helps to keep the municipal transport system running by providing a feeder service to other modes of municipal transport. Despite this, NMT's contribution to municipal transport is largely overlooked (Jain, 2013). The integration of NMT with municipal modes of transport contributes to a more environmentally sustainable and efficient transport system.

Brussel (2014) maintains that travellers are encouraged to use municipal transport through a well-integrated NMT system. According to Jain (2013), introducing additional park and ride amenities, stations, and introducing single multimodal ticketing would help to integrate NMT with bus, taxi, and rail, and provide integrated multimodal transport. NMT has various advantages in terms of economics, health, the environment, and transport. According to Menin (2015) cities around the world are replacing driving lanes with dedicated lanes for municipal transport, pedestrian, and cycling infrastructure. Municipalities must build creative and strategies to address the obstacles that can arise because of providing sufficient infrastructure for NMT.

The urban population of South Africa is increasing. As a result, the country is considering NMT as a viable mode of alternative transport. Climate change has opened the door to developing mitigation measures such as promoting a green economy in South Africa (Mashamaite 2018). NMT is an aspect of green strategies that emphasizes the importance of increasing accessibility and mobility for low - income communities. Sustainable municipal transport can be described as the provision of infrastructure and services for the movement of goods and people, as well as the development of social and economic growth, in a way that is open, secure, affordable, durable, and effective for current and future generations. Furthermore, much of this is accomplished thus lowering carbon and other climate change effects and emissions (UN, 2016:10). Mashamaite (2018) claims that sustainable municipal transport provides people with effective and healthy mobility while having a low environmental impact.

## CHALLENGES OF MUNICIPAL TRANSPORT SYSTEM IN SOUTH AFRICA

Thirty years into the democratic era, South Africa's hopes for an efficient, open, and integrated municipal transport system have remained unfulfilled. According to Mthimkhulu (2017), the underlying issues stem from years of poorly provided, but heavily subsidized programs and networks, as well as spatial segregation and other roots of unequal infrastructure provision. For various reasons, captured users are forced to use municipal transport services that are dangerous, costly, or inaccessible, creating a bleak and underwhelming picture.

Many of the challenges facing South African municipalities, such as service delivery protests, infrastructure damage, political interference in municipal governance and corruption scandals, tend to be complex and not apparent. Due to limited financial resources, there are many different opinions on how to solve traffic problems. While politicians have policy solutions to planning difficulties and planners focus on shaping transport patterns, there seem to be no solutions to the uneven and negative physical features of the land. The country's transport planning is hampered by inadequate coordination between transport demands and settlement sprawl, as well as planned and unplanned land uses. The inherited and ongoing shortage of trained, experienced, and skilled staff continues to impede the essential institutional capacity to conduct analytical transport planning.

Commuters prioritize "service punctuality, crowding levels, distance from the station, and train security" before using accessible modes of transport (Dikgang 2013). Trains are always overcrowded and poorly policed. The main issue, however, is that Metrorail trains have always been plagued by a lack of schedule structure. The minibus taxi industry in South Africa is one of the most lucrative, as well as a major economic pillar. The contribution of the industry to the country's Gross Domestic Product is rising. Minibus taxis provide more flexibility to many passengers than trains due to their obvious route and network versatility. On the other hand, many minibus taxis operate without licenses and are often driven by unlicensed drivers. Mtizi (2017) contends that commuters have expressed their displeasure with the violence of this mode of transport. Most taxi drivers' driving conduct is typically reckless, as they have a habit of violating most of the rules of the road. The municipal transport sector in South Africa is unstructured and inefficient. Gopaul (2015) outlines the following issues in the municipal transport industry:

- Lack of control (or enforcement) over transport modes, which gives rise to illegal and poor driving practices and duplicate services.
- Insufficient services and inadequate capital for upgrades.
- Lack of integration of services between modes, resulting in inconvenient and expensive travel.
- Limited ability to provide safety at public pick-up and drop-of zones; and
- Detrimental environmental impact such as air and noise pollution, extreme land reserve required for road lanes.

BRT is a specialized bus system that aims to provide high-quality rapid mass transit. However, the system faced various obstacles in achieving this goal. The other municipal transport industries such as minibus taxi industry and private bus companies did not support the system. Since it is competitive, they did not endorse the project because they feared losing commuting customers. Munoz and Paget-Seekins (2016) indicate that BRT has a difficult time securing users, particularly private vehicle users, since buses primarily serve cities and do not access most surrounding neighbourhoods. Minibus taxis are not permitted to use the system BRT's dedicated lanes. Since there are less lanes than before, the minibus taxis create traffic congestion in the affected areas, resulting in inefficient transport. Commuters will be delayed as a result. The BRT is a costly project to maintain, and designing a financial model for potential system maintenance is difficult.

Municipalities must make tough decisions to strike a balance between conflicting community desires and limited resources and funding. Furthermore, a lack of political will to overcome the obstacles to project and program implementation is a problem in and of itself. High transaction costs, competition, cost of pollution reductions, availability of investment resources, and slow technological growth are among the other challenges. To overcome these barriers to implementation, policy action and incentives are needed.

## RECOMMENDATIONS

Many economic and societal practices are made possible by municipal transport. As a result, one of the primary issues that must be addressed is the gap in levels of accessible and reliable municipal transport or those in lower income brackets. Solutions to municipal transport issues must be contextualized. Broad planning is needed to improve mobility and provide an integrated transport system for communities. People living in remote areas need fewer motorized modes of transport, emphasizing the value of non-motorized transport.

According to Mtimkhulu (2017), emphasizing the use of vehicles such as bicycles will increase people's accessibility to amenities such as clinics, schools and malls. Cycling, according to this scholar, would not necessitate a significant investment in infrastructure and has the added benefit of being environmentally sustainable, making it an important choice to consider. NMT should be considered when upgrading infrastructure. Cyclists and pedestrians should have protected safe zones. Furthermore, safety should be a top priority, and the municipality should form alliances with security service providers to ensure the safety of NMT users. To tackle the negative stigma associated with the use of NMT, successful education and awareness programs should be created and enforced.

Mthimkhulu (2017) suggests that South African government should introduce and implement strict rules for taxi drivers to manage the minibus taxi industry. The scholar further suggests that there should be a taxi driver registration that lists the licenses and the vehicle's roadworthiness; drivers should be required to complete defensive driving and first-aid training. Mthimkhulu (2017) goes on to say that, as the number of road accidents rises, drivers must be mindful of how to save passengers' lives and be accountable to them. GPS sensors installed on taxis should also be part of the rules to track speed and driving pattern.

The provision of infrastructure and services to citizens of urban areas is the responsibility of local governments. Transport costs are influenced by the position of physical infrastructure such as homes, factories, and commercial centres. Any of the municipal transport issues would be greatly alleviated by appropriate land use planning policies that incorporate residential and job areas. Finally, transport infrastructure is normally built after an area has been developed. As a result, new projects must be built alongside existing infrastructure, reducing the need for large capital investments in transport infrastructure.

Since the BRT system faces various problems, this chapter suggests that it be updated and applied in a new way. A much more versatile implementation model that allows for the inclusion of all other modes as well as human settlements. Starting from scratch with a new BRT system was not a good idea; instead, divide the municipal transport system into stages, empower and restructure existing municipal transport operators, build and increase current system efficiencies, and improve existing infrastructure.

## CONCLUSION

This chapter concludes that for a more equitable, affordable, and efficient municipal transport system to exist in South Africa, many pressing issues must be addressed. The chapter also described the difficulties associated with municipal transport, as well as amicable solutions to public transport issues in the context of South Africa. It should be noted that at the strategic, tactical, and institutional level, there is a need for greater incorporation of social outcomes into municipal transport policy. According to this chapter, if South Africa has access to emerging transport infrastructure and technologies, it can become an experiment and testing ground for tomorrow's municipal transport systems. To improve or substitute current services, new municipal transport systems may be introduced.

## ACKNOWLEDGEMENT

The financial assistance of the National Institute for the Humanities and Social Sciences (NIHSS), in collaboration with the South African Humanities Deans Association (SAHUDA) towards this research is hereby acknowledged. Opinions expressed and conclusions arrived at are those of the author and are not necessarily to be attributed to the NIHSS and SAHUDA.

## REFERENCES

Banister, D. (2008). The sustainable mobility paradigm. *Transport Policy*, 15(2), 73–80. 10.1016/j.tranpol.2007.10.005

Bannister, S., & Esteves, C. (2015). *Implementing BRT in eThekwini: challenges, lessons and opportunities. [online]. BRT in eThekwini.* ERLN. http://www.erln.org.za/images/jevents/5624b4c361e9f6.60912785.pdf.

Bickford, G. (2013). South African Cities Network: Literature review on public transport and mobility in municipalities. ARUP. Board, Washington, DC.

Brussel, M. (2014). *Integration of public transport and NMT-UNEP. Principles and application in an East African context.* University of Twente PDF Presentation. http://staging.unep.org/transport/sharetheroad/PDF/courseware_nmt/Lecture8_Integration_Publictransport_NMT_Brussel.pdf

City of Cape Town. (2023). *MyCiTi Bus Rapid Transit System.* City of Cape Town. https://www.capetown.gov.za/en/MyCiti/Pages/default.

City of Polokwane. (2020). *Leeto la Polokwane: Enhancing Public Transportation in Polokwane.* (Polokwane Government Report).

Dariusz, M., Kinga, K., & Ewa, K. (2021). Management of Municipal Public Transport Vehicle Journeys by Using the PERT Method. *Energies*, 14(15), 4403. 10.3390/en14154403

Department of Transport. (2020). *Road Infrastructure Strategic Framework for South Africa.* (Government Report). Department of Transport.

Diaz, R. B. (2009). *Characteristics of Bus Rapid Transit for Decision-Making, Federal Transit Administration (FTA), United States Department of Transportation.* U.S. DOT.

Dikgang, J. (2013). *Passenger modal shift: From road to rail – the Gautrain NAMA case.* Department of Transport, Republic of South Africa. www.transport2020.org /file/Jacob-dikgang-ppt.pdf.

Enoch, M. P., & Potter, S. (2006). Developing indicators of transport sustainability: A multi-criteria analysis of UK cities. *Transport Policy*, 13(3), 265–276.

Flick, U. (2018). *Designing qualitative research.* Sage publications. 10.4135/9781529622737

Fobosi, S. C. (2023). The Minimum Effect of the Taxi Recapitalisation Programme on Precarious Working Conditions in South Africa's Minibus Taxi Sector: An Industry Full of Pitfalls. *South African Review of Sociology*, 53(1), 28–46. 10.1080/21528586.2023.2198497

Gajbhiye, P., Maaz, M., Gedam, S., & Patil, Y.M. (2023). Smart BRT Management System. *International Journal of Advanced Research in Science, Communication and Technology, 3*(7), 9-12.

Givoni, M., & Banister, D. (2010). *Integrated Transport: From Policy to Practice* (1st ed.). Routledge. 10.4324/9780203850886

Gopaul, A. (2015). *Operational Greenhouse Gas Emissions of Public Transportation in the eThekwini Municipality.* [Partial Dissertation, University of Kwazulu-Natal].

Jain, A. (2013). *Sustainable urban mobility in Southern Asia.* (Technical report) UNHabitat, Nairobi, Kenya. https://unhabitat.org/wpntent/uploads/2013/06/GRHS .2013.Regional.Southern.Asia_.pdf

Jennings, G. (2014). Finding our balance: Considering the opportunities for public bicycle systems in Cape Town, South Africa. *Research in Transportation Business & Management*, 1–9.

Jennings, G. (2015). *Public Transport Interventions and Transport Justice in South Africa: A Literature and Policy Review.*

Levinson, H., Zimmerman, S., Clinger, J., Gast, J., Rutherford, S., & Bruhn, E. (2003). Litman, T. 2013. *The New Transportation Paradigm.ITE Journal*, 1(83), 20–27.

Mashamaite, M. M. (2018). *Assessing the inclusion of climate change strategies in the integrated transport plans of South African metropolitan municipalities.* IPADA conference proceedings, Cape Town.

McKay, T. (2020). South Africa's key urban transport challenges. In A. Gunter & R. Massey (Eds.), (pp. 189–207). *Urban Geography in South Africa - Perspectives and Theory.* Research Gate.

Menon, A. (2015). *Bicycling innovations. [online]. SAICA and professional news – young member's page*. Koleko. http://www.koleko.co.za/wp-content/uploads/2015/10/2015-Jan-Bicycling-Innovations.pdf

Munoz, C., & Paget-Seekins, L. (2016). Restructuring public transport through bust rapid transit: An international and interdisciplinary perspective. *Journal of the American Planning Association*, 83(1), 107.

National Treasury. (2016). *Division of Revenue Bill*. National Treasury.

Netshisaulu, M. S. (2021). *How do Urban cities manage road traffic congestion?* The 6th International Conference on Public Administration and Development Alternatives, Virtual conference.

Nijkamp, P., & Pepping, G. C. (2003). Integrated land use and transport modelling: Decision chains and hierarchies. In *Integration of land use and transport* (pp. 3–12). Springer.

Rodriguez, D. (2019). *Intelligent Transport Systems: Technologies and Applications*. Springer.

Saunders, M., Lewis, P., & Thornhill, A. (2019). *Research methods for business students*. Pearson.

Scorcia, H., & And Munoz-Raskin, R. (2019). Why South African cities are different? Comparing Johannesburg's Rea Vaya bus rapid transit system with its Latin American siblings. *Case Studies on Transport Policy*, 7(2), 395–403. 10.1016/j.cstp.2019.01.010

Simões, V. (2014). *An evaluation of the inclusion of principles of corridor development, transit-oriented development and non-motorised transportation within Johannesburg's Corridors of Freedom: the case of Turffontein Corridor*. Wired Space. http://wiredspace.wits.ac.za/xmlui/bitstream/handle/10539/20470/Final%20Research%20Report_Vanessa%20Simoes.pdf?sequence=1&isAllowed=y

Soto, J. J., Orozco-Fontalvo, M., & Useche, S. A. (2022). Public transportation and fear of crime at BRT Systems: Approaching to the case of Barranquilla (Colombia) through integrated choice and latent variable models. *Transportation Research Part A, Policy and Practice*, 155, 142–160. 10.1016/j.tra.2021.11.001

South Africa Republic. (1996). *The Constitution of the Republic of South Africa*. Government Printers.

South Africa Republic. (2014). *Department of Transport Roads Infrastructure Policy: Policy framework*. Government printers.

Thomas, D. P. (2016). Public Transportation in South Africa: Challenges and Opportunities. *World Journal of Social Science Research, 3*(3).

Todes, A. (2012). New Directions in Spatial Planning? Linking Strategic Spatial Planning and Infrastructure Development. *Journal of Planning Education and Research*, 32(4), 400–414. 10.1177/0739456X12455665

UN - United Nations. (2016). *Mobilizing sustainable transport for development: analysis and policy recommendations from the United Nations Secretary-General's High-Level Advisory Group on sustainable transport.* UN. https://sustainabledevelopment.un.org/content/documents/2375Mobilizing%20Sustainable%20Transport.pdf

Walker, J. (2012). *Human Transit. How Clearer Thinking about Public Transit Can Enrich Our Communities and Our Lives*. Island Press.

Walters, J. (2013). Overview of public transport policy developments in South Africa. *Research in Transportation Economics*, 39(1), 34–45. 10.1016/j.retrec.2012.05.021

Walters, J. (2014). Public transport policy implementation in South Africa: Quo Vadis? Original research. *Journal of Transport and Supply Chain Management*, 8(1), 1–10. 10.4102/jtscm.v8i1.134

Wang, X. (2018). *Urban Transportation Planning in the era of Intelligent Transport Systems*. Elsevier.

Zimmerman, S., & Fang, K. (2015). *Public transport service optimisation and system integration. China Transport Topics No. 14*. World Bank Office.

# Chapter 13
# The Impact of Civil Society Organisations (CSOs) on the Effectiveness and Quality of Municipal Service Delivery

**Kutu Ramolobe**
*Nelson Mandela University, South Africa*

**Murendeni Praise Ramaru**
*Nelson Mandela University, South Africa*

## ABSTRACT

*Municipalities are the level of government closest to the people, and their primary function is to deliver essential services to local communities. However, effectively achieving this goal requires prioritizing the interests of those communities. A key factor in improving municipal service delivery is strong collaboration with civil society organizations (CSOs). Therefore, this chapter investigates the impact of CSOs on the effectiveness and quality of municipal services. Qualitative research methodologies were used, largely through desktop research to analyse the influence of CSOs on municipal service delivery. CSOs are crucial, in improving the efficiency and quality of services provided by local governments. They engage communities to promote involvement and hold authorities accountable for their actions. Through encouraging engagement and fostering accountability measures CSOs make contributions, to upholding democratic principles and enhancing the welfare of residents.*

DOI: 10.4018/979-8-3693-3617-5.ch013

## INTRODUCTION

Municipalities are the level of government closest to the people, and their primary function is to deliver essential services to local communities. However, effectively achieving this goal requires prioritizing the interests of those communities. A key factor in improving municipal service delivery is strong collaboration with civil society organizations (CSOs) (Masiya, Davids, & Mangai, 2021). CSOs act as watchdogs, holding governments accountable to the people they serve (Smith, Buse & Gordon, 2016). They fulfil a range of critical roles, including advocacy, monitoring government performance, building civic capacity, and even directly delivering services (Mavee, 2022). Therefore, this paper investigates the impact of CSOs on the effectiveness and quality of municipal services.

South Africa's Constitution mandates municipalities to provide sustainable services and promote social and economic development in the communities they serve. The Bill of Rights further guarantees citizens' fundamental right to access essential social services. Furthermore, White Paper on Local Government 1998, empowers municipalities to work collaboratively with residents and community groups to find sustainable ways to meet social, economic, and material needs while enhancing overall quality of life (Masiya et al., 2021). Service delivery is a prominent and sometimes contentious aspect of CSOs' work in society. CSOs are often well-positioned to provide essential services like healthcare, education, and social welfare, particularly when governments struggle to deliver effectively and CSOs have strong relationships within the communities they serve (Mavee, 2022). In developing countries, CSOs are considered crucial partners for development, primarily fulfilling advocacy, monitoring, and service delivery roles (Masiya et al., 2021). The emphasis on civil society participation is driven by the need for good governance within the public sector, especially in partnerships focused on service delivery (Brinkerhoff, 2003:105). CSOs can serve as watchdogs to ensure governments are effective and responsive to the needs of the people, ultimately improving governance (Mlambo et al., 2020; Ndou & Sebola, 2014, as cited in Thusi & Mashabela, 2023).

## Understanding Civil Society Organizations (CSOs)

Civil society organizations (CSOs) are a diverse group working for the benefit of citizens. Graham et al. (2018) defines them as encompassing "the total diversity of human voluntary endeavor; the mechanism through which people come together to pursue their wants and needs". In simpler terms, they are organizations created to address the needs and interests of citizens. Mangogo (2018) emphasizes that CSOs are independent from government control and operate on a non-profit basis. They function in the political, economic, and cultural spheres, distinct from both the market and the state. Importantly, CSOs can bridge the gap between the government and society, fostering public participation (Mangogo, 2018). Over the years, CSOs have played a crucial role in improving the lives of the underprivileged, promoting community development, and giving voice to marginalized groups. Laine (2014) offers a broader perspective on civil society, encompassing various stakeholders. This includes non-governmental organizations (NGOs), social movements, community-based organizations (CBOs), community members, trade unions, academics, community leaders, and justice groups. These groups collectively form a powerful force for social cohesion (Laine, 2014). The Asian Development Bank (2009) further highlights that CSOs prioritize accessible, high-quality service delivery while promoting accountability. Their inclusivity stems from the varying sizes, structures, and roles that governments play within society. Ultimately, CSOs foster unity by bringing people together around shared goals and interests (ADB, 2009).

There are different types of CSOs, each with its specific focus. Community-based organizations (CBOs), as described by the World Bank (2019), primarily address the concerns of their local communities. They provide support to residents and create platforms for them to connect with stakeholders offering resources (World Bank, 2019). For instance, developmental NGOs, on the other hand, concentrate on social and humanitarian development issues. Faith-based organizations (FBOs), as noted by the World Bank (2020), are rooted in religion and focus on development activities aligned with their religious missions. The World Bank (2020) also highlights that FBOs' unique strategies are particularly effective due to the high number of people who identify with a religion (over 80% globally). FBOs are prevalent in many countries and create opportunities for partnerships and advocacy on a wide range of development challenges (World Bank, 2020). Koehrsen and Heuser (2019) emphasize the effectiveness of FBOs in serving those in need. They play a significant role in providing essential services like healthcare, education, and promoting sustainable development (Koehrsen & Heuser, 2019). Lastly, non-governmental organizations (NGOs) operate independently from the state and are non-profit driven. They offer a variety of services that contribute to the general well-being of society.

## METHODOLOGY

The paper provides context for the impact of CSOs on the effectiveness and quality of municipal services. For this paper, qualitative research methodologies were used, largely through desktop research and secondary data analysis. Relevant materials used in this review consisted of documents, reports, journals and other papers were retrieved from the Nelson Mandela University Library database and the internet. Relevant materials were identified by using a database keyword search for phrases related with CSOs' impact on the effectiveness and quality of municipal services. Search terms included municipal services, and civil society organisations (CSOs). The primary search was performed between March 2024 and 20 April 2024. More recent material was preferred in order to reflect current research and approaches to the topic. Several of the references cited in the initial texts were also reviewed for their relevance to this topic in order to increase the relevant material for review. The scarcity of relevant material, combined with the exploratory and evaluative nature of the current research activity, necessitated a substantial reliance on grey literature for its review. This data mostly comprises of reports and policy documents from both governmental and non-governmental agencies, which were located and sourced either through internet search terms or because they were cited or referred to in the sourced journal articles.

## Impact of CSOs on the Effectiveness of Municipal Service Delivery

CSOs are essential for effective local governance (Ullah et al., 2023). They bridge the gap between citizens and the government, empowering citizens to participate in decision-making and ensuring they receive necessary services. CSOs raise public awareness and advocate for human rights, peace, and harmony, creating a crucial partnership with the public sector. This collaboration is vital because government spending on development projects alone is often ineffective (Brass, 2016). Through community mobilization and participatory approaches, CSOs identify local needs. Community gatherings, awareness dialogues, and seminars facilitate discussions and prioritization of these needs (Ullah et al., 2023). For instance, development projects are often approved based on the demands raised by CSOs. In recent times, local governments have even mandated community identification of development projects, frequently facilitated by CSO meetings. These contributions make CSOs a vital platform for socioeconomic betterment and local governance. Their role in local development and community empowerment is undeniable (Ullah et al., 2023; Cammett & MacLean, 2014).

A strong and vibrant democracy requires CSOs to promote democratic values (Ullah et al., 2023). Understanding how a municipality's administrative capacity, CSOs, and collaborative governance influence service delivery is crucial, especially when local governments have weak bureaucracies and rely on CSOs (De la Riva Aguero, 2020). CSO involvement can enhance or even replace government limitations, potentially improving service delivery (Auerbach, 2017; Loeffler & Bovaird, 2016). However, transparency in the relationship between CSOs, communities, and the government is essential for effective involvement (Devas & Grant, 2003). Transparent engagement is believed to build trust, collaboration, social support networks, and pressure on authorities over time, especially with high participation levels. This can lead to more responsive service provision, even in weak or non-democratic contexts (Tsai, 2007, cited by de la Riva Aguero, 2020). Finally, CSOs play a vital role in ensuring the voices of the urban poor are heard in discussions about urban development. Effective advocacy requires collaboration with other organizations working on various urban affairs issues (Bandauko, 2015).

## Development of Civil Society Organisations in South Africa

The dismantling of apartheid and the shift towards a democratic system presented a significant challenge for local government (Mangongo, 2018). Newly elected officials faced the daunting task of translating the profound socio-political aspirations of marginalized and impoverished communities into tangible improvements and functional service delivery (Mogale, 2003). Many municipalities established during the transition period grappled with the enormous problems inherited from the apartheid era. Moreover, the Local Government: Municipal Structures Act of 1988 established the ward system to foster sustainable service delivery through community participation. This system mandates the creation of ward committees to facilitate communication between municipalities and local communities. These committees play a crucial role in identifying community needs and ensuring municipal programs and projects are tailored to local circumstances and interests. In essence, the Act provides a platform for local communities to express their needs and preferences to the municipalities (Masiya, Davids, & Mangai, 2021). Additionally, municipalities are encouraged to consult with citizens about the level and quality of services offered, and whenever possible, give them a choice in the services they receive (Masiya, Davids, & Mangai, 2021).

Civil society organizations (CSOs) have emerged as crucial players in community development. These organizations, composed of stakeholders and residents within communities, collaborate to identify and maintain social development systems (Bappi, 2018). Citizen participation is paramount, as CSOs alone cannot drive community development (Mangogo, 2018). Research by Graham et al. (2018) highlights the role of CSOs in creating space for public voices and fostering "the practice of citizenship and for the building of social cohesion." South Africa's local governments continue to grapple with the enduring effects of apartheid. Moving forward requires a clear vision that acknowledges the role of history, promotes active citizen participation, and leverages the strengths of civil society organizations.

## Challenges and Considerations for CSO Advocacy

While CSOs are often seen as bridges between citizens and policymakers, the effectiveness of their advocacy efforts depends on several factors. The level of space provided by the government, the resources available to CSOs from sponsors, and their own internal capacity all significantly impact their success (Neumayr & Meyer, 2010). Weaknesses within citizen organizations advocating for civic engagement and social accountability can pose a risk. Internal governance and accountability issues within CSOs themselves can also undermine civic engagement efforts (Ahmad, 2008). Nevertheless, the policy advocacy function of CSOs is becoming increasingly important in democracies around the world (Thusi & Mashabela, 2023). CSOs play a vital role in representing individuals who have been historically marginalized by the state. Some CSOs have unique organizational structures and decision-making processes designed to address these political concerns. Additionally, CSOs may join coalitions or policy networks to amplify their advocacy efforts (Sabi, 2013).

# IMPACT OF CSOs ON THE EFFECTIVENESS OF MUNICIPAL SERVICE DELIVERY

## Increased Community Participation

Community participation is a crucial aspect of effective local governance. Defined as a process and outcome where individuals and communities actively engage in decisions impacting their lives (Burns et al., 2004), it empowers communities and grants them a significant voice. This participation fosters a sense of ownership and increases the legitimacy of local government decisions. Mikkelsen (2005) highlights how public participation empowers communities in development projects. This fosters capacity building, allowing communities to manage projects more effectively and efficiently. Katz (2017) emphasizes the transformative potential of community participation within local government, underlining its vital role in fostering positive change.

Effective service delivery is another key benefit. As Potter (2015) explains, community participation allows local government to identify the specific needs and expectations of residents. This clarity minimizes disputes and ensures local government prioritizes the most pressing community concerns. The advantages of public participation extend beyond service delivery. Cogan and Sharpe (cited in Maphazi et al., 2013) identify five key benefits: improved planning, conflict management and avoidance, better future decision-making, enhanced cooperation, and increased trust between government and the public. Additionally, Creighton (cited in Maphazi et al., 2013) emphasizes how public participation leads to more meaningful decisions, reduced costs and delays, easier implementation, minimized confrontation, and a more credible and well-maintained development process.

Furthermore, Plummer (2021) underscores the importance of sustainable public participation for community development. Policymaking that prioritizes participation is essential for enhancing government capacity and incorporating indigenous knowledge. By actively engaging with citizens and civil society, governments can move beyond traditional top-down approaches and embrace a more inclusive and democratic model of governance. Community participation is a cornerstone of effective local government. It empowers communities, improves service delivery, fosters better decision-making, and strengthens the relationship between government and the public. By embracing sustainable participation practices, local governments can work collaboratively with citizens to build stronger, more vibrant communities.

## Accountability

Local governments play a crucial role in a well-functioning democracy, particularly due to their proximity to the people they serve. Accountability is essential for good governance at this level (Ballestone & Sanchez, 2016:6). Citizens need ways to assess how effectively their local government is using public resources and fulfilling its legal and managerial responsibilities. Civil society organizations (CSOs) play a vital role in holding governments accountable through various monitoring and oversight mechanisms (Ballestone & Sanchez, 2016). Transparency is a key pillar of accountability (Christensen & Laegreid, 2016). By providing citizens with reliable and timely information about public policies and government actions, transparency helps to prevent dishonest behavior and the misuse of public resources (Christensen & Laegreid, 2016). This is especially important in local government, where corruption has historically been an issue (Sikhakane & Reddy, 2011).

In a democratic South Africa, transparency and accountability are essential at all levels of government. However, due to their close relationship with the people they serve, local governments have a particular responsibility to be open and accountable (Ballestone & Sanchez, 2016). Transparency in local government finances, for example, allows citizens to see how their tax dollars are being spent. This can lead to greater development and improved service delivery, as local officials are held responsible for their actions (Ballestone & Sanchez, 2016).

## CONCLUSION

Non-governmental organizations (NGOs) are crucial, in improving the efficiency and quality of services provided by governments. They engage communities promote involvement and hold authorities accountable for their actions. This involvement enhances planning processes resolves conflicts effectively and strengthens the bond between citizens and the government. NGOs also play a role in ensuring transparency and integrity in government operations through monitoring and oversight activities. By promoting openness and responsible resource management they deter corruption. Encourage the use of public funds, which ultimately results in better service delivery. Moreover, building partnerships between governments and NGOs is vital for successful governance at the grassroots level. Through encouraging engagement and fostering accountability measures NGOs make contributions, to upholding democratic principles and enhancing the welfare of residents.

## REFERENCES

Ahmed, S. A. (2008). *Transparency and accountability in the public sector in the Arab Regin.Arab: UNDESA Asian Development Bank., 2009. ADB Cooperation with Civil Society: Annual Report 2008.* Asian Development Bank. www.adb.org/Documents/Reports/NGO annualreport/2008/2008report.pdf

Asian Further Development Bank. (2009). *Civil Society Organisation Source book. A staff guide to cooperation with Civil Society*. Catologing in Publication Data: Philipines

Auerbach, A. M. (2017). Neighbourhood associations and the urban poor: India's slum development committees. *World Development*, 96, 119–135. 10.1016/j.worlddev.2017.03.002

Ballesteros, B. C., & Sanchez, M. G. (2016). *Local government in the digital era: looking for accountability*. Nova Science publishers.

Bandauko, E. (2015). Civil society organizations (CSOs) in Urban planning advocacy: Lessons from Zimbabwe. *Journal of Advocacy. Research in Education*, 3(2), 104–109.

Bappi. U. (2018). Governance and Community Development in Nigeria. *International Journal of Research in Business studies, 3.*

Brass, J. N. (2016). *Allies or adversaries: NGOs and the state in Africa*. Cambridge University Press. 10.1017/CBO9781316678527

Bray, J. (2003). decision making in government. *Special Conference Issues: Decision-Making*, 19, 25–35.

Brinkerhoff, J. M. (2003). Donor-funded government—NGO partnership for public service improvement: Cases from India and Pakistan. *Voluntas*, 14(1), 105–122. 10.1023/A:1022997006704

Burns, D., Heywood, F., Taylor, M., Wilde, P., & Wilson, M. (2004). *Making Community Participation Meaningful: A Handbook for Development and Assessment.* Policy Press.

Cammett, M., & MacLean, L. M. (Eds.). (2014). *The politics of non-state social welfare*. Cornell University Press. 10.7591/9780801470349

de la Riva Aguero, R. (2020). *Is governance enough? Assessing municipal capacity and CSO participation for complex service delivery.*

Devas, N., & Grant, U. (2003). Local government decision-making—citizen participation and local accountability: Some evidence from Kenya and Uganda. *Public Administration and Development*, 23(4), 307–316. 10.1002/pad.281

Donahue, J. H., & Zeckhauser, R. J. (2012). *Collaborative Governance, Private Roles for Public Goals in Turbulent Times*. Princeton University Press. 10.1515/9781400838103

Gamble, H. (2021). *Contesting French West Africa: Battles Over schools and the colonial order*. Library of Congress Cataloguing in Publication Data.

Graham, L, Himlin, R., Engel, H., Mathoho, M., Reddy, J., & Delany, D. (2018). *Review of the State of Civil Society Organisations in South Africa*. National Development Agency: Braamfontein.

Koehrsen, J., & Heuser, A. (2019). *Faith-Based Organisation in Development Discourses and Practice*. Taylor & Francis. 10.4324/9780429351211

Laine, L. (2014). Debating civil society: Contested conceptualisations and development trajectories. *International Journal of Not-for-profit Law*, 16(1).

Makoti, M.Z., & Odeku. (2021). Impetus for Fostering Effective Inter-Governmental Relationships. *Co-operative Governance in South Africa, 12*

Mangogo, B. (2018). *Enhancing Civil Society Participation in the South Africa Development Agenda: The role of civil Society Organisations*. National Development Agency: Parktown.

Masiya, T., Davids, Y. D., & Mangai, M. S. (2021). Factors affecting the performance of South African municipal officials: Stakeholders' perspectives. *Commonwealth Journal of Local Governance*, (25), 97–115. 10.5130/cjlg.vi25.7701

Mavee, S. E. A. (2022). The Relevance of Civil Society Participation in Democratic Governance. *Administratio Publica*, 30(3), 171–191.

Mbaku, J. M. (2020). *Good and inclusive governance is imperative for Africa's future*. Bookings.

Michels, A. (2011). Innovations in democratic governance: How does citizen participation contribute to a better democracy? *International Review of Administrative Sciences*, 77(2), 275–293. 10.1177/0020852311399851

Mlambo, V. H., Zubane, S. P., & Thusi, X. (2022). Interrogating governance challenges and cadre deployment in South Africa. *Cihan University-Erbil Journal of Humanities and Social Sciences*, 6(1), 11–18. 10.24086/cuejhss.v6n1y2022.pp11-18

Ndou, S. D., & Sebola, M. P. (2014). Civil Society in Context of a Legal Temperament: Is the Watchdog a Capable Person? *Mediterranean Journal of Social Sciences*, 5(27), 908–915. 10.5901/mjss.2014.v5n27p908

Neumayr, M., & Meyer, M. (2010). *In search of civicness: an empirical investigation of service delivery, public advocacy, and community building by civil society organizations* (pp. 201-226). Nomos Verlagsgesellschaft mbH & Co. KG.

Plummer, J. (2021). *Municial and community participation. A source for Capacity building*. Earthsczn.

Sabi, S. C. (2013). The role of civil society in policy advocacy: A case study of the Treatment Action Campaign and health policy in South Africa [Doctoral dissertation,. University of KwaZulu-Natal (UKZN)].

Smith, J., Buse, K., & Gordon, C. (2016). Civil society: *T*he catalyst for ensuring health in the age of sustainable development. *Globalization and Health*, 12(1), 1–6. 10.1186/s12992-016-0178-427424031

Thusi, X., & Mashabela, M. (2023). The role of civil society organizations in promoting public accountability: The perspective of the South African local government. *IAHRW International Journal of Social Sciences Review*, 11(2), 175–180.

Ullah, T., Ullah, S., Khan, N., & Ellahi, M. B. (2023). The Role of Civil Society in Local Governance and Service Delivery: An Analysis of Local Government System of Khyber Pakhtunkhwa. *Journal of Policy Research*, 9(2), 540–547.

# Chapter 14
# Addressing Corruption and Mismanagement in South African Municipalities:
## Strategies for Effective Governance

**Martin Mulunda Kabange**
*Durban University of Technology, South Africa*

**Hlengiwe Mabizela**
https://orcid.org/0000-0001-8538-635X
*Durban University of Technology, South Africa*

**Lesha Joseph Judell**
*Durban University of Technology, South Africa*

**Zwelithini Michael Zwane**
https://orcid.org/0000-0003-3953-5662
*Durban University of Technology, South Africa*

## ABSTRACT

*Corruption and mismanagement pose significant challenges to effective governance and service delivery within South African municipalities. A systematic literature review was conducted using the preferred reporting items for systematic reviews and meta-analyses (PRISMA) framework to address these issues, and interventions supported by empirical evidence were suggested. The results emphasised the need*

DOI: 10.4018/979-8-3693-3617-5.ch014

*to address systemic obstacles, encourage community involvement, and strengthen civil society's responsibility. Capacity-building initiatives and institutional reform were also identified as indispensable instruments in the fight against corruption. Municipalities can achieve more transparent, accountable, and effective governance by addressing these issues. Policymakers and stakeholders should prioritise these interventions to restore public confidence in municipal management and promote sustainable development.*

## INTRODUCTION

Municipalities are vital in providing essential services and managing local communities in South Africa. They are responsible for directly delivering services such as water, sanitation, electricity, housing, and transportation to residents. However, ensuring efficient service delivery and effective governance in municipalities has been challenging, with issues such as corruption, mismanagement, and inefficiency often hindering progress (Tshishonga, 2019; Fagbadebo, 2019). These issues have deep historical roots that date back to the apartheid era, which was marked by discrimination and a lack of accountability (Du Plessis, 2018). Many practices from the apartheid regime, such as patronage networks, lack of transparency in decision-making and discriminatory resource allocation (Madumo, 2015), have persisted, leading to significant governance challenges despite the transition to democracy in 1994 (Steyn, 2016).

Similarly, South Africa has struggled with major socio-economic disparities in the post-apartheid era, worsening corruption and mismanagement in various sectors, including municipalities (Mlambo, 2023). These challenges are further exacerbated by a widespread culture of impunity, inadequate supervision mechanisms, and weak regulatory frameworks (Fagbadebo, 2019). South Africa's international reputation has been damaged, and public trust has been steadily eroded by high-profile corruption scandals involving public officials and private sector entities (Adetiba, 2016), which impede service delivery in several municipalities.

A deeper exploration of the root causes of corruption and mismanagement in South African municipalities reveals a complex interplay of historical and social contexts, resource constraints, and power dynamics. Within municipal governance, power dynamics often manifest as entrenched political interests prioritising personal or factional gains over public service delivery. This issue is further intensified by patronage systems and the politicisation of administrative roles, resulting in inefficiencies and a lack of accountability (Madumo, 2015; de Visser, 2010). Resource constraints also play a significant role, with many municipalities facing substantial financial challenges, inadequate funding, and misallocation of resources, which hinder their ability to deliver essential services. Poor revenue collection practices and reliance on irregular and insufficient national government transfers often lead to financial instability (Khan, 2020; Erika and Elda, 2015).

The background information to this research further highlights that the long-lasting social and economic inequalities created by apartheid, such as racial segregation and economic marginalisation, still impact communities today (Madumo, 2015). Corruption and mismanagement mainly harm marginalised communities, which struggle with limited access to healthcare, education, and job opportunities (Tshishonga, 2019; John and Nhlamulo, 2023). Despite initiatives like the Batho Pele initiative, aimed at improving public service delivery and fighting corruption by setting service standards, offering redress mechanisms, ensuring equal access, promoting respectful interactions, providing accurate information, promoting transparent decision-making, and ensuring value for money, South African municipalities still face challenges in delivering essential services and establishing effective governance (Mojapelo, Modiba & Saurombe, 2023).

Considering the above arguments, the research is, thus, motivated by an urgent need to systematically provide an in-depth understanding of the hurdles South African municipalities encounter regarding corruption and mismanagement. Furthermore, it seeks to critically review governance pointers prioritising transparency, accountability, and enhanced service delivery by suggesting strategic interventions and governance reforms. In a nutshell, the significance of the research lies in systematically providing effective solutions to improve governance effectiveness and promote positive change in South Africa's municipal sector.

Despite growing awareness of the identified problem in this research, there is a significant knowledge gap regarding the optimal strategies to eradicate corruption and foster effective and efficient governance at the municipal level in South Africa. This research intended to bridge this divide by investigating corruption and mismanagement in South African municipalities using case studies and illustrations from selected literature per the Preferred Reporting Items for Systematic Reviews and Meta-Analyses (PRISMA) framework. Furthermore, the research analysed diverse approaches to address corruption, promote openness, and stimulate responsibility. By examining these widespread issues and proposing viable approaches to resolve them, this research aims to make a scholarly contribution to the broader dialogue surrounding the enhancement of governance in municipalities across South Africa.

The study is organised into sections covering the research problem, a brief literature review on corruption and mismanagement in South African municipal governance, methodology approach, results, discussion, and conclusion.

## Research Problem

Over the years, the local government, regarded as the sphere of government closer to the people and at the coalface of service delivery, has come under intense scrutiny since the advent of democracy and during the ongoing process of local government reforms in South Africa (Chilenga-Butao, 2020). Moreover, many South African local governments have been engulfed in service delivery challenges and political infighting, compromising service delivery (Ndou, 2022). In Addition, corruption and mismanagement are widespread in South African municipalities, hindering effective governance and public service delivery. For instance, Corruption Watch (2021:1) recorded over 5,000 reported corruption cases within local government sectors since its inspection in 2012, including bribery, procurement irregularities, and misappropriation of public funds. This evidence highlights the pervasive nature of corrupt practices within municipal establishments. Dlomo (2017) also found that many South African municipalities were at significant risk of financial mismanagement, mainly dominated by unacceptable tender processes and inability to follow procedures and variations in the procurement of goods, all regulated by the law. Other scholars associate such financial mismanagement with poor supply chain management, performance reporting and risk management and inefficient internal control measures (Monkam, 2014; Sibanda et al., 2020).

In spite of the increasing recognition of the above issues, there is still a lack of knowledge about the most effective approaches to address them. McKenzie and Marx (2024) revealed that about 64% of South African municipalities have been classified as financially distressed by the National Treasury in the State of Local Government Finances report for 2021 issued on December 07 2022, implying that most South African municipalities require urgent intervention and turnaround. This evidence underscores a significant deficiency in implementing critical anti-corruption protocols, indicating a lack of understanding or capability to counter corruption and mismanagement at the local level effectively.

Additionally, several authors found systemic challenges, such as inadequate oversight mechanisms, political interference, and weak institutional capacity, perpetuate corruption and mismanagement in South African municipalities despite efforts to improve governance (Mbandlwa, Dorasamy, and Fagbadebo, 2020; Mamokhere, 2022; Thusi and Selepe, 2023). There is a need to develop innovative and context-specific approaches to address these fundamental systemic challenges and promote sound governance practices at the grassroots level. Hence, this study aims to analyse the factors contributing to corruption and mismanagement in South African municipalities, assess their impact on service delivery and infrastructure development, and propose evidence-based strategies to alleviate these challenges and promote effective governance. We (researchers), therefore, argue that the study would contribute to the broader conversation on governance reform and institutional improvement in South Africa and establish accountable and resilient municipal institutions.

## BRIEF LITERATURE REVIEW ON CORRUPTION AND MISMANAGEMENT IN SOUTH AFRICAN MUNICIPAL GOVERNANCE

An extensive academic literature review on corruption and mismanagement in South African municipalities reveals many scholarly perspectives and recommended solutions. Van Rensburg and Botes (2017), as well as Mkhize, Makau, and Madumi (2020), suggest that the persistence of corruption in South African municipalities can be attributed to several factors, including inadequate governance structures, political patronage and a lack of accountability mechanisms. They propose that structural reforms and the creation of efficient supervision entities are essential strategies to mitigate corrupt practices. Khan (2020) agrees with this viewpoint, highlighting the critical significance of political elites and their networks in sustaining corruption in municipal administration. This scholar further emphasised that political determination and responsibility dedication are essential to counteract corruption effectively.

However, the literature also presents critical viewpoints regarding the effectiveness of specific strategies to combat corruption and mismanagement. Naidoo (2018) suggests that although oversight bodies and structural reforms are essential, they might not be sufficient to combat corruption unless underlying socio-economic inequalities and systemic injustices are addressed. This argument highlights the drawbacks of exclusively prioritising institutional reforms while neglecting the influence of broader societal elements that contribute to corruption. Similarly, Ndlela and Duncan (2019) offer a critical analysis of the prevalent top-down methodology used in anti-corruption endeavours among municipalities in South Africa. The latter scholars argue that this approach may fail to recognise the importance of community-driven solutions and specific local circumstances. They further suggest implementing decentralised decision-making processes, which enable local communities to engage actively in governance and ensure that municipal officials are held responsible.

Nonetheless, local empowerment efforts may face obstacles such as limited resources and capabilities, particularly in marginalised communities (Jamatia, 2023). Additionally, the complexities of addressing corruption in municipalities where political interference and patronage networks are deeply ingrained are illuminated by Mkhize, Makau, and Madumi (2020). They explain that more extensive political and cultural transformations are necessary to challenge existing power dynamics and advance ethical leadership alongside efforts to combat corruption. However, the execution of these changes may face opposition from vested interests situated in political and bureaucratic spheres. These diverse viewpoints emphasise the need for comprehensive and situation-specific strategies that consider socio-economic inequalities, community participation, and systemic changes when attempting to eradicate corruption and mismanagement in South African municipalities.

An extensive scholarly discourse exists regarding the strategic utility of effective governance in addressing corruption and mismanagement. This strategic instrument requires governing bodies to manage resources effectively, provide services transparently, and interact with citizens (Patience and Nel, 2022). In South African municipalities, effective governance is of the utmost importance for many reasons, including the provision of vital services such as water, sanitation, and electricity, which require fair allocation and easy access (Mlambo, 2019). Moreover, other scholars assert that effective governance is vital for fostering inclusive growth, addressing socio-economic inequalities, promoting local economic development, and establishing trust and legitimacy among the populace, considering the nation's historical context of apartheid and persistent socio-political obstacles (Mlambo 2019; Sebopetsa and Odeku 2021; Mamokhere 2022). Therefore, it is crucial to establish effective governance to address corruption and mismanagement issues and ensure the moral and productive use of public funds for the benefit of all individuals.

Evidence from real-life cases revealed that corruption and mismanagement severely affect South African municipalities' public trust and service delivery. For instance, Municipal officials' involvement in the Venda Building Society (VBS) Mutual Bank scandal resulted in a financial crisis and the disruption of essential services due to municipal funds being deposited in exchange for bribes (VBS, 2018). In the Investigators' Report, it was alleged that VBS executives paid millions in bribes to municipal officers to secure substantial deposits from their municipalities. Furthermore, VBS executives and employees were accused of generating fraudulent deposits totalling hundreds of millions of Rands to benefit affiliated parties. This included a fraudulent deposit of 250 million for the Insure Group that was recorded in a journal entry (Course sidekick, 2023). The Special Investigating Unit (SIU) expressed satisfaction with the imprisonment of former City of Ekurhuleni officials for tender fraud, corruption, and money laundering involving R21.8 million in the case of the Ekurhuleni Metropolitan Municipality. Also, the Pretoria Commercial Crimes Court sentenced businessman Velero David and former Ekurhuleni IT executive Nilesh Singh to 10 years and 15 years, respectively, for fraud and corruption, with a total of R21,806,331 and R12,678,602 (SIU, 2022). In the Nelson Mandela Bay Municipality, irregular expenditure and unauthorised contracts for infrastructure projects were identified, underscoring the widespread nature of procurement corruption (Steyn Kotze et al., 2020; Thusi and Selepe, 2023). The Emfuleni Local Municipality's substantial challenges with unauthorised, irregular, and wasteful expenditures resulted in severe service delivery backlogs and financial instability

(Sape, 2019). Moreover, allegations of corruption and mismanagement, attributed to irregular tender awards and fund misappropriation, led to the suspension of several senior officials in the City of Tshwane (Lekubu, 2015).

Additionally, the Auditor-General of South Africa (AGSA, 2021) reported that the COVID-19 pandemic was marked by significant corruption and mismanagement, exploiting emergency procurement processes. The irregularities included non-delivery and overpricing of essential products and services. Supply chain rule violations resulted in R21.10 billion in irregular expenditures by local governments in 2020–21. However, the actual amount may be higher, as 31% of municipalities had qualified audit findings, suggesting improper spending was underreported or unrecognised (AGSA, 2021).

These few selected cases show the urgent need for solid anti-corruption measures and effective governance frameworks. Mantzaris and Pillay (2017) reiterated the need to strengthen institutional capabilities, foster a culture of accountability, and enhance transparency. Other scholars claim that engaging local communities in governance processes to address residents' needs and priorities could enhance accountability (Smith, 2020; Moloi, 2020). For instance, the participatory budgeting initiative in the eThekwini Municipality empowered residents to influence budget allocations directly, resulting in more responsive and transparent governance (Smith, 2020). Successful municipal reforms offer valuable lessons. In Cape Town, a comprehensive anti-corruption strategy, including establishing an independent audit committee, enhancing whistleblower protections, and implementing rigorous procurement oversight, significantly improved transparency and reduced corruption prevalence (Fourie, 2019). Similarly, implementing digital governance tools in the City of Johannesburg, such as e-procurement systems, has heightened transparency and accountability while reducing opportunities for corruption (Moloi, 2020).

As far as theories are concerned, they address complex challenges such as mismanagement and corruption in public administration. For example, the Systems Theory of Management (STM) analyses the functioning and influence of organisations as interconnected systems. In their research, Saul, Shopola, and Mlambo (2023) applied this theory to understand how effective management systems can improve governance. Another relevant theory is the Afrocentricity Theory (AT), which acknowledges indigenous knowledge and cultural values and prioritises African perspectives in governance. John and Nhlamulo (2023) utilised this theoretical framework to emphasise the impact of culture on governance practices. Mamokhere and Meyer (2023) establish a hierarchy of citizen engagement in public affairs in accordance with the Ladder of Citizen Participation Theory (LCP). While these theories are crucial for understanding governance dynamics, they have limitations. For instance, the AT might fail to consider the principles of universal governance, while the LCP could oversimplify the intricacies of citizen engagement.

In contrast, the Public Choice Theory (PCT) examines the impact of individual self-interest on the decision-making process, while the Theory of Reasoned Action (TRA) investigates the influence of psychological factors on behaviour. The significance of these theories in understanding responsible public financial management is emphasised by Makhanya (2023) and Zweni, Yan, and Juta (2022). Although the AT may fail to consider systemic concerns, Collective Action Theory (CAT) and Institutional Theory (IT) illuminate structural elements which contribute to corruption, as demonstrated by Sebake's (2020) research study. Thus, although there are numerous theories, the selected ones provide essential frameworks for understanding the underlying factors and devising effective interventions to combat corruption and mismanagement in South African municipalities.

## METHODOLOGY APPROACH

This research study employs the PRISMA framework to systematically review interventions addressing corruption and mismanagement in South African municipalities. PRISMA ensures methodical identification, screening, and synthesis of relevant literature, enhancing transparency and reproducibility (Page et al., 2021). By synthesising existing knowledge, the study fills a significant gap in understanding municipal governance practices in South Africa. It critically reveals recurring patterns, emerging trends, and optimal anti-corruption strategies. The PRISMA protocol facilitates a comprehensive investigation, guiding the identification and screening of pertinent literature, as depicted in the flowchart below in Figure 1.

*Figure 1. PRISMA flowchart for publication selection*

## Information Sources

To conduct this study, we selected several databases, including ProQuest Social Science, Scopus, and EBSCOhost. We chose these databases based on their compliance with indexation standards, broad coverage of various subjects, and popularity among scholars. These platforms offer comprehensive access to relevant scholarly works, user-friendly interfaces, and complete articles. By avoiding repetitive information and thoroughly examining the available literature, we aimed to improve the quality and relevance of the research outcomes. We conducted the most recent searches or consultations of each database on the following dates: ProQuest on March 10, 2024; Scopus on March 14, 2024; and EBSCOhost on March 15, 2024.

## Search Strategy

We developed a comprehensive strategy to retrieve academic journal articles on corruption and mismanagement in South African municipalities from the three selected databases (ProQuest Social Science, Scopus, and EBSCOhost). We used search queries incorporating different iterations of *corruption*, *mismanagement*, and *"South African municipalities"* to ensure inclusivity (see Appendix 1). We consistently applied refined search criteria, including the availability of complete texts and publication dates from 2013 to 2024, and only included English-language journal articles. These filters aimed to optimise the search results by prioritising scholarly articles that met the predetermined criteria and significantly contributed to the research area.

## Selection Process

The selection process involved a comprehensive screening and eligibility assessment to identify studies that met the predetermined inclusion criteria. Four independent reviewers applied a title and abstract vetting process to all records obtained from database searches. Then, each reviewer evaluated the relevance of each record based on predetermined inclusion criteria, including publications in English academic journals, pertinence to corruption and mismanagement in South African municipalities, and publications within the designated timeframe of 2013 to 2024. The reviewers resolved any data inconsistencies or uncertainties during the screening procedure through consensus discussion to ensure uniformity and dependability.

To promote objectivity and reduce bias, we utilised the Ryyan software, a web-based application that facilitates systematic reviews through blinded peer review. This tool anonymised study records throughout the screening and eligibility assessment, effectively mitigating reviewer bias and bolstering the study's dependability, thereby contributing to the selection process for credible and high-quality findings. After this preliminary evaluation, potentially pertinent records underwent a comprehensive text review by the same four reviewers. In this stage, the complete texts of the articles were independently assessed by each reviewer to ascertain their compliance with the inclusion criteria.

As illustrated in Figure 1, a comprehensive compilation of 298 records was obtained from three databases during the identification stage of the PRISMA framework: EBSCOhost (4), ProQuest Social Science (283 records), and Scopus (11 records). One duplicate record was eliminated before screening, leaving 297 distinct records for subsequent evaluation. No records have been excluded or declared ineligible by automation tools. Commencing with this preliminary stage, a thorough dataset was gathered in preparation for the subsequent screening and evaluation of eligibility.

In the screening phase, 297 records were evaluated to determine whether or not they met the objectives of the study. A critical evaluation of the abstracts and topics of 224 records resulted in their exclusion from consideration, as they failed to pertain to the research focus directly. Following that, 73 reports were identified for retrieval; however, the full texts of 11 of these reports remained inaccessible. In the end, 62 reports were evaluated for eligibility; 3 were deemed ineligible because of ambiguous subject matter, and 5 were excluded due to an imprecise scope of investigation. Implementing this screening procedure guaranteed that relevant and meaningful literature would be considered for subsequent analysis and synthesis.

A comprehensive selection of 54 studies, presented in Table 1, met the predetermined criteria for eligibility and were incorporated into the review due to their pertinence to the research objectives. These studies were considered suitable for further analysis and synthesis, contributing valuable insights to the study's objectives and enhancing the comprehensiveness of the review.

## RESULTS OF THE STUDY

Table 1 summarises the selected articles, including information on authors, study titles/codes, theoretical frameworks, methodologies employed, and publication years. This comprehensive overview presents the research landscape, facilitates the synthesis of the findings and allows for critical discussion on effective governance strategies addressing corruption and mismanagement in South African municipalities.

*Table 1. Summary of selected articles*

| Code | Author/s | Title of the article | Theoretical framework | Methodology | Year of publication |
|---|---|---|---|---|---|
| A1 | Mudzusil; Munzhedzi and Mahole (2024) | Governance challenges in the provision of municipal services in the Vhembe District Municipality | | Mixed method | 2024 |
| A2 | Saul; Shopola, and Mlambo (2023) | Human Resource Management System as Enabling Tool for Good Governance in South Africa's Local Government Sector | Systems theory of management | Secondary data | 2023 |

continued on following page

*Table 1. Continued*

| Code | Author/s | Title of the article | Theoretical framework | Methodology | Year of publication |
|---|---|---|---|---|---|
| A3 | John and Nhlamulo (2023) | Questioning the Practice of Corruption in the Attainment of the Selected Sustainable Development Goals (SDGs) in South Africa | Afrocentricity theory, | Qualitative method | 2023 |
| A4 | Bhuda, Motswaledi; and Marumo, (2023 | . Moral Decay, Government, and Looting in South Africa during COVID-19 | | Secondary data | 2023 |
| A5 | Mokhutso,; Marumo; and Motswaledi, (2023) | Ubuntu: An Antidote to Service Delivery Crisis and Political Instability in South Africa | | Secondary data | 2023 |
| A6 | Lavhelani and Lavhelani, (2023) | Assessing the Legal Framework for Service Delivery in the Vhembe District Municipality | | Qualitative method | 2023 |
| A7 | Thusi and Mashabela, (2023) | The role of civil society organisations in promoting public accountability: The perspective of the South African local government | | Qualitative method | 2023 |
| A8 | Mamokhere and Meyer (2023) | The Integrated Development Planning Process's Impact as a Tool for Increasing Community Participation in South Africa | Ladder of Citizen Participation Theory | Mixed method | 2023 |
| A9 | Yende (2023) | Towards Sustainable Service Delivery by South African Local Authorities: A Community Participation Strategy | | Secondary data | 2023 |
| A10 | Makhanya (2023) | The role of accounting officers in ensuring responsible public financial management: A PFMA-centric approach | Public Choice Theory | Case study method | 2023 |
| A11 | Alence and Pitcher (2019) | Resisting state capture in South Africa | | Secondary data | 2019 |
| A12 | Hendrickse (2023) | Ethnic leadership in the age of disruption: implications for South African municipalities | | Secondary data | 2023 |
| A13 | Erika and Elda (2015) | The corruption Bogey in South Africa: Is Public Education safe | | Secondary data | 2015 |
| A14 | Mamokhere (2022) | Pragmatic implementation and promotion of good governance principles in realising Sustainable Development Goal Six (6) in South Africa | | Systematic Literature review | 2022 |
| A15 | Maseko; Robbetze and Masungini (2023) | Association between municipal credit management, responsiveness and service delivery | | Quantitative method | 2023 |
| A16 | Schoeman and Chakwizira (2023) | Advancing a performance management tool for service delivery in local government | | Secondary data | 2023 |
| A17 | Asuelime and Ndimande-Hlongwa, (2022) | Civil society, COVID-19 pandemic and state corruption implications for nation building in South Africa | | Secondary data | 2022 |
| A18 | Ogunlela; Ojugbele and Tengeh (2021) | Blockchain technology as a panacea for procurement corruption in digital era | | Secondary data | 2021 |
| A19 | Zweni; Yan and Juta, (2022) | The malady of perpetual municipal-finance mismanagement: Designing a leadership framework as a Panacea. *African Journal of Development Studies*. | Theory of Reasoned Action, Theory of Financial Control, and Agency Theory | Qualitative method | 2022 |

continued on following page

*Table 1. Continued*

| Code | Author/s | Title of the article | Theoretical framework | Methodology | Year of publication |
|---|---|---|---|---|---|
| A20 | Mamokhere (2022) | Leaving no one behind in a participative integrated development planning process in South Africa | Democratic Decision-Making Theory | Mixed method approach | 2022 |
| A21 | Mamokhere (2022) | Mamokhere, J., 2022. Accountability, inclusivity, effectiveness, and leaving no one behind: An exploration of effective governance principles in ensuring clean water and sanitation in South African municipalities | Human rights-based approach | Secondary data | 2022 |
| A22 | Magagula; Mukonza; Manyaka; and Moeti (2022) | The role of district municipalities in service provision in South Africa: Dissecting challenges faced by Ehlanzeni District Municipality | | Qualitative method | 2022 |
| A23 | Maluleke (2022) | Alleged corrupt practices on stock theft by public sector officials in the selected rural areas of Giyani, Limpopo Province: Exploring the causes and experiences | | Qualitative method | 2022 |
| A24 | Vyas-Doorgapersad and Mothabi (2022) | Overview of misconduct influencing ethical culture in the Local Government Sector Education Training Authority, South Africa | | Secondary data | 2022 |
| A25 | Mubangizi (2022) | The Interplay between Civil Society and Local Government in South Africa: Conflict and Collaboration in the Delivery of Public Services | | Secondary data | 2022 |
| A26 | Ncamphalala and Vyas-Doorgapersad (2022) | The role of information and communication technology (ICT) on the transformation of municipalities into smart cities for improved service delivery | | Qualitative method | |
| A27 | Patience and Nel (2022) | Governance, democracy and accountability from a network governance perspective within the city of Ekurhuleni | | Qualitsitive method | 2022 |
| A28 | Rulashe and Ijeoma, (2022) | An exploration of public accountability and service delivery at the Buffalo City Metropolitan Municipality in the Eastern Cape province, South Africa | | Mixed-method approach | 2022 |
| A29 | Zerihun and Mashingo, (2022) | The quest for service delivery: The case of a rural district municipality in the Mpumalanga province of South Africa | The New Public Management | Quantitative method | 2022 |
| A30 | Gasela (2022) | The impact of material irregularity provisions of the *Public Audit Act* on accountability, oversight and governance in the Northern Cape province of South Africa | Agency Theory and Contigency Theory | Quantitative method | 2022 |
| A31 | Mamokhere; Kgobe; Lavhelani and Richard (2021) | Give to Caesar what belongs to caesar: The provision of water and sanitation service in South African rural areas | | Qualitative method | 2021 |
| A32 | Sebopetsa and Odeku, (2021) | Safeguarding the Right to Protest and Prohibition of Violent Protests in South Africa: Issues and Perspectives | | Qualitative method | 2021 |
| A33 | Enaifoge and Abosede (2021) | Enhancing Good Governance in South Africa Through Youth Protest: A Catalyst for Social Change | | Qualitative method | 2021 |
| A34 | Mashaine and Odeku (2021) | Transformative Interventions Fostering the right to access to Adequate Housing in South Africa | | Secondary data | 2021 |

continued on following page

*Table 1. Continued*

| Code | Author/s | Title of the article | Theoretical framework | Methodology | Year of publication |
|---|---|---|---|---|---|
| A35 | Sebola (2021) | Monitoring for Good Governance in South Africa: the Complex of a Fair Public Administration | | Secondary data | 2021 |
| A36 | Kanjere and Koto (2021) | Public Procurement Corruption and Corporate Scandals in Limpopo Province, South Africa: A Content Analysis Perspective | | Qualitative method | 2021 |
| A37 | Ngumbela (2021) | Troubled municipalities, municipality troubles: An implementation of Back to Basics programme in the Eastern Cape province, South Africa | Theory of change | Mixed-method approach | 2021 |
| A38 | Sebake (2020) | Crime against Humanity: Social Perception of Public Service Corruption in South Africa | Institutional Theory and Corruption; Collective Action Theory and Corruption; Public Value Theory and Corruption | | 2020 |
| A39 | Ndlovu; Maramura; and Enaifoghe (2020) | Moral and Ethical Leadership Challenges in South African Public Service: The Case of the Eastern Cape, Department of Education | | Mixed method approach | 2020 |
| A40 | Mabizela and Matsiliza (2020) | Uncovering the gaps in the provision of services in the rural Okhahlamba Municipality of KwaZulu-Natal province | | Mixed method approach | 2020 |
| A41 | Mathebula and Sebola (2019) | Evaluating the Integrated Development Plan for Service Delivery within the Auspices of the South African Municipalities | | Secondary method | 2019 |
| A42 | Mlambo (2019) | Governance and Service Delivery in the Public Sector: The Case of South Africa under Jacob Zuma (2009 – 2018) | | Secondary method | 2019 |
| A43 | Govender and Reddy (2019) | Effectiveness of governance towards digitalisation at eThekwini Metropolitan Municipality in KwaZulu-Natal province, South Africa | New Public Management | Qualitative method | 2019 |
| A44 | Sithole and Mathonsi (2015) | Local Governance Service Delivery Issues during Apartheid and Post-Apartheid South Africa | | Secondary method | 2015 |
| A45 | Marutlulle and Ijeoma (2015) | Obstacles to Housing Delivery in Ekurhuleni Metropolitan Municipality: A Critical Review of Output and Input | | Secondary method | 2015 |
| A46 | Mamogale (2014) | Financial Performance of Local Government in Limpopo Province, 2010-2012 | Citizenry engagement and participation theory | Secondary method | 2014 |
| A47 | Akinboade; Mokwena; and Kinfack (2014) | Protesting for Improved Public Service Delivery in South Africa's Sedibeng District | | Quantitative method | 2014 |
| A48 | Kanyane (2014) | Exploring challenges of municipal service delivery in South Africa (1994-2013) | | Qualitative method | 2014 |
| A49 | Mofolo; Mkuyane; and Skade (2014) | Actions and behaviours essential for monitoring & evaluation to succeed in South African public service | | Secondary method | 2014 |

continued on following page

*Themes generated from the selected articles*

Continued

| Code | Author/s | Title of the article | Theoretical framework | Methodology | Year of publication |
|---|---|---|---|---|---|
| A50 | Kroukamp and Cloete (2018) | Improving professionalism in South African local government | | Qualitative method | 2018 |
| A51 | Zengethwa; Thakhathi and Oyelana (2019) | Challenges Faced by the Raymond Mhlaba Municipality in Implementing the Back-to-Basics Programme | | Qualitative method | 2019 |
| A52 | Ndlovu and Mutambara (2023) | Manifestations of corruption within the Kwazulu-Natal municipalities: A thorn in the flesh | Ethical leadership theory | Quantitative method | 2023 |
| A53 | Muzekenyi; Nyika; and Hoque (2022) | Decentralisation of Authority and its Implications for Inclusive Economic Development strategies in South Africa: A critical review | | Secondary data | 2022 |
| A54 | Mbazira, C., 2013. | Service delivery protests struggle for rights and the failure of local democracy in South Africa and Uganda: parallels and divergences. | | Secondary data | 2013 |

Source: Authors' compilation

*Themes generated from the selected articles*

| Themes | Authors | No of articles |
|---|---|---|
| 1. Legislative Duty of local government; governance, accountability and ethical leadership | Mathebula and Sebola (2019) – A41<br>Mamokhere (2022) – A21; A14<br>Enaifoghe; Abosede (2021) –A33<br>Ndlovu; Maramura and Enaifoghe (2020) – A39<br>Hendrickse (2023) – A12<br>Rulashe and Ijeoma (2022)- A28<br>Mamokhere, Kgobe and Chauke (2021) – A31 | 8 |

*Themes generated from the selected articles*

Continued

| Themes | Authors | No of articles |
|---|---|---|
| 2. Governance challenges in municipal service delivery | Mudzusi1; Munzhedzi and Mahole (2024) – A1<br>Magagula; Mukonza; Manyaka and Moeti (2022) – A22<br>Bhuda; Motswaled and Marumo (2023) – A4<br>Mashiane and Odeku (2021) – A34<br>Mabizela and Matsiliza (2020) – A40<br>Mathonsi and Sithole (2015) – A44<br>Kanyane (2014) – A48<br>Marutlulle and Ijeoma (years) – A45<br>Zerihum, and Mashingo (2022) – A29:<br>Akinboade, Mokwena, and Kinfack (2014) – A47 | 10 |
| 3. Community Participation and Civil Society Accountability | Mbazira (2013) – A54<br>Thusi and Mashabela (2023) – A7<br>Asuelime and Hlongwa (2022)- A17<br>Mamokhere and Meyer (2023) – A8<br>Yende (2023) – A9<br>Mamokhere (2022) – A20<br>Mubangizi (2022)- A25<br>Jerome, Patience; Danielle Nel (2021) – A27<br>Akinboade, Mokwena, and Kinfack (2014) – A47<br>Zengethwa1, Thakhathi and Oyelana (2019) – A51 | 10 |

| Themes | Authors | No of articles |
|---|---|---|
| 4. Anti-corruption measures and institutional reform & capacity building | Gasela (2022) – A30; Mlambo (2019) – A42<br>Pinky Mothabi and Shikha Vyas-Doorgapersad (2022) – A24<br>Ndlovu and Mutambara (2023) – A13; A52<br>Mamokhere and Nhlamulo (2023) – A3<br>Mokhutso; Marumo and Motswaledi (2023) – A5<br>Muzekenyi, Farai Nyika and Hoque (2022) – A53<br>Rod Alence, Anne Pitcher (2019) – A11<br>Rozenda Hendrickse (2023); Witness Maluleke (2022) – A23<br>Koto and Kanjere (2021) – A36; Mamogale (2014) – A46<br>Xolisile G. Ngumbela1 (2020) – A37<br>Mofolo, Mkuyane and Skade (2014) – A49<br>Sebake (2020) – A38<br>Ilse Schoeman and James Chakwizira (2023) – A16<br>Sebola (2021) – A35<br>Saul; Shopola, and Mlambo (2023) – A2<br>Oyebanjo; Olabode and Robertson (2021) – A18<br>Maseko; Robbetze and Masungini (2023)- A15<br>Njabulo Makhanya (2023)- A10<br>Zweni; Yan, and Juta (2022)- A19<br>Lavhelani; Lavhelani (2023) – A6<br>Sebopetsa; Odeku (2021) – A32<br>Govender and Reddy (2019) – A43<br>Ncamphalala; Doorgapersad (2022) – A26<br>Kroukamp and Cloete (2018) – A50 | 26 |

Source: Authors compilation

1. Legislative Duty of Local Government: Governance, Accountability, and Ethical Leadership

The theme focuses on the critical responsibilities of local government in South African municipalities. The emphasis is on ethical leadership, accountability, and efficient governance. The process involves complying with legislative mandates, promoting transparency, instilling public confidence, and encouraging ethical behaviour among government personnel. Moreover, it highlights the crucial role of local government in promoting community welfare by facilitating socio-economic progress, ensuring service delivery, and combating corruption and mismanagement. The significance of integrated planning instruments, such as the Integrated Development Plan (IDP), in improving service provision in South African municipalities is emphasised by Mathebula and Sebola (2019). The IDP is critical to achieving effective governance, accountability, and ethical leadership.

Mamokhere (2022) argues that effective governance principles are essential to achieving Sustainable Development Goal 6: clean water and sanitation. Implementing systems that foster constitutionalism, accountability, democracy, and good governance can help attain this goal. Rulashe and Ijeoma (2022) examine the public accountability strategies used by the Buffalo City Metropolitan Municipality. They identify communication deficiencies and inadequate implementation of accountability mechanisms as factors contributing to service delivery and public accountability problems. Enaifoghe and Abosede (2021) advocate for youth participation in governance processes to promote good governance. Ndlovu, Maramura, and Enaifoghe (2020) emphasise the significance of ethical leadership in the fight against maladministration and corruption.

In examining these viewpoints, several criticisms emerge, emphasising accountability, ethical leadership, and governance. Although Mamokhere (2022) and Ndlovu et al. (2020) emphasise the importance of ethical leadership and constitutionalism, these concepts may not adequately address systemic problems because they disregard structural obstacles and power dynamics that sustain corruption. Furthermore, while Enaifoghe and Abosede (2021) emphasise youth participation in governance, it may not be sufficient to effect change independently; systemic obstacles such as limited resources, exclusion from decision-making processes, and political marginalisation must also be confronted. Similarly, the scholarly work of Rulashe and Ijeoma (2022) primarily focuses on public accountability strategies while neglecting the fundamental deficiencies in governance. Failure to confront systemic challenges such as institutional fragility and lack of transparency may result in these strategies superficially addressing matters that ultimately remain unresolved.

2. Governance challenges in municipal service Delivery.

The theme of governance challenges in municipal service delivery focuses on identifying and addressing obstacles that hinder effective governance and providing services at the local government level. Several authors share similar views on the challenges of corruption and mismanagement in South African municipalities. For example, Mudzusi, Munzhedzi, and Mahole (2024) highlight problems such as poor service provision, lack of resources, insufficient accountability, and low efficiency in the Vhembe District Municipality. Similarly, Bhuda, Motswaled, and Marumo (2023) identify the negative consequences of cadre deployment and financial constraints on municipal services. Zengethwa, Thakhathi, and Oyelana (2019) describe corruption and ineptitude in the Raymond Mhlaba Municipality, leading to inadequate service provision and unfulfilled community needs. Other authors, such as Marutlulle and Ijeoma (2015) and Mabizela and Matsiliza (2020), point to systemic obstacles such as strict government policies, limited capacity, and declining public trust in municipal officials as contributing factors to poor service delivery. Mashiane and Odeku (2021) also highlight the culture of impunity among those responsible for adequate housing, which underscores the lack of accountability in addressing housing needs. Bhuda, Motswaled, and Marumo (2023) conclude that corruption and non-service delivery have wider social consequences, such as moral decay and social unrest. Most authors collectively stress the urgent need for reforms to address corruption, mismanagement, and institutional weaknesses in South African municipalities to improve service delivery and restore public trust.

3. Community Participation and Civil Society Accountability

Community participation and civil society accountability are crucial in promoting transparency and accountability in South African municipalities. The theme of community engagement and civil society accountability emphasises this importance. Scholars such as Mamokhere (2022) emphasise the significance of public engagement in procedures like the Integrated Development Plan (IDP) to ensure that municipal policies align with the community's needs. Yende (2023) underscores the importance of proactive community engagement to improve service delivery, highlighting that sustainable progress requires transparency and accountability.

Furthermore, Asuelime and Hlongwa (2022) and Thusi and Mashabela (2023) examine the importance of civil society in opposing corruption and maladministration, advocating for accountability mechanisms that prevent the misallocation of government resources. However, Mbazira (2013) cautions that effective community participation requires the development of civic competence and the establishment of operational structures. He suggests that just engaging with communities is not enough; they must also be equipped with the necessary resources and competencies. Additionally, Akinboade, Mokwena, and Kinfack (2014) emphasise the correlation between protest participation and public perception of governance, indicating that it is essential to cultivate public confidence in municipal authorities by addressing development challenges identified by residents.

Although community engagement and civil society responsibility are crucial for promoting good governance and combating corruption, they are insufficient to empower communities and ensure their opinions are considered and implemented. Transparent decision-making processes, easily accessible platforms for citizen engagement, and strong oversight mechanisms are also necessary.

4. Anti-corruption measures and institutional reform & capacity building

Anti-corruption measures, institutional reform, and capacity building seek to detect, prevent, and address corruption in government institutions. These initiatives aim to strengthen institutional frameworks, enhance transparency, foster accountability, and develop the capacity to combat corrupt practices effectively. Several authors address the issue of corruption and mismanagement in South African municipalities, presenting a range of solutions to improve governance and service provision. Mathebula and Sebola (2019) state that inadequate performance management tools and legislative frameworks contribute to persistent service delivery gaps. On the other hand, Mofolo, Mkuyane, and Skade (2014) highlight the importance of Monitoring and Evaluation (M&E) in ensuring effective governance. Sebola (2021) emphasises the need for institutions to conduct effective governance monitoring, while Koto and Kanjere (2021) provide insight into the damaging effects of recruitment patterns on financial performance. Saul, Shopola, and Mlambo (2023) advocate for human resource management systems free from political manipulation to improve municipal performance. Oyebanjo, Olabode, and Robertson (2021) suggest implementing blockchain technology to digitise governance to reduce corruption.

Kroukamp and Cloete (2018) stress the importance of professional behaviour and responsibility, while Ncamphalala and Doorgapersad (2022) focus on using Information Communication and Technology (ICT) to facilitate intelligent governance. Govender and Reddy (2019) find governance frameworks and digitalisation inadequate, while Maseko, Robbetze, and Masungini (2023) highlight the positive correlation between credit management and service provision. Makhanya (2023) emphasises the need to strengthen municipal financial management, while Zweni, Yan, and Juta (2022) propose a leadership framework to improve financial management operations. In sum, arguments from several authors emphasise the importance of a comprehensive strategy to combat corruption and mismanagement that includes legal frameworks, human resources, technology, governance, and financial management. Additionally, the selected studies for analysis show that a substantial number used qualitative methodology. While this approach can provide valuable insights, it has some potential drawbacks. For instance, the subjective nature of participant responses and the possibility of interview bias can limit the extent of the analysis. Moreover, the methodology's dependence on secondary data can also constrain the analysis. Therefore, empirical investigation is necessary to enhance our understanding of the fundamental issues related to mismanagement and corruption in South African municipalities.

5. Discussion of Findings

After carefully analysing different perspectives on governance, accountability, and ethical leadership, Mamokhere (2022) and Ndlovu et al. (2020) studies might not thoroughly address the issue of systemic corruption even though they stress the importance of ethical leadership and constitutionalism. While constitutionalism and ethical leadership emphasise the significance of adhering to legal principles and ethical standards in governance processes to promote transparency and integrity in decision-making, their effectiveness in fighting corruption may be limited due to systemic challenges such as institutional deficiencies and power asymmetry. Similarly, systemic barriers such as power dynamics and structural obstacles contribute significantly to the perpetuation of corruption in South African municipalities. Structural barriers refer to inherent deficiencies or constraints within the institutional structure, such as ambiguous mandates, overlapping jurisdictions, and insufficient enforcement mechanisms. On the other hand, power dynamics involve unequal power distributions among various stakeholders, which promote individualistic objectives at the expense of society's collective well-being. These systemic barriers create an environment conducive to corruption by fostering secrecy, patronage, and impunity, which allows corruption to persist within municipal governance structures.

Furthermore, Enaifoghe and Abosede (2021) argue that systemic obstacles like resource constraints and exclusion from decision-making procedures hinder youth participation in governance. Youth engagement has the potential to bring novel insights, inventive solutions, and inclusive representation to decision-making processes. However, if systemic obstacles such as restricted resource accessibility and exclusionary governance practices are not addressed, youth engagement may remain symbolic rather than substantial. In order to optimise the effects of youth engagement, it is crucial to confront these systemic obstacles by adopting strategies that ensure fair and equal access to resources, encourage inclusive participation in decision-making procedures, and create a nurturing atmosphere conducive to youth involvement.

Although it is important to hold public officials and institutions accountable for their actions, fundamental governance failures hinder the effectiveness of such strategies. Through audits, transparency measures, and whistleblower protections, public accountability strategies promote transparency, integrity, and responsiveness in governance processes. However, addressing governance shortcomings, such as inadequate enforcement mechanisms, institutional capacity, and transparent practices, is crucial to tackling corruption and mismanagement. Therefore, comprehensive reforms are necessary to strengthen institutional capacity, promote transparency and accountability mechanisms, and foster a culture of integrity and ethics among municipalities in South Africa.

Civil society accountability and community participation are crucial factors in promoting good governance and combating corruption. Transparent decision-making processes facilitate the openness and accountability of government actions, allowing the public to scrutinise and question officials' choices. Citizen engagement platforms, such as online portals and public forums, ensure diverse community voices are heard during decision-making. By establishing citizen watchdog groups and independent audits, government actions are subject to checks and balances, ultimately increasing accountability.

However, these mechanisms must confront systemic obstacles, including political marginalisation and resource constraints. Political marginalisation occurs when specific societal groups, including minority or marginalised communities, are excluded from decision-making procedures due to power asymmetry or discriminatory policies. Inclusive environments that enable meaningful participation in governance activities by all community members, irrespective of socio-economic status or personal history, are essential to address political marginalisation. Resource constraints, such as restricted access to information or technology and financial limitations, may impede community engagement. Therefore, governments and civil society organisations should invest in capacity-building initiatives and provide adequate resources to support citizen participation.

Establishing an environment of openness and responsibility within civil society organisations is essential to ensure their efficacy in holding local administrations accountable. Civil society organisations function as watchdogs, promoting ethical behaviour, transparency, and accountability within governance procedures. By implementing these principles internally, civil society organisations bolster their legitimacy and credibility as change agents. Furthermore, enhancing transparency and accountability within civil society organisations strengthens their ability to observe governmental activities and advocate for reforms. Therefore, initiatives to promote accountability and transparency within civil society organisations should be integrated into efforts to strengthen community participation and civil society accountability.

The finding also revealed that a multifaceted approach is indispensable in addressing corruption and mismanagement comprehensively within South African municipalities. Firstly, by strengthening institutional capacity, which involves enhancing the capabilities and resources of local government entities to fulfil their mandates effectively. This gives local government entities adequate resources and capabilities to carry out their mandates efficiently. Effective staff training programs, improved recruitment and retention procedures, and clearly defined chains of command and responsibility are key elements of institutional capacity enhancement. Strengthening institutional capacity can make municipalities more resilient to external pressures and better equipped to tackle challenges. This, in turn, can reduce the likelihood of corruption and mismanagement (Mamokhere, 2022).

Secondly, leveraging technological advancements is another important means to enhance governance, promote transparency and efficiency, and combat corruption. Incorporating digital platforms into public procurement, financial management, and citizen engagement can increase transparency, optimise operations, and reduce the risks of corrupt practices. Blockchain technology, for example, can create immutable transaction ledgers, minimising the risk of deception and ensuring accountability.

Technological solutions can also improve service delivery and encourage greater citizen engagement in governance processes (Ndlovu et al., 2020).

Thirdly, it is essential to establish clear rules and regulations that govern the behaviour of public officials and institutions by implementing robust legal frameworks. Effective legislation can provide the necessary instruments and penalties to deter corrupt activities, ensure accountability of offenders, and protect whistleblowers. Legal frameworks should also promote transparency in decision-making processes, ensure information accessibility, and establish independent oversight mechanisms. By reinforcing legal frameworks, municipalities can foster an ethical culture and promote effective governance (Enaifoghe & Abosede, 2021).

However, achieving sustainable progress in governance and accountability requires coordination and collaboration among stakeholders. This includes international collaborators, government agencies, and civil society organisations. Coordination and alignment of strategies with overarching goals and objectives can prevent redundant efforts and promote collaboration. Through collaborative efforts, stakeholders can optimise outcomes related to governance and achieve sustainable progress (Rulashe & Ijeoma, 2022).

## 6. Conclusion

In conclusion, this systematic review sheds light on the multifaceted nature of corruption and mismanagement in South African municipalities, highlighting the critical importance of addressing systemic issues to ensure effective governance. The study emphasises the need for reforms that target corruption, ineptitude, and institutional deficiencies within South African municipalities. Evidence from various scholars suggests that achieving efficient governance, accountability, and ethical leadership is crucial but may not be enough to confront profoundly ingrained corruption if fundamental structural obstacles and power dynamics are not addressed.

It is necessary to overcome systemic barriers, including resource constraints and exclusionary practices, in youth participation in governance and public accountability initiatives. A comprehensive approach is needed to enhance institutional capabilities and harness technological advancements to promote transparency and efficiency, establish strong legal structures, and cultivate an environment characterised by integrity and ethical conduct within civil society organisations. Suggestions include adopting strategies to confront systemic obstacles, strengthening mechanisms to ensure transparency and accountability, and advocating for inclusive governance processes that empower communities and amplify their voices. The policy implications include the need for legislative reforms, institutional restructuring, and capacity-building initiatives to combat corruption effectively and strengthen governance structures. By adopting a holistic approach, municipalities in South Africa can cultivate an environment characterised by openness, responsibility, and effective administration, which improves the provision of services and reinstates public confidence.

## REFERENCES


Adetiba, O. F. (2016). *The challenges of curbing corruption in a democracy: The case of the Public Protector and Nkandla* [Doctoral dissertation, Stellenbosch: Stellenbosch University].

Akinboade, O. A., Mokwena, M. P., & Kinfack, E. C. (2014). Protesting for improved public service delivery in South Africa's Sedibeng District. *Social Indicators Research*, 119(1), 1–23. 10.1007/s11205-013-0377-9

Alence, R., & Pitcher, A. (2019). Resisting state capture in South Africa. *Journal of Democracy*, 30(4), 5–19. 10.1353/jod.2019.0065

Asuelime, R. A., & Ndimande-Hlongwa, N. (2022). Civil society, COVID-19 pandemic and state corruption implications for nation building in South Africa. *Journal ofNation-Building and Policy Studies*, 1(1, si1), 163–181. 10.31920/2516-3132/2022/s1s1a9

Auditor-General of South Africa. (2021). *Consolidated general report on local government audit outcomes - FMA 2020-21*. Auditor General of South Africa. Pretoria.

Bhuda, M.T., Motswaledi, T., & Marumo, P. (2023). Moral Decay, Government, and Looting in South Africa during COVID-19. *African Journal of Development Studies, 13*.

Chilenga-Butao, T. (2020). Decentralisation and recentralisation in South Africa's local government: Case studies of two municipalities in Limpopo. *Transformation (Durban)*, 103(1), 12–35. 10.1353/trn.2020.0011

Corruption Watch. (2021). *South Africa needs clean hands*. Corruption Watch. https://www.corruptionwatch.org.za/wp-content/uploads/2021/08/CW-localgovt-sectoral-report-August2021.pdf

Course Sidekick. (2023). *Comprehensive Case Study report on the alleged irregularities committed at VBS Bank during 2014 to 2018*. Course Sidekick. https://www.coursesidekick.com/accounting/3383328 [Accessed 15 June 2024].

De Visser, J. (2010). The political-administrative interface in South African municipalities assessing the quality of local democracies. *Commonwealth Journal of Local Governance*, (5), 86–101. 10.5130/cjlg.v0i5.1473

Dlomo, P. A. (2017). *The impact of irregular expenditure in the South African public finance with specific reference to the National Department of Public Works*, 1–125. CPUT. http://etd.cput.ac.za/handle/ 20.500.11838/2453

Enaifoghe, A., & Abosede, D. A. (2021). Enhancing good governance in South Africa through youth protest: A catalyst for social change. *Research World*, 12(2), 1–11.

Erika, S., & Elda, W. (2015). The corruption Bogey in south Africa: Is public education safe. *South African Journal of Education*, 5(9), 16–44.

Fagbadebo, O. (2019). Corruption and the challenge of accountability in the post-colonial African states: A discourse. *Journal of African Union Studies*.

Gasela, M. M. (2022). The impact of material irregularity provisions of the *Public Audit Act* on accountability, oversight and governance in the Northern Cape province of South Africa. *Africa's Public Service Delivery and Performance Review*, 10(1), a601. 10.4102/apsdpr.v10i1.601

Govender, N., & Reddy, P. S. (2019). Effectiveness of governance towards digitalisation at eThekwini Metropolitan Municipality in KwaZulu-Natal province, South Africa. *Africa's Public Service Delivery and Performance Review*, 7(1), a336. 10.4102/apsdpr.v7i1.336

Hendrickse, R. (2023). Ethnic leadership in the age of disruption: implications for South African municipalities. *International Journal of Research in Business and Social Science (2147-4478), 12*(7), 224-234.

Jamatia, P. L. (2023). The Role of Youth in Combating Social Inequality: Empowering the Next Generation. *International Journal of Social Science, Educational, Economics. Agricultural Research & Technology: Open Access Journal*, 2(8), 229–238.

John, D., & Nhlamulo, T. (2023). The Impact of Corruption on Governance and Development in South Africa. *Southern African Journal of Public Affairs*, 30(1), 47–65.

John, M., Lavhelani, K. F. K., & Richard, C. K. (2021). Give to Caesar what belongs to Caesar: The provision of water and sanitation service in South African Rural areas. *Gender & Behaviour*, 19(3), 18323–18330.

John, M., & Nhlamulo, M. (2023). Questioning the Practice of Corruption in the Attainment of the Selected Sustainable Development Goals (SDGs) in South Africa. *IAHRW International Journal of Social Sciences Review, 11*(3).

Kanjere, M. & Koto, A. (2021). Public Procurement Corruption and Corporate Scandals in Limpopo Province, South Africa: A Content Analysis Perspective. *Acta Universitatis Danubius. Relationes Internationales, 14*(2).

Kanyane, M. (2014). Exploring challenges of municipal service delivery in South Africa (1994-2013). *Africa's Public Service Delivery & Performance Review*, 2(1), 90–110. 10.4102/apsdpr.v2i1.45

Khan, F. (2020). Corruption and Mismanagement in South African Municipalities: A Critical Evaluation. *Journal of Public Administration*, 55(2), 284–298.

Kroukamp, H., & Cloete, F. (2018). Improving professionalism in South African local government. *Acta Academica*, 50(1), 61–80. 10.18820/24150479/aa50i1.4

Lavhelani, P. N., & Lavhelani, P. D. (2023). Assessing the Legal Framework for Service Delivery in the Vhembe District Municipality. *Gender & Behaviour*, 21(1), 20959–20972.

Lekubu, B. K. (2015). *Manifestations of corruption in the City of Tshwane Metropolitan Municipality* [Doctoral dissertation, University of South Africa].

Mabizela, H. & Matsiliza, N.S. (2020). Uncovering the gaps in the provision of services in the rural Okhahlamba Municipality of KwaZulu-Natal province. *Africa's Public Service Delivery and Performance Review,8*(1), a390. . v8i1.390.10.4102/apsdpr

Madumo, O. S. (2015). Developmental Local Government Challenges and Progress in South Africa. *Administration Publica*, 23(4), 153–166.

Magagula, D. N., Mukonza, R. M., Manyaka, R. K., & Moeti, K. (2022). The role of district municipalities in service provision in South Africa: Dissecting challenges faced by Ehlanzeni District Municipality. *Africa's Public Service Delivery and Performance Review*, 10(1), a628. 10.4102/apsdpr.v10i1.628

Makhanya, N., 2023. The role of accounting officers in ensuring responsible public financial management: A PFMA centric approach. *International Journal of Research in Business and Social Science (2147-4478), 12*(10), 241-247.

Maluleke, W. (2022). Alleged corrupt practices on stock theft by public sector officials in the selected rural areas of Giyani, Limpopo Province: Exploring the causes and experiences. *International Journal of Research in Business and Social Science (2147-4478), 11*(5), 472-481.

Mamogale, M. J. (2014). Financial Performance of Local Government in Limpopo Province, 2010-2012. *African Studies Quarterly*, 15(1).

Mamokhere, J. (2022). Pragmatic implementation and promotion of good governance principles in realising Sustainable Development Goal Six (6) in South Africa. *International Journal of Research in Business and Social Science (2147-4478), 11*(6), 20-32.

Mamokhere, J. (2022). Leaving no one behind in a participative integrated development planning process in South Africa. *International Journal of Research in Business and Social Science (2147-4478), 11*(10), 277-291.

Mamokhere, J. (2022). Accountability, inclusivity, effectiveness, and leaving no one behind: An exploration of effective governance principles in ensuring clean water and sanitation in South African municipalities. *International Journal of Research in Business and Social Science (2147-4478), 11*(10), 191-205.

Mamokhere, J., 2022. Understanding the Complex Interplay of Governance, Systematic, and Structural Factors Affecting Service Delivery in South African Municipalities. *Commonwealth Youth & Development, 20*(2).

Mamokhere, J., & Meyer, D. F. (2023). The Integrated Development Planning Process's Impact as a Tool for Increasing Community Participation in South Africa. *African Journal of Development Studies*, 13(2), 7–34. 10.31920/2634-3649/2023/v13n2a1

Mantzaris, E., & Pillay, P. (2017). Procurement and Corruption: The Case of the Ekurhuleni Metropolitan Municipality. *African Journal of Public Affairs*, 9(5), 78–92.

Marutlulle, N. K., & Ijeoma, E. O. C. (2015). Obstacles to housing delivery in Ekurhuleni Metropolitan Municipality: A critical review of output and input. *Africa's Public Service Delivery & Performance Review*, 3(4), 141–163. 10.4102/apsdpr.v3i4.101

Maseko, G. J., Robbetze, N., & Masungini, A. W. (2023). 'Association between municipal credit management, responsiveness and service delivery'. *Africa's Public Service Delivery and Performance Review*, 11(1), a686. 10.4102/apsdpr.v11i1.686

Mashiane, K. & Odeku, K.O. (2021). Transformative interventions fostering the right to access to adequate housing in South Africa. *African Journal of Development Studies (formerly AFFRIKA Journal of Politics, Economics and Society), 2021*(si1), 265-287.

Mathebula, N.E. & Sebola, M.P. (2019). Evaluating the Integrated Development Plan for Service Delivery within the Auspices of the South African Municipalities. *African Renaissance (1744-2532), 16*(4).

Mbandlwa, Z., Dorasamy, N. & Fagbadebo, O.M. (2020). Leadership challenges in the South African local government system. *Journal of Critical Reviews.*

Mbazira, C. (2013). Service delivery protests, struggle for rights and the failure of local democracy in South Africa and Uganda: Parallels and divergences. *South African Journal on Human Rights*, 29(2), 251–275. 10.1080/19962126.2013.11865074

McKenzie, M. & Marx, B. (2024). Turnaround for municipal distress resolution: An audit outcomes approach. *South African Journal of Accounting Research.*

Mkhize, M. C., Makau, K. L., & Madumi, P. (2020). *Good Governance Under Zuma Administration: Fad or Reality?* Governance and Societal Adaptation in Fragile States.

Mlambo, D. (2023). Fighting public sector corruption in post-apartheid South Africa: Progress on paper, hurdles on the ground. In *Mbali Conference 2023 Proceedings* (p. 326).

Mlambo, D. N. (2019). Governance and service delivery in the public sector: The case of South Africa under Jacob Zuma (2009–2018). *African Renaissance*, 16(3), 207–224. 10.31920/2516-5305/2019/V16n3a11

Mofolo, M., Mkuyane, L., & Skade, T. (2014). Actions and behaviours essential for monitoring & evaluation to succeed in South African public service. *Africa's Public Service Delivery & Performance Review*, 2(3), 5–24. 10.4102/apsdpr.v2i3.58

Mojapelo, M., Modiba, M., & Saurombe, N. (2023). Applying Batho Pele principles in South African public archives–Do public programming initiatives count? *Information Development*, 39(2), 357–375. 10.1177/02666669211049382

Mokhutso, J., Marumo, P. O., & Motswaledi, T. R. (2023). Ubuntu: An Antidote to Service Delivery Crisis and Political Instability in South Africa. *Journal of Nation-building &. Policy Studies*, 7(2).

Moloi, T. (2020). Digital Governance in the City of Johannesburg: E-Procurement and Transparency. *Journal of Urban Affairs*, 42(4), 523–541.

Monkam, N. F. (2014). Local municipality productive efficiency and its determinants in South Africa. *Development Southern Africa*, 31(2), 275–298. 10.1080/0376835X.2013.875888

Mubangizi, B. C. (2022). The Interplay between Civil Society and Local Government in South Africa: Conflict and Collaboration in the Delivery of Public Services. *African Journal of Development Studies*, (si1), 39. 10.31920/2634-3649/2022/SIv2a3

Mudzusi, T. N., Munzhedzi, P. H., & Mahole, E. (2024). Governance challenges in the provision of municipal services in the Vhembe District Municipality. *Africa's Public Service Delivery & Performance Review*, 12(1), 10. 10.4102/apsdpr.v12i1.749

Muzekenyi, M., Nyika, F., & Hoque, M. (2022). Decentralisation of Authority and its Implications for Inclusive Economic Development strategies in South Africa: A critical review. *Journal of Nation-Building and Policy Studies*, 6(3), 47–66. 10.31920/2516-3132/2022/v6n3a3

. Ncamphalala, M. Vyas-Doorgapersad, S. 2022. The role of information and communication technology (ICT) on the transformation of municipalities into smart cities for improved service delivery. *International Journal of Research in Business and Social Science (2147-4478), 11*(2), 318-328.

Ndlovu, M., Maramura, T. C., & Enaifoghe, A. (2020). Understanding the moral and ethical leadership challenges in South African public service: The case of the Eastern Cape, Department of Education. *Journal of Nation-Building and Policy Studies*, 4(2), 21. 10.31920/2516-3132/2020/v4n2a2

Ndlovu, S. L., & Mutambara, E. (2023). Manifestations of corruption within the Kwazulu-Natal municipalities: A thorn in the flesh. *Corporate Governance and Organizational Behavior Review*, 7(1), 81–93. 10.22495/cgobrv7i1p8

Ndou, L. L. (2022). *An analysis of a coalition government: a new path in administration and governance at local government level in South Africa* [Doctoral dissertation, North-West University, South Africa].

Ngumbela, X. G. (2021). Troubled municipalities, municipality troubles: An implementation of Back to Basics programme in the Eastern Cape province, South Africa. *Africa's Public Service Delivery & Performance Review*, 9(1), 8. 10.4102/apsdpr.v9i1.405

Ogunlela, O.G., Ojugbele, O.H., & Tengeh, R.K. (2021). Blockchain technology as a panacea for procurement corruption in digital era. *International Journal Research Business Social Science, 10*(4).

Page, M.J., Moher, D., Bossuyt, P.M., Boutron, I., Hoffmann, T.C., Mulrow, C.D., Shamseer, L., Tetzlaff, J.M., Akl, E.A., Brennan, S.E. & Chou, R. (2021). PRISMA 2020 explanation and elaboration: updated guidance and exemplars for reporting systematic reviews. *BMJ, 372.*

Patience, J. J., & Nel, D. (2022). Governance, democracy and accountability from a network governance perspective within the city of Ekurhuleni'. *Africa's Public Service Delivery and Performance Review*, 10(1), a554. 10.4102/apsdpr.v10i1.554

Pillay, P. (2020). Forensic Investigation into Procurement Fraud in Ekurhuleni Metropolitan Municipality. *South African Journal of Public Administration*, 55(2), 112–130.

Rulashe, T. & Ijeoma, E.O.C. (2022). An exploration of public accountability and service delivery at the Buffalo City Metropolitan Municipality in the Eastern Cape province, South Africa. *Africa's Public Service Delivery and Performance Review,10*(1), a535. . v10i1.535.10.4102/apsdpr

Sape, J. T. (2019). *The efficacy of the Emfuleni local municipality procurement system* [Doctoral dissertation, North-West University, South Africa].

Saul, T. F., Shopola, M. A., & Mlambo, V. H. (2023). Human Resource Management System as Enabling Tool for Good Governance in South Africa's Local Government Sector. *IAHRW International Journal of Social Sciences Review*, 11(4), 514–520.

Schoeman, I., & Chakwizira, J. (2023). Advancing a performance management tool for service delivery in local government. *Administrative Sciences*, 13(2), 31. 10.3390/admsci13020031

Sebake, B. K. (2020). Crime against humanity: Social perception of public service corruption in South Africa. *African Journal of Development Studies*, 10(3), 167.

Sebola, M. P. (2021). Monitoring for good governance in south africa: The complex of a fair public administration. *Acta Universitatis Danubius.Administratio*, 13(1), 39–55.

Sebopetsa, M. A., & Odeku, K. O. (2021). Safeguarding the Right to Protest and Prohibition of Violent Protests in South Africa: Issues and Perspectives. *African Journal of Peace and Conflict Studies*, 10(2), 45. 10.31920/2634-3665/2021/v10n2a3

Sibanda, M. M., Zindi, B., & Maramura, T. C. (2020). Control and accountability in supply chain management: Evidence from a South African metropolitan municipality. *Cogent Business & Management*, 7(1), 1785105. 10.1080/23311975.2020.1785105

Sithole, S. L., & Mathonsi, N. S. (2015). Local governance service delivery issues during apartheid and post-Apartheid South Africa. *Africa's Public Service Delivery & Performance Review*, 3(3), 5–30. 10.4102/apsdpr.v3i3.87

Smith, B. (2020). Participatory Budgeting in eThekwini Municipality: Enhancing Community Engagement and Transparency. *Commonwealth Journal of Local Governance*, 23(1), 58–72.

Special Investigating Unit (SIU). (2022). *Two former Ekurhuleni officials, businessman jailed for tender fraud, money laundering, and corruption.* SIU. https://www.siu.org.za/two-former-ekurhuleni-officials-businessman-jailed-for-tender-fraud-money-laundering-and-corruption/

Steyn Kotze, J., Davids, Y. D., Fokou, G., & Sanchez Betancourt, D. (2020). *Spoils politics: the case of Nelson Mandela Bay: case study report.*

Thusi, X., & Mashabela, M. (2023). The role of civil society organisations in promoting public accountability: The perspective of the South African local government. *IAHRW International Journal of Social Sciences Review*, 11(2), 175–180.

Thusi, X., & Selepe, M. M. (2023). The impact of poor governance on public service delivery: A case study of the South African local government. *International Journal of Social Science Research and Review*, 6(4), 688–697.

Tshishonga, N. (2019). Prospects and challenges of transforming local government into a learning organisation. *African Journal of Public Affairs*, 11(1), 157–175.

Van Rensburg, M., & Botes, V. (2017). The Political Economy of Corruption in South Africa's Municipalities: The Case of Nelson Mandela Bay Metropolitan Municipality. Alternation. *Interdisciplinary Journal for the Study of the Arts and Humanities in Southern Africa*, 24(1), 133–158.

Venda Building Society (VBS) 101. (2018). *From the masterminds to the mass fraud*. VBS. https://www.news24.com/Fin24/vbs-allegations-unpacked-from-the-masterminds-to-the-mass-fraud-20180717 [Accessed 15 June 2024].

Vyas-Doorgapersad, S. & Mothabi, P. (2022). Overview of misconduct influencing ethical culture in the Local Government Sector Education Training Authority, South Africa. *International Journal of Research in Business and Social Science (2147-4478), 11*(4), 365-374.

Yende, N. E. (2023). Towards Sustainable Service Delivery by South African Local Authorities: A Community Participation Strategy. *African Journal of Development Studies*, 13(1), 197.

Zengethwa, N. P., Thakhathi, D. R., & Oyelana, A. A. (2019). *Challenges Faced by the Raymond Mhlaba Municipality in Implementing the Back-to-Basics Programme*. University of Fort Hare. 10.31901/24566608.2019/68.1-3.3176

Zerihun, M. F., & Mashingo, M. P. (2022). The quest for service delivery: The case of a rural district municipality in the Mpumalanga province of South Africa. *Africa's Public Service Delivery and Performance Review*, 10(1), a512. 10.4102/apsdpr.v10i1.512

Zweni, A., Yan, B. Juta, L.B., 2022. The malady of perpetual municipal-finance mismanagement: Designing a leadership framework as a Panacea. *African Journal of Development Studies.*

# APPENDIX: SEARCH STRATEGY

*Appendix table*

| Databases | Keywords |
|---|---|
| EBSCohost – 4 | AB (Corruption OR Bribery OR Fraud OR Embezzlement OR Graft OR Nepotism OR Kickbacks OR Patronage OR Cronyism OR "Abuse of power" OR Collusion OR Misappropriation OR Favoritism OR Malfeasance OR "Illicit enrichment" OR "Influence peddling" OR Racketeering OR Extortion OR "Money laundering" OR "Insider trading" OR Sleaze) AND AB (Mismanagement OR "Poor governance" OR Negligence OR Ineptitude OR Misadministration OR Oversight failure OR Inefficiency OR Wastefulness) AND AB (south africa* OR municipalit* OR "Local government" OR "Township governance" OR "Local authorities" OR "Municipal services" OR "Municipal administration") |
| Scopus 11 | (TITLE-ABS-KEY ((corruption OR bribery OR fraud OR embezzlement OR graft OR nepotism OR kickbacks OR patronage OR cronyism OR "Abuse of power" OR collusion OR misappropriation OR favoritism OR malfeasance OR "Illicit enrichment" OR "Influence peddling" OR racketeering OR extortion OR "Money laundering" OR "Insider trading" OR sleaze)) AND TITLE-ABS-KEY ((mismanagement OR "Poor governance" OR negligence OR ineptitude OR misadministration OR oversight AND failure OR inefficiency OR wastefulness)) AND TITLE-ABS-KEY (("south africa*" OR municipalit* OR "Local government" OR "Township governance" OR "Local authorities" OR "Municipal services" OR "Municipal administration"))) |
| ProQuest – Social Science Journal 283 | summary((Corruption OR Bribery OR Fraud OR Embezzlement OR Graft OR Nepotism OR Kickbacks OR Patronage OR Cronyism OR "Abuse of power" OR Collusion OR Misappropriation OR Favoritism OR Malfeasance OR "Illicit enrichment" OR "Influence peddling" OR Racketeering OR Extortion OR "Money laundering" OR "Insider trading" OR Sleaze)) AND (Mismanagement OR "Poor governance" OR Negligence OR Ineptitude OR Misadministration OR "Oversight failure" OR Inefficiency OR Wastefulness) AND ("south africa*" OR municipal* OR "Local government" OR "Township governance" OR "Local authorities" OR "Municipal services" OR "Municipal administration") |

Source: Authors compilation.

# Compilation of References


Abbas, Z., Aziz, A., & Hameed, R. (2023). *Toward Sustainable Urban Transportation: Examining the Potential of Transport Departments in Lahore, Pakistan.* SAE Technical Papers. 10.4271/2023-01-5074

Abiddin, N. Z., Ibrahim, I., & Abdul Aziz, S. A. (2022). Non-governmental organisations (NGOs) and their part towards sustainable community development. *Sustainability (Basel)*, 14(8), 4386. 10.3390/su14084386

Abubakari, M., Hussain, J., Arhin, P., Paul, B. N., & Uwayisenga, V. (2023). Inner-city development experiences of Germany: Lessons for Pakistan, Ghana, Kenya, and Rwanda in urban development. In *Cogent Social Sciences, 9*(2). 10.1080/23311886.2023.2282487

Abush, C., & Mwita, A. B. (2021). COVID-19 pandemic, a war to be won: Understanding its economic implications for Africa. *Applied Health Economics and Health Policy*, 18(3), 325–328.33368032

Academy of Science of South Africa. (2022). The District Development Model as a platform for inclusive innovation and innovative districts. Academy of Science of South Africa. [http://hdl.handle.net/20.500.11911/240]. Accessed on. [07 February 2023]

Academy of Science of South Africa. (2022). *The District Development Model as a platform for innovation for inclusivity.* Academy of Science of South Africa.

Acharya, K. K., & Zafarullah, H. (2017). Service delivery and development at the grassroots: The evolution and contribution of community-based organisations in Nepal. *Asia Pacific Journal of Public Administration*, 39(4), 276–286. 10.1080/23276665.2017.1408268

Ackerman, J. (2011). Co-governance for accountability: Beyond 'exit' and voice. In Cornwall, A. (Ed.), *The Participation Reader*. Zeb Books.

Adetiba, O. F. (2016). *The challenges of curbing corruption in a democracy: The case of the Public Protector and Nkandla* [Doctoral dissertation, Stellenbosch: Stellenbosch University].

African National Congress (ANC). (1994). *The Reconstruction and Development Programme: A Policy Framework.* ANC.

Afrin, M., MacGregor, H., Scoones, I., & Wilkinson, A. (2021). Post-pandemic transformations: How and why COVID-19 requires us to rethink development. *World Development*, 138, 105233. 10.1016/j.worlddev.2020.10523333100478

Agrawal, A. (2001). Common Property Institutions and Sustainable Governance of Resources. *World Development*, 29(10), 1649–1672. 10.1016/S0305-750X(01)00063-8

Agrawal, A., & Ribot, J. C. (1999). Accountability in decentralization: A framework with South Asian and West African cases. *Journal of Developing Areas*, 33(4), 473–502.

Ahmad, I., & Islam, M. R. (2024). Empowerment and Participation: Key Strategies for Inclusive Development. In *Building Strong Communities: Ethical Approaches to Inclusive Development* (pp. 47-68). Emerald Publishing Limited.

Ahmad, J., & Devarajan, S. (2005). *Decentralisation and Service Delivery.* (World Bank Policy Research Working Paper 3603). World Bank. https://documents1.worldbank.org/curated/en/606871468139500265/pdf/wps3603.pdf

Ahmad, M. (2023). Leveraging Blockchain for Spatial Data Infrastructure: Challenges and Opportunities. *Supporting Technologies and the Impact of Blockchain on Organizations and Society*, 177–194. 10.4018/978-1-6684-5747-4.ch011

Ahmad, M., Ali, A., & Khiyal, M. S. H. (2023). Fog Computing for Spatial Data Infrastructure: Challenges and Opportunities. In D. P. Acharjya & K. Ahmed P. (Eds.), *Multi-Disciplinary Applications of Fog Computing: Responsiveness in Real-Time* (pp. 152–178). IGI Global. 10.4018/978-1-6684-4466-5.ch008

Ahmad, M., Ali, A., Mobo, F. D., & Hussain, H. (2024). *Spatial Data Infrastructure for Information Governance: The Case Study From Pakistan.* Research Gate. https://doi.org/10.4018/979-8-3693-0472-3.ch011

Ahmad, M., & Ali, A. (2023a). A Review of Governance Frameworks for National Spatial Data Infrastructure. In Correia, A., & Agua, P. B. (Eds.), *Innovation, Strategy, and Transformation Frameworks for the Modern Enterprise* (pp. 186–207). IGI Global. 10.4018/979-8-3693-0458-7.ch008

Ahmad, M., & Ali, A. (2023b). Integrated Geospatial Information Management in the World of Metaverse. In Lekhi, P., & Kaur, G. (Eds.), *Concepts, Technologies, Challenges, and the Future of Web 3* (pp. 248–270). IGI Global. 10.4018/978-1-6684-9919-1.ch013

Ahmad, M., Ali, A., Nawaz, H., Arslan, M., & Kumar, N. (2024). Optimizing Integrated Spatial Data Management Through Fog Computing: A Comprehensive Overview. In Prakasha, G. S., Lapina, M., Balakrishnan, D., & Sajid, M. (Eds.), *Digital Technologies in Modeling and Management: Insights in Education and Industry* (pp. 263–283). IGI Global. doi.org/10.4018/978-1-6684-9576-6.ch013

Ahmad, M., Ali, A., Tin, T. T., & Ali, A. (2024). Harnessing the Power of Geospatial Data: The Convergence of SDI, Big Data, and Cloud Computing. In Darwish, D. (Ed.), *Emerging Trends in Cloud Computing Analytics, Scalability, and Service Models* (pp. 312–330). IGI Global. 10.4018/979-8-3693-0900-1.ch016

Ahmad, M., Khayal, M. S. H., & Tahir, A. (2022). Analysis of Factors Affecting Adoption of Volunteered Geographic Information in the Context of National Spatial Data Infrastructure. *ISPRS International Journal of Geo-Information*, 11(2), 120. 10.3390/ijgi11020120

Ahmad, N., & Anjum, G. A. (2012). Legal and institutional perplexities hampering the implementation of urban development plans in Pakistan. *Cities (London, England)*, 29(4), 271–277. 10.1016/j.cities.2011.07.006

Ahmed, N. (2008). Karachi in 2020: Approaching planning as a project. *Proceedings of the Institution of Civil Engineers. Urban Design and Planning*, 161(3), 123–129. 10.1680/udap.2008.161.3.123

Ahmed, S. A. (2008). *Transparency and accountability in the public sector in the Arab Regin. Arab: UNDESA Asian Development Bank., 2009. ADB Cooperation with Civil Society: Annual Report 2008*. Asian Development Bank. www.adb.org/Documents/Reports/NGO annualreport/2008/2008report.pdf

Akinboade, O. A., Mokwena, M. P., & Kinfack, E. C. (2014). Protesting for improved public service delivery in South Africa's Sedibeng District. *Social Indicators Research*, 119(1), 1–23. 10.1007/s11205-013-0377-9

Alence, R., & Pitcher, A. (2019). Resisting state capture in South Africa. *Journal of Democracy*, 30(4), 5–19. 10.1353/jod.2019.0065

Ali, A., Ahmad, M., Nawaz, M., & Sattar, F. (2024). Spatial data infrastructure as the means to assemble geographic information necessary for effective agricultural policies in Pakistan. *Information Development*, 02666669241244503, 02666669241244503. 10.1177/02666669241244503

Ali, A., & Imran, M. (2021). National Spatial Data Infrastructure vs. Cadastre System for Economic Development: Evidence from Pakistan. *Land (Basel)*, 10(2), 188. 10.3390/land10020188

Allen, V. (2021). Comparative analysis of international crisis management in Covid-19 pandemic. *Mednarodno inovativno poslovanje (Journal of Innovative Business and Management), 13*(2), 65-73.

Alma'arif, A.A. & Wargadinata, E.L. (2022). Adopting Open Government in Local Development Planning. *Jurnal Kebijakan dan Administrasi Publik, 26*(1), 18-26.

Alon-Barkat, S. (2020). Can Government Public Communications Elicit Undue Trust? Exploring the Interaction between Symbols and Substantive Information in Communications. *Journal of Public Administration: Research and Theory*, 30(1), 77–95. 10.1093/jopart/muz013

Altaf, M. A. (1994). Household demand for improved water and sanitation in a large secondary city. Findings from a study in Gujranwala, Pakistan. *Habitat International*, 18(1), 45–55. 10.1016/0197-3975(94)90038-8

Amathole District Municipality. (2014). *ASPIRE Annual Report 2013-2014.* East London: Amathole.

Amlaev, K. R., & Karabakhtsyan, G. A. (2022). The municipal planning for the benefit of health. *Problemy Sotsial'noi Gigieny. Problemy Sotsial'Noi Gigieny i Istoriia Meditsiny*, 30(2). 10.32687/0869-866X-2022-30-2-244-24635439383

Amtaika, A. (2013). *Local government in South Africa since 1994: Leadership, democracy, Development and Service Delivery in Post-Apartheid Era.* Carolina Academic Press.

Andama, F. A. (2020). Decentralisation and Public Policy implementation in Uganda: the case Of West Nile Sub-Region [Doctoral dissertation, North-West University, South Africa].

Anjorin, A. A. (2020). The coronavirus disease 2019 (COVID-19) pandemic: A review and an update on cases in Africa. *Asian Pacific Journal of Tropical Medicine*, 13(5), 199. 10.4103/1995-7645.281612

Ansell, C., & Gash, A. (2008). Collaborative Governance in Theory and Practice. *Journal of Public Administration Research and Theory: J-PART*, 18(4), 543–571. https://www.jstor.org/stable/25096384. 10.1093/jopart/mum032

Anwar, M. M., Fayyaz, F., Aziz, A., & Mahmood, M. R. (2021). Socio-Ecological and Ethical Economic Demand of Urban Parks in Gujrat City, Punjab, Pakistan. *Arid Ecosystems*, 11(2), 141–148. 10.1134/S2079096121020037

Anwar, N. H. (2014). Urban transformations: Brokers, collaborative governance and community building in Karachi's periphery. *South Asian History and Culture*, 5(1), 75–92. 10.1080/19472498.2013.863011

Arcilla, G. R., Co, F. F., & Occampo, R. S. (2011). Correlates of poverty: Evidence from the community-based-monitoring system (CBMS) data. *DLSU Business & Economics Review*, 20(2), 33–43. 10.3860/ber.v20i2.1912

Arends, H. (2020). The dangers of fiscal decentralization and public service delivery: A review of arguments. *Politische Vierteljahresschrift*, 61(3), 599–622. 10.1007/s11615-020-00233-7

Armstrong, P. (2001). Science, enterprise, and profit: Ideology in the knowledge-driven economy. *Economy and Society*, 30(4), 524–552. 10.1080/03085140120089081

Arndt, S., Chowdhury, F. J., & Rahman, M. M. (2020). COVID-19 pandemic: Rethinking strategies for resilient urban design, perceptions, and planning. *Frontiers in Sustainable Cities*, 3, 668263.

Arta, D. N. C., Leuhery, F., Abubakar, H., Yusuf, M., & Cakranegara, P. A. (2023). Literature Review: Analisis Hubungan Antara Pelatihan dan Kinerja Karyawan di Sebuah Perusahaan. [MSEJ]. *Management Studies and Entrepreneurship Journal*, 4(1), 162–168.

Asghar, J. (2013). Critical paradigm: A preamble for novice researchers. *Life Science Journal*, 10(4), 3121–3127.

Asha, A. A., & Makalela, K. I. (2020). Challenges in the implementation of the integrated development plan and service delivery in Lepelle-Nkumbi Municipality, Limpopo province. *International Journal of Economics and Finance Studies*, 12(1), 1–15. 10.34109/ijefs.202012101

Asian Further Development Bank. (2009). *Civil Society Organisation Source book. A staff guide to cooperation with Civil Society*. Catologing in Publication Data: Philipines

Asuelime, R. A., & Ndimande-Hlongwa, N. (2022). Civil society, COVID-19 pandemic and state corruption implications for nation building in South Africa. *Journal of Nation-Building and Policy Studies*, 1(1, si1), 163–181. 10.31920/2516-3132/2022/s1s1a9

Atisa, G., Zemrani, A., & Weiss, M. (2021). Decentralized governments: Local empowerment and sustainable development challenges in Africa. *Environment, Development and Sustainability*, 23(3), 3349–3367. 10.1007/s10668-020-00722-0

Attygall, L. (2020). *Understanding community-led approaches to community change*. Tamarack Institute.

Auditor General of South Africa (AGSA). (2021). *Municipal Finance Management Act (MFMA) Consolidated General Report on Local Government Audit Outcomes 2019–2020*. AGSA. https://www.agsa.co.za/Portals/0/Reports/MFMA/201920

Auditor General South Africa (AGSA). (2022). *Auditor-General calls on municipal leaders to transform local government to improve people's lives—media release*. AGSA. https://www.agsa.co.za/Portals

Auditor-General of South Africa. (2021). *Consolidated general report on local government audit outcomes - FMA 2020-21*. Auditor General of South Africa. Pretoria.

Auel, K. (2014). Intergovernmental relations in German federalism: Cooperative federalism, party politics and territorial conflicts. *Comparative European Politics*, 12(4), 422–443. 10.1057/cep.2014.13

Auerbach, A. M. (2017). Neighbourhood associations and the urban poor: India's slum development committees. *World Development*, 96, 119–135. 10.1016/j.worlddev.2017.03.002

Ayele, Z., & May, A. 2010. *Withholding rates: a new culture of non-payment*. Dullahomar Institute. https://dullahomarinstitute.org.za/multilevel-govt/local-government-bulletin/archives/volume-11-issue-2-april-may-2009/lgb-iss11-2-withholding-rates-a-culture-of-non-payment.pdf

Bahiigwa, G., De Pinto, A., Birner, R., & Ball, V. (2017). Strengthening agricultural education and training in sub-Saharan Africa from an innovation systems perspective: Case studies of Kenya, Nigeria, and South Africa. *European Journal of Development Research*, 29(4), 784–808.

Baholo, N. (2023). *Community participation in an integrated development planning process life cycle: the case of Matlosana Local Municipality* [Doctoral dissertation, North-West University (South Africa].

Baiocchi, G. (2015). The Citizens of Porto Alegre. In Miraftab, F., & Kudva, H. (Eds.), *Cities of the Global South: Reader*. Routledge.

Baiocchi, G., & Ganuza, E. (2014). Participatory Budgeting as if Emancipation Mattered. *Politics & Society*, 42(1), 29–50. 10.1177/0032329213512978

Baker, L., Cristancho, S., Kennedy, T. J., & Lingard, L. 2018. Qualitative research in medical education: methodologies and methods. *Understanding medical education: Evidence, theory, and practice*. Wiley.

Baker, D., Crescenzi, R., Roller, E., Anguelovski, I., Datta, A., & Harrison, J. (2021). Regions in COVID-19 recovery. *Regional Studies*, 55(12), 1955–1965. 10.1080/00343404.2021.2003768

Ballesteros, B. C., & Sanchez, M. G. (2016). *Local government in the digital era: looking for accountability*. Nova Science publishers.

Balmford, F., Smaidi, K., Salles, M. P., Lopes Neto, A. C., Heilberg, I. P., & Glina, S. (2022). COVID-19: The impact on urolithiasis treatment in Brazil. *International Braz J Urol*, 48(1), 101–109. 10.1590/s1677-5538.ibju.2021.040534735086

Bambo, S. (2022). *South African Local Government Challenges and Prospects. Polokwane*. Empore Publishers.

Bandauko, E. (2015). Civil society organizations (CSOs) in Urban planning advocacy: Lessons from Zimbabwe. *Journal of Advocacy. Research in Education*, 3(2), 104–109.

Banerjee, C. (2020). *Guidelines on Integrity and Transparency in Governance and Responsible Code of Conduct*. New Delhi, India: Confederation of Indian Industry (CII). https://www2.deloitte.com/content/dam/Deloitte/in/Documents/risk/inrisk-cii-guidelines-on-integrity-transparency-in-governance-and-responsible-code-of-conduct-noexp.pdf.

Banister, D. (2008). The sustainable mobility paradigm. *Transport Policy*, 15(2), 73–80. 10.1016/j.tranpol.2007.10.005

Bannister, S., & Esteves, C. (2015). *Implementing BRT in eThekwini: challenges, lessons and opportunities. [online]. BRT in eThekwini*. ERLN. http://www.erln.org.za/images/jevents/5624b4c361e9f6.60912785.pdf.

Bappi. U. (2018). Governance and Community Development in Nigeria. *International Journal of Research in Business studies, 3*.

Barchiesi, F. (2011). *Precarious Liberation: Workers, the State and Contested Social Citizenship in Post-Apartheid South Africa. Scottsville*. UKZN Press. 10.1515/9781438436128

Bardhan, P., & Mookherjee, D. (2006). *Decentralization and Local Governance in Developing Countries: A Comparative Perspective*. The MIT Press. https://EconPapers.repec.org/RePEc:mtp:titles:0262524546

Bardhan, P. (2002). Decentralization of governance and development. *The Journal of Economic Perspectives*, 16(4), 185–205. 10.1257/089533002320951037

Barnett, C. C., Minis, H. P., & VanSant, J. (1997). *Democratic Decentralization*. Research Triangle Institute. https://pdf.usaid.gov/pdf_docs/pnada635.pdf

Basson, A., & Hunter, Q. (2023). *Who will Rule South Africa? The Demise of the ANC and the Rise of a New Democracy*. Flyleaf Publishing & Distribution.

Baud, I., & Nainan, N. (2012). Negotiated Spaces for Representation in Mumbai. In Pouw, N., & Baud, I. (Eds.), *Local Governance and Poverty in Developing Nations*. Routledge.

Beall, J. (2005). *Funding Local Governance: Small Grants for Democracy and Development*. ITDG Publishing. 10.3362/9781780443287

Bergström, T., Kuhlmann, S., Laffin, M., & Wayenberg, E. (2022). Special issue on comparative intergovernmental relations and the pandemic: How European devolved governments responded to a public health crisis. *Local Government Studies*, 48(2), 179–190. 10.1080/03003930.2022.2039636

Bertalanffy, L. (1950). An Outline of General System Theory. *The British Journal for the Philosophy of Science*, 1(2), 134–165. 10.1093/bjps/I.2.134

Bertalanffy, L. V. (1968). *General system theory: Foundations, development, applications*. G. Braziller.

Berthin, G. (2018). *Service Delivery in Municipal governments: Some Lessons*. 4Democraticgovernance. https://4democraticgovernance.com/2018/03/31/service-delivery-in-local-governments-some-lessons/

Beyers, L. J. E. (2016). Service delivery challenges facing municipalities: A case study of Fetakgomo Local Municipality in Sekhukhune District Municipality, Limpopo Province. *Bangladesh e-Journal of Sociology*, 13(2), 167–178.

Beyers, L. J. E. (2016). Service Delivery challenges facing municipalities: A case study of Fetakgomo Local Municipality in Sekhukhune District Municipality, Limpopo Province. *Bangladesh e-Journal of Sociology*, 13(2), 167–178.

Bhorat, H., Cassim, A., & Tseng, D. (2019). Local economic development in South Africa: A review of policies and practices. *Suid-Afrikaanse Tydskrif vir Ekonomiese en Bestuurswetenskappe*, 22(1), 1–11.

Bhuda, M.T., Motswaledi, T., & Marumo, P. (2023). Moral Decay, Government, and Looting in South Africa during COVID-19. *African Journal of Development Studies, 13*.

Bianchi, C., Nasi, G., & Rivenbark, W. C. (2021). Implementing collaborative governance: Models, experiences, and challenges. *Public Management Review*, 23(11), 1581–1589. 10.1080/14719037.2021.1878777

Bibri, S. E., Krogstie, J., & Kärrholm, M. (2020). Compact city planning and development: Emerging practices and strategies for achieving the goals of sustainability. Developments in the built environment, 4, 100021.

Bickford, G. (2013). South African Cities Network: Literature review on public transport and mobility in municipalities. ARUP. Board, Washington, DC.

Bishop, I. D., Escobar, F. J., Karuppannan, S., Williamson, I. P., Yates, P. M., Suwarnarat, K., & Yaqub, H. W. (2000). Spatial data infrastructures for cities in developing countries. Lessons from the Bangkok experience. *Cities (London, England)*, 17(2), 85–96. 10.1016/S0264-2751(00)00004-4

Bjuremalm, H., Gibaja, A. F., & Molleda, J. V. (2015). *Democratic Accountability in Service Delivery. A practical guide to identify improvements through assessment.* IDEA Int, 23–24 November 2015, Pretoria, South Africa. https://www.idea.int/sites/default/files/publications/democratic-accountability-in-service-delivery.pdf

Blakely, E. J. (1994). *Planning Local Economic Development: Theory and Practice*. Sage.

Blinova, E. A. (2017, June). Participatory budgeting and social inclusion in modern Brazil. In *Proceedings of the International Conference IMS-2017* (pp. 230-236). ACM. 10.1145/3143699.3143723

Böcher, M. (2008). Regional governance and rural development in Germany: the implementation of LEADER+. *Sociologia Ruralis, 48*(4), 372-388.

Boerboom, I. (2010). Integrating spatial planning and decision support system infrastructure and spatial data infrastructure. *GSDI 12 World Conference Singapore*. http://www.gsdi.org/gsdiconf/gsdi12/papers/82.pdf

Bordvik, M. B. (2022). *Ethical Code of Conduct and its impact on decision making among managers in local government in Zimbabwe*. Walden University.

Bormann, N. C. (2019). Uncertainty, cleavages, and ethnic coalitions. *The Journal of Politics*, 81(2), 471–486. 10.1086/701633

Borzacchiello, M. T., & Craglia, M. (2013). Estimating benefits of spatial data infrastructures: A case study on e-Cadastres. *Computers, Environment and Urban Systems*, 41, 276–288. 10.1016/j.compenvurbsys.2012.05.004

Bosch, O. J. H. (2013). *Systems Thinking for Local Economic Development (LED) in Developing Countries*. (LEDNA Working Paper Series). LEDNA.

Bouckaert, G., Chawdhry, U., Fraser-Moleketi, G., Meuleman, L., & Pizani, M. (2018). *Effective Governance for Sustainable Development: 11 Principles to Put in Practice*. International Institute for Sustainable Development.

Bradley, A. (2017) *Strengthening local democracy: Empowering municipal governments*. International IDEA. https://www.idea.int/news/strengthening-local-democracy-empowering-local-authorities

Brand, A., & Drewes, E. (2020). Structuring South Africa's national economic space: A regional corridor network model approach. *Town and Regional Planning*, 77, 120–135.

Brass, J. N. (2016). *Allies or adversaries: NGOs and the state in Africa*. Cambridge University Press. 10.1017/CBO9781316678527

Bratton, M., & Van de Walle, N. (1997). *Democratic Experiments in Africa: Regime Transitions and the Consequences of Elections*. Cambridge University Press. 10.1017/CBO9781139174657

Bray, J. (2003). decision making in government. *Special Conference Issues: Decision-Making*, 19, 25–35.

Breakfast, N., Bradshaw, G., & Nomarwayi, T. (2019). Violent service delivery protests in post-apartheid South Africa, 1994–2017-a conflict resolution perspective. *African Journal of Public Affairs*, 11(1), 106–126.

Brinkerhoff, D., & Goldsmith, A. (2002). *Clientelism, Patrimonialism and Democratic Governance: An Overview and Framework for Assessment and Programming.*

Brinkerhoff, D. W., & Wetterberg, A. (2013). Performance-based public management reforms: Experience and emerging lessons from service delivery improvement in Indonesia. *International Review of Administrative Sciences*, 79(3), 433–457. 10.1177/0020852313491059

Brinkerhoff, J. M. (2003). Donor-funded government—NGO partnership for public service improvement: Cases from India and Pakistan. *Voluntas*, 14(1), 105–122. 10.1023/A:1022997006704

Brown, J. S. (2022). *Unmasking the impact of COVID-19 on businesses: Firm level evidence from across the world*. The World Bank.

Brumatti, L. M. (2022). *Institutional roots inertia and participatory governance in Brazil* [Doctoral dissertation, Universidade de São Paulo].

Brussel, M. (2014). *Integration of public transport and NMT-UNEP. Principles and application in an East African context.* University of Twente PDF Presentation. http://staging.unep.org/transport/sharetheroad/PDF/courseware_nmt/Lecture8_Integration_Publictransport_NMT_Brussel.pdf

BTI. (2024). *Zimbabwe Country Report 2024*. BTI Transformation Index, Country Dashboard Zimbabwe. https://bti-project.org/en/reports/country-report/ZWE

Burke, B. F. (2014). Understanding intergovernmental relations, twenty-five years hence. *State & Local Government Review*, 46(1), 63–76. 10.1177/0160323X13520461

Burns, D., Heywood, F., Taylor, M., Wilde, P., & Wilson, M. (2004). *Making Community Participation Meaningful: A Handbook for Development and Assessment*. Policy Press

Busengdal, E. (2022). Prioritising Integration of Refugees in Municipal Planning at a Local Political Level. *Scandinavian Journal of Public Administration*, 26(4), 3–17. 10.58235/sjpa.v26i4.10576

Butt, M. A., Li, S., & Javed, N. (2016). Towards Co-PPGIS—a collaborative public participatory GIS-based measure for transparency in housing schemes: A case of Lahore, Pakistan. *Applied Geomatics*, 8(1), 27–40. 10.1007/s12518-015-0160-5

Cammett, M., & MacLean, L. M. (Eds.). (2014). *The politics of non-state social welfare*. Cornell University Press. 10.7591/9780801470349

Carney, D., Drinkwater, M., Rusinow, T., Neefjes, K., Wanmali, S., & Singh, N. (1999). *Livelihoods approaches compared: A brief comparison of the livelihoods approaches of the UK Department for International Development (DFID), CARE, Oxfam and the United Nations Development Programme (UNDP)*. Department for International Development (DFID).

Carney, D., Drinkwater, M., Rusinow, T., Neefjes, K., Wanmali, S., & Singh, N., 1999. *Livelihoods approaches compared: A brief comparison of the livelihoods approaches of the UK Department for International Development (DFID), CARE, Oxfam and the United Nations Development Programme (UNDP)*. Department for International Development (DFID).

Carney, D. (1998). *Sustainable Livelihoods Approaches: Progress and Possibilities for Change*. Institute of Development Studies.

Carothers, T., & Brenchenmacher, S. (2014). *Accountability, Transparency, Participation, and Inclusion: A New Development Consensus?* Carnegie Endowment for International Peace. https://carnegieendowment.org/2014/10/20/accountability-transparency-participation-and-inclusion-new-development-consensus-pub-56968

Cebekhulu, E. (2018). *Umhlaba Uyahlaba! The World is Thorny. Wandsbeck*. Reach Publishers.

Cejudo, G. M., & Michel, C. L. (2021). Instruments for policy integration: How policy mixes work together. *SAGE Open*, 11(3), 21582440211032161. 10.1177/21582440211032161

Cermeño, H. (2021). Living and planning on the edge: Unravelling conflict and claim-making in peri-urban lahore, pakistan. *Urban Planning*, 6(2), 189–201. 10.17645/up.v6i2.3858

Cetl, V., Ivić, S. M., & Tomić, H. (2009). Improvement of national spatial data infrastructure as a public project of permanent character. *Kartografija i Geoinformacije, 8*(11).

Chakunda, V. (2018). *A Critical Analysis of The Dynamics of Intergovernmental Relations in Zimbabwe*. 10.4172/2332-0761.1000326

Chakunda, E. (2018). Local governance in Zimbabwe: A review of literature. *Journal of Public Administration and Governance*, 8(2), 14–26.

Chakunda, V., & Chakaipa, S. (2015). Local Government Capacity Building and Development: Lessons, Challenges and Opportunities. Journal of Political Sciences and Public Affairs. *Review Article*, 3(1).

Chambers, R., & Conway, G. (1992). *Sustainable rural livelihoods: Practical concepts for the 21st century*. (IDS Discussion Paper, 296). IDS.

Chambers, R. (1997). *Whose Reality Counts? Putting the First Last.* Intermediate Technology Publications. 10.3362/9781780440453

Chambers, R. B., & Conway, D. (2017). How to construct a mixed methods research design. *Kölner Zeitschrift für Soziologie und Sozialpsychologie*, 69(S2, Suppl 2), 107–131. 10.1007/s11577-017-0454-128989188

Chatiza, K. (2008). *Opportunities and challenges in institutionalising participatory development: the case of rural Zimbabwe.*

Chatzichristos, G., & Perimenis, A. (2022). Evaluating the social added value of LEADER: Evidence from a marginalised rural region. *Journal of Rural Studies*, 94, 366–374. 10.1016/j.jrurstud.2022.07.016

Chigwata, T. C., & Marumahoko, S. (2018). Intergovernmental planning and budgeting in Zimbabwe: learning the lessons of the past. *Commonwealth Journal of Local Governance, 20.* http://dx.doi.org/cjlg.v0i20.6140

Chigwata, T. C., & Marumahoko, S. 2018. Intergovernmental planning and budgeting in Zimbabwe: learning the lessons of the past. *Commonwealth Journal of Local Governance, 20,* 1-15. http://dx.doi.org/cjlg.v0i20.6140

Chigwata, T. C., & Marumahoko, S. (2018). *Intergovernmental planning and budgeting in Zimbabwe: learning the lessons of the past.* Commonwealth Journal of Local Governance. 10.5130/cjlg.v0i20.6140

Chikozho, C., & Kanyangarara, M. (2015). Decentralisation and service delivery in Zimbabwe: The case of education. *Journal of Public Administration and Governance*, 5(1), 1–12.

Chikulo, B. C. (2013). Developmental local governance and service delivery in South Africa: Progress, achievements and challenges. *Journal of Social Development in Africa*, 28(1), 35.

Chilenga-Butao, T. (2020). Decentralisation and recentralisation in South Africa's local government: Case studies of two municipalities in Limpopo. *Transformation (Durban)*, 103(1), 12–35. 10.1353/trn.2020.0011

Chiunye, T. M. (2018). *An Impact- assessment of the Rural District Council's Capacity Building Programme (RDCCBP) on organisational performance: the case of Chaminuka Rural District Council.* Shamva Administrative District.

Chiwara, A. G. (2022). Assessing COVID-19's economic impact in sub-Saharan Africa: Insights from a CGE model. *COVID-19 in developing economies, 53.*

Chiyamwaka, B. (2007). *The role of the media in fostering good governance, transparency, and accountability.* Media Council of Malawi.

City of Cape Town. (2023). *MyCiTi Bus Rapid Transit System.* City of Cape Town. https://www.capetown.gov.za/en/MyCiti/Pages/default.

City of Polokwane. (2020). *Leeto la Polokwane: Enhancing Public Transportation in Polokwane.* (Polokwane Government Report).

Claire, M. (2015). The Politics of What Works in Service Delivery in S. Hickey, K. Sen, & B. Bukenya (eds), *The Politics of Inclusive Development: Interrogating the Evidence.* Oxford Press. https://doi.org/10.1093/acprof:oso/9780198722564.003.0005

Clark, A. S. (2020). Coronavirus infections—More than just the common cold. *Journal of the American Medical Association*, 323(8), 707–709. 10.1001/jama.2020.075731971553

Cleary, M. R. (2007). Electoral Competition, Participation, and Government Responsiveness in Mexico. *American Journal of Political Science*, 51(2), 283–299. https://www.jstor.org/stable/4620066. 10.1111/j.1540-5907.2007.00251.x

CLGF (Commonwealth Local Government Forum). (2005). *Good governance and local government.* CLGF.

Coelho, T. R., Pozzebon, M., & Cunha, M. A. (2022). Citizens influencing public policy-making: Resourcing as a source of relational power in e-participation platforms. *Information Systems Journal*, 32(2), 344–376. 10.1111/isj.12359

Cole, M. J., Bailey, R. M., Cullis, J. D., & New, M. G. (2018). Spatial inequality in water access and water use in South Africa. *Water Policy*, 20(1), 37–52. 10.2166/wp.2017.111

Coleman, D. J., & Nebert, D. D. (1998). Building a North American Spatial Data Infrastructure. *Cartography and Geographic Information Systems*, 25(3), 151–160. 10.1559/152304098782383098

Colombo, C. (2018). Justifications and citizen competence in direct democracy: A multilevel analysis. *British Journal of Political Science*, 48(3), 787–806. 10.1017/S0007123416000090

Comins, L. (2023). *Durban rates revolt: tempers flare at meeting with mayor.* CO. https://mg.co.za/news/2023-08-14-durban-rates-revolt-tempers-flare-at-meeting-with-mayor/

Comins, L. (2023a). *Durban rates boycotters in court to stop city from cutting their water and lights.* CO. https://mg.co.za/news/2023-09-12-durban-rates-boycotters-in-court-to-stop-city-from-cutting-their-water-and-lights/

Conyers, D. (2003). Decentralisation in Zimbabwe: A Local Perspective. *Public Administration and Development*, 23(1), 115–124. 10.1002/pad.265

Cooperative Governance and Traditional Affairs. (2020). *District development model progress.* Pretoria: COGTA. Republic of South Africa.

Cooperative Governance and Traditional Affairs. (2020). *Update on the roll-out of the DDM approach. Presentation at the dialogue on the institutionalisation of the District Development Model.* Pretoria: COGTA. RSA.

Corruption Watch. (2021). *South Africa needs clean hands*. Corruption Watch. https://www.corruptionwatch.org.za/wp-content/uploads/2021/08/CW-localgovt-sectoral-report-August2021.pdf

Cotella, G., & Brovarone, E. V. (2020). The Italian National Strategy for Inner Areas: A Place-based approach to Regional Development. In *Dilemmas of regional and local development* (pp. 50-71). Routledge.

Cotella, G., & Dąbrowski, M. (2021). EU Cohesion Policy as a driver of Europeanisation: A comparative analysis. In *EU Cohesion Policy and Spatial Governance* (pp. 48–65). Edward Elgar Publishing. 10.4337/9781839103582.00013

Council of Europe. (2022). *Twelve Principles of Good Governance*. Strasbourg Cedex, France: Council of Europe. https://www.coe.int/en/web/good-governance/12-principles

Course Sidekick. (2023). *Comprehensive Case Study report on the alleged irregularities committed at VBS Bank during 2014 to 2018*. Course Sidekick. https://www.coursesidekick.com/accounting/3383328 [Accessed 15 June 2024].

Creswell, J. W., & Poth, C. N. (2017). Qualitative inquiry and research design: Choosing among five approaches. *Sage (Atlanta, Ga.)*.

Crompvoets, J., Vancauwenberghe, G., Bouckaert, G., & Vandenbroucke, D. (2011). Practices to develop spatial data infrastructures: Exploring the contribution to e-government. In *Practical Studies in E-Government*. Best Practices from Around the World. 10.1007/978-1-4419-7533-1_13

Crompvoets, J., Vancauwenberghe, G., Ho, S., Masser, I., & Timo De Vries, W. (2018). Governance of national spatial data infrastructures in Europe. *International Journal of Spatial Data Infrastructures Research*, 13, 253–285.

Crook, R. C., & Manor, J. (1998). *Democracy and Decentralisation in South Asia and West Africa: Participation, Accountability and Performance*. Cambridge University Press. 10.1017/9780511607899

Crous, M. (2002). Service delivery in the South African public service: implementation of the Batho Pele principles by Statistics South Africa. [Thesis, University of Pretoria].

Crush, J. (2000). *Migration in Southern Africa: A paper prepared for the Policy Analysis and Research Programme of the Global Commission on International Migration*. Global Commission on International Migration.

Crush, J., Chikanda, A., & Tawodzera, G. (2017). South-South migration and the labour market in South Africa. *European Journal of Development Research*, 29(3), 533–548.

Curato, N., Hammond, M., & Min, J. B. (2019). *Power in deliberative democracy*. Palgrave Macmillan. 10.1007/978-3-319-95534-6

Currie, A. (2021). Industry engagement on DDM implementation. *IMIESA*, 46(2), 20–21.

Da Cruz, N. F., Tavares, A. F., Marques, R. C., Jorge, S., & De Sousa, L. (2016). Measuring local government transparency. *Public Management Review*, 18(6), 866–893. 10.1080/14719037.2015.1051572

Dąbrowski, M. (2014). Towards place-based regional and local development strategies in Central and Eastern Europe? EU cohesion policy and strategic planning capacity at the sub-national level. *Local Economy*, 29(4-5), 378–393. 10.1177/0269094214535715

Dagnino, E. (2008). Challenges to Participation, citizenship, and democracy: Perverse Confluence and displacement of Meanings. In Bebbington, A., Hickey, S., & Miltlin, D. (Eds.), *Can NGOs Make a Difference? The Challenge of Development Alternatives*. Zed Books.

Dahl, R. (1971). *Polyarchy. Participation and Opposition.* Yale University Press.

Dariusz, M., Kinga, K., & Ewa, K. (2021). Management of Municipal Public Transport Vehicle Journeys by Using the PERT Method. *Energies*, 14(15), 4403. 10.3390/en14154403

de la Riva Aguero, R. (2020). *Is governance enough? Assessing municipal capacity and CSO participation for complex service delivery.*

De Visser, J. (2005). *Developmental local government: A case study of South Africa*. Intersentia nv.

De Visser, J. (2010). The political-administrative interface in South African municipalities assessing the quality of local democracies. *Commonwealth Journal of Local Governance*, (5), 86–101. 10.5130/cjlg.v0i5.1473

De Vries, M. S. (2016). *Understanding public administration.* Bloomsbury Publishing. 10.1007/978-1-137-57546-3

Della Porta, D. (2013). *Can Democracy be Saved? Cambridge CB2.* Polity Press.

Dellepiane-Avellaneda, S. (2010). Good governance, institutions, and economic development: Beyond the conventional wisdom. *British Journal of Political Science*, 40(1), 195–224. 10.1017/S0007123409990287

Delmastro, C., Lavagno, E., & Schranz, L. (2016). Underground urbanism: Master Plans and Sectorial Plans. *Tunnelling and Underground Space Technology*, 55, 103–111. 10.1016/j.tust.2016.01.001

Department for International Development (DFID). (1999). *Sustainable Livelihoods Guidance Sheets*. DFID.

Department of Cooperative Governance and Traditional Affairs (CoGTA). (2019). *Coordinated Service Delivery Model, President Coordinating Council.* CoGTA. https://www.thepresidency.gov.za

Department of Cooperative Governance and Traditional Affairs (CoGTA). (2020). *Implementation Framework of DDM*. CoGTA. www.cogta.gov.za/ddm/index

Department of Cooperative Governance and Traditional Affairs (CoGTA). (2021). *How is the DDM Aligned to the IUDF?* CoGTA. www.cogta.gov.za/ddm/index

Department of Cooperative Governance and Traditional Affairs (CoGTA). (2023). *Implementation of DDM*. CoGTA. https://www.cogta.gov.za/cgta

Department of Cooperative Governance. (2020). *General guidelines on the Local Government: Municipal Property Rates Act no.6 of 2004*. Department of Cooperative Governance.

Department of Cooperative Governance. (2021). *State of local government*. Department of Cooperative Governance.

Department of National Treasury. (2004). *Annual Report: 2004-2005*. Government Printers.

Department of National Treasury. (2015). *Local Government Revenue and Expenditure*. Cape Town: Press Release.

Department of Planning, Monitoring and Evaluation (DPME) (2020). *The Impact of COVID-19 on South African Municipalities Survey Results*. DPME.

Department of Planning, Monitoring and Evaluation. (2019). *Khawuleza District Development Model*. Pretoria: DPME. RSA.

Department of Planning, Monitoring, and Evaluation. (DPME) (2019). *Presidential launch of DDM*. DPME. https://www.dpme.gov.za/news

Department of Provincial and Local Government. (2003). *Local Economic Development*. DPLG.

Department of Transport. (2020). *Road Infrastructure Strategic Framework for South Africa*. (Government Report). Department of Transport.

Devas, N., & Grant, U. (2003). Local government decision-making—citizen participation and local accountability: Some evidence from Kenya and Uganda. *Public Administration and Development*, 23(4), 307–316. 10.1002/pad.281

Development Bank of Southern Africa (DBSA). (2020). *Integrated Urban Development Framework (IUDF): Integrated Local Economic Development (LED)*. Toolkit.

Dhimitri, E., & Burda, M. (2019). The participatory budgeting for local governance. Case study municipality of Korca (Albania). *Journal of Applied Economic Sciences*, 2(64), 605–611.

Diaz, L., Remke, A., Kauppinen, T., Degbelo, A., Foerster, T., Stasch, C., Rieke, M., Schaeffer, B., Baranski, B., Bröring, A., & Wytzisk, A. (2012). Future SDI - Impulses from Geoinformatics research and IT trends. *International Journal of Spatial Data Infrastructures Research*, 7. 10.2902/1725-0463.2012.07.art18

Diaz, R. B. (2009). *Characteristics of Bus Rapid Transit for Decision-Making, Federal Transit Administration (FTA), United States Department of Transportation*. U.S. DOT.

Dikgang, J. (2013). *Passenger modal shift: From road to rail – the Gautrain NAMA case.* Department of Transport, Republic of South Africa. www.transport2020.org /file/Jacob-dikgang-ppt.pdf.

Dimock, J. P. (2021). The Critical Paradigm. In *Understanding Communication Research Methods* (pp. 35–47). Routledge. 10.4324/9781003109129-5

Dipela, M. P., & Mohapi, B. J. (2021). Barriers affecting effective monitoring and evaluation of poverty alleviation projects within Waterberg District. *Social Work*, 57(3), 287–301.

Dlomo, P. A. (2017). *The impact of irregular expenditure in the South African public finance with specific reference to the National Department of Public Works*, 1–125. CPUT. http://etd .cput.ac.za/handle/ 20.500.11838/2453

Donahue, J. H., & Zeckhauser, R. J. (2012). *Collaborative Governance, Private Roles for Public Goals in Turbulent Times*. Princeton University Press. 10.1515/9781400838103

Dosoudil, M. (2012). A case study of street committees in enhancing participatory democracy in the Emfuleni Local Municipality and the need for civil education. *Journal of African & Asian Local Government Studies*, 1(1), 62–85.

Douglass, T. J., Chassot, O., Chaudhary, S., Cordova, L.Jr, Cruz-Trinidad, A., & Wong, M. (2020). COVID-era policies and economic recovery plans: Are governments building back better for protected and conserved areas. *Parks*, 27(Special Issue), 5.

Dring, C. C., Newman, L., & Wittman, H. (2023). Assessing governability of agricultural systems: Municipal agricultural planning in Metro Vancouver, Canada. *Frontiers in Sustainable Food Systems*, 6, 855684. 10.3389/fsufs.2022.855684

Du Toit, A., Kirsten, J., & Mabaya, E. (2018). Public expenditure on agriculture in South Africa: A provincial analysis. *Agrekon*, 57(3), 297–313.

Dua, V., Kumar, M., Verma, A., & Pais, J. (2020). COVID-19 lockdown. *Social scientist, 48*(562-565), 67-82.

Duarte, F., & Ratti, C. (2018). The impact of autonomous vehicles on cities: A review. *Journal of Urban Technology*, 25(4), 3–18. 10.1080/10630732.2018.1493883

Dube, S., & Kirsten, J. (2019). Participatory approaches in local economic development: Lessons from LED initiatives in rural South Africa. *Development Southern Africa*, 36(6), 777–793.

Duncan, J. (2015). *Protest Nation: The Right to Protest in South Africa*. Scottville: UKZN Press.

Duvel, G. (1996). Institutional Linkages for Effective Coordination and Cooperation In Participative Rural Development. *Journal of International Agricultural and Extension Education*, 3(2), 3. 10.5191/jiaee.1996.03204

Džinić, J., Svidroňová, M. M., & Markowska-Bzducha, E. (2016). Participatory budgeting: A comparative study of Croatia, Poland and Slovakia. *NISPAcee Journal of Public Administration and Policy*, 9(1), 31–56. 10.1515/nispa-2016-0002

Dzvimbo, M. A., Monga, M., & Mashizha, T. M. (2017). The Link between Rural Institutions and Rural Development: Reflections on Smallholder Farmers and Donors in Zimbabwe. *IOSR Journal of Humanities and Social Science*, 22(6), 46–53. 10.9790/0837-2206064653

Echessa, G. M. (2010). *The role of residents' associations in urban service delivery: the case of Nairobi City, Kenya*. [Thesis, Kenyatta University]. https://www.durban.gov.za/pages/government/about-ethekwini

ECSECC. (2006). *Annual Report 2006*. Bhisho.

Eicher, C.K. (1999). Institutions and the African farmer. *Issues in agriculture, 14*(1), 1-2.

Eidelman, T. A. 2021. *Reclaiming Cape Town: Spatial Justice and the (Post) Apartheid City* [Doctoral dissertation, Vanderbilt University].

Eikelenboom, M., & Long, T. B. (2023). Breaking the cycle of marginalisation: How to involve local communities in multi-stakeholder initiatives? *Journal of Business Ethics*, 186(1), 31–62. 10.1007/s10551-022-05252-5

Ellis, F. (2000). *Rural Livelihoods and Diversity in Developing Countries*. Oxford University Press. 10.1093/oso/9780198296959.001.0001

Emerson, K., Nabatchi, T., & Balogh, S. (2012). An Integrative Framework for Collaborative Governance. *Journal of Public Administration: Research and Theory*, 22(1), 1–29. https://www.jstor.org/stable/41342607. 10.1093/jopart/mur011

Enaifoghe, A. (2023). The Role of Ethical Behavior and Public Value Creation in the Local Government System in South Africa. *International Journal of Social Science Research and Review*, 6(1), 471–483.

Enaifoghe, A., & Abosede, D. A. (2021). Enhancing good governance in South Africa through youth protest: A catalyst for social change. *Research World*, 12(2), 1–11.

Enoch, M. P., & Potter, S. (2006). Developing indicators of transport sustainability: A multi-criteria analysis of UK cities. *Transport Policy*, 13(3), 265–276.

Erika, S., & Elda, W. (2015). The corruption Bogey in south Africa: Is public education safe. *South African Journal of Education*, 5(9), 16–44.

eThekwini Metropolitan Municipality. (2023). *Court rules in favour of eThekwini in Westville rates boycott battle*. Durban. https://www.durban.gov.za/news/Court+rules+in+favour+of+eThekwini+in+Westville+rates+boycott+battle

Everatt, D. (2021). South Africans are revolting against inept local government. Why it matters. *The Conversation*. https://theconversation.com/south-africans-are-revolting-against-inept-local-government-why-it-matters-155483

Fagbadebo, O. (2019). Corruption and the challenge of accountability in the post-colonial African states: A discourse. *Journal of African Union Studies*.

Faguet, J. P. (2014). Decentralization and Governance. *World Development*, 53, 2–13. 10.1016/j.worlddev.2013.01.002

FAO. (2006). *Institutional analysis of trade liberalization and agriculture*. FAO. http://www.fao.org/documents/show_cdr.asp?url_file

Ferry, L., Eckersley, P., & Zakaria, Z. (2015). Accountability and transparency in English local government: Moving from "matching parts" to "awkward couple"? *Financial Accountability & Management*, 31(3), 345–361. 10.1111/faam.12060

Fine, J. (2018). *Understanding local economic development*. Routledge.

Flick, U. (2018). *Designing qualitative research*. Sage publications. 10.4135/9781529622737

Fobosi, S. C. (2023). The Minimum Effect of the Taxi Recapitalisation Programme on Precarious Working Conditions in South Africa's Minibus Taxi Sector: An Industry Full of Pitfalls. *South African Review of Sociology*, 53(1), 28–46. 10.1080/21528586.2023.2198497

Folke, C., Carpenter, S., Elmqvist, T., Gunderson, L., Holling, C. S., & Walker, B. (2005). Regime shifts, resilience, and biodiversity in ecosystem management. *Annual Review of Ecology, Evolution, and Systematics*, 35(1), 557–581. 10.1146/annurev.ecolsys.35.021103.105711

Foss, D. J., & Fay, D. (1975). Linguistic theory and performance models. *Testing linguistic hypotheses*, 65–91.

Fowler, A. (2000). NGDOs as a moment in history: Beyond aid to social entrepreneurship or civic innovation? *Third World Quarterly*, 21(4), 637–654. 10.1080/713701063

Franklin, A. L., & Ebdon, C. (2020). Participatory budgeting in the Philippines. *Chinese Public Administration Review*, 11(1), 60–74. 10.22140/cpar.v11i1.250

Fraser, G. C. G. (1991). *Agricultural marketing in less developed countries with special reference in Ciskei.* [Unpublished PhD thesis, University of Stellenbosch: Stellenbosch].

Froud, J. (2003). The Private Finance Initiative: Risk, Uncertainty and the State. *Accounting, Organizations and Society*, 28(6), 567–589. 10.1016/S0361-3682(02)00011-9

Gajbhiye, P., Maaz, M., Gedam, S., & Patil, Y.M. (2023). Smart BRT Management System. *International Journal of Advanced Research in Science, Communication and Technology, 3*(7), 9-12.

Gamble, H. (2021). *Contesting French West Africa: Battles Over schools and the colonial order.* Library of Congress Cataloguing in Publication Data.

Gargano, G. (2021). The bottom-up development model as a governance instrument for the rural areas. The cases of four local action groups (LAGs) in the United Kingdom and in Italy. *Sustainability (Basel)*, 13(16), 9123. 10.3390/su13169123

Gasela, M. M. (2022). The impact of material irregularity provisions of the *Public Audit Act* on accountability, oversight and governance in the Northern Cape province of South Africa. *Africa's Public Service Delivery and Performance Review*, 10(1), a601. 10.4102/apsdpr.v10i1.601

Gasela, M. M. (2022). The influence of organizational culture on performance in public entities of South Africa. *Africa's Public Service Delivery and Performance Review*, 10(1), 563. 10.4102/apsdpr.v10i1.563

Gelderblom, D. (2020). The limits to bridging social capital: Power, social context and the theory of Robert Putnam. *The Sociological Review*, 00(0), 1–16. 10.1177/0038026118765360

Germann, M., & Serdult, U. (2017). Internet voting and turnout: Evidence from Switzerland. *Electoral Studies*, 47, 1–12. 10.1016/j.electstud.2017.03.001

Gibson, N. (2011). *Fanonian Practices in South Africa: From Steve Biko to Abahlali baseMjondolo*. University of KwaZulu-Natal Press.

Gidden, T. H. (2018). National minorities between protection and empowerment: Towards a theory of empowerment. *JEMIE*, 13, 11.

Giles-Corti, B., Vernez-Moudon, A., Reis, R., Turrell, G., Dannenberg, A. L., Badland, H., Foster, S., Lowe, M., Sallis, J. F., Stevenson, M., & Owen, N. (2016). City planning and population health: a global challenge. In *The Lancet* (Vol. 388, Issue 10062). 10.1016/S0140-6736(16)30066-6

Gilman, H., & Wampler, B. (2019). The difference in design: Participatory budgeting in Brazil and the United States. *Journal of Deliberative Democracy*, 15(1). 10.16997/jdd.318

Gimenes, F. de S. F., De Oliveira, A. A. F., Noberto, L. V. V., Sabino, C. W. C., & Cavalcante, J. R. V. (2024). The experience of the Municipal Finance Department of Fortaleza in implementing spatial data infrastructure as an integrated management tool for the real estate registry. *CONTRIBUCIONES A LAS CIENCIAS SOCIALES, 17*(2). 10.55905/revconv.17n.2-055

Givoni, M., & Banister, D. (2010). *Integrated Transport: From Policy to Practice* (1st ed.). Routledge. 10.4324/9780203850886

Goba, N. S. (2018). *The architecture of non-grievability: a critical race spatial analysis of the continuance of apartheid spatial planning into (post) apartheid South Africa*. University of Pretoria.

Goldsmith, J. (2014). *Government outsourcing: a practical guide for safe and local governments*. India: School of public and environmental affairs Press.

Gopaul, A. (2015). *Operational Greenhouse Gas Emissions of Public Transportation in the eThekwini Municipality*. [Partial Dissertation, University of Kwazulu-Natal].

Gordon, V., Osgood, J. L.Jr, & Boden, D. (2017). The role of citizen participation and social media platforms in the participatory budgeting process. *International Journal of Public Administration*, 40(1), 65–76. 10.1080/01900692.2015.1072215

Goswami, D., Tripathi, S. B., Jain, S., Pathak, S., & Seth, A. 2019. Towards building a district development model for India using census data. In *Proceedings of the 2nd ACM SIGCAS Conference on Computing and Sustainable Societies* (pp. 259-271). ACM. 10.1145/3314344.3332491

Govender, N., & Reddy, P. S. (2019). Effectiveness of governance towards digitalisation at eThekwini Metropolitan Municipality in KwaZulu-Natal province, South Africa. *Africa's Public Service Delivery and Performance Review*, 7(1), a336. 10.4102/apsdpr.v7i1.336

Government of Zimbabwe. (1998). Rural District Councils Act [Printflow / Government Printers.]. *Pub.*, L(29), 13.

Government of Zimbabwe. (2009). Public Finance and Management Act [Printflow / Government Printers.]. *Pub.*, L(22), 19.

Government of Zimbabwe. (2013). Constitution of Zimbabwe Amendment 20 of 2013, Printflow / Government Printers, Harare Government of Zimbabwe. (1998). *Traditional Leaders Act Chapter 29:17*. Harare.

Government of Zimbabwe. (2020). Devolution and Decentralisation Policy of 2020. In *Government Gazzette*. Printflow, Harare.

Graham, L, Himlin, R., Engel, H., Mathoho, M., Reddy, J., & Delany, D. (2018). *Review of the State of Civil Society Organisations in South Africa*. National Development Agency: Braamfontein.

Granell, C., Schade, S., & Hobona, G. (2011). Linked Data: Connecting Spatial Data Infrastructures and Volunteered Geographic Information. In *Geospatial Web Services: Advances in Information Interoperability*.

Green, F. M. (2008). *Constitutional Development in the South Atlantic States, 1776-1860: A Study in the Evolution of Democracy*. The Lawbook Exchange, Ltd.

Green, T. (2015). *Social Exclusion in South African Cities: Urbanization, Housing and Social Cohesion*. Routledge.

Guamba, J. M. E. (2016). Municipal Management in a Systemic Perspective. *International Journal of Management*. 10.18535/ijmei/v2i9.03

Gumede, V. (2022). *South Africa Sate & Development. Soshanguve & Pretoria: SAAPAM & Unisa Press*. RSA.

Guner, H. R., Hasanoğlu, İ., & Aktaş, F. (2020). COVID-19: Prevention and control measures in community. *Turkish Journal of Medical Sciences*, 50(9), 571–577. 10.3906/sag-2004-14632293835

Guyadeen, D., Henstra, D., Kaup, S., & Wright, G. (2023). Evaluating the quality of municipal strategic plans. *Evaluation and Program Planning*, 96, 102186. 10.1016/j.evalprogplan.2022.10218636410094

Gwala, S. N. (2023). *Municipal planning in dense rural settlements: a case of Mzinyathi in eThekwini Metropolitan Municipality* [Doctoral dissertation, Durban University of Technology]. DUT Library.

Hadley, O., & Serrat, O., & Oliver, N. (2017). The sustainable livelihoods approach. *Knowledge solutions: Tools, methods, and approaches to drive organizational performance*, 21-26.

Haider, M., & Badami, M. G. (2010). Urbanization and Local Governance Challenges in Pakistan. *Environment & Urbanization Asia*, 1(1), 81–96. 10.1177/097542530900100107

Hall, S. (2003). New Labour's double-shuffle. *Soundings*, 24(24), 10–24. 10.3898/136266203820467680

Hammond, M. (2021). Democratic innovations after the post-democratic turn: Between activation and empowerment. *Critical Policy Studies*, 15(2), 174–191. 10.1080/19460171.2020.1733629

Haque, M. S. (2005). Corrupt Organizations. *Journal of Economic Behavior & Organization*, 57(4), 473–495.

Harvey, D. (1989). From managerialism to entrepreneurialism: The transformation of urban governance in late capitalism. *Geografiska Annaler. Series B, Human Geography*, 71B(1), 3–17. 10.1080/04353684.1989.11879583

Harvey, D. (2005). *A Brief History of Neoliberalism*. Oxford University Press. 10.1093/oso/9780199283262.001.0001

Hassenforder, E., & Barone, S. (2018). Institutional arrangements for water governance. *International Journal of Water Resources Development.*

Healey, P. (1992). Planning through debate. *The Town Planning Review*, 63(2), 143–163. 10.3828/tpr.63.2.422x602303814821

Held, D. (2010). Models of Democracy (3rd Ed). Cambridge CB2: Polity Press.

Heller, P. (2001). Moving the State: The Politics of Democratic Decentralisation in Kerala, South Africa, and Porto Alegre. *Politics & Society*, 29(1), 131–163. 10.1177/0032329201029001006

Heller, P. (2012). Democracy, Participatory Politics, and Development: Some Comparative Lessons from Brazil, India, and South Africa. *Polity*, 44(4), 643–665. 10.1057/pol.2012.19

Helmsing, A. H. J. (1990). Transforming Rural Local Government: Zimbabwe's Postindependence Experience. *Environment and Planning. C, Government & Policy*, 8(1), 87–110. 10.1068/c080087

Hendrickse, R. (2023). Ethnic leadership in the age of disruption: implications for South African municipalities. *International Journal of Research in Business and Social Science (2147-4478), 12*(7), 224-234.

Herbert, M. M. 2021. *An Analysis of the Integrated Development Planning Process in Blouberg Local Municipality* [Master's thesis, University of Pretoria (South Africa)].

Hickey, S & Mohan, G. (2008). Relocating participation without a radical politics of development: insight from political action and practice. In S, Hickey & G, Mohan (eds.) *Participation from 18.*

Hilbert College. (2023). *Electoral Integrity: Challenges, Goals and Resources*. Hilbert College. https://online.hilbert.edu/blog/electoral-integrity/

Hlati, T. (2020). *Local economic development policies*. UpJohn Research.

Hocevar, S. P., Jansen, E., & Thomas, G. F. (2011). Inter-Organizational Collaboration: Addressing the Challenge. *Homeland Security Affairs, 7.* https://www.hsaj.org/articles/64

Holloway, G., Agapitova, N., & Chamberlain, W. (2018). Agri-Parks in South Africa: A case study of Eastern Cape Province. In Sandrey, R., & Bhorat, H. (Eds.), *State of the Nation: Poverty & Inequality: Diagnosis, Prognosis and Responses* (pp. 139–159). HSRC Press.

Homsy, G. C., Liu, Z., & Warner, M. E. (2019). Multilevel governance: Framing the integration of top-down and bottom-up policymaking. *International Journal of Public Administration*, 42(7), 572–582. 10.1080/01900692.2018.1491597

Houston, S., Brannan, G. D., Brannan, J. M., & Sharts-Hopko, N. C. (2021). Qu*alitative study*. NIH.

Hussain, Z., & Nadeem, O. (2021). The nexus between growth strategies of master plans and spatial dynamics of a metropolitan city: The case of Lahore, Pakistan. *Land Use Policy*, 109, 105609. 10.1016/j.landusepol.2021.105609

Hussnain, M. Q., Waheed, A., Anjum, G. A., Naeem, M. A., Hussain, E., Wakil, K., & Pettit, C. J. (2020). A framework to bridge digital planning tools' utilization gap in peri-urban spatial planning; lessons from Pakistan. *Computers, Environment and Urban Systems*, 80, 101451. 10.1016/j.compenvurbsys.2019.101451

Huxham, C., & Vangen, S. (2005). *Managing to collaborate: The theory and practice of collaborative advantage*. Routledge.

Imran, M. (2009). Public transport in Pakistan: A critical overview. *Journal of Public Transportation*, 12(2), 53–83. 10.5038/2375-0901.12.2.4

International Idea. (2015). Democracy and Service Delivery. *International IDEA Policy Dialogue*. IDEA. https://www.idea.int/sites/default/files/publications/democracy-and-service-delivery.pdf

Iqbal, A., Yasar, A., Nizami, A. S., Haider, R., Sharif, F., Sultan, I. A., Tabinda, A. B., Kedwaii, A. A., & Chaudhary, M. M. (2022). Municipal Solid Waste Collection and Haulage Modeling Design for Lahore, Pakistan: Transition toward Sustainability and Circular Economy. *Sustainability (Basel)*, 14(23), 16234. 10.3390/su142316234

Irfan, M., Kazmi, S. J. H., & Arsalan, M. H. (2018). Sustainable harnessing of the surface water resources for Karachi: A geographic review. *Arabian Journal of Geosciences*, 11(2), 24. 10.1007/s12517-017-3365-6

ITDG. (2005). *Ministerial conference and expo on agricultural science and technology*. FAS. http://www.fas.usda.gov/icd/stconf/pubs/conf_fact.html

Jachi, M., Makumbe, M., & Mandongwe, L. (2019). Public Procurement and Public Service Delivery in Zimbabwe Local Authorities. A Non-systematic Review. *Public Policy and Administration Research*. 10.7176/PPAR/9-12-05

Jain, A. (2013). *Sustainable urban mobility in Southern Asia.* (Technical report) UNHabitat, Nairobi, Kenya. https://unhabitat.org/wpntent/uploads/2013/06/GRHS.2013.Regional.Southern.Asia_.pdf

Jamatia, P. L. (2023). The Role of Youth in Combating Social Inequality: Empowering the Next Generation. *International Journal of Social Science, Educational, Economics. Agricultural Research & Technology: Open Access Journal*, 2(8), 229–238.

James, J. (2021). *A simple decision analysis of a mandatory lockdown response to the COVID-19 pandemic.*

Javed, N., & Farhan, K. (2020). Access to urban services for political and social inclusion in Pakistan. In *Advances in 21st Century Human Settlements.* Springer. 10.1007/978-981-15-2973-3_10

Javed, N., Hasan, R., & Qureshi, N. N. (2020). Developing a National Urban Policy: A Case Study of Pakistan. In *Developing National Urban Policies.* Springer. 10.1007/978-981-15-3738-7_5

Jennings, G. (2015). *Public Transport Interventions and Transport Justice in South Africa: A Literature and Policy Review.*

Jennings, G. (2014). Finding our balance: Considering the opportunities for public bicycle systems in Cape Town, South Africa. *Research in Transportation Business & Management*, 1–9.

John, M., & Nhlamulo, M. (2023). Questioning the Practice of Corruption in the Attainment of the Selected Sustainable Development Goals (SDGs) in South Africa. *IAHRW International Journal of Social Sciences Review, 11*(3).

John, D., & Nhlamulo, T. (2023). The Impact of Corruption on Governance and Development in South Africa. *Southern African Journal of Public Affairs*, 30(1), 47–65.

John, M., Lavhelani, K. F. K., & Richard, C. K. (2021). Give to Caesar what belongs to Caesar: The provision of water and sanitation service in South African Rural areas. *Gender & Behaviour*, 19(3), 18323–18330.

Jones, P., King, N., & Eynon, R. (2018). *Interpretative phenomenological analysis: A guide to conducting and reporting.* Routledge.

Joseph, J. E. (2022). Unequal, undiversified and underrepresented: Women on the backburner in local decision making in South Africa's local government. *ScienceRise*, (3 (80)), 24–37. 10.21303/2313-8416.2022.002533

Kabizwe, A. (2021). COVID-19 pandemic–an African perspective. *Emerging Microbes & Infections*, 9(1), 1300–1308.34176429

Kalonda, J. K., & Govender, K. (2021). 'Factors Affecting Municipal Service Delivery: A Case Study Of Katima Mulilo Town Council, Namibia'. *African Journal of Public Affairs*, 12(2), 1–26.

Kalwar, S., Sahito, N., Memon, I. A., Hwang, J., Mangi, M. Y., & Lashari, Z. A. (2019). National Planning Strategies for Agro-based Industrial Development in Secondary Cities of Sindh Province, Pakistan. *Sustainability (Basel)*, 11(24), 7066. 10.3390/su11247066

Kambuwa, M., & Wallis, M. (2002). *Public Management*. University of Durban-Westville.

Kanjere, M. & Koto, A. (2021). Public Procurement Corruption and Corporate Scandals in Limpopo Province, South Africa: A Content Analysis Perspective. *Acta Universitatis Danubius. Relationes Internationales, 14*(2).

Kanyane, M. (2014) Exploring Challenges of Municipal Service Delivery in South Africa (1994-2013). *Africa's public service delivery and performance review*, *2*(1), 90-110.

Kanyane, M. (2014). Exploring challenges of municipal service delivery in South Africa (1994-2013). *Africa's Public Service Delivery & Performance Review*, 2(1), 90–110. 10.4102/apsdpr.v2i1.45

Kanyane, M., & Koma, S. (2014). *Developmental Local Government in South Africa: Issues for Considerations. Wandsbeck*. Reach Publishers.

Kaplan, A. (1996). *The Development Practitioners' Handbook*. Pluto Press.

Kaywood, L. (2021). Exploring the History and Development of the Local Government System in South Africa. *African Journal of Public Affairs.*, 1(3), 42–61.

Keating, M. (2012). Intergovernmental relations and innovation: From co-operative to competitive welfare federalism in the UK. *British Journal of Politics and International Relations*, 14(2), 214–230. 10.1111/j.1467-856X.2011.00484.x

Kenton, W. (2022). *What Is Social Capital? Definition, Types, and Examples*. Investiopedia. https://www.investopedia.com/terms/s/socialcapital.asp

Kgobe, F. K. L., & Mamokhere, J. (2021). Interrogating The Effectiveness Of Public Accountability Mechanisms In South Africa: Can Good Governance Be Realized? *International Journal of Entrepreneurship*, 25(2), 1–12.

Kgobe, F. K. L., & Mamokhere, J. (2021). The value of public participation in land-use planning for redeeming congestion in South African municipalities. *Technium Soc. Sci. J.*, 26, 17–31. 10.47577/tssj.v26i1.5020

Khalo, T. (2013). Accountability and Oversight in Municipal Financial Management: The Role of Municipal Public Accounts Committees. *Journal of Public Administration*, 48(4), 589–501.

Khambule, I. (2021). The DDM: Towards a Capable Local Development State in South Africa. The University of KwaZulu-Natal. *Journal of Public Administration*, 56(3), 507–523.

Khambule, I. (2021). The District Development Model: Towards a Capable Local Developmental State in South Africa. *Journal of Public Administration*, 56(3), 507–523.

Khan, F. (2020). Corruption and Mismanagement in South African Municipalities: A Critical Evaluation. *Journal of Public Administration*, 55(2), 284–298.

Khan, H. A. (2008). Application of systems theory in agriculture. *World Applied Sciences Journal*, 4(1), 100–106.

Khan, H. F., Arif, M. A., Intikhab, S., & Arshad, S. A. (2023). Quantifying Household Water Use and Its Determinants in Low-Income, Water-Scarce Households in Karachi. *Water (Basel)*, 15(19), 3400. 10.3390/w15193400

Khorommbi, K. C. 2019. *The establishment of catchment management agencies in South Africa: an organisational design perspective* [Doctoral dissertation, North-West University, South Africa].

Khoza, M. (2003). *Being Yourself, Representing Others: A Guide for Local Government Councillors in South Africa*. Flame Tree Media.

Kiefer, K., & Ranganathan, M. (2020). The politics of participation in cape Town's slum upgrading: The role of productive tension. *Journal of Planning Education and Research*, 40(3), 263–277. 10.1177/0739456X18761119

Kitano, H. (2002). Systems Biology: A Brief Overview. *Science*, 295(5560), 1662–1664. 10.1126/science.106949211872829

Klasen, S. (1997). Poverty, Inequality and Deprivation in South Africa: An Analysis of the 1993 SALDRU Survey. *Social Indicators Research*, 41(1/3), 64–66. 10.1023/A:1006892216864

Knight, B., Chigudu, H., & Tandon, R. (2002). *Reviving Democracy: Citizens at the Heart of Governance*. Earthscan Publications Limited.

Koehrsen, J., & Heuser, A. (2019). *Faith-Based Organisation in Development Discourses and Practice*. Taylor & Francis. 10.4324/9780429351211

Koetter, T., Sikder, S. K., & Weiss, D. (2021). The cooperative urban land development model in Germany-An effective instrument to support affordable housing. *Land Use Policy*, 107, 105481. 10.1016/j.landusepol.2021.105481

Kooiman, J. (2003). Governing as governance. *Sage (Atlanta, Ga.)*.

Kosec, K., & Wantchekon, L. (2020). Can information improve rural governance and service delivery? *World Development*, 125, 104376. 10.1016/j.worlddev.2018.07.017

Kraai, S., Ndevu, Z., & Matsiliza, N. (2023). Participatory Budgeting to Foster Inclusivity, Transparency, and Accountability in Local Government: A case study of the City of Ekurhuleni Metropolitan Municipality of South Africa. *African Journal of Public Affairs*, 14(1), 63–88.

Krane, D., & Wright, D. S. (2018). Intergovernmental relations. In *Defining public administration* (pp. 83–101). Routledge. 10.4324/9780429501074-8

Krantz, S. B. (2011). N of I? Issues of Validity and Reliability in. *PAACE Journal of Lifelong Learning*, 4, 51–60.

Krieger, J. (2007). The Political Economy of New Labour: The Failure of a Success Story. *New Political Economy*, 12(3), 421–432. 10.1080/13563460701485664

Kroukamp, H., & Cloete, F. (2018). Improving professionalism in South African local government. *Acta Academica*, 50(1), 61–80. 10.18820/24150479/aa50i1.4

Kucukpehlivan, T., Cetin, M., Aksoy, T., Senyel Kurkcuoglu, M. A., Cabuk, S. N., Isik Pekkan, O., Dabanli, A., & Cabuk, A. (2023). Determination of the impacts of urban-planning of the urban land area using GIS hotspot analysis. *Computers and Electronics in Agriculture*, 210, 107935. 10.1016/j.compag.2023.107935

Kumo, L. W., Omilola, B., & Minsat, A. (2015). *African Economic Outlook*. Oxford University Press.

Kunene, B., Mashau, P., & Nyawo, J. (2022). Ascertaining The Challenges Faced By Women Entrepreneurs in Ethekwini Municipality, KwaZulu-Natal Province. *Gender & Behaviour*, 20(1), 19060–19083.

Kurebwa, J. (2015). Decentralisation and central government control: Experiences from the local government reform in Zimbabwe. *African Journal of Governance and Development*, 9(2), 73–84.

Kusek, J. Z., & Rist, R. C. (2004). *Ten steps to a Result-Based Monitoring and Evaluation. A Handbook for Developing Practitioners*. D.C. The World Bank. 10.1596/0-8213-5823-5

Kusters, K., Buck, L., de Graaf, M., Minang, P., van Oosten, C., & Zagt, R. (2018). Participatory planning, monitoring and evaluation of multi-stakeholder platforms in integrated landscape initiatives. *Environmental Management*, 62(1), 170–181. 10.1007/s00267-017-0847-y28324144

Kusters, K., De Graaf, M., Buck, L., Galido, K., Maindo, A., Mendoza, H., Nghi, T. H., Purwanto, E., & Zagt, R. (2020). Inclusive landscape governance for sustainable development: Assessment methodology and lessons for civil society organisations. *Land (Basel)*, 9(4), 128. 10.3390/land9040128

La Foy, G. B. (2020). *Local government in the constitutional dispensation: defining the limits of local government's legislative and executive authority* [Doctoral dissertation].

Lachapelle, P. R., & Austin, E. K. (2014). *Community Participation: Encyclopaedia of Quality of Life and Well-Being Research*. Springer: Dordrecht publisher. 10.1007/978-94-007-0753-5_471

Lafont, C. (2015). Deliberation, participation, and democratic legitimacy: Should deliberative mini-publics shape public policy? *Journal of Political Philosophy*, 23(1), 40–63. 10.1111/jopp.12031

Laine, L. (2014). Debating civil society: Contested conceptualisations and development trajectories. *International Journal of Not-for-profit Law*, 16(1).

Lakuma, C. P., Katunze, M., Nagawa, M., Mawejje, J., Lwanga, M., Mbowa, S., & Shinyekwa, I. (2017). *Country reviews of capacity development: The case of Uganda*.

Lalu, P. (2022). *Undoing apartheid*. John Wiley & Sons.

Lavhelani, P. N., & Lavhelani, P. D. (2023). Assessing the Legal Framework for Service Delivery in the Vhembe District Municipality. *Gender & Behaviour*, 21(1), 20959–20972.

Leach, O. A., Derevianko, Y. M., Kozlov, D. V., & Mukorez, A. I. (2021). *Regional Economic Development in The Context of the COVID-19 Pandemic and the Economic Crisis*.

Leduka, M. (2009). *Participatory budgeting in the South African local government context: The case of the Mantsopa local municipality, Free State province* [Doctoral dissertation, Stellenbosch: University of Stellenbosch].

Ledwith, M., & Springett, J. (2022). Participatory practice: Community-based action for transformative change. *Practice*. Policy Press.

Lee, A., Martin, R., Thomas, G., Guilaume, Y., & Maio, G. R. (2015). Conceptualiz2ing leadership perceptions as attitudes: Using attitude theory to further understand the leadership process. *The Leadership Quarterly*, 26(6), 28–31. 10.1016/j.leaqua.2015.10.003

Leibbrandt, M., Finn, A., Woolard, I., & Argent, J. (2019). Trends in South African income distribution and poverty since the fall of apartheid. *The World Bank Economic Review*, 33(2), 251–273.

Lekubu, B. K. (2015). *Manifestations of corruption in the City of Tshwane Metropolitan Municipality* [Doctoral dissertation, University of South Africa].

Levinson, H., Zimmerman, S., Clinger, J., Gast, J., Rutherford, S., & Bruhn, E. (2003). Litman, T. 2013. *The New Transportation Paradigm.ITE Journal*, 1(83), 20–27.

Lincoln, Y. S., & Guba, E. G. (1985). Naturalistic inquiry. *Sage (Atlanta, Ga.)*.

Linton, T. (2021). Coronavirus is proving we need more resilient supply chains. *Harvard Business Review*, 5.

Lodge, T. (2001). South African Politics and Collective Action, 1994-2000. In B. Klandermans, M. Roefs, & J. Olivier. (Eds). *The State of the People: Citizens, Civil Society and Governance* (pp, 1-26). Pretoria: Human Sciences Research Council.

Lodi, J. D. (2020). *Implementation of the DDM. Department of Cooperative Governance and Traditional Affairs.* CoGTA. http://www.cogta.gov.za

Loha, W. (2023). Community-led development: perspectives and approaches of four member organizations. *Qeios, CC-BY 4.0.*

Lubuulwa, K. B. (2021). *Putting decentralisation policy into practice in Uganda: a participatory action research study of local government empowerment for local economic development.*

Lu, D. (2024). *Regional development and its spatial structure*. Springer. 10.1007/978-981-99-7683-6

Ludbrook, K. (2021). Local government in South Africa is broken: but giving the job to residents carries risks. *The Conversation*.https://theconversation.com/local-government-in-south-africa-is-broken-but-giving-the-job-to-residents-carries-risks-155970

Luhmann, N. (1995). *Social Systems*. Stanford University Press.

Luthuli, T. B. (2005). *Performance Measurement as a Public Policy Implementation Tool in the South African Public Service*. University of Pretoria.

Ly, B. (2023). Social media and political involvement in Cambodia. *Cogent Social Sciences*, 9(1), 2194565. 10.1080/23311886.2023.2194565

Mabizela, H. & Matsiliza, N.S. (2020). Uncovering the gaps in the provision of services in the rural Okhahlamba Municipality of KwaZulu-Natal province. *Africa's Public Service Delivery and Performance Review,8*(1), a390. . v8i1.390.10.4102/apsdpr

Madlala, S. (2020). Reconceptualizing Public Participation in Local Government: The District Development Model. Kariuki and Reddy, 2020 (Ed). *The Covid-19 Pandemic in South Africa: A Review of Selected Local Governance and Policy Responses, 2,* 81-100.

Madumo, O. S. (2015). Developmental Local Government Challenges and Progress in South Africa. *Administration Publica*, 23(4), 153–166.

Madzimure, T. (2021). A Case for Decentralization in Zimbabwe's Local Government System: Challenges and Opportunities. *Archives of Business Research*, 9(2), 1–21. 10.14738/abr.92.9580

Maela, K. D., Matloga, S. T., & Zitha, H. E. (2024). Nurturing Development Administration in South African Local Government. *International Journal of Social Science Research and Review*, 7(3), 170–188. 10.47814/ijssrr.v7i3.1987

Magagula, D. N., Mukonza, R. M., Manyaka, R. K., & Moeti, K. (2022). The role of district municipalities in service provision in South Africa: Dissecting challenges faced by Ehlanzeni District Municipality. *Africa's Public Service Delivery and Performance Review*, 10(1), a628. 10.4102/apsdpr.v10i1.628

Magau, A. (2017). Understanding the implementation of local economic development (LED) programmes in the Eastern Cape, South Africa. *Journal of Economics and Behavioral Studies*, 9(2), 102–114.

Magingxa, L. L., & Kamara, A. B. 2003. *Institutional perspectives of enhancing smallholder market access in South Africa.* Contributed Paper Presented at the 41st Annual Conference of the Agricultural Economic Association of South Africa (AEASA), Pretoria, South Africa.

Maila, H. M. (2006). *Public Management and Service Delivery in the Department of Water Affairs and Forestry.* [Unpublished MTech Dissertation. UNISA].

Main Street America. (2023). *The Mainstreet Approach.*Main Street America. https://www.mainstreet.org/ourwork/theapproach

Majola, T., Mkhize, N., & Mwaura, F. (2020). Impact of COVID-19 on Agriculture and Food Security in Africa: Policy Responses and Opportunities for Post-Pandemic Recovery. *Journal of Agricultural and Resource Economics*, 45(3), 407–424.

Majola, T., & Naidu, S. (2022). Digital Agriculture: A Potential Catalyst for Rural Development in South Africa. In Antwi-Agyei, A., Adiku, D., Vrieling, A., & Adimassu, F. (Eds.), *Digital Agriculture: Sustainable Crop Production and Food Security* (pp. 455–475). Springer.

Makalela, K. I. 2019. *The efficacy of integrated development plan in enhancing service delivery in Lepelle-Nkumpi Local Municipality, Limpopo Province* [Doctoral dissertation].

Makalela, K. I., Masenya, M. J., & Mokoele, N. J. (2021). Women in South Africa's development trajectory: Disjuncture between Voice, Participation and integrated Development Planning. *European Journal of Economics*, 5(3).

Makhanya, N., 2023. The role of accounting officers in ensuring responsible public financial management: A PFMA centric approach. *International Journal of Research in Business and Social Science (2147-4478), 12*(10), 241-247.

Makhura, M. N. (2009). *Rural Development in SA: Repetition, Revision & Rethink.* Paper presented to HSRC/Land Bank seminar. Pretoria.

Makhura, M., & Mokoena, M. (2003). Market access for small-scale farmers in South Africa. In Nieuwoudt, L., & Groenewald, J. (Eds.), *The Challenges of Change: Agriculture, Land and the South African Economy.* University of Natal Press.

Makoni, T. (2021). Africa after the covid-19 lockdowns: Economic impacts and prospects.

Makoti, M.Z., & Odeku. (2021). Impetus for Fostering Effective Inter-Governmental Relationships. *Co-operative Governance in South Africa, 12*

Makoti, M. Z., & Odeku, O. K. (2018). Critical perspective on the complexity and functionality of intergovernmental relations between provincial and local governments in South Africa. *African Journal of Public Affairs*, 10(1), 98–112.

Malan, L. P. (2012). *Intergovernmental relations in South Africa: a revised policy approach to co-operative government.* University of Pretoria.

Malinga, W., Moyo, P. M., Sikhosana, N., & Moyo, M. (2017). Decentralisation and Rural Development: Is it a Policy of Empowering or Disempowering Rural Communities in Zimbabwe? *International Journal of Innovative Research and Development*, 6(4). 10.24940/ijird/2017/v6/i4/APR17061

Maluleke, W. (2022). Alleged corrupt practices on stock theft by public sector officials in the selected rural areas of Giyani, Limpopo Province: Exploring the causes and experiences. *International Journal of Research in Business and Social Science (2147-4478), 11*(5), 472-481.

Mamogale, M. J. (2014). Financial Performance of Local Government in Limpopo Province, 2010-2012. *African Studies Quarterly*, 15(1).

Mamokhere, J. (2022). Accountability, inclusivity, effectiveness, and leaving no one behind: An exploration of effective governance principles in ensuring clean water and sanitation in South African municipalities. *International Journal of Research in Business and Social Science (2147-4478), 11*(10), 191-205.

Mamokhere, J. (2022). Leaving no one behind in a participative integrated development planning process in South Africa. *International Journal of Research in Business and Social Science (2147-4478), 11*(10), 277-291.

Mamokhere, J. (2022). Pragmatic implementation and promotion of good governance principles in realising Sustainable Development Goal Six (6) in South Africa. *International Journal of Research in Business and Social Science (2147-4478), 11*(6), 20-32.

Mamokhere, J. (2022). Understanding the Complex Interplay of Governance, Systematic, and Structural Factors Affecting Service Delivery in South African Municipalities. *Commonwealth Youth & Development, 20*(2).

Mamokhere, J., 2022. Understanding the Complex Interplay of Governance, Systematic, and Structural Factors Affecting Service Delivery in South African Municipalities. *Commonwealth Youth & Development, 20*(2).

Mamokhere, J. (2019). An exploration of reasons behind service delivery protests in South Africa: A case of Bolobedu South at the Greater Tzaneen Municipality. *International Conference on Public Administration and Development Alternatives (IPADA).* IEEE.

Mamokhere, J., & Kgobe, F. K. L. (2023). One District, One Approach, One Budget, One Plan: Understanding District Development Model as an Initiative for Improving Service Delivery and Socio-economic Development in South Africa. *IAHRW International Journal of Social Sciences Review*, 11(3), 362–370.

Mamokhere, J., & Meyer, D. F. (2022). Comprehending stakeholders' involvement in the integrated development planning process as a tool for improved community participation. *EUREKA: Social and Humanities*, (4), 18–32.

Mamokhere, J., & Meyer, D. F. (2023). The Integrated Development Planning Process's Impact as a Tool for Increasing Community Participation in South Africa. *African Journal of Development Studies*, 13(2), 7–34. 10.31920/2634-3649/2023/v13n2a1

Mamokhere, J., Musitha, M. E., & Netshidzivhani, V. M. (2022). The implementation of the basic values and principles governing public administration and service delivery in South Africa. *Journal of Public Affairs*, 22(4), e2627. 10.1002/pa.2627

Managa, A. (2012). Unfulfilled promises and their consequences: A reflection on local government performance and the critical issue of poor service delivery in South Africa. Africa Institute of South Africa. AISA. *Policy Brief*, 76, 1–8.

Mandaza, B. (2005). The State and the Crisis of Zimbabwean Nationalism. In Raftopoulos, B., & Muzondidya, A. (Eds.), *Becoming Zimbabwe: A History from the Pre-colonial Period to 2009* (pp. 277–292). Weaver Press.

Mandondo, A. (2000). Environmental policy and law in Zimbabwe: Issues and challenges. In Moyo, S., & Rosalie, P. S. (Eds.), *Zimbabwe's environment: Issues and policies* (pp. 95–110). University of Zimbabwe Publications.

Mandondo, A. (2001). Allocation of governmental authority and responsibility in Tiered governance regimes: The case of the Chivi Rural District Council land use planning and conservation by-laws. *African Studies Quarterly*, 5, 41–56.

Manfré, L., Hirata, E., Silva, J. B., Shinohara, E. J., Giannotti, M., Larocca, A. P. C., & Quintanilha, J. (2012). An Analysis of Geospatial Technologies for Risk and Natural Disaster Management. *ISPRS International Journal of Geo-Information*, 1(2), 166–185. 10.3390/ijgi1020166

Mangcu, X. (2002). *The democratic moment: South Africa's prospects under Jacob Zuma.* Sunnyside: Jacana Media.

Mangogo, B. (2018). *Enhancing Civil Society Participation in the South Africa Development Agenda: The role of civil Society Organisations.* National Development Agency: Parktown.

Mangwanya, M. G., & Shava, E. (2023). Intergovernmental relations as an accelerator for the local government planning in South Africa. *Journal of Southwest Jiaotong University*, 58(2).

Mansuri, G., & Rao, V. (2003). *Evaluating community driven development: a review of the evidence.* Development Research Group, World Bank.

Mansuri, G., & Rao, V. (2013). *Accountability, transparency, participation, and inclusion: A new development consensus?* Carnegie Endowment for International Peace. https://carnegieendowment.org/files/development_consensus_brief.pdf

Mantzaris, E., & Pillay, P. (2017). Procurement and Corruption: The Case of the Ekurhuleni Metropolitan Municipality. *African Journal of Public Affairs*, 9(5), 78–92.

Manungufala, T. (2020). Overview of the District Development Model – A framework for co-Operative service delivery. Parliament, Research Unit: 9. [https://www.parliament.gov.za/storage/app/media/Pages/2020/september/02-09- 2020_National_Council_of_Provinces_Local_Government_Week/docs/Overview_of_the_district _development_model_a_framework_for_co-operative_service_delivery.pdf]

Manzini, S. (2016). *The views of government officials on the Integrated Development Plan as a framework for local government that is developmental and responsive to peoples' needs.* Gauteng.

Mapuva, J. (2011). Enhancing local governance through local initiatives: Residents' associations in Zimbabwe. *African Journal of History and Culture*, 3(1), 1–12.

Marks, G. (1993). Structural policy and multi-level governance in the EC. In Sbragia, A. (Ed.), *Euro-politics: Institutions and policymaking in the "new" European Community* (pp. 391–410). Brookings Institution Press.

Martin, C. (2023). *Municipalities embrace the phased design build delivery method.* Burns McDonnell. https://blog.burnsmcd.com/municipalities-embrace-the-phased-design-build-delivery-method

Martin, S. (2003). Engaging with citizens and other stakeholders. In Bovaird, T., & Loffler, E. (Eds.), *Public Management and Governance.* Routledge.

Marumaholo, S., Chigwata, T. C., & Nhede, N. T. (2018). Participatory Budgeting in the City of Kwekwe (Zimbabwe). *African Journal of Public Affairs.*, 10(4), 196–211.

Marutlulle, N. K., & Ijeoma, E. O. C. (2015). Obstacles to housing delivery in Ekurhuleni Metropolitan Municipality: A critical review of output and input. *Africa's Public Service Delivery & Performance Review*, 3(4), 141–163. 10.4102/apsdpr.v3i4.101

Maseko, G. J., Robbetze, N., & Masungini, A. W. (2023). 'Association between municipal credit management, responsiveness and service delivery'. *Africa's Public Service Delivery and Performance Review*, 11(1), a686. 10.4102/apsdpr.v11i1.686

Maserumule, M. H. (2017). 'Editorial: Just a thought'. *Journal of Public Administration*, 52(2), 308–502.

Mashamaite, M. M. (2018). *Assessing the inclusion of climate change strategies in the integrated transport plans of South African metropolitan municipalities.* IPADA conference proceedings, Cape Town.

Mashiane, K. & Odeku, K.O. (2021). Transformative interventions fostering the right to access to adequate housing in South Africa. *African Journal of Development Studies (formerly AFFRIKA Journal of Politics, Economics and Society), 2021*(si1), 265-287.

Masilo, T., & Gershwin, G. (2020). *The Perceived Impact Of Integrated Development Planning (Idp).* On The Social And Economic Development Of Local Communities Of Magareng Local Municipality, Northern Cape Province.

Masipa, M. H. (2021). *An analysis of the Integrated Development Planning (IDP) process in Blouberg Local Municipality* [Doctoral dissertation, University of Pretoria].

Masiya, T., Davids, Y. D., & Mangai, M. S. (2019). Assessing service delivery. *Theoretical and Empirical Researches in Urban Management*, 14(2), 20–40.

Masiya, T., Davids, Y. D., & Mangai, M. S. (2019). Assessing Service Delivery: Public Perception of Municipal Service Delivery in South Africa. *Theoretical and Empirical Research in Urban Management*, 14(2), 20–40.

Masiya, T., Davids, Y. D., & Mangai, M. S. (2021). Factors affecting the performance of South African municipal officials: Stakeholders' perspectives. *Commonwealth Journal of Local Governance*, (25), 97–115. 10.5130/cjlg.vi25.7701

Masser, I. (2019). Geographic Information Systems to Spatial Data Infrastructure. In *Geographic Information Systems to Spatial Data Infrastructure*. Taylor & Francis. 10.1201/9780429505904

Masuku, M. B., & Kirsten, J. F. (2021). Capacity development for agricultural innovation systems in South Africa: Lessons from case studies in the Eastern Cape Province. *Agrekon*, 60(2), 161–180.

Masuku, M. M., & Jili, N. N. (2019). Public service delivery in South Africa: The political influence at local government level. *Journal of Public Affairs*, 19(4), e1935. 10.1002/pa.1935

Masuku, M. M., Jili, N. N., & Selepe, B. M. (2015). The implementation of Local Economic Development initiatives towards poverty alleviation in Big 5 False Bay Local Municipality. *African Journal of Hospitality, Tourism and Leisure*, 5(4), •••.

Matasi, A. N. (2021). *" Not a Good Time": Economic Impact of COVID-19 in Africa* (*Vol. 17*, No. 1). African Development Bank.

Matebesi, S. (2023). Transactional autism: Effect of the engagement practices of protest leaders on community protest in South Africa. In H, Brooks, R, Chikane & S, Mottiar (Eds.). *Johannesburg: Mapungubwe Institute for Strategic Reflection (MISTRA).*

Mathebula, N.E. & Sebola, M.P. (2019). Evaluating the Integrated Development Plan for Service Delivery within the Auspices of the South African Municipalities. *African Renaissance (1744-2532), 16*(4).

Matlhoahela, R. K. (2022). *Public participation in the Integrated Development Planning process at local government sphere in South Africa: a literature study* [Doctoral dissertation, North-West University (South Africa)].

Matloga, S. T., Mahole, E., & Nekhavhambe, M. M. (2024). Challenges of public participation in improving basic service delivery in Vhembe District Municipality, Limpopo, South Africa. *Journal of Local Government Research and Innovation*, 5, 11. 10.4102/jolgri.v5i0.160

Mavee, S. E. A. (2022). The Relevance of Civil Society Participation in Democratic Governance. *Administratio Publica*, 30(3), 171–191.

Mawonde, C. (2021). Citizen participation in decision-making in Zimbabwe: The case of rural district councils. *Journal of Public Administration and Policy Research*, 13(1), 12–25.

May, A. (2010). The withholding of rates in five local municipalities. Good Governance Learning Network (GGLN).

Mazele, O., & Amoah, C. (2022). The causes of poor infrastructure management and maintenance in South African municipalities. *Property Management*, 40(2), 192–206. 10.1108/PM-06-2021-0042

Maziwisa, N. T. (2020). A review of the SA's tourism recovery plans post COVID-19. *Athens Journal of Tourism*, 9(1), 9–18.

Mazzucato, M., Kattel, R., & Ryan-Collins, J. (2020). Challenge-driven innovation policy: Towards a new policy toolkit. *Journal of Industry, Competition and Trade*, 20(2), 421–437. 10.1007/s10842-019-00329-w

Mazzucato, M., Qobo, M., & Kattel, R. (2022). Building state capacities and dynamic capabilities to drive social and economic development: The case of South Africa. In *The Future of the South African Political Economy Post-COVID 19* (pp. 43–74). Springer International Publishing. Midtown Manhattan. New York. 10.1007/978-3-031-10576-0_3

Mbaku, J. M. (2020). *Good and inclusive governance is imperative for Africa's future*. Bookings.

Mbandlwa, Z., Dorasamy, N. & Fagbadebo, O.M. (2020). Leadership challenges in the South African local government system. *Journal of Critical Reviews*.

Mbatha, S. (2022). *Informal Transactions of Low-Income Houses in South Africa: A Case Study of eThekwini Municipality*. [Doctoral Thesis, Habitat International]. V26/ transcript.

Mbazira, C. (2013). Service delivery protests, struggle for rights and the failure of local democracy in South Africa and Uganda: Parallels and divergences. *South African Journal on Human Rights*, 29(2), 251–275. 10.1080/19962126.2013.11865074

Mboneni, A. (2023). *Political instability affects service delivery: an assessment of Dr Beyers Naude Local Municipality from 1994-2017* [Doctoral dissertation, Stellenbosch: Stellenbosch University].

McCarthy, C., van Walbeek, C., & Goldstein, S. (2020). *Estimating the impact of COVID-19 on poverty in South Africa: An analysis using the first five waves of NIDS-CRAM data*. (Stellenbosch Economic Working Papers: WP21/2020).

McGraw, G. S. (2011). MINIMUM CORE: LEGAL CONSTRUCTION AND THE ROLE OF NATIONAL JURISPRUDENCE. *Loyola University Chicago International Law Review*, 8(2), 127–204.

McKay, T. (2020). South Africa's key urban transport challenges. In A. Gunter & R. Massey (Eds.), (pp. 189–207). *Urban Geography in South Africa - Perspectives and Theory*. Research Gate.

McKenzie, M. & Marx, B. (2024). Turnaround for municipal distress resolution: An audit outcomes approach. *South African Journal of Accounting Research*.

Mehlape, M. M. (2022). *Community participation in the Integrated Development Planning processes as a means of improving local governance: a case of Polokwane Municipality* [Doctoral dissertation].

Menon, A. (2015). *Bicycling innovations. [online]. SAICA and professional news – young member's page*. Koleko. http://www.koleko.co.za/wp-content/uploads/2015/10/2015-Jan-Bicycling-Innovations.pdf

Meyer, D. F., & Venter, A. (2014). An analysis of the effectiveness of the Local Government Turnaround Strategy (LGTAS): The case of the Fezile Dabi District Municipality, *South Africa. African Journal of Public Affairs*, 7(1), 80–93.

Michels, A. (2011). Innovations in democratic governance: How does citizen participation contribute to a better democracy? *International Review of Administrative Sciences*, 77(2), 275–293. 10.1177/0020852311399851

Miggels, A., & Rulashe, T. (2022). Organisational Change as a Tool for Transforming Governance in a Local Municipality, Nelson Mandela Bay Municipality in the Eastern Cape. *Journal of Public Administration.*, 57, 508–528.

Miller, G. (2020). Mitigating the wider health effects of covid-19 pandemic response. *BMJ (Clinical Research Ed.)*, 369.32341002

Miraftab, F., & Kudva, H. (2015). *"Participation" Cities of the Global South: Reader*. London & New York: Routledge.

Mirosa, O., & Harris, L. M. (2012). Human right to water: Contemporary challenges and contours of a global debate. *Antipode*, 44(3), 932–949. 10.1111/j.1467-8330.2011.00929.x

Misi, J. (2014). *Donor Funding and Sustainable Rural Development and its Challenges in Zimbabwe; A Case Study of Mudzi District: 2000-2012*. Semantic Scholar.

Miyandazi, V. (2023). Human Rights and Equality Commissions in Kenya and their role in tackling poverty and economic inequality. *Federal Law Review*, 51(4), 422–441. 10.1177/0067205X231212026

Mkhize, E. M. (2020). Economic impact of COVID-19 pandemic on healthcare facilities and systems: International perspectives. *Best Practice & Research. Clinical Anaesthesiology*, 35(3), 293–306.34511220

Mkhize, M. C., Makau, K. L., & Madumi, P. (2020). *Good Governance Under Zuma Administration: Fad or Reality?* Governance and Societal Adaptation in Fragile States.

Mkhize, N., Ngcwabe, C., & Kirsten, J. (2020). The Role of the Industrial Development Corporation in Financing Agribusiness: The Case of South Africa. *Development Southern Africa*, 37(6), 883–898.

Mlambo, D. (2023). Fighting public sector corruption in post-apartheid South Africa: Progress on paper, hurdles on the ground. In *Mbali Conference 2023 Proceedings* (p. 326).

Mlambo, P., & Tshishonga, N. (2018). Operation Sukuma Sakhe (OSS) at Ugu District: Towards Democratizing Participatory Spaces for Decentralized Service Delivery. In G, Szell & D, Chetty (eds,). *Making Popular Participation Real* (pp. 227-241). Berlin & New York; Peter Lang.

Mlambo, D. N. (2019). Governance and service delivery in the public sector: The case of South Africa under Jacob Zuma (2009–2018). *African Renaissance*, 16(3), 207–224. 10.31920/2516-5305/2019/V16n3a11

Mlambo, V. H., Zubane, S. P., & Thusi, X. (2022). Interrogating governance challenges and cadre deployment in South Africa. *Cihan University-Erbil Journal of Humanities and Social Sciences*, 6(1), 11–18. 10.24086/cuejhss.v6n1y2022.pp11-18

Mnguni, E. S. (2022). Pollution of the vaal river system in South Africa: A case study. *WIT Transactions on Ecology and the Environment*, 257. 10.2495/WMEI220021

Modisha, N. J. (2013). *The role of rural-based municipalities to promote socio-economic development: The case of Molemole and Blouberg Municipalities in Limpopo province* [Doctoral dissertation, University of Limpopo].

Moeti, K. (2007). Budget reform and management of public money through budgeting. In Moeti, K. (Ed.), *Public Finance Fundamentals* (pp. 122–133). Juta & Co.

Mofokeng, W. N. (2019). *Assessment of budget allocation and funding of community food security projects in Emfuleni Local Municipality* [Doctoral dissertation, North-West University (South Africa)].

Mofolo, M., Mkuyane, L., & Skade, T. (2014). Actions and behaviours essential for monitoring & evaluation to succeed in South African public service. *Africa's Public Service Delivery & Performance Review*, 2(3), 5–24. 10.4102/apsdpr.v2i3.58

Mojapelo, M., Modiba, M., & Saurombe, N. (2023). Applying Batho Pele principles in South African public archives–Do public programming initiatives count? *Information Development*, 39(2), 357–375. 10.1177/02666669211049382

Mokgopo, T. I. (2017). The decentralised nature of the sphere of local government in South Africa. [JPADA]. *Journal of Public Administration and Development Alternatives*, 2(1), 82–102.

Mokhutso, J., Marumo, P. O., & Motswaledi, T. R. (2023). Ubuntu: An Antidote to Service Delivery Crisis and Political Instability in South Africa. *Journal of Nation-building &. Policy Studies*, 7(2).

Mokoele, N. J. (2022). Fragmented Governance in South African Cities: The Dilemmas of Planning and Management. *African Renaissance*, 19(2), 13–30.

Moloi, T. (2020). Digital Governance in the City of Johannesburg: E-Procurement and Transparency. *Journal of Urban Affairs*, 42(4), 523–541.

Monaco, S. (2008). Neighbourhood Politics in Transition: residents' associations and local government in post-apartheid Cape Town. [Dissertation, Uppsala University].

Mongae, M. (2024). *30 years: Democracy isn't a once-off achievement*. Mail & Guardian.

Monkam, N. F. (2014). Local municipality productive efficiency and its determinants in South Africa. *Development Southern Africa*, 31(2), 275–298. 10.1080/0376835X.2013.875888

Moore, C. (2020). The impact of COVID-19 on small business outcomes and expectations. *Proceedings of the National Academy of Sciences of the United States of America*, 117(30), 17656–17666. 10.1073/pnas.200699111732651281

Morato, L. C. (2022). Opportunities and Challenges of Municipal Planning in Shaping Vertical Neighbourhoods in Greater London. *Urban Planning*, 7(4). 10.17645/up.v7i4.5757

Moriarty, P., Smits, S., Butterworth, J., & Franceys, R. (2013). Trends in rural water supply: Towards a service delivery approach. *Water Alternatives*, 6(3), 329.

Motshabi, P. T. 2023. *Exploring bulk water services delivery challenges in the Dr. Ruth Segomotsi Mompati district municipality in the North West Province* [Doctoral dissertation, North-West University (South Africa)].

Moyo, P., & Ncube, C. (2014). Devolution of power in Zimbabwe's new constitutional order: Opportunities and potential constraints. *Journal of Public Administration*, 49(1), 1–14. http://www.scielo.org.za/scielo.php?script=sci_arttext&pid=S2077-49072014000100014

Moyo, S., Mhlanga, N., & Mavhura, E. (2019). Decentralisation and development: A case study of rural municipal governments in Zimbabwe. *International Journal of Public Administration and Management Research*, 7(1), 1–12.

Mpofu, N. (2022). *Impact of COVID-19: Nowcasting and big data to track economic activity in Sub-Saharan Africa*. International Monetary Fund.

Mpya, M. I. 2020. *The implementation of the National Development plan and its impact on the Provision of Sustainable Human Settlements: the case of Gauteng Province* [Doctoral dissertation, Doctoral dissertation].

Msemburi, W. T. (2020). *A Subnational Analysis of Burden of Disease in South Africa: Mortality Levels, Causes of Death and Their Forecasts*. University of Washington.

Mubangizi, B. C. (2019). Monitoring and evaluation processes critical to service provision in South Africa's rural-based municipalities. *Journal of Reviews on Global Economics*, 8, 555–565. 10.6000/1929-7092.2019.08.48

Mubangizi, B. C. (2022). The Interplay between Civil Society and Local Government in South Africa: Conflict and Collaboration in the Delivery of Public Services. *African Journal of Development Studies*, (si1), 39. 10.31920/2634-3649/2022/SIv2a3

Mudege, N. N., & Ansell, N. (2013). Women's representation in rural councils in Zimbabwe: The significance of local government structures. *Journal of International Women's Studies*, 14(2), 202–218.

Mudimu, G.T., Ting, Z., & Nalwimba, N. (2019). *Contested Terrain: Local Governance and Development in Post-Land Reform Zimbabwe*.

Mudzusi, T. N., Munzhedzi, P. H., & Mahole, E. (2024). Governance challenges in the provision of municipal services in the Vhembe District Municipality. *Africa's Public Service Delivery & Performance Review*, 12(1), 10. 10.4102/apsdpr.v12i1.749

Mueller, S., Vatter, A., & Schmid, C. (2016). Self-Interest or Solidarity? *Statistics, Politics, and Policy*, 7(1-2), 3–28. 10.1515/spp-2016-0003

Muiu, M. (2023). *Politics and Government in South Africa*. Routledge, Taylor & Francis Group. 10.4324/9781003377962

Mukoyi, J. (2021). Local Governance as a Creature of the Statute: Decentralization and Local Governance in Zimbabwe. *International Journal of Scientific and Research Publications*, 11(3), 66–72. Advance online publication. 10.29322/IJSRP.11.03.2021.p11109

Mullaly, B. (2007). The new structural social work (3rd ed.). Don Mills, Ontario: Oxford University Press.

Municipality, A. D. (2010). Integrated Development Plan (IDP) [East London: Amathole.]. *RE:view*, 2009–2010.

Munoz, C., & Paget-Seekins, L. (2016). Restructuring public transport through bust rapid transit: An international and interdisciplinary perspective. *Journal of the American Planning Association*, 83(1), 107.

Munungufala, T. (2019). *Overview of the DDM – A Framework for Co-operative Service Delivery*. South African Parliament Research Unit. www.parliament.gov.za

Munwana, P. (2020). *The effectiveness of the Integrated Development Planning (IDP) on service delivery: a case of Kagiso Township in Mogale City Local Municipality*. University of Johannesburg.

Munzhedzi, P.H. and Makwembere, S., 2019. Good governance as a solution to local economic development challenges in South African municipalities. *Journal of Public Administration, 54*(4-1), 659-676.

Munzhedzi, P. H. (2020). Evaluating the efficacy of municipal policy implementation in South Africa: Challenges and prospects. *African Journal of Governance and Development*, 9(1), 89–105.

Munzhedzi, P. H. (2021). An evaluation of the application of the new public management principles in the South African municipalities. *Journal of Public Affairs*, 21(1), e2132. 10.1002/pa.2132

Munzhedzi, P. H. (2022). The top-down approach in intergovernmental relations in South Africa: Challenges and prospects. *Journal of Public Affairs*, 22(2), e2431.

Munzhelele, M., Van Niekerk, A., & Mafongoya, P. (2019). The Fourth Industrial Revolution: Potential Contributions to Sustainable Agriculture in Africa. *Sustainability*, 11(13), 3533.

Mutua, M. W. (2017). The ideology of human rights. In *International Law of Human Rights* (pp. 103–172). Routledge. 10.4324/9781315092492-6

Muzekenyi, M., Nyika, F., & Hoque, M. (2022). Decentralisation of Authority and its Implications for Inclusive Economic Development strategies in South Africa: A critical review. *Journal of Nation-Building and Policy Studies*, 6(3), 47–66. 10.31920/2516-3132/2022/v6n3a3

Mwale, A. O. (2021). The impact of COVID-19 on African economies: An introduction. *African Development Review*, 33(Suppl 1), S1.34149237

Naal, H., El Koussa, M., El Hamouch, M., Hneiny, L., & Saleh, S. (2020). Evaluation of global health capacity building initiatives in low-and middle-income countries: A systematic review. *Journal of Global Health*, 10(2), 020412. 10.7189/jogh.10.02041233110574

Nadeem, O., Hameed, R., & Afzal, M. (2020). Is peri-urban structure plan likely to be a viable approach to manage development in urban peripheries?–Case studies from Punjab, Pakistan. *Pakistan Journal of Engineering and Applied Sciences*.

Nadeem, K., Shahzad, S., Hassan, A., Usman Younus, M., Asad Ali Gillani, S., & Farhan, K. (2023). Municipal solid waste generation and its compositional assessment for efficient and sustainable infrastructure planning in an intermediate city of Pakistan. *Environmental Technology*, 44(21), 3196–3214. Advance online publication. 10.1080/09593330.2022.205437035302920

Naeem, S., Waheed, A., & Khan, M. N. (2020). Drivers and barriers for successful special economic zones (SEZs): Case of SEZs under China Pakistan economic corridor. *Sustainability (Basel)*, 12(11), 4675. 10.3390/su12114675

Naidu, S., & Selier, J. (2019). Rural infrastructure investment and agricultural productivity in South Africa: Evidence from Kwazulu-Natal and Eastern Cape provinces. *Agrekon*, 58(2), 129–147.

Narayan, D. (1995). The contribution of people's participation: Evidence from 121 rural water supply projects. *Environmentally Sustainable Development Occasional Paper Series, 1*(5).

Narayan-Parker, D. (2000). *Voices of the poor: Can anyone hear us?* World Bank Publications.

Nardi, P. M. (2018). *Doing survey research: A guide to quantitative methods*. Routledge. 10.4324/9781315172231

National Development Plan (NDP). (2012). *Vision for 2030: Our future – make it work*. NDP.

National Planning Commission (NPC). (2019). *Our future - make it work National Development Plan*. NPC. (www.gov.za)

National Treasury. (2016). *Division of Revenue Bill*. National Treasury.

National Treasury. (2020). *Estimates of National Expenditure 2020*. National Treasury.

Nawaz, M., & Tahir, Z. (2022). Roles and Responsibilities of Urban Planners to Address the Issues of Built-up areas in Pakistan. *Global Sociological Review*, VII(I), 9–15. 10.31703/gsr.2022(VII-I).02

Nawaz, M., Yousafzai, M. T., Khan, S., Ahmad, W., Salman, M., Han, H., Ariza-Montes, A., & Vega-Muñoz, A. (2021). Assessing the formal and informal waste recycling business processes through a stakeholders lens in Pakistan. *Sustainability (Basel)*, 13(21), 11717. 10.3390/su132111717

Ncetezo, N., & Kirsten, J. F. (2017). Project Management of Irrigation Schemes in South Africa: Lessons from Case Studies in Eastern Cape Province. *Water (Basel)*, 9(3), 205.

Ncube, C. (2020). *Regional Economic Development in The Context of the COVID-19 Pandemic and the Economic Crisis.*

Ndevu, Z. J., & Muller, K. (2018). Operationalising performance management in local government: The use of the balanced scorecard. *SA Journal of Human Resource Management*, 16(1), 1–11. 10.4102/sajhrm.v16i0.977

Ndevu, Z., & Muller, K. (2017). A conceptual framework for improving service delivery at local government in South Africa. *African Journal of Public Affairs*, 9(7), 13–24.

Ndlovu, M., Maramura, T. C., & Enaifoghe, A. (2020). Understanding the moral and ethical leadership challenges in South African public service: The case of the Eastern Cape, Department of Education. *Journal of Nation-Building and Policy Studies*, 4(2), 21. 10.31920/2516-3132/2020/v4n2a2

Ndlovu, S. L., & Mutambara, E. (2023). Manifestations of corruption within the Kwazulu-Natal municipalities: A thorn in the flesh. *Corporate Governance and Organizational Behavior Review*, 7(1), 81–93. 10.22495/cgobrv7i1p8

Ndou, L. L. (2022). *An analysis of a coalition government: a new path in administration and governance at local government level in South Africa* [Doctoral dissertation, North-West University, South Africa].

Ndou, S. D., & Sebola, M. P. (2014). Civil Society in Context of a Legal Temperament: Is the Watchdog a Capable Person? *Mediterranean Journal of Social Sciences*, 5(27), 908–915. 10.5901/mjss.2014.v5n27p908

Nedović-Budić, Z., Crompvoets, J., & Georgiadou, Y. (2011). Spatial data infrastructures in context: North and South. In *Spatial Data Infrastructures in Context*. North and South. 10.1201/b10857

Nefale, M. D. (2018). *An investigation into Citizens' trust in service delivery in Makhado Municipality, Limpopo province, South Africa.* [Unpublished Thesis, University of Limpopo].

Nel, V., & Minnie, S. (2022). Can the district development model deliver development in South African local governments? *Rozwój Regionalny i Polityka Regionalna, 15*(60), 39-53.

Nel, E. (2004). *Evolving Participatory Governance and Developmental Local Government in Post-Apartheid South Africa. Participatory Governance Planning, Conflict Mediation and Public Decision-Making in Civil Society.* Ashgate Publishing Limited.

Nel, E., & Rogerson, C. M. (2016). The contested trajectory of applied local economic development in South Africa. *Local Economy*, 31(1-2), 109–123. 10.1177/0269094215623729

Nelson Mandela Metropolitan Municipality. (2022). *Integrated Development Plan 2022/2023*. Nelson Mandela Metropolitan Municipality.

Netshisaulu, M. S. (2021). *How do Urban cities manage road traffic congestion?* The 6th International Conference on Public Administration and Development Alternatives, Virtual conference.

Neumayr, M., & Meyer, M. (2010). *In search of civicness: an empirical investigation of service delivery, public advocacy, and community building by civil society organizations* (pp. 201-226). Nomos Verlagsgesellschaft mbH & Co. KG.

Ngcamu, B. S. (2019). Exploring service delivery protests in post-apartheid South African municipalities: A literature review. The Journal for Transdisciplinary Research in Southern Africa, 15(1), Nkuna N.W., Nemutanzhela T.L. (2012). Locating the role of service delivery within powers and functions of local government in South Africa. *Journal of Public Administration*, 47(si-1), 355–368.

Ngcinela, S., Mushunje, A., Taruvinga, A., Ngarava, S., & Mutengwa, C. S. (2019). Determinants of genetically modified (GM) maize adoption and the intensity of adoption in OR Tambo District Municipality, Eastern Cape Province, South Africa. *GM Crops and Food: Biotechnology in Agriculture and the Food Chain*, 10(1), 1–11. 10.1080/21645698.2019.158012730913974

Ngcobo, N. N., Idsardi, E. F., & van Rensburg, H. C. J. (2019). Budgetary allocation and expenditure in the Eastern Cape Department of Rural Development and Agrarian Reform. *Suid-Afrikaanse Tydskrif vir Ekonomiese en Bestuurswetenskappe*, 22(1), 1–11.

Ngcwabe, C., & Kirsten, J. (2021). The Role of Public Finance Institutions in Supporting Emerging Farmers in South Africa: The Case of Eastern Cape Development Corporation. *Agrekon*, 60(3), 342–358.

Ngcwabe, C., & Masuku, M. B. (2020). Challenges of Local Economic Development in South Africa: Perspectives from Eastern Cape Province. *Africa's Public Service Delivery & Performance Review*, 8(1), 1–15.

Ngqwala, N. S. (2019). *Leadership imperatives for local government service delivery: case of a selected local municipality inthe Eastern Cape, South Africa* [Doctoral dissertation, Cape Peninsula University of Technology].

Ngumbela, X. G. (2021). Troubled municipalities, municipality troubles: An implementation of Back to Basics programme in the Eastern Cape province, South Africa. *Africa's Public Service Delivery & Performance Review*, 9(1), 8. 10.4102/apsdpr.v9i1.405

Nijkamp, P., & Pepping, G. C. (2003). Integrated land use and transport modelling: Decision chains and hierarchies. In *Integration of land use and transport* (pp. 3–12). Springer.

Norris, P., & Nai, A. (Eds.). *Election watchdogs: transparency, accountability and integrity.* Electoral Integrity Project. https://www.electoralintegrityproject.com/election-watchdogs

Nsingo, S. (2006). Assessing the performance of public sector institutions in Zimbabwe: a case study approach.

Ntliziywana, P. (2019). Professionalization of Local Government Management in South Africa. In C, Chigwata, J, De Visser & L, Kaywood (Eds.). *The Journey to Transform Local Government.* Cape Town: Juta @ Co. Ltd.

Nussbaum, M. C. (2011). *Creating Capabilities: The Human Development Approach.* Belknap Press. 10.4159/harvard.9780674061200

Nyakurukwa, K., & Seetharam, Y. (2022). *Corporate governance in a weak legal environment: a systematic review focusing on Zimbabwe.* Qualitative Research in Financial Markets.

Nyawo, J. C., & Mubangizi, B. C. (2021). An exploration of government administrative processes in supporting agro-smallholders' access to municipal markets in eThekwini Municipality, KwaZulu-Natal Province. *Africa's Public Service Delivery & Performance Review*, 9(1), 12. 10.4102/apsdpr.v9i1.528

Nyembezi, N. (2024). 30 years on, unity in diversity is in trouble. *The Mercury*, 6.

Nyikadzino, M. (2019). Zimbabwe's transition to a devolved system of government: Critical factors for success. *Africa's Public Service Delivery & Performance Review, 7*(3), 154-173. https://journals.co.za/doi/abs/10.4102/apsdpr.v10i1.604

Nyikadzino, T., & Vyas-Doorgapersad, S. (2022). Zimbabwe's transition to a devolved system of government: Critical factors for success. *Africa's Public Service Delivery and Performance Review*, 10(1), a604. 10.4102/apsdpr.v10i1.604

Nyoni, V. G. (2017). *An investigation on the role played by Local Authorities in service delivery: A case of Kadoma City Council.* [Unpublished Thesis, Midlands State University].

O'Neill, O. (2006). Transparency and the Ethics of Communication. *Ratio Juris*, 19(2), 173–193.

October, L. (2018). *Ward Councillors are key players.* Mail & Guardian.

Odaro, E. D. (2012). 'Causes of Poor Service Delivery in Africa and Their Impact on Development'. Consilience. *Journal of Sustainable Development*, 7(1), 34–45.

Odum, E. P. (1983). *Systems Ecology: An Introduction.* John Wiley & Sons.

OECD. (1996). *The Knowledge-Based Economy.* Organisation for Economic Cooperation and Development.

OECD. (2010). *OECD Rural Policy Reviews.* OECD. 10.1787/9789264082151-

OECD. (2023). *Multi-level governance tools: Enabling sound regional governance.* OECD. https://www.oecd-ilibrary.org/sites/df3fa2fe-en/index.html?itemId=%2Fcontent%2Fcomponent%2Fdf3fa2fe-en# 3310.1007/s11115-019-00452-6

Ogunlela, O.G., Ojugbele, O.H., & Tengeh, R.K. (2021). Blockchain technology as a panacea for procurement corruption in digital era. *International Journal Research Business Social Science, 10*(4).

Ojo, M. O. (2012). Rural-urban migration: A livelihood pathway for the poor: A case study of migration from Amakohia in Imo State, Nigeria to Owerri. *Journal of Sustainable Development in Africa*, 14(4), 238–256.

Olowu, D., & Wunsch, J. S. (2004). *Local Governance in Africa: The Challenges of Democratic Decentralisation*. Lynne Rienner Publishers.

Onyalo, P. O. (2021). The Decentralised Governance in Kenya: Implications on Citizen Participation in Local Governance. *European Journal of Behavioral Sciences*, 4(4), 22–39. 10.33422/ejbs.v4i4.692

Orlando, L. (2020). Ancient genomes reveal unexpected horse domestication and management dynamics. *BioEssays*, 42(1), 1–8. 10.1002/bies.20190016431808562

Ouwencamp, S. (2023). *Fostering public participation in integrated development planning: the case of the City of Matlosana* [Doctoral dissertation, North-West University (South Africa)].

Padayachee, V., & Van Niekerk, R. (2019). *Shadow of Liberation: contestation and compromise in the economic and social policy of the African National Congress, 1943-1996*. Wits University Press.

Paderewski, D., Levitsky, S., & Yashar, D. J. (2021). Inequality, democracy, and the inclusionary turn in Latin America. *The inclusionary turn in Latin American democracies*, 1-56.

Page, M.J., Moher, D., Bossuyt, P.M., Boutron, I., Hoffmann, T.C., Mulrow, C.D., Shamseer, L., Tetzlaff, J.M., Akl, E.A., Brennan, S.E. & Chou, R. (2021). PRISMA 2020 explanation and elaboration: updated guidance and exemplars for reporting systematic reviews. *BMJ, 372*.

Pandeya, G. P. (2015). Does citizen participation in local government decision-making contribute to strengthening local planning and accountability systems? An empirical assessment of stakeholders' perceptions in Nepal. *International Public Management Review*, 16(1), 67–98.

Paradis, E., Nimmon, L., Wondimagegn, D., & Whitehead, C. R. (2020). Critical theory: Broadening our thinking to explore the structural factors at play in health professions education. *Academic Medicine*, 95(6), 842–845. 10.1097/ACM.000000000000310831809292

Pateman, C. (1970). *Participation and Democratic Theory*. Cambridge University Press. 10.1017/CBO9780511720444

Patience, J. J., & Nel, D. (2022). Governance, democracy and accountability from a network governance perspective within the city of Ekurhuleni'. *Africa's Public Service Delivery and Performance Review*, 10(1), a554. 10.4102/apsdpr.v10i1.554

Pekkola, S., Ylinen, M. and Mavengere, N. (2022). Consortium of Municipalities Co-tailoring a Governmental e-Service Platform: What could go wrong? *Digital Government: Research and Practice, 3*(6) 1–16. 10.1145/3511889

Peng, Y., Peng, X., Li, X., Lu, M., & Yin, M. (2023). Effectiveness in Rural Governance: Influencing Factors and Driving Pathways—Based on 20 Typical Cases of Rural Governance in China. *Land (Basel)*, 12(7), 1452. 10.3390/land12071452

Peterson, Z. A. (2021). Beyond informed consent. *Bulletin of the World Health Organization*, 82, 771–777.15643799

Phago, K. (2009). An integrated development plan in South African local government: The case of the City of Tshwane Metropolitan Municipality. *Journal of Public Administration*, 44(3), 483–491.

Phillimore, J. (2013). Understanding Intergovernmental Relations: Key Features and Trends. *Australian Journal of Public Administration*, 72(3), 228–238. 10.1111/1467-8500.12025

Phillips, C., & Conteh, C. (2021). *Neighbourhood associations and the municipality: supporting citizen engagement in the city*. (Niagara Community Observatory Working Paper).

Picard, L. A., & Mogale, T. (2015). *The Limits of Democratic Governance in South Africa*. UCT Press.

Pickles, J. (2011). Transparency and Accountability in Local Government. *Local Government Studies*, 37(4), 427–447.

Piesse, J., Gouse, M., & Thirtle, C. (2005). Agricultural technology, productivity and employment: Policies for poverty reduction. *Agrekon*, 44(1), 37–59. 10.1080/03031853.2005.9523702

Pillay, D., & Bass, O. (2015). Addressing government's role in South Africa's development: A capabilities approach. *Development Southern Africa*, 32(1), 47–64.

Pillay, P. (2020). Forensic Investigation into Procurement Fraud in Ekurhuleni Metropolitan Municipality. *South African Journal of Public Administration*, 55(2), 112–130.

Plummer, J. (2021). *Municial and community participation. A source for Capacity building*. Earthsczn.

Poirier, L., Antonio, D., Dettmann, M., Eng, T., Ganata, J., Ghosh, S., Lopez, M., Karma, R., Natekal, A., & Brinkley, C. (2024). Making plans findable, accessible, interoperable, and reusable with data infrastructure: A search engine for constructing, analyzing, and visualizing planning documents. *Environment and Planning. B, Urban Analytics and City Science*, 23998083241227471. 10.1177/23998083241227471

Poniatowicz, M., Dziemianowicz, R., & Kargol-Wasiluk, A. (2020). Good governance and institutional quality of public sector. *Theoretical and empirical implications, 23*(2), 529-556.

Powell, D., May, A., & Ntliziywana, P. (2010). The withholding of rates and taxes in five local municipalities. *Local Government Bulletin*, 12(4), 9–12.

Pretty, J. (1995). Participatory learning for sustainable agriculture. *World Development*, 23(8), 1247–1263. 10.1016/0305-750X(95)00046-F

Prota, F., Viesti, G., & Bux, M. (2020). 10. The Contribution of European Cohesion Policy to Public Investment. *A European Public Investment Outlook*, 175.

Purfield, C. (2016). *Developing an Intergovernmental Fiscal Framework. Making It Happen, 13*. The World Bank.

Putnam, R. D. (1993). *Making Democracy Work: Civic Traditions in Modern Italy*. Princeton University Press.

Radin, B. A. (1992). Rural Development Councils: An Intergovernmental Coordination Experiment. *Publius*, 22(3), 111–127. https://www.jstor.org/stable/3330255

Raftopoulos, B., & Mhute, E. (2009). The Politics of Local Government in Zimbabwe. In Raftopoulos, B., & Muzondidya, A. (Eds.), *Reflections on Zimbabwe's Liberation War: Politics, economics and society* (pp. 243–268). Weaver Press.

Raihan, A. (2024). A Systematic Review of Geographic Information Systems (GIS) in Agriculture for Evidence-Based Decision Making and Sustainability. *Global Sustainability Research*, 3(1), 1–24. Advance online publication. 10.56556/gssr.v3i1.636

Rajabifard, A., Binns, A., Masser, I., & Williamson, I. (2006). The role of sub-national government and the private sector in future spatial data infrastructures. *International Journal of Geographical Information Science*, 20(7), 727–741. 10.1080/13658810500432224

Rajabifard, A., Feeney, M. E. F., & Williamson, I. P. (2002). Future directions for SDI development. *International Journal of Applied Earth Observation and Geoinformation*, 4(1), 11–22. 10.1016/S0303-2434(02)00002-8

Ramodula, T. M., & Govender, K. K. (2021). Developmental local government: A framework for implementation. *Africa Journal of Public Sector Development and Governance*, 4(1), 45–72. 10.55390/ajpsdg.2021.4.1.3

Rana, I. A., & Bhatti, S. S. (2018). Lahore, Pakistan – Urbanization challenges and opportunities. *Cities (London, England)*, 72, 348–355. 10.1016/j.cities.2017.09.014

Randolph, R. (2019). Regional development policies and the challenge to reduce spatial inequalities in Brazil. *Area Development and Policy*, 4(3), 271–283. 10.1080/23792949.2019.1570824

Rawat, F., & Dobie, K. (2021). *The local government Ethics Committee Guidebook*. The Ethics Institute, Canada.

Rayan, M., Gruehn, D., & Khayyam, U. (2021). Green infrastructure indicators to plan resilient urban settlements in Pakistan: Local stakeholder's perspective. *Urban Climate*, 38, 100899. 10.1016/j.uclim.2021.100899

Reddy, P. S. (2016). The politics of service delivery in South Africa: The local government sphere in context. *TD: The Journal for Transdisciplinary Research in Southern Africa*, 12(1), 1–8. 10.4102/td.v12i1.337

Reddy, P. S., Sing, D., & Moodley, S. (2003). *Local Government Financing and Development in Southern Africa*. Oxford University Press.

Reinar, M. B., & Lundberg, A. K. (2023). Goals à la carte: Selective translation of the Sustainable Development Goals in strategic municipal planning in Norway. *Journal of Environmental Planning and Management*, 1–17. 10.1080/09640568.2023.2191816

Republic of South Africa (RSA). (1998). *White Paper on Local Government*. RSA.

Republic of South Africa. (1996). *Constitution of the Republic of South Africa, 1996*. Government Printers.

Republic of South Africa. (1996). *Constitution of the Republic of South, 1996*. Government Printer.

Republic of South Africa. (1998). *Local Government: Municipal Structures Act, 1998 (Act No. 117 of 1998)*. Government Printers.

Republic of South Africa. (1998). *White Paper on Local Government (Notice 423 of 1998)*. Pretoria: Government Printers.

Republic of South Africa. (1998). *White Paper on Local Government*. Pretoria: Government Printers.

Republic of South Africa. (2000). *Local Government: Municipal Systems Act, (Act 32 of 2000)*. Government Printer.

Republic of South Africa. (2000). *Local Government: Municipal Systems Act, 2000 (Act No. 32 of 2000)*. Government Printers.

Republic of South Africa. (2003). *Local Government: Municipal Finance Management Act, (Act 56 of 2003)*. Government Printer.

Republic of South Africa. (2003). *Municipal Finance Management Act, 2001 (Act No. 56 of 2003)*. Government Printers.

Republic of South Africa. (2004). *Local Government: Municipal Property Rates Act, (Act 6 of 2004)*. Government Printer.

Republic of South Africa. (2005). *Intergovernmental Relations Framework Act, 2005 (Act No. 13 of 2005)*. Government Printers.

Republic of South Africa. (2007). *Growth and Development Summit Report*. Pretoria, South Africa.

Ribot, J. C. (2004). *Rural Governance and Decentralization: Evidence from Southeast Asia*. Agricultural Decentralization & Rural Institutions.

Rice, L. (2022). Against climate apartheid: Confronting the persistent legacies of expendability for climate justice. *Environment and Planning. E, Nature and Space*, 5(2), 625–645. 10.1177/2514848621999286

Richards, N. (2023). *Veil of secrecy' lifted: vaal NPO has court order against Emfuleni municipality*. EWN. https://ewn.co.za/2023/06/29/veil-of-secrecy-lifted-vaal-npo-has-court-order-against-emfuleni-municipality

Rizwan, H., & Obaidullah, N. (2006). Challenges of Implementing Urban Master Plans: The Lahore Experience. *World Academy of Science, 24: 101, 108.*

Robbins, G. (2012). *Public Participation in Municipal Budgeting*. UKZN.

Robert, L. (2022). *"Direct Democracy: Definition, Examples, Pros and Cons." ThoughtCo, Feb. 2, 2022. Accessed from* [thoughtco.com/what-is-direct-democracy-3322038.]. Accessed on. [19 April 2024]

Roberts, G. (2022). Policy responses to the COVID-19 pandemic. *International Journal of Environmental Research and Public Health*, 18(2), 559.33440841

Roberts, K., Dowell, A., & Nie, J. B. (2019). Attempting rigour and replicability in thematic analysis of qualitative research data; a case study of codebook development. *BMC Medical Research Methodology*, 19(1), 1–8. 10.1186/s12874-019-0707-y30922220

Rodriguez, D. (2019). *Intelligent Transport Systems: Technologies and Applications*. Springer.

Rodrik, D. (1998). *Trade Policy and Economic Performance in Sub-Saharan Africa*. (NBER Working Paper Series No. 6562). National Bureau of Economic Research, Massachussets.

Rogerson, C. M. (2012). Local economic development in South Africa: The role of municipalities. *Development Southern Africa*, 29(2), 190–204.

Rogerson, C. M. (2014). Reframing place-based economic development in South Africa: The example of local economic development. *Bulletin of Geography. Socio-Economic Series*, 24(24), 203–218. 10.2478/bog-2014-0023

Rogerson, C. M. (2018). Pro-poor local economic development in South Africa: the application of public procurement. In *Local economic development in the developing world* (pp. 101–130). Routledge.

Rogerson, C. M. (2018). Towards pro-poor local economic development: the case for sectoral targeting in South Africa. In *Local Economic Development in the Changing World* (pp. 75–100). Routledge.

Roser, M. (2016). *'World Poverty'. Published online at OurWorldInData.org*. Retrieved.

Rousseau, J.J. (1998). *The Social Contract. Hertfordshire SG12 9HJ: Words Editions.*

Rulashe, T. (2022). 'A luta continua', will it ever end? The reality of local government in South Africa. *Journal of Local Government Research and Innovation*, 3. 10.4102/jolgri.v3i0.97

Rulashe, T., & Dyan, M. (2023). A Critical Review of the Municipal Public Accounts Committee and Financial Management at Amahlathi Municipality, South Africa. *Journal of Public Administration Studies*, 8(1), 56–65. 10.21776/ub.jpas.2023.008.01.7

Rulashe, T., & Ijeoma, E. O. (2022). An exploration of public accountability and service delivery at the Buffalo City Metropolitan Municipality in the Eastern Cape province, South Africa. *Africa's Public Service Delivery and Performance Review*, 10(1), 535. 10.4102/apsdpr.v10i1.535

Ryan, C. (2021). *The revolt of the ratepayers.* MoneyWeb. https://www.moneyweb.co.za/news/south-africa/the-revolt-of-the-ratepayers/

Sabi, S. C. (2013). The role of civil society in policy advocacy: A case study of the Treatment Action Campaign and health policy in South Africa [Doctoral dissertation,. University of KwaZulu-Natal (UKZN)].

Safwan, M. (2020). *Building healthy cities in the global south: A case study of the City of Lahore.* University of Waterloo.

Sanders, A. (2018). *Different types of assessment and what you need to know about them.* Edulastic.

Santos, F., Tanscheit, T., & Ventura, T. (2020). The Workers' Party and Participatory institutions: The influence of intra-party dynamics in the adoption of Participatory budgeting. *Dados*, 63, e20180152. 10.1590/dados.2020.63.3.202

Sape, J. T. (2019). *The efficacy of the Emfuleni local municipality procurement system* [Doctoral dissertation, North-West University, South Africa].

Sasseville, D. N. (1988). *Harvesting and handling produce: Plan now for high quality.* Guide.

Satuku, S. (2020). *What is a residents association?* Repobackend. https://repobackend.zimcitizenswatch.org/uploads/What_is_a_Resident_Association_156284d880.pdf

Saul, T. F., Shopola, M. A., & Mlambo, V. H. (2023). Human Resource Management System as Enabling Tool for Good Governance in South Africa's Local Government Sector. *IAHRW International Journal of Social Sciences Review*, 11(4), 514–520.

Saunders, M., Lewis, P., & Thornhill, A. (2019). *Research methods for business students.* Pearson.

Sausi, K., Kanyane, M., Gumede, N., Mchunu, N., Davids, D., Zondi, T., Houston, G., Ngqwala, N., Bohler-Muller, N., & Cosser, M. (2023). Implementation of the DDM in South Africa.https://repository.hsrc.ac.za/bitstream/handle/20.500.11910/20128/9812719

Sausi, K., Kanyane, M., Davids, Y. D., Gumede, N., Houston, G., Mchunu, N., & Bohler-Muller, N. (2022). *Evaluating the District Development Model: a review, with case studies. Developmental, capable & ethical state research division human sciences research council.* Human Sciences Research Council.

Savage, A., Brune, S., Hovis, M., Spenser, S. E., Dinan, M., & Seekamp, E. (2023). *Working Together: A Guide to Collaboration in Rural Revitalization.* North Carolina State University. https://content.ces.ncsu.edu/show_ep3_pdf/1710596944/24402/

Save the Vaal Environment. (2020). *The aim of save the Vaal environment.* Save the Vaal Environment. https://www.save.org.za/about-us/

Scheba, S. (2022). Viewpoint–The South African Water Sector: Municipal Dysfunction, Resistance and Future Pathways. *Water Alternatives*, 15(3), 632–649.

Schiller, P. L., & Kenworthy, J. (2017). *An introduction to sustainable transportation: Policy, planning and implementation*. Routledge. 10.4324/9781315644486

Schmitter, P. C. (2004). Decentralization and the future of democracy. *Studies in Comparative International Development*, 39(1), 14–31.

Schnabel, J., & Hegele, Y. (2021, June 15). Explaining Intergovernmental Coordination during the COVID-19 Pandemic: Responses in Australia, Canada, Germany, and Switzerland. *Publius*, 51(4), pjab011. 10.1093/publius/pjab011

Schoeman, I., & Chakwizira, J. (2023). Advancing a performance management tool for service delivery in local government. *Administrative Sciences*, 13(2), 31. 10.3390/admsci13020031

Schutte, A. R. (2020). COVID-19: Rethinking the lockdown groupthink. *Frontiers in Public Health*, 9, 625778.33718322

Schwella, E. (2017). *South African Governance*. Oxford University Press Southern Africa. RSA.

Scoones, I. (1998). *Sustainable rural livelihoods: A framework for analysis*. (IDS Working Paper, 72).

Scoones, I. (2009). Livelihoods perspectives and rural development. *The Journal of Peasant Studies*, 36(1), 171–196. 10.1080/03066150902820503

Scoones, I. (2010). *Zimbabwe's land reform: Myths and realities*. James Currey.

Scorcia, H., & And Munoz-Raskin, R. (2019). Why South African cities are different? Comparing Johannesburg's Rea Vaya bus rapid transit system with its Latin American siblings. *Case Studies on Transport Policy*, 7(2), 395–403. 10.1016/j.cstp.2019.01.010

Scudder, M. F. (2020). The ideal of uptake in democratic deliberation. *Political Studies*, 68(2), 504–522. 10.1177/0032321719858270

Sebake, B. K. (2020). Crime against humanity: Social perception of public service corruption in South Africa. *African Journal of Development Studies*, 10(3), 167.

Sebake, B. K., & Mukonza, R. M. (2020). Integrated Development Plan, Monitoring and Evaluation in the City of Tshwane: A confluence question for optimising service delivery. *Journal of Public Administration*, 55(3), 342–352.

Sebola, M. P. (2021). Monitoring for good governance in south africa: The complex of a fair public administration. *Acta Universitatis Danubius.Administratio*, 13(1), 39–55.

Sebopetsa, M. A., & Odeku, K. O. (2021). Safeguarding the Right to Protest and Prohibition of Violent Protests in South Africa: Issues and Perspectives. *African Journal of Peace and Conflict Studies*, 10(2), 45. 10.31920/2634-3665/2021/v10n2a3

Seekings, J., & Nattrass, N. (2015). *Policy, politics and poverty in South Africa*. New Africa Books. 10.1057/9781137452696

Seligson, M. A., & Passe-Smith, J. J. (1998). *Development and Underdevelopment: The political economy of global inequality*. Lynne Rienner publishers.

Sen, A. (1999). *Development as freedom*. Oxford University Press.

Sethu, M. J. (2021). *The role of performance, monitoring and evaluation within municipal service delivery: A case study of Capricorn District Municipality, Limpopo Province* [Doctoral dissertation].

Sharon, C., Faitira, M., & Zororo, M. (2023). *Local Authorities' Performance in Zimbabwe Systematic Review of Related Literature*. International Journal of Research in Commerce and Management Studies., 10.38193/IJRCMS.2023.5204

Shaukat, N., Ullah, Z., Khan, B., Ali, S. M., & Waseem, A. (2019). An Information-Based Waste Management Approach for Pakistan. *1st International Conference on Electrical, Communication and Computer Engineering, ICECCE 2019*. IEEE. 10.1109/ICECCE47252.2019.8940796

Shongwe, B. R., & Meyer, D. F. (2023). Service Delivery Challenges within Rural Communities. The Case of the Nkomazi Local Municipal Area. *Administratio Publica, 31*(4). https://journals.co.za/doi/abs/10.10520/ejc-adminpub_v31_n2_a8

Shongwe, B. R., & Meyer, D. F. (2023). Service Delivery Challenges within Rural Communities. The Case of the Nkomazi Local Municipal Area. Johannesburg. University of Johannesburg, School of Public Management, Governance and Public Policy.

Shopola, A.M., 2022. Management of District-Local Relations through the District Intergovernmental Forum in Mopani District Municipality, South Africa. *African Journal of Governance & Development, 11*(1.1), 25-46.

Sibanda, M. M. (2017). Control, ethics, and accountability in the financial management performance of Eastern Cape municipalities. *Journal of Public Administration*, 52(2), 313–339.

Sibanda, M. M., Zindi, B., & Maramura, T. C. (2020). Control and accountability in supply chain management: Evidence from a South African metropolitan municipality. *Cogent Business & Management*, 7(1), 1785105. 10.1080/23311975.2020.1785105

Siddle, A., & Koelble, T. A. (2012). *The Failure of Decentralisation in South African Local Government: complexity and unanticipated consequences*. UCT Press. 10.58331/UCTPRESS.51

Sikhosana, N. (2022). *Outcomes-based participatory gender planning and budgeting in South African local government context: a case of selected municipalities in the Eastern Cape Province*.

Simbi, T. (1998). *Agricultural policy in South Africa*. NDA. http://www.nda.agric.za/docs/policy98.htm. Accessed on 16 /05/2012

Simões, V. (2014). *An evaluation of the inclusion of principles of corridor development, transit-oriented development and non-motorised transportation within Johannesburg's Corridors of Freedom: the case of Turffontein Corridor*. Wired Space. http://wiredspace.wits.ac.za/xmlui/bitstream/handle/10539/20470/Final%20Research%20Report_Vanessa%20Simoes.pdf?sequence=1&isAllowed=y

Singh, K. (2023). *Durban revolts: Civic groups launch eThekwini rates boycott in what the city calls a 'mob mentality'*. News24. https://www.news24.com/news24/southafrica/news/durban-revolts-civic-groups-launch-ethekwini-rates-boycott-in-what-the-city-calls-a-mob-mentality-20230802

Sintomer, Y., Herzberg, C., & Rocke, A. (2008). Participatory Budgeting in Europe: Potential and Challenges. *International Journal of Urban and Regional Research*, 32(1), 164–178. 10.1111/j.1468-2427.2008.00777.x

Sithole, S. L., & Mathonsi, N. S. (2015). Local governance service delivery issues during apartheid and post-Apartheid South Africa. *Africa's Public Service Delivery & Performance Review*, 3(3), 5–30. 10.4102/apsdpr.v3i3.87

Slater, D. (2021). DDM to improve planning, implementation as South Africa Embarks on economic recovery: African News. https://www.polity.org.za/article/district-development-model

Smith, B. (2020). Participatory Budgeting in eThekwini Municipality: Enhancing Community Engagement and Transparency. *Commonwealth Journal of Local Governance*, 23(1), 58–72.

Smith, I. J. (2021). Cross-country comparisons of COVID-19: Policy, politics, and the price of life. *Environmental and Resource Economics*, 76, 525–551.32836862

Smith, J., Buse, K., & Gordon, C. (2016). Civil society: The catalyst for ensuring health in the age of sustainable development. *Globalization and Health*, 12(1), 1–6. 10.1186/s12992-016-0178-427424031

Smoke, P. (2015). Accountability and service delivery in decentralising environments: Understanding context and strategically advancing reform. *A Governance Practitioner's Notebook: Alternative Ideas and Approaches*. OECD.

Smoke, P., & Lewis, B. D. (1996). *Fiscal Decentralization in Developing Countries: Issues, Challenges, and the Search for Solutions*. Urban Institute Press.

Soto, J. J., Orozco-Fontalvo, M., & Useche, S. A. (2022). Public transportation and fear of crime at BRT Systems: Approaching to the case of Barranquilla (Colombia) through integrated choice and latent variable models. *Transportation Research Part A, Policy and Practice*, 155, 142–160. 10.1016/j.tra.2021.11.001

South Africa Republic. (1996). *The Constitution of the Republic of South Africa*. Government Printers.

South Africa Republic. (2014). *Department of Transport Roads Infrastructure Policy: Policy framework*. Government printers.

South African Broadcasting Authority Digital News. (2021). *Kgetlengrivier Municipality take back charge of sewage and water plants*. SABC News. https://www.sabcnews.com/sabcnews/kgetlengrivier-municipality-take-back-charge-of-sewage-and-water-plants/

South African Government. (2020). *Economic Transformation and Inclusive Growth*. South African Government.

Souza, C. (2001). Participatory budgeting in Brazilian Cities: Limits and Possibilities in building democratic institutions. *Environment and Urbanization*, 13(1), 159–184. 10.1177/095624780101300112

Special Economic Zones (SEZs). (2019). *SEZ Annual Performance Report 2019*. Government of South Africa.

Special Investigating Unit (SIU). (2022). *Two former Ekurhuleni officials, businessman jailed for tender fraud, money laundering, and corruption*. SIU. https://www.siu.org.za/two-former-ekurhuleni-officials-businessman-jailed-for-tender-fraud-money-laundering-and-corruption/

*State of Nation Address*. (2024). South African Government. https://www.gov.za/SONA2024#

*State of the Nation Address*. (2019). South African Government. https://www.stateofthenation.gov.za/

*State of the Nation Address*. (2023). South African Government. https://www.stateofthenation.gov.za/

Statistics South Africa (Stats SA). (2020). *Poverty trends in South Africa: An examination of absolute poverty between 2006 and 2015*. Statistics South Africa.

Statistics South Africa. (2022). https://www.statssa.gov.za/wp-content/uploads/

Stephen, S., Charron, N., & Justesen, M. K. (2023). Electoral competition, political parties and clientelism: Evidence from local elections in South Africa. *Democratization*, 30(3), 479–500. 10.1080/13510347.2022.2155143

Steyn Kotze, J., Davids, Y. D., Fokou, G., & Sanchez Betancourt, D. (2020). *Spoils politics: the case of Nelson Mandela Bay: case study report*.

Such, E., Smith, K., Woods, H. B., & Meier, P. (2022). Governance of Intersectoral Collaborations for Population Health and to Reduce Health Inequalities in High-Income Countries: A Complexity-Informed Systematic Review. *International Journal of Health Policy and Management*, 11, 2780–2792. 10.34172/ijhpm.2022.655035219286

Sullivan, L. (2019). Conservation in context: Toward a systems framing of decentralised governance and public participation in wildlife management. *The Review of Policy Research*, 36(2), 242–261. 10.1111/ropr.12326

Suryanto, S., & Asri, A. R. F. (2020). Analysis of Money Market Mutual Fund Performance and Its Influencing Factors. *Journal of Finance and Banking Studies*, 10(1), 1–16.

Sutrisno, P. (2023). Literature review: Risk Mitigation and Rescue Procedures in the People's Credit System Literature Review: Mitigasi Resiko Dan Prosedur. *COSTING: Journal of Economic, Business and Accounting, 6*(2).

Swanepoel, H., Cloete, P., van Niekerk, J., & van Rooyen, J. (2016). Rural development challenges in the Eastern Cape Province, South Africa: Sustainable livelihoods in the face of social and environmental crises. *Agrekon*, 55(1-2), 104–125.

Syvrud, A., Pohlner, H., Punthakey, J. F., Grant, M., & Green, T. (2021). Advancing urban water security in the indus basin, pakistan—Priority actions for karachi and lahore. *Water (Basel)*, 13(23), 3399. 10.3390/w13233399

Tapscott, C. (2008). The challenges of deepening democracy in post-apartheid South Africa. In *Foundations for local governance: Decentralization in comparative perspective* (pp. 213–231). Physica-Verlag HD. 10.1007/978-3-7908-2006-5_10

Taruvinga, A., Kambanje, A., Mushunje, A., & Mukarumbwa, P. (2022). Determinants of livestock species ownership at household level: Evidence from rural OR Tambo District Municipality, South Africa. *Pastoralism*, 12(1), 8. 10.1186/s13570-021-00220-6

Tasci, A. D. A., Wei, W., & Milman, A. (2020). Uses and misuses of the case study method. *Annals of Tourism Research*, 82, 102815. 10.1016/j.annals.2019.102815

Tata Sustainability Group. (2018). *Social capital – an eclectic literature survey*. Aequitas Consulting Pvt. Ltd.

Thabethe, L. R. 2023. *The efficacy of integrated development plan implementation towards the enhancement of basic service delivery: case of Mpakeni Village, Mbombela Local Municipality, South Africa* [Doctoral dissertation].

Thirtle, C., Lin, L., & Piesse, J. (2003). The impact of research-led agricultural productivity growth on poverty reduction in Africa, Asia and Latin America. *World Development*, 31(12), 1959–1976. 10.1016/j.worlddev.2003.07.001

Thomas, D. P. (2016). Public Transportation in South Africa: Challenges and Opportunities. *World Journal of Social Science Research, 3*(3).

Thompson, L., & Nleya, N. (2010). Passivity or protest? Understanding the dimensions of mobilisation on rights to services in Khayelitsha, Cape Town. In Coelho, V. S. P., & Von Lieres, B. (Eds.), *Mobilising for Democracy: Citizen Action and the Political of Public Participation (pp* (pp. 223–242). Zed Books. 10.5040/9781350221413.ch-011

Thusi, X., & Mashabela, M. (2023). The role of civil society organisations in promoting public accountability: The perspective of the South African local government. *IAHRW International Journal of Social Sciences Review*, 11(2), 175–180.

Thusi, X., & Mashabela, M. (2023). The role of civil society organizations in promoting public accountability: The perspective of the South African local government. *IAHRW International Journal of Social Sciences Review*, 11(2), 175–180.

Thusi, X., & Selepe, M. M. (2023). The impact of poor governance on public service delivery: A case study of the South African local government. *International Journal of Social Science Research and Review*, 6(4), 688–697.

Thwala, S. 2022. *The role of municipal budget in service delivery for Local Economic Development: the case of Ekurhuleni* [Doctoral dissertation, University of Johannesburg].

Tirivanhu, P. (2022). A framework for facilitating holistic interventions for building community resilience to climate change for sustainable community development. In *Sustainable Rural Development Perspective and Global Challenges*. IntechOpen.

Tobi, A. A., & Oikhala, G. I. (2021). Local government reforms and grassroots development in Nigeria. *The Journal of American Science*, 18(1), 113–133.

Todes, A. (2012). New Directions in Spatial Planning? Linking Strategic Spatial Planning and Infrastructure Development. *Journal of Planning Education and Research*, 32(4), 400–414. 10.1177/0739456X12455665

Torjman, S., & Makhoul, A. (2012). *Community-Led Development*. Caledon Institute of Social Policy.

Tsheola, J. P. (2012). Theorising a democratic developmental state: Issues of public service delivery planning and violent protests in South Africa. *Journal of Public Administration*, 47(1), 161–179.

Tshishonga, N. (2018). The War Room as a Platform for Public Participation: Views from Stakeholders. In Szell, G., & Chetty, D. (Eds.), *Making Popular Participation Real; African and International Experiences*. Peter Lang.

Tshishonga, N. (2019). Prospects and challenges of transforming local government into a learning organisation. *African Journal of Public Affairs*, 11(1), 157–175.

Tshishonga, N. (2019). The Legacy of Apartheid on Democracy and Citizenship in Post-Apartheid South Africa: An Inclusionary and Exclusionary Binary? AFFRIKA: Journal of Politics. *Economics and Society.*, 9(1), 167–191.

Turok, I., & Borel-Saladin, J. (2014). Is urbanisation in South Africa on a sustainable trajectory? *Development Southern Africa*, 31(5), 675–691. 10.1080/0376835X.2014.937524

Ubisi, S. V. (2018). Accountability as one of the basic values and principles governing public administration in South Africa. *International Conference on Public Administration and Development Alternatives (IPADA)*. Research Gate.

UCLG and OECD. (2016). *Zimbabwe Unitary Country*. OECD. https://www.oecd.org/regional/regional-policy/profile-Zimbabwe.pdf

Uddin, N. (2019). Empowerment through participation in local governance: the case of Union Parishad in Bangladesh. *Public Administration and Policy: An Asia-Pacific Journal, 22*(1). https://www.emerald.com/insight/content/doi/10.1108/PAP-10-2018-0002/full/html

ul Hussnain, M. Q., Waheed, A., Wakil, K., Pettit, C. J., Hussain, E., Naeem, M. A., & Anjum, G. A. (2020). Shaping up the future spatial plans for urban areas in Pakistan. *Sustainability (Switzerland), 12*(10). 10.3390/su12104216

Ullah, T., Ullah, S., Khan, N., & Ellahi, M. B. (2023). The Role of Civil Society in Local Governance and Service Delivery: An Analysis of Local Government System of Khyber Pakhtunkhwa. *Journal of Policy Research*, 9(2), 540–547.

UN - United Nations. (2016). *Mobilizing sustainable transport for development: analysis and policy recommendations from the United Nations Secretary-General's High-Level Advisory Group on sustainable transport.* UN. https://sustainabledevelopment.un.org/content/documents/2375Mobilizing%20Sustainable %20Transport.pdf

United Nations Department of Economic and Social Affairs. (2019). *Principles of Effective Governance for Sustainable Development.* New York: United Nations Department of Economic and Social Affairs.

United Nations Development Programme (UNDP). (2003). *South Africa Human Development Report 2003: the Challenge of Sustainable Development in SouthAfrica-Unlocking People's Creativity*. Oxford University Press.

United Nations Development Programme. (2000). *South Africa: transformation for Human Development, 2000.* UNDP.

US Department of State. (2022*). U.S. Relations With Zimbabwe. Bilateral Relations Fact Sheet, Bureau of African Affairs*. US DoS. https://www.state.gov/u-s-relations-with-zimbabwe/

Van Averbeke, W., Sigwela, A., & Groenewald, J. A. (2017). The Impact of Irrigation Infrastructure on Smallholder Farming Income: Evidence from Rural South Africa. *Water (Basel)*, 9(11), 880.

Van Der Waldt, G. (2020). London Government. In C, Landsberg & S, Graham (Eds.) (5th Eds.) *Government and Politics in South Africa: Coming of Age*. Pretoria: Van Schaik Publishers.

Van Rensburg, M., & Botes, V. (2017). The Political Economy of Corruption in South Africa's Municipalities: The Case of Nelson Mandela Bay Metropolitan Municipality. Alternation. *Interdisciplinary Journal for the Study of the Arts and Humanities in Southern Africa*, 24(1), 133–158.

Venda Building Society (VBS) 101. (2018). *From the masterminds to the mass fraud.* VBS. https://www.news24.com/Fin24/vbs-allegations-unpacked-from-the- masterminds-to-the-mass-fraud-20180717 [Accessed 15 June 2024].

Vendemmia, B., Pucci, P., & Beria, P. (2021). An institutional periphery in discussion. Rethinking the inner areas in Italy. *Applied Geography (Sevenoaks, England)*, 135, 102537. 10.1016/j.apgeog.2021.102537

Venot, E. J. (2017). *Planning local economic development: Theory and practice*. SAGE publications.

Vila Pouca de Aguiar, Portugal (2023). *Good democratic governance as tool to challenge desertification and promote attractivity of rural communities*. Council of Europe. https://www.coe.int/en/web/good-governance/-/good-democratic-governance-as-tool-to-challenge-desertification-and-promote-attractivity-of-rural-communities

Vincent, C. (2015). The Context of Inter-Governmental Relations in Zimbabwe. Reflections from the Constitution of Zimbabwe Amendment Number 20 Of 2013. *IOSR Journal of Humanities and Social Science (IOSR-JHSS), 20*(1), 37-41.

Vincent, C. (2017). *Central-local Government Relations*. Implications on the Autonomy and Discretion of Zimbabwe's Local Government.

Vincent, C., & Stephen, C. (2015). Local government capacity building and development: Lessons, challenges and opportunities. *Journal of Political Sciences & Public Affairs*, 3(1), 1–5. 10.4172/2332-0761.1000149

Vivek, N. D. (2024). Transformation Deferred: Disparate Development in Post-Apartheid South Africa (1994-2004). [PJGD]. *PanAfrican Journal of Governance and Development*, 5(1), 128–155. 10.46404/panjogov.v5i1.5364

Vungu Rural District Council. (2017). *About.* Rural District Development Committee (RDDC). http://www.vungurdc.org.zw/RDDC.html

Vyas-Doorgapersad, S. & Mothabi, P. (2022). Overview of misconduct influencing ethical culture in the Local Government Sector Education Training Authority, South Africa. *International Journal of Research in Business and Social Science (2147-4478), 11*(4), 365-374.

Waardenburg, M., Groenleer, M., de Jong, J., & Keijser, B. (2020). Paradoxes of collaborative governance: Investigating the real-life dynamics of multi-agency collaborations using a quasi-experimental action-research approach. *Public Management Review*, 22(3), 386–407. 10.1080/14719037.2019.1599056

Wadesango, N., Mhaka, C., Chikomo, T., & Wadesango, V. O. (2018). 'Causes of Poor Service Delivery and the Feasibility of Outsourcing to Improve Services in Local Authorities'. *Journal of Economics and Behavioral Studies*, 10(2), 88–198.

Waheeb, S. A., Zerouali, B., Elbeltagi, A., Alwetaishi, M., Wong, Y. J., Bailek, N., AlSaggaf, A. A., Abd Elrahman, S. I. M., Santos, C. A. G., & Majrashi, A. A. (2023). Enhancing Sustainable Urban Planning through GIS and Multiple-Criteria Decision Analysis: A Case Study of Green Space Infrastructure in Taif Province, Saudi Arabia. *Water (Basel)*, 15(17), 3031. 10.3390/w15173031

Walker, J. (2012). *Human Transit. How Clearer Thinking about Public Transit Can Enrich Our Communities and Our Lives*. Island Press.

Wallis, M. (2018). Case Studies from eThekwini Municipality. In G, Szell & D, Chetty (eds,). Making Popular Participation Real (pp. 263-275). Berlin & New York; Peter Lang.

Walters, J. (2013). Overview of public transport policy developments in South Africa. *Research in Transportation Economics*, 39(1), 34–45. 10.1016/j.retrec.2012.05.021

Walters, J. (2014). Public transport policy implementation in South Africa: Quo Vadis? Original research. *Journal of Transport and Supply Chain Management*, 8(1), 1–10. 10.4102/jtscm.v8i1.134

Wampler, B. (2000). *A Guide to Participatory Budgeting*. A Paper presented at the third conference of the International Budget Project, Mumbai. www.internationalburget.org/cdrom/papers/systems/ParticcipatoryBudget/Wampler. pdf

Wampler, B., McNulty, S., & Touchton, M. (2021). *Participatory budgeting from a global perspective*. Oxford University Press. 10.1093/oso/9780192897756.001.0001

Wang, X. (2018). *Urban Transportation Planning in the era of Intelligent Transport Systems*. Elsevier.

Wassenhoven, L. C., & Wassenhoven, L. C. (2019). Introduction, Historical Periods, and Examples. *The Ancestry of Regional Spatial Planning: A Planner's Look at History*. Research Gate.

Watson, M. (2001). Embedding the 'new economy' in Europe: A study in the institutional specificities of knowledge-based growth. *Economy and Society*, 30(4), 504–523. 10.1080/03085140120089072

Welsh, D. (2021). Apartheid and its legacies. In N, De Jager (Ed.). *South African Politics: An Introduction* (pp. 29-55). Cape Town: Oxford University Press.

Wester, M. (2022). Robust municipal decision making? A pilot study of applying robust decision making in three Swedish municipalities. *Journal of Environmental Planning and Management*, 65(4), 745–758. 10.1080/09640568.2021.1914560

Wiener, N. (1948). *Cybernetics: Or Control and Communication in the Animal and the Machine*. MIT Press.

Wilson, F. M. (2021). The early impacts of the COVID-19 pandemic on business sales. *Small Business Economics*, 1–12.38624577

Woodhouse, J. A. (2017). *Designing a qualitative study*. SAGE.

Woulfin, S.L. & Allen, C.D. (2022). The institution of schooling. *The Foundational Handbook on Improvement Research in Education, 67*.

Xulu, G., & Kirsten, J. F. (2018). Enhancing Smallholder Market Access through Local Economic Development: Evidence from South Africa. *Development Southern Africa*, 35(5), 629–644.

Xuza, P. H. (2005). Renewal of small-town economies: The case of Alice, Eastern Cape Province, South Africa. *Africa Insight*, 35(4), 90–96.

Yende, N. E. (2023). Towards Sustainable Service Delivery by South African Local Authorities: A Community Participation Strategy. *African Journal of Development Studies*, 13(1), 197.

Young, I. M. (2002). *Inclusion and Democracy*. Oxford University Press. 10.1093/0198297556.001.0001

Zabala, L., Febres, J., Sterling, R., López, S., & Keane, M. (2020). Virtual testbed for model predictive control development in district cooling systems. *Renewable & Sustainable Energy Reviews*, 129, 109920. 10.1016/j.rser.2020.109920

Zantsi, L. K. 2020. *The approach of the African National Congress to dealing with participatory spaces in post-apartheid South African local government* [Doctoral dissertation, Keele University].

Zengethwa, N. P., Thakhathi, D. R., & Oyelana, A. A. (2019). *Challenges Faced by the Raymond Mhlaba Municipality in Implementing the Back-to-Basics Programme*. University of Fort Hare. 10.31901/24566608.2019/68.1-3.3176

Zerihun, M.F., & Mashingo M.P. (2022). The quest for service delivery: The case of a rural district municipality in the Mpumalanga province of South Africa. *Africa's Public Service Delivery and Performance Review 10*(1), a512. (1). 10.4102/apsdpr.v10i1.512

Zhou, S. (2000). *Understanding The Inter-Relationships for The Creation of a Local Land Information System: The Zimbabwean Local Government Experience at Growth Points*. University of Kwa-Zulu-Natal.

Zimbwa, Y. (2020). Analyzing the ultimate impact of COVID-19 in Africa. *Case Studies on Transport Policy*, 9(2), 796–804.33842205

Zimmerman, S., & Fang, K. (2015). *Public transport service optimisation and system integration. China Transport Topics No. 14*. World Bank Office.

Zinyama, T. (2021). Local Government, Decentralisation, Devolution, and Service Delivery in Zimbabwe. In *Encyclopedia of Information Science and Technology*. IGI Global. 10.4018/978-1-7998-3479-3.ch109

Zondo, T. (2020). The positive impact of lockdown on containing the COVID-19 outbreak in China. *Journal of Travel Medicine*, 27.32181488

Zweni, A. G. (2022). *Critical evaluation of service delivery in selected South African municipalities: the role of budget management* [Doctoral dissertation, Cape Peninsula University of Technology].

Zweni, A., Yan, B. Juta, L.B., 2022. The malady of perpetual municipal-finance mismanagement: Designing a leadership framework as a Panacea. *African Journal of Development Studies*.

# About the Contributors

**Pandelani Harry Munzhedzi** holds a doctorate from University of KwaZulu Natal, and is the Associate Professor of Public Administration at the University of Venda in South Africa. He is a Head of Department of Public and Development Administration. Prof Munzhedzi is also a C2 Rated Scientist by the National Research Foundation (NRF). He has worked in the public service for almost 10 years before joining academia at the University of Limpopo.

**Ntwanano Erasmus Mathebula** is a Senior Lecturer at the University of Limpopo in South Africa. He has worked for the University of Venda prior joining the University of Limpopo. Dr Mathebula published extensively in different journals.

**Ntsako Idris Makamu** holds a doctorate from Tshwane University of Technology, and is an Associate Professor of Public Administration and Management at the University of South Africa (UNISA). He was a senior lecturer and subsequently an Associate Professor at the North West University before joining UNISA.

***

**Munir Ahmad** is a seasoned professional in the realm of Spatial Data Infrastructure (SDI), Geo-Information Productions, Information Systems, and Information Governance, boasting over 25 years of dedicated experience in the field. With a PhD in Computer Science, Dr. Ahmad's expertise spans Spatial Data Production, Management, Processing, Analysis, Visualization, and Quality Control. Throughout his career, Dr. Ahmad has been deeply involved in the development and deployment of SDI systems specially in the context of Pakistan, leveraging his proficiency in Spatial Database Design, Web, Mobile & Desktop GIS, and Geo Web Services Architecture. His contributions to Volunteered Geographic Information (VGI) and Open Source Geoportal & Metadata Portal have significantly enriched the geospatial community. As a trainer and researcher, Dr. Ahmad has authored over 50 publications, advancing the industry's knowledge base and fostering innovation in Geo-Tech, Data Governance, and Information Infrastructure, and Emerging Technologies. His commitment to Research and Development (R&D) is evident in his role as a dedicated educator and mentor in the field.

## *About the Contributors*

**Asmat Ali** is PhD in Remote Sensing & GIS. He is Director of Cartography and GIS at Survey of Pakistan. He is also Project Director Feasibility Study for Establishment of National Spatial Data Infrastructure (NSDI) for Pakistan. In, 1998 he earned Professional Master Degree in Geoinformatics from Faculty of Geo-Information Science and Earth Observation (ITC), University of Twente, Enschede The Netherlands. The title of his IFA was, "*Digital Production Line in The Context of Survey of Pakistan*". Later on, he got MSc Degree in Geo-information Science and Earth Observation, with Specialization in Geo-Information Management from the same university. The title of his MSc thesis was, "*Potential of Public Private Partnership for NSDI Implementation In Pakistan*". In 2022, he got PhD degree in Remote Sensing and GIS from PMAS-Arid Agriculture University Rawalpindi, Pakistan. The title of his dissertation was "*Spatial Data Infrastructure as The Means to Assemble Geographic Information Necessary for Effective Agricultural Policies in Pakistan*". He has 35 years of experience in geospatial information production and management discipline as practitioner, trainer and educator. He has served on several operational, administrative and instructional appointments. He was in-charge of the team which started GIS mapping and digital cartography at Survey of Pakistan in 1999. His more than 30 research papers including four book chapters and articles on Spatial Data Infrastructure (SDI), GIS, Remote Sensing, E-governance, as well as Land Administration have been published in various internationally renowned journals and conferences. In 2008, SDI Asia-Pacific identified him as *Focal Point for SDI Development in Pakistan*. GSDI in 2016, acknowledged and awarded him as *SDI Implementer from Pakistan*. He is on the visiting faculty of Bahria University Islamabad and PMAS- Arid Agriculture University Rawalpindi, Pakistan.

**Hammad Hussain** is a final year student of software engineering at COMSATS University Islamabad, Wah campus Pakistan. In 2023, he successfully completed an internship at Survey of Pakistan. During the internship, he worked on: i) Geospatial data development using GIS and Remote Sensing techniques. ii) Assessment of National Spatial Data Infrastructure (NSDI) websites and their improvement with respect to SDI services.

**Martin Kabange** is a lecturer in Economics at the Durban University of Technology in South Africa. He has published extensively on Informality, Macroeconomics Financial Inclusion and Public Administration.

**Tendai Kaponda** is a seasoned local governance practitioner with a passion for rural development, he is a public policy scholar with a decade of experience working in local governance. His professional career has focused on empowering rural communities through sustainable practices and effective policy implementation. His research interests lie at the intersection of sustainable agriculture, rural governance, and public policy, with a particular focus on facilitating sustainable rural development. Currently pursuing a Doctorate in Public Administration at Central China Normal University, his doctoral research delves into the complexities of rural governance, aiming to bridge the gap between theory and practice. This research aligns with his extensive experience working within local governance structures, where firsthand exposure to the challenges and opportunities faced by rural communities has fueled his academic pursuits. His dedication to sustainable development extends beyond academia. His experience as a local governance practitioner demonstrates a commitment to translating theory into action, fostering positive change for rural communities. This combination of academic rigour and practical expertise positions. He is making significant contributions to the field of rural governance and sustainable development.

**Emmanuel Maemu** holds a doctorate from the University of Venda in South Africa where he is a lecturer. Dr Maemu worked for the public service before joining academia. He is a very passionate researcher who continues to public on development issues.

**Maijane Mashamaite** holds a D.Admin Degree from the University of South Africa and is currently Senior Lecturer in the Department of Public Administration and Management at UNISA. Prior to joining UNISA, she was a lecturer at the University of Limpopo in the Faculty of Management and Law teaching modules of the degree of Bachelor of Administration in Local government and Transport Management. Her research interests are in Public Policy, Project Management, Local Government, Transportation and Climate Change. Dr Mashamaite is a member of the South African Association of Public Administration and Management (SAAPAM) and received an award for Best conference paper for 2023 (22nd Annual Conference of the SAAPAM). Furthermore, she received an Award for UNISA- College of Economics Management and Sciences (CEMS) for developing researcher producing the most output in 2018.

**Sanah Matloga** is a Doctor of Administration, Lecturer at the University of Venda Department of Public and Development Administration since 2020. Holder of Master of Administration ("Cum laude") from the University of Venda. Teacher, researcher and supervisor of Honors, Masters and Doctorate (PhD)

**Nandiswa Mpolweni** is a dedicated professional from the Eastern Cape, South Africa, with a strong passion for public administration and service delivery. She has pursued her academic journey with a focus on local government finance, public management, and public administration. Nandiswa's educational foundation was laid at Walter Sisulu University, where she completed her National Diploma in Local Government Finance. Eager to expand her knowledge and skills, she continued her studies at the same university and obtained a Bachelor of Technology in Public Management. These degrees provided her with a solid understanding of the intricacies of local governance and public administration. Driven by her desire to make a positive impact in her community, Nandiswa embarked on further academic pursuits. She pursued a Masters of Management Science in Public Administration, specializing in the challenges of service delivery in selected townships within the Nelson Mandela Metropolitan Municipality. Throughout her academic journey, Nandiswa demonstrated exceptional dedication and a commitment to understanding the complexities of public administration and service delivery. She conducted in-depth research, utilizing qualitative methods such as interviews and document reviews to gain valuable insights into the barriers impeding effective service delivery in townships. Nandiswa's research focused on identifying critical challenges, such as limited community participation, insufficient budget allocation, human resource constraints, and strained intergovernmental relations. Through her meticulous study, she recognized the interconnected nature of these challenges and their impact on the municipality's capacity to deliver services effectively and achieve strategic goals. Beyond her academic pursuits, Nandiswa is known for her strong work ethic, attention to detail, and her ability to collaborate effectively with stakeholders. She possesses a deep understanding of the importance of community engagement and participatory decision-making processes in promoting sustainable development and community well-being. With her extensive academic background and research expertise, Nandiswa is poised to become a valuable asset in the field of municipal planning and service provision. Her findings and insights offer valuable guidance for policymakers and practitioners seeking to address the challenges of service delivery in townships and improve the lives of community members. Nandiswa Mpolweni's commitment to public administration and service delivery, backed by her academic achievements and research contributions, positions her as a dedicated professional ready to make a meaningful impact in her community and beyond.

**Mpfareleni Netswera** holds a doctorate from University of South Africa (UNISA) in South Africa. She is currently a postdoctoral fellow at UNISA where she contributes on research matters.

**Praise Ramaru** is an associate Lecturer at Nelson Mandela University currently doing her PhD in Public Administration, she teaches and provides research supervision, her research areas include Government transactions, Public Policy, Leadership and many other areas.

**Ramolobe Kutu Sam** is a South African academic and researcher. He is currently a lecturer in the Department of Public Management and Leadership at Nelson Mandela University in Gqeberha, Eastern Cape. His research interests include local government, traditional leadership, disability, and service delivery. He holds a PhD in Public Administration from Nelson Mandela University. His research has been published in a number of academic journals and presented his research at several conferences.

**Tando Rulashe** is a Senior Lecturer at the Faculty of Humanities' Department of Public Management & Leadership at Nelson Mandela University. He holds a Doctor of Public Administration from the University of Fort Hare. His research niche areas include Public Policy, Local Government Administration and Organisation Development.

## *About the Contributors*

**Bernard Karabo Sebake** is a Director for Student Governance and Development at Nelson Mandela University, based in Gqeberha, in the Eastern Cape Province of South Africa. He holds a Doctoral Degree qualification in Public Management specialising in Monitoring and Evaluation of Integrated Development Plan. He is a researcher and a political analyst which his areas of interest are amongst the following: - Public administration theories; Governance, politics and conflicts; Local government contemporary issues; Public sector transformation and reform; service delivery; public policy, enterprise and youth development. He participated in numerous national and international conferences and published sufficiently in the area of his interest. He also played a leading role in a number of Review Panels for strategic effectiveness of Student Affairs in various Universities including the review of scholarship in his field of interest. He edited a number of books that were taking an intellectual posture of development praxis which position his remarkable scholarly work thus far.

**Mahlodi Joyce Sethu** has a PHD, and is Senior Lecturer at the University of Venda South Africa. Faculty of Management and Law, Department of Public and Development Administration. Teacher, researcher and supervisor of Honors, Masters and Doctorate (PhD)

**Slungile Sigwebela** is a young African lady who was born and bred in Harding (KwaZulu-Natal). Slungile Sigwebela Holds a Bachelor of Social Science Degree, an Honours degree in Community and Development Studies. She is also Master of Social Science (Research) Graduand. All these qualifications were obtained at the University of KwaZulu Natal.

**Ndwakhulu Tshishonga** (PhD) is an Africanist academic and a research fellow within the School of Built Environment & Development Studies at the University of KwaZulu-Natal. He specialises in political economy, Community Development, decolonized development and developmental state, local economic development, local governance and citizenship, and African Politics. Over the past two decades, more than 70 scholarly papers and book chapters were contributed to local and international journals and edited books. His academic citizenship includes presenting at both national and international conferences as well engaging government departments in policy issues relating governance, democracy and professionalising community development in South Africa.

**Zwelithini Zwane** is currently a Lecturer at Durban University of Technology. Previously taught at Mangosuthu University of Technology and at the University of Zululand in the field of Publication Administration. My areas of expertise are in local government, human resource management and public policy

# Index


## A

accessible grievance 26, 42, 43, 45, 46, 50
agricultural development 80, 81, 92, 95, 97
agricultural growth 77, 83, 90, 91, 92, 94, 95, 97, 98, 100
agricultural productivity 83, 90, 96, 98, 100, 105, 108, 163
Agriculture 64, 77, 78, 79, 80, 81, 82, 83, 85, 91, 92, 97, 102, 103, 104, 105, 106, 138, 163, 178, 192, 193, 213, 214, 236, 244
alternative solutions 4, 6
Anti-corruption measures 300, 310, 312

## B

BRT system 264, 271, 272, 277
budget allocation 4, 10, 16, 59, 66, 67, 68, 69, 70, 73

## C

capacity building 40, 41, 42, 45, 53, 62, 94, 97, 171, 176, 200, 205, 208, 217, 224, 226, 254, 288, 293, 310, 312
Citizen Participation 3, 4, 6, 7, 8, 9, 11, 15, 16, 17, 19, 22, 25, 26, 27, 28, 29, 31, 34, 37, 40, 41, 42, 43, 44, 45, 46, 47, 48, 49, 50, 55, 159, 186, 287, 292, 300, 305, 315
civil society 7, 8, 9, 10, 11, 12, 13, 14, 15, 20, 22, 38, 45, 46, 48, 51, 72, 86, 97, 134, 198, 234, 283, 284, 285, 286, 287, 289, 291, 292, 293, 295, 305, 306, 309, 312, 314, 315, 316, 317, 321, 323
civil society organizations 8, 10, 13, 38, 45, 48, 51, 86, 283, 284, 287, 289, 291, 293
climate change 75, 122, 180, 183, 187, 211, 217, 271, 275, 280
coalition governance 67, 68, 69, 70
communication methods 204, 212
Community development projects 234
Community-led initiatives 129, 130, 131, 132, 137, 141
community participation 17, 59, 61, 62, 63, 68, 70, 72, 73, 86, 92, 130, 134, 135, 137, 161, 162, 163, 164, 167, 168, 210, 222, 287, 288, 289, 291, 293, 299, 305, 309, 312, 314, 315, 320, 324
Coronavirus 110, 112, 117, 125, 126, 128
COVID-19 pandemic 82, 97, 98, 114, 123, 125, 126, 127, 138, 157, 173, 210, 242, 300, 305, 317

## D

decision-making processes 3, 4, 5, 11, 26, 28, 29, 31, 32, 33, 34, 37, 38, 43, 44, 48, 49, 63, 68, 80, 92, 94, 100, 133, 148, 149, 150, 152, 153, 154, 155, 156, 159, 176, 178, 185, 186, 288, 298, 311, 312, 314, 316
deliberative democracy 3, 4, 6, 8, 9, 11, 15, 18, 19
Democratic governance 6, 7, 10, 14, 15, 22, 25, 26, 27, 28, 29, 30, 31, 32, 33, 34, 38, 39, 42, 43, 44, 45, 46, 47, 48, 49, 50, 53, 57, 232, 237, 292
democratic practices 26
Devolution 5, 10, 27, 28, 29, 54, 55, 57, 157, 159, 161, 162, 163, 164, 168, 266
direct democracy 3, 5, 15, 18, 22
District Development Model 195, 196, 197, 198, 199, 201, 202, 203, 204, 205, 210, 212, 213, 214, 216, 217, 218, 219, 220, 223, 227, 228, 233, 234, 235, 240, 241, 242, 244, 245

## E

economic constraints 145, 164, 168
Economic Development 40, 62, 63, 66, 73, 74, 75, 77, 78, 79, 85, 86, 87, 89, 90, 91, 92, 94, 95, 98, 99, 100, 101, 102, 104, 106, 107, 108, 109, 110, 111, 112, 114, 116, 119, 120, 123, 124, 126, 127, 128, 179, 189, 196, 200, 203, 206, 214, 217, 218, 219,

223, 229, 230, 231, 234, 235, 236, 243, 244, 253, 254, 258, 261, 284, 299, 308, 321
economic growth 61, 77, 78, 82, 84, 89, 109, 112, 116, 117, 122, 123, 124, 128, 165, 174, 204, 205, 206, 211, 213, 214, 219, 264, 265, 275
educational levels 5, 15
employment opportunities 64, 80, 82, 84, 116, 122
Entrepreneurs 109, 110, 128, 195, 242
equal opportunity 4, 8
equitable distribution 15, 68, 82
expenditure reports 26, 42, 43, 45, 46, 50

## F

farming practices 79, 92
financial resources 12, 13, 15, 35, 41, 42, 43, 46, 48, 50, 62, 64, 79, 86, 96, 157, 158, 166, 179, 182, 185, 231, 234, 275

## G

geospatial datasets 175, 184, 186
Good governance 36, 53, 74, 143, 206, 210, 247, 248, 251, 253, 255, 256, 257, 258, 259, 284, 289, 304, 305, 306, 307, 311, 312, 314, 318, 319, 321, 323
Governance challenges 191, 292, 295, 304, 309, 311, 321
government agencies 95, 96, 150, 151, 155, 167, 169, 177, 179, 184, 186, 187, 217, 263, 316
grievance procedures 26, 43, 45, 46, 50

## H

human resource 59, 62, 70, 74, 205, 304, 313, 323

## I

inclusive growth 82, 92, 97, 107, 210, 216, 217, 299
Informal Economy 128
informed decision-making 175, 185, 186
Institutional reform 295, 310, 312
Integrated Development 16, 17, 21, 58, 59, 60, 61, 62, 65, 67, 69, 71, 72, 73, 74, 75, 78, 105, 137, 199, 200, 205, 210, 211, 216, 220, 229, 235, 236, 245, 249, 250, 258, 259, 305, 306, 307, 311, 312, 320
Integrated Development Planning 17, 60, 61, 71, 72, 73, 74, 137, 216, 305, 306, 320
Integrated development plans 16, 58, 59, 62, 78, 200, 205
Integrated service delivery 204, 212, 227, 228, 234, 238, 245
inter-governmental coordination 145, 146, 147, 148, 160, 162, 163, 164, 165, 166, 167, 235
Inter-governmental Relations 163, 173, 211, 217

## L

LED initiatives 86, 89, 90, 91, 94, 96, 97, 98, 102, 113, 129, 130, 131, 132, 137, 141
Local authority 133, 233, 250
local democratic Governance 10, 14
Local Economic Development (LED) 74, 75, 77, 78, 79, 85, 86, 87, 89, 90, 91, 92, 94, 95, 98, 99, 100, 101, 102, 104, 106, 107, 108, 109, 110, 111, 112, 114, 116, 119, 120, 123, 124, 126, 127, 128, 196, 200, 206, 223, 230, 231, 234, 236, 244, 299
local governance 2, 3, 6, 7, 8, 9, 10, 11, 12, 17, 18, 20, 22, 23, 26, 27, 28, 33, 34, 38, 39, 44, 45, 48, 49, 52, 55, 56, 60, 73, 132, 143, 158, 159, 170, 172, 191, 205, 229, 240, 242, 286, 288, 292, 293, 307, 317, 323
Local Government 2, 6, 7, 10, 12, 15, 17, 18, 20, 21, 22, 23, 26, 27, 28, 34, 35, 37, 38, 39, 40, 42, 43, 47, 53, 54, 56, 57, 60, 68, 69, 71, 72, 73, 74, 76, 84, 85, 97, 102, 106, 107, 112, 120, 133, 134, 135, 137, 138, 139, 142, 143, 147, 158, 159, 160, 162, 164, 171,

172, 173, 179, 180, 183, 196, 198, 199, 200, 201, 203, 204, 205, 207, 208, 209, 210, 211, 212, 215, 217, 218, 219, 220, 221, 223, 224, 225, 226, 227, 228, 229, 230, 231, 232, 234, 235, 237, 238, 239, 240, 241, 242, 244, 245, 252, 253, 258, 259, 266, 268, 284, 287, 288, 289, 291, 292, 293, 297, 304, 305, 306, 307, 308, 310, 311, 315, 317, 319, 320, 321, 322, 323, 324, 325

## M

Management 7, 10, 11, 21, 22, 23, 26, 34, 48, 52, 53, 54, 55, 60, 68, 72, 74, 75, 76, 85, 90, 97, 98, 100, 103, 105, 107, 110, 123, 125, 131, 132, 136, 137, 143, 156, 158, 159, 170, 173, 176, 178, 179, 181, 182, 183, 184, 185, 186, 187, 188, 191, 192, 194, 198, 199, 200, 207, 208, 209, 218, 220, 222, 223, 225, 226, 228, 229, 230, 235, 236, 237, 240, 242, 243, 245, 250, 251, 258, 259, 260, 261, 262, 263, 264, 279, 280, 282, 288, 290, 295, 297, 300, 301, 304, 305, 306, 307, 313, 315, 319, 320, 323
marginalised communities 63, 134, 296, 298, 315
mismanagement 2, 163, 203, 294, 295, 296, 297, 298, 299, 300, 301, 303, 304, 305, 311, 312, 313, 314, 315, 316, 319, 324, 325
multi-faceted approach 29, 61, 70, 120, 128
municipal governments 26, 27, 28, 29, 33, 36, 37, 38, 39, 40, 41, 42, 43, 44, 45, 46, 47, 48, 49, 50, 52, 55, 180, 198, 252
municipal planning 68, 69, 175, 176, 177, 178, 179, 180, 181, 182, 183, 184, 185, 186, 189, 190, 192, 194, 222, 247, 248, 249, 251, 253, 254, 255, 256, 257
municipal services 129, 130, 131, 135, 182, 209, 233, 254, 283, 284, 285, 286, 304, 311, 321, 325
Municipal Systems 7, 60, 137, 143, 198, 199, 200, 201, 225, 249, 250, 252, 269
municipal transport system 260, 261, 264, 270, 271, 272, 273, 274, 275, 277, 278

## N

National Development 73, 78, 84, 105, 196, 198, 203, 211, 219, 224, 235, 236, 292
negative externalities 146, 148, 167

## P

participatory budgeting 1, 2, 3, 4, 5, 6, 7, 8, 9, 10, 11, 12, 13, 14, 15, 16, 17, 18, 19, 20, 21, 23, 24, 44, 45, 50, 81, 300, 323
participatory Governance 3, 5, 8, 10, 17, 18, 22, 216
power dynamics 12, 28, 151, 162, 169, 202, 212, 295, 298, 311, 314, 316
project implementation 59, 70, 253
public expenditure 4, 102, 218
public resources 4, 5, 8, 9, 40, 248, 289
public trust 43, 46, 49, 50, 155, 295, 299, 312

## R

ratepayers' association 139, 140
rates and taxes 143, 208
resource allocation 13, 25, 34, 36, 40, 41, 43, 44, 45, 46, 48, 50, 59, 62, 63, 66, 67, 69, 70, 81, 84, 175, 185, 197, 206, 219, 295
resource management 34, 48, 74, 185, 186, 218, 290, 304, 313, 323
road safety 262, 267, 271
Rural governance 31, 32, 33, 36, 37, 39, 40, 54, 56, 145, 146, 147, 148, 149, 150, 151, 152, 153, 157, 158, 159, 160, 161, 162, 163, 164, 167, 168, 172
Rural Infrastructure 105

## S

SDI 175, 176, 177, 178, 179, 181, 184, 185, 186, 187, 188, 190, 193
service delivery 2, 7, 11, 12, 13, 14, 17, 21,

25, 26, 27, 28, 33, 34, 35, 36, 38, 39, 40, 41, 42, 43, 44, 45, 46, 47, 48, 49, 50, 51, 52, 53, 54, 55, 56, 57, 58, 59, 65, 66, 67, 68, 69, 70, 72, 73, 74, 75, 76, 78, 98, 106, 130, 131, 133, 134, 136, 142, 157, 160, 171, 172, 183, 185, 195, 196, 197, 198, 199, 200, 201, 202, 203, 204, 205, 206, 207, 208, 209, 210, 211, 212, 213, 215, 217, 218, 219, 220, 221, 222, 223, 224, 226, 227, 228, 229, 230, 232, 234, 235, 236, 237, 238, 240, 241, 242, 243, 244, 245, 254, 256, 258, 259, 275, 283, 284, 285, 286, 287, 288, 289, 290, 291, 293, 294, 295, 296, 297, 299, 305, 306, 307, 308, 309, 311, 312, 313, 316, 317, 318, 319, 320, 321, 322, 323, 324
small-scale farmers 79, 80, 83, 96, 100, 104
social contract 2, 13, 14, 23
social development 79, 240, 261, 266, 287
social exclusion 13, 16, 80, 82, 103, 113
social justice 8, 9, 15, 60, 146
society organizations 8, 10, 13, 38, 45, 48, 51, 86, 283, 284, 287, 289, 291, 293
socioeconomic difficulties 204, 218
Spatial Data 175, 177, 178, 179, 181, 184, 185, 186, 188, 189, 190, 191, 192, 193
Stakeholder Collaboration 77
stakeholder engagement 65, 66, 67, 89, 97, 148, 149, 155, 167
strategic planning 60, 81, 111, 179, 221, 234, 250
supply chains 110, 111, 114, 118, 124, 126
sustainable development 12, 17, 25, 32, 38, 44, 45, 49, 51, 60, 61, 63, 66, 69, 70, 72, 78, 84, 86, 90, 91, 92, 93, 94, 97, 100, 105, 106, 108, 114, 116, 117, 131, 132, 141, 182, 194, 211, 216, 217, 219, 224, 255, 256, 258, 259, 285, 293, 295, 305, 311, 318, 319
sustainable growth 62, 86
sustainable outcomes 156
sustainable provision 129, 130, 131, 262

# T

taxi industry 262, 269, 276, 277
transparency measures 26, 42, 43, 46, 314

# U

Urban Development 102, 160, 175, 182, 183, 184, 186, 188, 189, 196, 203, 211, 218, 235, 262, 287
Urban Planning 176, 182, 190, 192, 194, 218, 291

# W

whistleblower protections 300, 314

www.ingramcontent.com/pod-product-compliance
Lightning Source LLC
LaVergne TN
LVHW080608300926
849162LV00005B/1080
* 9 7 9 8 3 6 9 3 3 6 1 7 5 *